Jeremy Tambling

Histories of the Devil

From Marlowe to Mann and the Manichees

palgrave
macmillan

Jeremy Tambling
London, United Kingdom

ISBN 978-1-137-51831-6 ISBN 978-1-137-51832-3 (eBook)
DOI 10.1057/978-1-137-51832-3

Library of Congress Control Number: 2016954799

Printed on acid-free paper

This Palgrave Macmillan imprint is published by Springer Nature
The registered company is Macmillan Publishers Ltd.
The registered company address is: The Campus, 4 Crinan Street, London, N1 9XW, United Kingdom

In memory of my brother, William Jonathan Francis Tambling, 1945–2015.

Preface and Acknowledgements

A quite favourable recent review of a book I wrote noted that there was no notice of any secondary literature at its start, and nor had I written any introduction. Obviously this will not do: it is customary to start with explanations rather than hope, as I tend to do, that these, and the terms of reference will emerge and be found, rather than being predefined. This particularly applies to a book on the devil where there can be no set terms of reference. This present book comes out of my university teaching, using some of what I wanted to say in lectures or seminars, and since it follows that, it references my writing at the time, so I hope the reader will forgive the autocitations, whose associated egocentrism I regret. (I notice in passing how my writing keeps coming back to certain Shakespeare plays: though I hope I have not repeated myself the same Shakespeare plays recur throughout this book.) This book finds the devil in literature, perhaps as a way of thinking what literature is: but it also works as a 'history of the devil' (title of a study by Defoe), and that idea challenges, perhaps uniquely, positivist assumptions: a history? And why the devil? This is not a history of ideas, nor of a concept: I accept Nietzsche's view that 'only that which has no history can be defined' (Nietzsche 1956: 212), which retroactively – since things *are* defined, and that usually gives them their history – means that an appeal to history is always metaphysical: attempting to create something definite that there can be a history of: believing in identity, continuity, and the identical and in either progress or cultural decline. Names endure, but that does not guarantee a history which links them. Though I may not escape generalisation, I have tried to avoid potted histories of Zoroastrianism, or

Manicheism, or Catharism, or combat myths, as so many previous books on the devil, some academic, have engaged with. I assume there is no single thing to be said about any of these hypostatisations, and nothing outside the text – nothing that can be discussed without close attention to specific texts. In the 'minute particulars' of texts and questions of how to read and discuss them, a universalising history may perhaps be avoided: texts will perhaps form a constellation with each other as they are brought into association with each other; these constellations allow for alternative histories, ways of reading. In these problems of reading literary texts or asking what a text may be, Old Nick lurks, the devil being in the detail; and my uses of Freud and of Derrida, in particular, will draw out the inherency of what Derrida (1978: 61) calls the 'demonic-hyperbole' within literature.

I do not follow the argument that though Christianity may have tended to give up on belief in a literal devil (Pope's cleric 'never mentions Hell to ears polite'), it remains a useful symbol to think about evil. Many of the book's texts are informed by Catholicism or Protestantism, but its subject is not the Christian devil, nor yet, quite, the devils of other faiths. The book takes theology seriously, as a discipline of thought, and I hope will be read by theologians; it admits its fascination, especially negative theology, but is, finally, I think, anti-theological. And it is not about 'evil', a term perhaps better dispensed with, for reasons which will become apparent, but which start with the point that the person who claims to know what evil is may not know what he or she is talking about. Although I hope theologians and philosophers of religion and historians will enjoy it, the book's likely readership will be those interested in visual images, or literature, both English and comparative, or critical theory, or post-Nietzschean philosophy. Some recurrent keywords may be flagged: e.g. nothing, *das Ding*, soliloquy, allegory, folly, and madness; genius and the daemon; carnival and melancholia and abjection; *différance*, nihilism, poverty, law, the double, laughter, temptation, banality, the death-drive, and the aesthetic. In how these familiar terms are used lies a sense of what 'the devil' includes. Scholarly books are written for people with specialist interests, which means that readers will cut to only the bits they want to read: quite right too, and I do it myself, but nonetheless the book thinks of itself as having an argument persevering and interweaving from end to beginning, and the best reader will forget that some bits are not her specialism, and will read it all.

This Preface announces the book's intentions, but the Introduction plunges in with discussion of four of the book's theoretical assumptions, on dualism, on the implications of the soliloquy, and what is meant by genius. It also comments on allegory, during the course of studying the shadowy figure of Simon Magus, first mentioned in the New Testament, and part of the prehistory of the Faust idea, a starting-point for this book, as its subtitle indicates. The modern history of Faust emerges in Germany in the sixteenth century, and it is discussed here through Marlowe, in *Doctor Faustus* (the substance of the first chapter), and then in later chapters on Goethe's two *Faust* plays, and in a last chapter on Bulgakov, and Thomas Mann. Other exfoliations from Goethe in particular involve the rewritings of *Faust* in Turgenev, and Dostoevsky.

A second starting point is Augustine (CE 354–430) on account of his contest with the Manichees. They believed in two opposing principles, of light and darkness, and confronted him with the challenge to deny the existence of evil as a positive and active force, or principle. Did God create the world from nothing? – a keyword for us throughout. But nothing will come of nothing. Did God create the world from something? Then something has equal status with God, as eternal – Aristotle believed in the eternity of the world – and if we ask about the existence of evil, then that must either be identified with God, if he created the world from nothing, or from a something which he cannot exclude. Augustine's *Confessions* say that after his conversion, he wrote the *Soliloquies*; the latter was then a new word, which lies at the heart of this book, and is discussed in Chapter 1, 'The Tempter or the Tempted, Who Sins Most?' in relation to Marlowe and Shakespeare, since soliloquy marks the speech of Marlowe's Faustus, or those other Marlovian or Shakespearian Lucifer-like overreaching self-asserters who become increasingly aware of themselves as divided subjects, so that to whom they speak when they soliloquise becomes ambiguous. Soliloquy risks the devil. It brings in someone else as the interlocutor: the daimon, or daemon, perhaps something other than the Christian demon, and the Genius. The Introduction and first Chapter trace soliloquy through *Doctor Faustus*, and into Shakespeare, while Chapter 2, 'Medieval and Early Modern Devils: Names and Images' approaches Shakespeare via the diabolical within Dante, and Chaucer, and medieval drama, i.e. within early modern literature, defining this as what is written in the vernacular. With these texts it becomes obvious that the devil cannot be thought of in Christian terms only, or that Christianity enacts a repression of another force which exceeds the place it gives to the diabolical, and whose instability, whether as as nature-spirit, or Folly or Vice runs throughout the texts discussed. It also shows itself in Chapter 3, on folly, and on fools, in Sebastian Brant and Bosch and Bruegel. I continue from there with Rabelais' carnival, his folk-devils, Pantagruel and Panurge, and with the body whose grotesquerie is threatened by newer sixteenth-century discourses, which make folly diabolical by labelling it madness. Such normalising forces exclude the *picaro*, the rogue and peasant slave, like Poor Tom in *King Lear*, the last text to be discussed in this Chapter, which draws much of its language of popular devils from then contemporary arguments about exorcism. But carnival, as the sphere of what cannot be controlled, with diabolical potential, offers a new and revolutionary possibility for the modern world, and extensions of carnival-thinking therefore run throughout the rest of the book.

Chapter 4, concentrates on Blake and Milton, initially via Freud's essay 'A Seventeenth-Century Demonological Neurosis' (1923), about the Bavarian painter, Christoph Haizmann who believed that he had sold his soul to the devil. It also includes discussion of the case of demon possession at Loudun in France, approaching this through Michel de Certeau, whose writings on the heterological within history are evoked several times, informing what is said about Bosch and Haizmann, and picking up on the ambiguity of a god who may be conceptualised as a wandering 'poor devil'. *Paradise Lost* is analysed alongside Blake, who also gives the opportunity to discuss the Book of Job, since he illustrated it. Here, the doubleness of Blake's own thoughts about the devil emerge: as rebel, poet, hermaphrodite, and figure of the accusing conscience together.

Chapter 5, 'Masks, Doubles, and Nihilism' concentrates on two other writers parallel with Blake, both fascinated by the double: James Hogg in *The Private Memoirs and Confessions of a Justified Sinner* (1824), and E.T.A. Hoffmann (1776–1822). The latter's writings on the devil, and on double psychic states and music attracted the attention of Baudelaire, whose essay on laughter takes that as a devilish going-on. Baudelaire starts the chapter and informs its interest in comedy, which is explored especially through Molière. Here again, carnival is central, as is masking, dissimulation, activities where the diabolical may or may not be present. Hoffmann became aware of carnival through Goethe, in the *Italian Journey*, not published until 1816–1817, but an influence on Hoffmann's fantastic short story *Princess Brambilla* (1820), a text I make central for considering relationships between the comic and the diabolic, as I do with his novel, *The Devil's Elixirs* (1815).

If meeting with the double – which threatens the subject's very sense of being an autonomous original – means meeting the devil, then Mephistopheles threatens with nihilism, as happens in *Faust*, the substance of Chapter 6. Here the diabolic – whether in Faust or in Mephisto – becomes the spirit of modernity, which is Goethe's subject. Chapter 7 extends those issues to Dostoevsky, and to his dialogic, polyphonic novels, which, following Bakhtin's arguments, rework carnival: Bakhtin is as relevant here as he was in Chapter 3. The emphasis falls on the double, and on feelings of devil-possession, and on suicide, taking these from *A Writer's Diary, Demons*, and *The Brothers Karamazov*. Russia remains prominent in Chapter 8, with *The Master and Margarita*, while a section on *Doctor Faustus* engages with Mann's sense of German culture as diabolical, and with music as its highest expression as much as Nazism threatens to be its logic. The questionableness of this thesis, and its asking, like Adorno, collaborator on Mann's text, about what art could be written after Auschwitz, brings the book to a close, though not before a note on Rushdie's *Satanic Verses.*

The material of this book started with a course I devised on carnival and tragedy. During its metamorphosings, in the on-off periods when I taught it, when I could not remember whether the title's copula was 'and' or 'or' or 'versus' – were carnival and tragedy opposites (so Bakhtin) or even the same? – I began to think the devil would make a good footnote to both terms. That produced a latter-day course on the devil. Thanks to all students who listened and discussed both, or either, and especial thanks to those who encouraged me to write the material up. Much reading has gone on since then, though I cannot hope to have mastered the secondary material on any, and especially on Rabelais, or Goethe, or Dostoevsky. Parts of Chapters 3 and 5 formed lectures at the National Taipei University of Technology, and the National Taiwan University in November 2014; part of Chapter 1, on soliloquy, to Hang Seng Management College in Hong Kong the same week. The E.T.A. Hoffmann material on *The Devil's Elixir's* revises an article in *Forum for Modern Language Studies* 51 (2015): 379–393: I thank Robin Mackenzie, the editor for his help, and also thank him and OUP for permission to reprint. Yet more on Hoffmann comes from a conference on opera and text at St Andrews in 2013, where I compared *Don Giovanni* and *Undine*: thanks to Emma Sutton for her organisation! Work on Mann's *Doctor Faustus*, which I have been wanting to write on since I excluded a chapter on it from my *Opera and the Culture of Fascism* (1997), appeared in

Forum for Modern Language Studies, 48 (2012): 208–221: phrases from that reappear here. I thank also Barbara Hardy, for conversation about Goethe in George Eliot; sadly she died a week before I completed a first draft of the manuscript, so ending an exchange of emails about *Daniel Deronda*. I thank Chris Terry for much help on Goethe, and Jonathan Hall for wholly inspirational thinking about carnival and Rabelais and Dostoevsky, and comments on the draft. Thanks to Priscilla Martin for most helpful comments, to Brian Worthington for Shakespeare, and Richard Heap for Chapter 4. Thanks to James Smith, Louis Lo, and Ian Fong, and Jack Sullivan for editorial assistance, Ben Doyle for taking on the book for Palgrave, and lastly, to Chris Barlow for wonderfully critical, exciting, and exacting comments on the book's first draft.

Two last details. All that I have referenced, and more that I have used but not had occasion to cite, appears in the Bibliography; footnotes give only supporting material. I have used the King James Bible (1611), and quoted extensively from Benjamin (*SW – Selected Writings*) and Freud as *SE*: i.e. *Standard Edition*, the only exceptions to the author-date system of referencing used elsewhere and used sparingly, often with just the first citation, to avoid cluttering the page with numbers. And for capitalisation and spelling: I have spelled daemon/daimon/demon interchangeably, and the context must command the meaning; 'devil' I have only capitalised when it seemed right, rather than following consistency. It does not seem possible to be more precise, bearing in mind the different irreconcilable usages from different authors, and the point holds with spellings, especially with those which involve working across languages. Even when I could work with a particular language, I have depended much for reassurance on good translations, but the devil has an affinity for translation, starting with Puck changing Bottom's head in *A Midsummer Night's Dream*, evoking the horrified reaction, 'Bless thee Bottom, thou art translated' (2.2.124–125). The malapropism translates transformation as does: 'by faith, Enoch was translated, that he should not see death, and was not found, because God had translated him' (Hebrews 11:5). Translation: transformation: there is no proper place, or proper word, nor even a proper type of head: the devil secures all that.

Contents

List of Figures

Introduction: Literature and Manicheism

In August 2014, news broke from Iraq and Syria of a new Islamist insurgent group, ISIS, taking on the Shias in northern Iraq, and persecuting the Yezidi minority, north of Mosul, killing or forcibly converting the men to Islam, selling women and children. Who were – and are – the Yezidis, these apparent anachronisms within modernity, threatened with genocide, their total number perhaps no more than 300,000? They will help in approaching what is meant by the devil, and lead into four related concepts which under different headings I want to discuss in this chapter, and which inform the book.

1 Dualism

In 1849, the Assyriologist Henry Layard described the Yezidi, noting their 'quiet and inoffensive demeanour':

> and the cleanliness and order of their villages . . . their known respect or fear for the evil principle has acquired for them the title 'Worshippers of the Devil'. Many stories are current as to the emblems by which this spirit is represented. They are believed by some to adore a cock, by others a peacock, but their worship, their tenets, and their origin were alike a subject of mystery . . . (quoted, Kreyenbroek 1995: 2).

A main figure in Yezidi religion seems to be Sheyk 'Ardi ibn Musafir, who was historically of the eleventh century, but reappears as the Peacock

J. Tambling, *Histories of the Devil*,
DOI 10.1057/978-1-137-51832-3_1

Angel, the executor for God on the earth (Awn 1983: 196–198). Associated with Satan, he taught that evil and the devil were created by God. That idea is a key to all theologies described in this book.[1] A certain veneration for Iblis, a name of Satan in Islam, was not unknown in Sufism; Iblis being both the jinn created thousands of years before Adam, who would not bow to Adam, and also a model for self-sacrifice (Awn 1983: 151). And Mithra, the Zoroastrian demiurge, was identical with the devil, 'the devil being better equipped than God to deal with the imperfections of this world' (Kreyenboek 1995: 3, 46, 47, 60). As 'poor devils' at the bottom of the pile in the politics at work in Syria, Iraq, and Turkey, the Yezidim may question the belief systems of three religions asserting themselves as monotheisms, and each with covert other secular agendas. To be monotheistic may name a desire: to possess one God, one truth; impossible, since this can only be by repressing the presence of any 'other' force against the monotheism, and there are too many of these others.

Layard thought the Yezidi beliefs were part of a Manichean view of the world, i.e. one where Good and Evil, Light and Darkness, play out an equal opposition to each other. This book is *not* about the Yezidis, but does take up the idea of the devil embodying evil/darkness within that polarised division, though remembering – to follow Derrida on 'supplementarity' – that creating any polarity or binary opposition involves assigning an ideological priority to the first term in the divide: the opposed terms are never equally balanced. I assume that maintaining any sense of identity depends on attempts to locate, define, and control a sense of the 'other', even when claims to identity are made from an embattled position. While critical work on 'the other' has expanded, as in the modernist Marxism of Benjamin and Adorno, or in psychoanalysis, or in the post-Nietzschean critical theory associated with Foucault and Derrida or Kristeva, and in the forms of history written by Michel de Certeau – all essential for this book – modernity, in spite of that, tends towards a political refusal of that 'other'. It requires a sometimes violent assertion of the values of a particular identity. Globalisation discards the other through an intense Manicheism, as when George Bush Jr in 2002 defined US foreign policy as working against an 'axis of evil'.

While the nineteenth century related Yezidism to Manicheism, the twentieth century related it to Zoroastrianism. Zoroaster (his Greek name) or Zarathustra (his Persian, and Nietzschean, name) lived between *c.*1500–1200 BCE (Cohn 1993: 75–104), or between the sixth and seventh centuries BCE (West 2010: 4). Zoroastrian cults in Western Iran survived in the isolation of the Kurdish mountains, as they also survived in Parsi.

Beyond Zarathustra, Zoroastrianism developed an intense 'dualism', a word apparently attributable to the Orientalist scholar Thomas Hyde (1636–1702) (Duchesse-Guillemin 1958: 10). Such dualism accepted two principles, Ahura Mazda (Lord Wisdom – Ohrmazd in Pahlavi), who forms a Heptad, by which the world was created; and Angra Mainyu, or Ahriman in Pahlavi, who is the Lie, or Falseness, his destiny a place of 'Worst Existence', an equivalent to hell (Boyce 1984: 35).

Dualism reappeared in the Parthian-born Mani (CE 216–*c*.276), aware of Buddhism, of Zoroaster, of Judaism, and Jesus of Nazareth, and the Greek Gnostic Marcion, (d. *c*.160); who separated the God of the Old from that of the New Testament. Manicheism's two principles are Light and Darkness, the latter being an active force, not what Milton, who refers to 'unessential night' (*Paradise Lost* 2.439), calls darkness:

> Privation mere of light and absent day
> (*Paradise Regained*, 4.400,
> Milton 1998: 456)

That line, by which Milton meant, reassuringly, to defang Manicheism, uncannily makes nothingness and absence threatening, a point observable throughout the examples in this book.

Mani thought Light and Darkness comprised an everlasting, eternal duality: 'there was no need to account for the origin of evil' (Gardner and Lieu 2004: 11). Light being trapped in matter, demons appear from these mixtures, and 'mankind has been deliberately fashioned by demonic forces in an attempt to prevent the redemption of the light'. How does this happen? Very simply: 'through the urge for sex humans will multiply, and further entrap the divine Soul in multitudes of material bodies' (Gardner and Lieu 2004: 16). The human soul is a repository of the trapped divine and needs saving; Jesus using for this salvation the 'Light Mind', who transforms and enlightens the human soul by freeing it from the body, which is the Gnostic aspect of Manichee belief. Manichees denied that Christ was human; he was not born of Mary. Like Plotinus (*c*.205–270) the Neoplatonist philosopher, for whom matter was the principle of evil, and like Gnostics, they appealed to an asceticism which believed that the sexual urge could be wholly transcended, a position resisted by St Augustine of Hippo (Lieu 1985: 117–153). Gnostics thought that creation, because material, and therefore imperfect, came from a lesser demiurge than the New Testament God: that view might command support from St John's Gospel, which separates God and the Logos, saying of the latter, not of God: 'All things were made by him, and without him was not any thing made' (John 1:3).

Manicheism's 'negative account of creation, and fierce antipathy to matter and sexuality as intrinsically demonic' and of marriage (Gardner and Lieu 2004: 21), affected Augustine (CE 354–430), who was a Manichee in his home town Carthage, until, increasingly uneasy, he left for Rome in 383, for a Chair of Rhetoric in Milan (Brown 2000: 35–49). Converted to Christianity in 386, he spent the rest of his life resisting Manichee dualism, as in the *Confessions* (Augustine 1992: 398), as something he could not deal with completely, but whose sense of evil as an active force threatened him, as when he had engaged in Carthage with Faustus of Milevis in Numidia, 'a great trap of the devil' says Augustine (1992: 73). This Faustus – first of many in this book – calling himself the apostle of Jesus Christ, accepted the New, but rejected the Old Testament (what would be better called the Hebrew Bible) for its immorality, and its adherence to matter, thus forcing Christians into a reaction: that of spiritualising away the materiality praised in the Old Testament by allegorising it, an interpretation which while ceding ground to Manicheism, caused Augustine some relief (*Confessions* 5.14.24, Augustine 1992: 88). In a way, Faustus, and the spirit of Marcion, had won: the Old Testament, the Jewish Bible, had its unacceptable parts turned into the reverse of what they meant, so ignoring its alterity: so *De doctrina Christiana* must hold that 'anything in the divine discourse that cannot be related either to good morals or the true faith should be taken as figurative' because 'scripture enjoins nothing but love, and censures nothing but lust [cupidity]' (Augustine 1997: 75–76, Robertson 1962: 295–300).

Augustine had to argue that matter was not independent of God, but had been created by God out of nothing, and that evil was nothing, the privation of good. But how did this account for the fall of Adam, if he had no evil? Augustine was compelled into holding that there was a weakness in unfallen man, that:

> the soul *qua* 'free' created being, rather than *qua* material is just not strong enough to stand out. Its weakness, which is a weakness of the will . . . is due to the very fact of its being created from that nothing to which all created opposites tend. (Rist 1994: 106)

For Rist (1994: 282), Augustine's *City of God* (post- CE 410), comes close to finding the fall of Adam inevitable. As Augustine writes:

> only a nature created out of nothing could have been distorted by a fault . . . although the will derives its existence, as a nature, from its creation by God, its falling away from its true being is due to its creation out of nothing. (Augustine 1972: 14.3.571)

The question whether matter could ever be fully justified was one that Augustine never solved; hence his dualism. In his binary view, spirits were angelic or demonic (Augustine 1972: 5.22). 'Darkness', as opposed to Light, becomes something substantial, because it maps onto the character of Evil Angels, as opposed to Good (Augustine 1972: 11.33, 11.18): darkness supports a covert Manichee position, which contradicts the sense of evil as negation. Augustine's dualism leads him into three positions:

1) Denying the reality of evil but making it 'nothing';
2) Denying darkness as something, but making it real;
3) Denying that matter can be other than tending towards a Fall; hence committing himself to negation of the material, especially the body.

Augustine gives point to Walter Benjamin's *The Origin of German Tragic Drama*, a study which is basic to this book. Benjamin calls the devil 'the original allegorical figure', a phrase to be expanded on (Benjamin 1977: 228) but at its simplest, meaning that allegory accepts and animates the unreal. Even personification-allegory, as when a character called Love or Time appears on stage, does that: it gives a mask, a face (Greek *prosopon*) to what has no existence other than as a concept. Manichee dualism compares with Yezidism: these are religions – they include the small print of Augustine's Christianity – which incorporate the devil, either within a dualistic and adversarial relationship to God and Light, or by coming near to ascribing matter to him, and making matter evil, however much evil may be seen as a negation.

That is where this book starts, thinking dualistically, 'thinking with demons': the title of Stuart Clark's book on witchcraft in European late medieval and early modern conditions. Like the Yezidim, witchcraft is not this book's subject, but Clark's *Thinking With Demons* (1997) considers the 'conditions of discourse' within early modern Europe which allowed such an apparent spike then in conceptualising the visible presence of demons and witchcraft. For Clark, to imagine a world where demons and demonology were accepted as everyday, and where demonology was part of a scientific mode of thought which persisted until the eighteenth century, requires conceptualising a different world, whose language and assumptions are different from the present, those of modernity, but based on the dominance of two tropes within its discourse. One is *inversion* and *reversibility*, and the other, *contrarieties*.

The first two of these supports the idea that the world is, or may be, upside down. That implies the world as containing its own carnival, and that is a topic which I discuss in Chapters 3 and 5, though it is implicit elsewhere in this study, subverting, like witchcraft, the order of the world. *Reversibility* evokes Derrida's concept of 'supplementarity', where, as said before, the second term in any binary opposite (e.g. man/woman; reason/emotion) is subordinated, or minoritised, so that the first term dominates: man over woman, reason over emotion (Derrida 1976: 141–164). Uncovering the supplement, within the project of deconstruction, as a political and discursive move, allows the priority of the subordinated term to emerge, and to be seen as essential in the constitution of the first term, which is actually its supplement.

'Inversion' means that in representations of witchcraft, women will dominate: riding horses, or goats, backwards, as in such artwork as Dürer's engraving *The Witch, c.*1502, or Hans Baldung Grien's *Witches' Sabbath* (1510). Witchcraft becomes a new subject for artists (Marrow and Shestack 1981: 114–119; Zika 2007: 11–35). Clark follows Foucault in considering the early modern as a separable 'episteme', whose conditions for discourse brought demons and witchcraft into a new visibility which then becomes essential for explaining mental illness (Clark 1997: 179). This is the territory of Foucault's *Histoire de la folie* (2006: (History of Madness)), again, a topic within Chapter 3; Foucault's subject was the construction in the seventeenth century of a new discourse of 'madness', as the other side of 'folly': *folie* means both. Madness morphs as the discursive conditions of the 'episteme' also shift into another 'episteme', discontinuous with the one before, and making any 'history' one of interruptions, and differences from what has gone before, the terms of reference being only apparently the same. A 'history of the devil' must show a deepening marginalisation and silencing of the mad; making madness appear in more virulent and morbid forms in modernity; as seen in Chapters 7 and 8, which pay attention to suicide, and to schizophrenia.

Clark perhaps does not account for the potentiality of these literary tropes. One explanation for the springiness of the terms 'inversion' and 'reversibility', which relates to comedy, is that they presuppose a prior demonism within language, destabilising concepts and creating oppositions to each. In Freud's essay 'The Antithetical Meaning of Primal Words' (1910, *SE* 11.154–161), every significant word means itself *and* its opposite. Clark's *contrarieties*, as antitheses, apparently separate in a binary opposite, already contain their 'other' inside each term. Conceptual thought works in binary pairs, such as 'good/evil' – terms which recall that 'the devil is a religious entity' (Clark 1997: 437), since only God is good (Matthew 19:17). Talk of the devil must then be theological, since 'evil' presupposes that there is a sovereign centring goodness, whose supremacy and actions must be justifiable – despite the evidence – as in Milton, or the Book of Job, one of those which excited eighteenth-century theodicies (see Chapter 4).

Thinking with demons, who had been seen, in Augustinian style, as devilish, was a work of late medievalism, but Gnosticism thought in terms of a range of spirits between the angelic and demonic, a view persisting into Goethe; and sometimes that view could be tolerated officially. Such spirits could be controlled by what Chaucer's 'The Franklin's Tale' (*c.*1390) in *The Canterbury Tales* criticises under the name of 'magyc natureel', which the Franklin, the narrator, says leads to 'illusion' (1988, Fragment V.1125, 1134).The magician who will remove the rocks so that the squire Aurelius can claim Dorigen, married to the knight Arveragus, is found on the road to Orleans, and entertains Aurelius with succeeding scenes, the last showing him 'his lady on a daunce':

> On which himself he daunced, as hym thoughte.
> And whan this maister that this magyk wroighte
> Saugh it was tyme, he clapte his hands two,
> And farewell! al oure revel was ago.
> (Chaucer, 1988, *CT* Fragment V. 1200–1204)

The gesture and words anticipate Prospero dismissing the Masque in *The Tempest*: 'our revels now are ended'. That masque was performed by 'spirits' impersonating gods (*The Tempest*, 4.1.148, 120–122), a scene which will be recalled in *Faust* Part Two.

The context in *The Tempest* (1611) is the revival over a hundred years previously of neo-Platonic magic within Italy, first, through the Florentine Marsilio Ficino (1433–1499), translating the *Corpus Hermeticum* for

Cosimo de' Medici. This comprised Gnostic texts, actually written between CE 100 and 300, but attributed to 'Hermes Trismegistus' who was considered the Egyptian equivalent to Moses, himself 'learned in all the wisdom of the Egyptians' (Acts 7:22), which, therefore, made that Egyptian hermiticism older than Moses, and the Pentateuch. Within this Hermetic literature, the *Corpus Hermeticum* and the *Asclepius*, was considered to lie a mystical knowledge (*gnosis*): the basis of Ficino's belief in 'natural magic', and that of Pico della Mirandola (1463–1494). It contested Augustine's attack on Hermes Trismegistus (Augustine 1972: *City of God* Book 8. 13–22), and on the supposed Latin translator of his *Asclepius*, Apuleius of Madura (born *c.*CE 123: author of *The Golden Ass*, a source for *A Midsummer Night's Dream*). Such neo-Platonism shows too in the controversial German Cornelius Agrippa von Nettesheim (1486–1535), author of *De Occulta Philosophia*, whose early form the art historian Erwin Panofsky considered a source for Dürer's print *Melencolia I* (*c.*1513): Dürer's prime treatment of the early modern subject as split, divided from the active life, and reduced to fruitless contemplation, by the power of melancholy. Rabelais (born *c.*1483–1494, d. 1553), in the Third Book of *Gargantua and Pantagruel*, satirised Agrippa as 'Herr Trippa', a cuckolded sage crazily unconscious of that detail of his life, but who assures Panurge, who is uncertain whether to get married, that marriage means cuckoldry (*Pantagruel* (1546), Third Book, Chapter 25). As Goethe read Cornelius Agrippa and used him in *Faust*, perhaps even adopting his first name, Heinrich, for Faust, so Agrippa influenced Marlowe's *Doctor Faustus* (Traister 1984: 12–15; Nauert 1965: 330–331). Faustus' magic will make him:

> as cunning as Agrippa was
> Whose shadows made all Europe honour him.
> (*Doctor Faustus* A1.1.119–120)

Another of these neo-Platonic believers in natural magic, which might also involve invocation of demons (Marlovian 'shadows'), Giordano Bruno, burned in Rome in 1600, may be the rival Pope in *Doctor Faustus*' Act 3 Scene 1 (B Text). Bruno was the subject of Frances Yates' ambitious, sometimes tendentious, researches, as was John Dee (1527–1608), satanic predecessor of Melmoth in Maturin's Romantic and demonic novel *Melmoth the Wanderer* (Yates 1964; Maturin 2000: 556). In these figures, whose 'natural magic' made demonology its analogue, the universe connects through spiritual essences running throughout it, which could be mastered. Demons could be bound by certain rites to do the magus' bidding, and not do harm.

Yet 'natural magic' for Agrippa and Bruno tended towards the demonic (Nauert 1965: 269–273). Dee wanted to find from angels the secrets of nature (Yates 1964: 149, 265). Pico della Mirandola, like Paracelsus (1493–1541), name of the Swiss physician Theophrastus von Hohenheim, took the Jewish Kabbala as mother and origin of astronomy, and as virtually synonymous with magic. Paracelsus believed in the Light of Nature, which was both reason, and a transcendental force with a status akin to angels, even as a personal protector, or domestic god or angel (Webster 2008: 155–159). Complementary to the Light of the Father, which communicated with the soul, it regulated natural forces. Since Satan and evil spirits were Kabbalists, Kabbalistic powers derived from harnessing the Light of Nature: in the 'application of kabbalistic or magical arts the practitioner was rightly called a magus' (Webster 2008: 153–156).

Frances Yates (1964: 160–161) emphasises the difference between Kabbalism and Renaissance Humanism. The latter was interested in literature and rhetoric and style, and in discarding Scholastic authority-bound medievalism in favour of thinking which was unconfined by those rules. This difference appears with Agrippa, whose scepticism about Renaissance intellectualism Nauret stresses: reason was fallen with Adam, whose sin was giving place to the flesh: i.e., in sexual intercourse. Agrippa felt the limitations of corporeality and of material nature, which pulled down reason; he must seek out esoteric revelation. His magic, then, tends towards the nihilistic; unsurprisingly his magnum opus was *De vanitate* (1526), which set the young Goethe's brains 'in a considerable whirl for a long time' (Goethe 1900: 1.135). Goethe in the mid-eighteenth century read it under the auspices of a tutor who told the young man 'Even in God I discover defects', and several features of *Faust* derive from Agrippa, not least the black dog (the *schwarze Pudel*) which Agrippa had as his familiar, and in which form Mephisto first appears. Agrippa's anti-clericalism and hatred of monks (the devil wore a cowl to tempt Christ) made him someone who believed there was no rational basis for faith; natural, or white magic is the privileged access to knowledge, via the magus (Nauert 1965: 175–177, 327, 330–331). Agrippa was accused of atheism after his death (Nauert 1965: 195); Paola Zambelli, calling Agrippa a 'magus turned sceptic' in *De vanitate*, quotes Frances Yates on

Dr Faustus as a refusal of everything of the Renaissance, 'an echo of Agrippa's *De vanitate*' (Zambelli 2007: 116). And indeed there seems nothing for Marlowe's Faustus to do once he has traded his soul.

Platonic philosophy was aware of Zoroastrian priests as 'magi', which the *OED* derives from an Old Persian word; 'magi' was the Vulgate's translation of the word for the Wise Men at Christ's Nativity (Matthew 2:1, 2). Paracelsus saw the Magi as Kabbalists, not astrologers, possessed of a secret, 'other' wisdom (Webster 2008: 64–68). They must be compared with Simon Magus, the New Testament sorcerer, who thought that the Holy Spirit was purchasable by money (Acts 8:9–24). If buying and selling is the way to divine power, Simon Magus, who is included in the *Legenda aurea* ('The Golden Legend') of the Genovese Dominican, Jacobus de Voragine (*c.*1280–1298) gives something to the sixteenth-century Master Doctor Faustus in the German *Faustbuch*, who buys by selling the soul, in a devilish pact. *The Golden Legend*'s 'Life of Saint Peter, Apostle' records Saint Peter's contestations before Nero in Rome with the diabolically aided Simon (Voragine 1993: 1. 340–350). Iraneus of Lyon (died *c.*202) had called Simon a Gnostic (Ferreiro 2005: 35–54). Legends accreting about Simon said he attempted to fly (the latter was a marker of Faust, devils, of witches, and the Antichrist, with whom Simon was also identified (Emmerson 1981: 27–30)), and that he associated with a woman called Helena, who was to be identified with Helen of Troy. She was a pure spirit in Gnostic thought, one of a series of emanations of the feminine principles, emanating from Deity (Brown 1939: 93). The Pope (88–99), Clement of Rome, in his apocryphal writings the *Recognitions* and the *Homilies*, described how he had been seduced by Simon Magus; that his own father was Faustinianus, and his brothers Faustinus and Faustus, or else that his father was Faustus, and indistinguishable from Simon Magus (Brown 1939: 89; Voragine 1993: 2.324). Not the least fascination in Faust is how traditions almost as old as Christianity turn out to be productive of a figure who in Goethe and Mann, if not in Marlowe, is entirely a figure of an aggressive forward-pressing modernity.

2 Soliloquy and the Genius

Thunder. Enter Lucifer and Four Devils, Faustus to Them with This Speech.

W.W. Greg, editor of Marlowe's play in 1950, with a preference for the B text, wrote this stage direction for the opening of Act 1 Scene 3, when

Faustus conjures up the devils.[2] It is evident that they are listening keenly to Faustus: Mephistopheles says so (A. 1.3. 48–50), and perhaps that stage direction has a general validity for drama. Who is talking, and who is listening to a soliloquy? For Ken Frieden, in medieval pageant plays, soliloquy is 'a concomitant of sin and separation from God. As drama develops, soliloquy appears as the device by which prayer can overcome the distance between human and divine realms' (Frieden 1985: 133). That theological situation, where a soliloquy is prayer-like, means that a Marlovian or Shakespearian soliloquy may become an engagement with the daimon or genius, who was classically considered the inseparable other of the self. Socrates had spoken of his *daimonion* who spoke to restrain him (*Phaedrus* 242, *Apology* 40, Nietzsche 1956: 77, 84). In Heraclitus, earlier, 'a man's character is his *daimon*' (Barnes 1987: 125). That changes by the eighteenth century: the Earl of Shaftesbury (1671–1713), in 'Soliloquy, or Advice to an Author' (1710) identifies the Greek *daimon* and the Latin *genius* with the effects of individual intelligence, and soliloquy in the Age of Reason is less a relationship with the daimon, than an expression of the self, no longer naming a transcending being, or power. 'As an individual has a personality, so individuals are characterized by a certain kind of genius'; a special capacity. Shaftesbury says that the ancient authors meant that, through soliloquy, 'we discover a certain *Duplicity* of Soul, and divide our-selves into *two Partys*'. In this dualist state, a 'genius' becomes no supernatural agency, but rather our 'self-dissecting' partner in 'the 'Home-*Dialect* of *Soliloquy*'.[3]

The genius, or the daemonic, is always likely in Christianity to be limited to the demonic, in a rejection of paganism or demand for monotheism, and within a post-Shakespearian increasing emphasis on the speaker as the single subject; a point which would silence soliloquy, so that it becomes, as now, when seen on stage, a way of addressing an audience. Should the distinction between the daemon and the demon be maintained? Lukacher's *Daemonic Figures*, whose subtitle is *Shakespeare and the Question of Conscience*, intentionally misleads on the words when rendering St Paul's words to the Corinthian Christians, 'I would not that ye should have fellowship with devils [RV: demons]' (I Corinthians 10:20) as 'I am unwilling that you should be partners with daemons', for though the Greek is the same (Lukacher wittily compares its silent *a* with the *a* of Derrida's *différance*), he is drawing out how St Paul has attempted, perhaps unsuccessfully, since the daemonic remains, to enact the characteristic closure of monotheism which could not admit the daemonic but which creates the category of evil (Lukacher 1994: 29, 30).

Angus Nicholl's comprehensive study, *Goethe's Concept of the Daemonic: After the Ancients* maintains that the daemonic for Goethe (1749–1832) meant the classical, not the Christian concept; this is contested by Kirk Wetters, whose view is that when Goethe speaks most comprehensively about the daemon, it is as the German 'etwas', i.e., as something undefinable, a 'something': Goethe not being confined to the ancients' definition. In Goethe's autobiography, *Dichtung und Wahrheit* (Poetry and Truth), he speaks of what Egmont, hero of his tragedy of 1788 discovers:

> [Egmont] thought he could detect in nature... something which manifests itself only in contradictions, and which, therefore, could not be comprehended under any idea, still less under one word. It was not godlike, for it seemed unreasonable; not human, for it had no understanding; nor devilish, for it was beneficent, nor angelic, for it often betrayed a malicious pleasure. It resembled chance, for it evolved no consequences; it was like Providence, for it hinted at connection. All that limits us it seemed to penetrate...
>
> To this principle, which seemed to come in between all other principles to separate them, and yet to link them all together, I gave the name of Daemonic.... (Goethe 1900: 2.157)

Wetters seems right in finding this daemonic a non-nameable principle, which, since it concludes Goethe's autobiography, brings into question its entire project, and contests the thought that life can be articulated biographically, in a non-ambiguous, single-minded sequential clarity obeying chronological time. Goethe says that 'with man, especially does [this daemonic power] stand in a most wonderful connection, forming in him a power which, if it be not opposed to the moral order of the world, nevertheless does often so cross it that one may be regarded as the warp, and the other as the woof' (Goethe 1900: 2.158).[4]

The daemonic's significance to Goethe comes out in his conversations with Johann Peter Eckermann.[5] On 11 March 1828, Napoleon – whom Goethe met at Erfurt in 1808 – is pronounced 'daemonic'; this is allied to 'genius' as the 'productive power' (Eckermann 1970: 245–253, Blumenberg 1985: 465–522). It may be noted that for Nietzsche, 'the event that made [Goethe] rethink his *Faust*, indeed the whole "human" problem, was the appearance of Napoleon' (Nietzsche 1999: 135). Similar discussions of genius with Eckermann appear on 2, 8 and 30 March 1831, when the daemonic is found within poetry, 'especially that which is unconscious, before which reason and understanding fall short, and which therefore produces effects far surpassing all conception'. The 'daemonic' and the 'genius' resist assimilation to Christianity, and to the theological. Walter Benjamin contends that its idea 'accompanies Goethe's vision all his life' (Benjamin *SW1*: 316), and its doubleness of meaning needs to be stressed for Goethe: it is to be discussed within the language of Christian theology, and it is outside that.

In an early poem, 'Mahomets Gesang' (A Song to Mahomet, 1772–1773), Goethe's tribute to a religion of genius, the 'genius' is the mountain torrent that leaps forth without an origin – for genius can have no historical origin – which pours forth in phallic power and lack of restraint, and takes other tributary rivers with it, which are fearful of death (Middleton 1983: 22–27; Wellbery 1996: 130–147). But in a later sonnet, 'Mächtiges Überraschen' (Immense Astonishment, 1807–1808), whose classical form contrasts with the violent Pindaric free verse-form of the 'Song to Mahomet' and its evocation of an originless absolutely new thing emerging in Islam, the language reappears of a river pouring forth: but the second stanza intercepts it:

> Dämonisch aber stürtz mit einem Male –
> Ihr folgen Berg und Wald in Wirbelwinden –
> Sich Oreas, Behagen dort zu finden
> Und hemmt den Lauf, begrenzt die weite Schale.
> (Middleton 1983: 176–177)

(Yet suddenly Oreas with daemonic swiftness, hillside and forest following her in whirlwinds, slides down and settles there, hems in his run, setting bounds to the wide bowl.)

Oreas was a mountain nymph, attendant on Artemis, who was herself a goddess of restraint. The force of the daemonic genius here is to check the wild run of the river, contain it in a bowl. The 'astonishment' comes from the interruption of one daemonic force, the river, by another. Goethe comes back to the daemonic in 'Urworte – Orphisch' (Primal Words – Orphic 1817), where the 'Dämon' is first of five forces, expressed in five prime words, attending the child at birth, the others being Chance (*Tyche*), Eros (*Liebe*), Necessity (*Anagké – Nötigung*), and Hope (*Elpis – Hoffnung*)

> Wie an dem Tag, der dich der Welt verliehen,
> Die Sonne stand zum Grusse der Planeten,
> Bist alsobald und fort und dort gediehen
> Nach dem Gesetz, wonach du angetreten.
> So musst du sein, dir kannst du nicht entfliehen,
> So sagten schon Sibyllen, so Propheten;
> Und keine Zeit und keine Macht zerstückelt,
> Geprägte Form, die lebend sich entwickelt.
> (Middleton 1983: 230–231)

(As to the day, which gave you to the world, the sun stood to the greeting of the planets, so quickly and strongly you began to grow and have continued to do so according to the law that prevailed over your beginning. So must it be, you cannot escape yourself, so said, completely, the Sibyls and the Prophets and no time and no might can destroy the minted/printed form, so stamped upon life.)

As the sybils and prophets in the Sistine Chapel watch over the birth of Adam, and his fall, so theatrically displayed in Michaelangelo's ceiling, so 'du' – the reader, the poet – starts out life under a 'Gesetz' (law) which imposes an 'es muss sein' (it must be) upon the human form which has been so impressed. The daemon is the law allotted to the individual; it both sets free and limits, being thus absolutely equivocal in character. It is not identifiable, in these last two poems, with the word 'genius' as this is currently used when Shakespeare is called a genius. It is both inside and outside the subjectivity which it questions and qualifies and produces to ambivalent effect: it is Socrates' Daemon as a restraining force. And Chance, Eros, Necessity, and Hope, are all part of it; perhaps the poem 'Urworte – Orphisch' moves in a circular form. The Daemon and Tyche seem opposed (male to female); if so, perhaps they oppose each other in art, as Lukács thinks (Wetters 2014: 135–159). There is no Romanticism here in this sense of the demonic, as in the idea of a romantic evil such as I think Euan Fernie contends for in claiming for 'evil' 'sheer vitality' and 'ambivalence' which intrudes onto 'the Good' (Fernie 2013: 21–22, 33). The demonic, as I shall call both the daemonic and demonic, names the unreadable, the ambiguous which Goethe sees as outlining, in the 'Urworte', 'a universal world of character development and socialisation, whereas *Poetry and Truth* presents the demonic as the inability of retrospective knowledge to give univocal meaning to a biographical-developmental narrative' (Wetters 2014: 136). With this contradiction in mind, the demonic, and the devil, cannot be regarded as one thing, nor regarded as interpretable in any pregiven way; rather Goethe's description of what Egmont found defeats figuration: what it resembles is what it is not.

Nor can the devil be labelled evil, save in a closed discourse that has prefixed the terms. 'Evil', as an allegorical personification, making the unreal real, identifies the 'other' with qualities I project from myself, or would separate from myself, creating a category to be expunged, in the name of the Good, or God. Allowing in a category of 'evil' creates a centring discourse, not reorientating, or disorganising thought which claims to understand what is 'Good'. It is true that 'evil' as a concept has received some fascinating treatment and attempts at a non-theological definition, as with Jean Nabert in 1955: as that 'which absolutely should not have occurred' (Dews 2008: 8). This recalls how many genocidal powers there have been in modernity; it challenges Augustine's evil as negation; nonetheless, it lacks explanatory value; it is a reification, which, accepting the term because it is already in use, prevents getting beyond the theological, or the metaphysical. In contrast to Goethe, it essentialises people and their acts. In connecting the daemonic with evil by conflating it with the demonic, the daemonic gets demonised; an unlucky history, part of this book's subject.

3 Allegory

And allegory may indeed be the devil's preferred genre. In T.F. Powys' minor classic novel, *Mr Weston's Good Wine* (1927), Mr Weston and his chauffeur, Michael, whose name implies the Archangel, visit the village of Folly Down to sell their wine, which speaks equally of love and death. Mr Weston is God who wishes to forget himself (Powys 1967: 39); he speaks of the Bible as poetry (46); but as unfinished indeed (183). As recalling, in the book's title, Jane Austen's *Emma*, Mr Weston speaks sympathetically of a poet admired by Austen: William Cowper (1731–1800), a Calvinist in the Age of Reason, whose madness and suicide attempts, and sense of himself as a 'castaway', the title of his most famous poem, derived from a literal reading of the Bible which convinced him he was damned (191). Cowper's 'Lines Written During a Period of Insanity' (1763 – an editor's title), beginning 'Hatred and Vengeance, my eternal portion', pronounce the sense of being an outcast, from a god who is diabolical in damning him, while he is, diabolically, refused the possibility of suicide (which he more than once attempted, out of despair):

> Man disavows, and Deity disowns me:
> Hell might afford my miseries a shelter;
> Therefore hell keeps her ever hungry mouths all
> Bolted against me.
>
> (Cowper 1934: 290)

His death-in-life is not to go down to hell alive, but to be 'buried above ground'. Mr Weston separates himself from this Calvinism, which is nonetheless implicit in the Bunyanesque idiom of the writing; the book becomes, as allegory – like Bunyan – a plea for allegory in the sense that no meanings are yet clinched for ever, nothing finished, giving point to the ending, where Mr Weston's 'old enemy' is to be disposed of: 'in his own element – fire' (222). Michael drops a burning match into the petrol tank, and he and Mr Weston vanish too in that element dear to Zoroastrianism; the constituting matter of Iblis. Does Powys suggest that the only God worth believing in is the one who is an allegory, not an entity, having no abiding quality to be hypostatised as good, or evil – certainly not one to be distinguished from the devil? That both forms of absolutism have to go at once?

Powys' wit recalls how vivid and acute has been the need to personify the 'other' as the devil in popular culture. Cowper's depressions and suicide attempts relate to a Calvinism and literalism in Biblical interpretation which I discuss with relation to Hogg (Chapter 5), but which recalls Benjamin's devil as 'the original allegorical figure'. Earlier in *The Origin of German Tragic Drama*, Benjamin distinguishes symbol from allegory:

> Whereas in the symbol destruction is idealised and the transfigured face of nature is fleetingly revealed in the light of redemption, in allegory the observer is confronted with the *facies hippocratica* of history as a petrified, primordial landscape. Everything about history that, from the very beginning, has been untimely, sorrowful, unsuccessful, is expressed in a face – or rather in a death's head. (Benjamin 1977: 166)

Here, allegory counters a sense of unity, such as the idea of the symbol proposes, allowing for the thought of progress, or success, or reconciliation. Where the symbol puts, or throws an image and concept together, as if not recognising the divided, dual nature of all concepts, and indeed of the single subject, the diabolic overthrows. Allegory gives history in images: for example the face which is a skull, a death's head. This is not the least of the devil's images, which shows not natural forces working for redeeming purposes in a Claude-like landscape of the golden age, but history as a continuing expression of things happening in the wrong time, of repeated disasters, which induce the melancholia which is at the heart of the seventeenth-century German *Trauerspiel* (mourning plays) Benjamin writes of, and, finally, of repeated failures. To write history as allegory, and to find allegories, which speak of transience and of what Benjamin (229) thinks of as one work of the devil, causing 'terror in mourning', as constitutive of history, is to confront disconnectedness. It implies that, since allegory is 'speaking other', all utterance is other, singular, not reducible to a narrative, nor to a law which generalises it, or unites it in the mode of the symbol. The symbolic mode of writing fits a narrative of progress, which Benjamin's Marxism opposes. History, which always has what Michel de Certeau calls 'heterology' inscribed within it – the foreign in the familiar, the past in the present and the vice versa; everything anachronous, which is the sphere of the devil – appears as allegory, images which do not have a 'natural' fit with each other, which cannot be worked into a consistent single narrative.

Here, two things need to be put together; the devil as not a name for 'evil', but as what has been dumped on as unacceptable, so that the devil may be the medieval comic, fool, clown, ass, vagabond, tinker, beggar, a 'poor devil' (a meaning of 'elf': *OED sb.*1.3.5), the cuckold, above all the *picaro*. Carnival could find a place for him, and for his complex relationship to laughter; hence the Russian critic and philosopher Mikhail Bakhtin inscribes him within Rabelais' work. But folly has been fought over, and interpreted as a madness to be excluded, and that single-mindedness which rejects the plural produces the devil in the modernity that so excludes. Folly shows in the Dostoevskian 'polyphonic novel', but Dostoevsky also shows how madness has politically excluded, as the embodiment of what is 'untimely, sorrowful, unsuccessful'; the 'petrifying' sense of history, having a Medusa-like face, which Benjamin refers to, may induce suicide. Yet madness may be a political weapon, fixing, and unfixing together, as in *The Master and Margarita*. Its most uncanny manifestation may be as music, as in Thomas Mann, heading up a discussion of where European modernity has arrived at. In his *Doctor Faustus*, music, as 'nothing', represents masculine abstract order, and feminine seduction both together (only the gender terms may also be switched): as figured in *Parsifal*'s Kundry; strangely diabolical. Folly, so often appearing with the death's head, is 'nothing', like Shakespeare's madness, but such negation articulates with the Augustinian sense of evil as nothing, as absence. In modernity, such nothingness shades into nihilism, which is suicidal in Dostoevsky; similarly, Goethe's Mephisto calls himself the spirit that negates. It is no coincidence that the age of reason, like Romanticism and realism, expunged allegory, in favour of symbolism; allegory responds to an older way of thinking which does not reject the catachresis of personification: where masks cover what might be something or nothing, what cannot be fixed in terms of identity. Symbolism, more positivist in drive, says that things are as they are described. The devil stands for the unfinished within history, and history as heterological, which means that it cannot be written at all without the devil's exclusion: which, indeed means history cannot be written, save by an ideological closure upon events.

That absolute ambiguity of the devil, ruining all forms of representation, prevents anyone being able to claim him or reject him. The last three chapters of this book present a modernity which has come close to ruin, to Benjamin's 'single catastrophe, which keeps piling wreckage upon wreckage' (Benjamin 2003: 392). As allegorical, asking whether something is something or nothing, the devil, in what follows, embodies whatever questions the being of entities; it is whatever 'default' marks the human. That works with Bernard Stiegler's argument that the human is definitionally lacking, requiring something additional to make it up as what Derrida would call the supplement: perhaps the prosthesis, as a smartphone or the powers of new technology which seems to guarantee presence while wiping out memory, may be the new devil (Stiegler 1998: 1.16). The devil is the supplement, always with the power of questioning what it is that it supplements, and implying that a Faustian bargain is within capitalist modernity, cause of all its collateral damage. And who, for Goethe, goes faster, who is more modern: Faust – 'for we must be absolutely modern', says Rimbaud in *Saison en Enfers* – or the devil? Yet Rimbaud's advice requires being able to read modernity; not simply accepting it as unavoidable; reading it for its ideological pretensions. And modernity may also be reactionary: exploitative, whether on a micro scale, individuating human subjects to make them even more accessible to the market, or to be disposable goods themselves, perhaps according to a secret theology within political discourse which assesses people as good or evil; or opening up everything on earth for 'development', with disastrous environmental effects. Certainly, in

Goethe, and the texts discussed after, modernity seems to be perfectly schizophrenic, and productive of madness.

Notes

1. For traditional studies of the devil, see, from a huge literature, for which they provide full bibliographies, the four volumes by Russell (1977, 1981, 1985, 1986), and by McGinn (2000) and Kelly (2006). These are thorough, and detailed, and outside what this book attempts to do, (a) because they systematically link the devil with evil, which is to concede the point to Christianity, whose story they are telling; for Kelly, 'the only true devil is the Christian devil' (2006: 4); (b) because they assume there is a history there of something discussable whereas this book has as subject the history of a non-concept; (c) because their agenda is so much pro-American in what it evaluates as evil and then passes off as a universal discourse: note the slippage in the title whereby McGinn's book on the Antichrist becomes in its subtitle 'the *human* fascination with evil'. Their nostalgia is that though talk of the devil has, largely, died down, there is still evil to be considered: 'the enemy within' (McGinn 2000: xvi). By far the best traditional study of the devil, putting him into narrative theory, is Forsyth (1987), while Fernie (2013) is engaging. Other overviews of the devil are noted as they appear and are discussed.
2. Marlowe's play exists in two versions *The Tragicall History of Dr Faustus* (A version, 1604), or *The Tragicall History of the Life and Death of Dr Faustus* (B version, 1616). 'A' shows Faust acting; 'B', which is longer, shows him acted upon, with evidence of censoring in religious passages ('God' becomes 'heaven'). It is more moralising, Calvinist, gloating in details confirming Faustus' damnation (Barber 1988: 87–130). Yet since Marlowe died in 1593, neither text possesses authority. Teasingly, Philip Henslowe commissioned revisions to the play in 1602, so perhaps both versions have suffered tampering. It seems unwise to commit to either A or B in isolation.
3. Quoted, Frieden (1985: 67, 68); he compares also the uses, and definitions, of 'Genius' in Addison's *Spectator* nos. 159, and 160.
4. *Dichtung und Wahrheit* was completed as to its first three books by 1813; its fourth, from which this comes, was written 1831–1832, and published posthumously in 1833.
5. Eckermann (1792–1854) met Goethe in Weimar in 1823, and began recording conversations with him in 1824, continuing until Goethe's death: they were published in 1836 and 1848.

Chapter 1: 'The Tempter or the Tempted, Who Sins Most?'

How art thou fallen from heaven, O Lucifer ['day star', margin], son of the morning! How art thou cut down to the ground, which didst weaken the nations.

For thou hast said in thine heart, I will ascend into heaven, I will exalt my throne above the stars of God, I will sit also upon the mount of the congregation in the sides of the north;

I will ascend above the heights of the clouds; I will be like the most High.

Yet thou shalt be brought down to hell, to the sides of the pit.

(*Isaiah* 14: 12–15)

Marlowe's *Doctor Faustus* is the subject then, and building on that, in moving to Shakespeare, the soliloquy, as the privileged medium for the devil's appearance.

Georg Helmstetter (or Georgius of Helmstadt – his family name unknown) was an apparently 'white' magician who was born *c.*1466, heard of in Heidelberg in 1483, known through some eight extant documents, and recorded as dead in Staufen-im-Breisgau around 1539. Helmstetter seems to have been 'Magister Georgius Sabellicus, Faustus junior, fons necromanticorum, astrologus, magus secundus, agromanticus, pyromanticus . . . ' and again, 'Georgius Faustus . . . a mere braggart and a fool' (quoted, Bevington and Rasmussen 1993: 4). So he called himself 'Faustus'. 'Sabellicus' is Latin: meaning north of Rome, land of the Sabines, associated with the occult. 'Magus' relates to Simon Magus. Luther seems to have been fascinated by the name, and implicitly aligned Helmstetter with the Faustus the Manichee who had oppressed Augustine, while Melanchthon (1497–1560), Luther's

J. Tambling, *Histories of the Devil*,
DOI 10.1057/978-1-137-51832-3_2

co-Reformer, linked Helmstetter with Simon Magus and Cornelius Agrippa (Laan and Weeks 2013: 129, 50–52, 67–91, 154–162).

Influenced by Melanchthon and Luther, who believed that every magician made a pact with the devil (Baron 1978: 78), the anonymous German *Faustbuch* appeared in 1587, and in an English version, by the possibly Calvinist 'P.F.', as *The Historie of the Damnable Life and Deserved Death of Doctor John Faustus.* Here appears Faustus' 'miserable and lamentable end' (chapter 62, title), Faustus confessing to his students, who find his written history after his death:

> I die both a good and bad Christian; a good Christian, for that I am heartily sorry, and in my heart always pray for mercy that my soul may be delivered: a bad Christian, for that I know the devil will have my body, and that would I willingly give him so that he would leave my soul in quiet . . . (Jones 1994: 178).

The translation appeared in 1592; perhaps earlier, according to John Henry Jones' edition of *The English Faust Book.* Jones prefers late 1588, followed by Marlowe's play in 1589. The year 1590 witnessed the production of Robert Greene's comic-historical play *Friar Bacon and Friar Bungay*, which borrows from the *Faust Book*, from an anonymous mid-sixteenth-century prose romance, *The Famous Historie of Friar Bacon*, and from Marlowe. It has dealings with the devil as its subject (Jones 1994: 66–72, 256–258). Marlowe's play, then, seems to be from one, or two, or many Faust versions, some predating Helmstetter, and which may even have their own English independent counterpart in the rhyme of Dr Forster who went to Gloucester; perhaps indicating too the pronunciation of the English Faustus, to suit with 'we must per*form*/The *form* of *Fau*stus' *for*tunes . . . ' (*Doctor Faustus*, Prologue A, 6–7). Similarly, the eponymous hero of the anonymous comedy *The Merry Devil of Edmonton* (1608) was the fifteenth-century Peter Fabell, who had 'beguiled the Devell by pollicie' (*ODNB*): he is the 'merry devil' himself, as Launcelot Gobbo is (*The Merchant of Venice* 2.3.2).

Jones' dating agrees with William Empson, for whom *Doctor Faustus* predates P.F.'s 1592 *Faustbuch*, saying it was acted *before* Henslowe's company gave its first recorded performance, i.e. 1594. The ambivalence within *Doctor Faustus* shows in the play's tensions between its forward daring and its debt to late medieval morality plays (see Chapter 2) (Brockbank 1962: 16–23). That is also apparent in *Friar Bacon and Friar Bungay.* Empson notes its double plot: one the wooing by the courtiers, including the future Edward the First, of Margaret, a Perdita-like country girl; the other comprises incidents from the thirteenth-century figure of the magus Roger Bacon ('wise Bacon', *Doctor Faustus* A.1.1.156), who seems a parallel to the later Peter Fabell. Bacon commands devils, having the power of a glass which can see things at a distance, and into the future; he desires to make a brazen head whose prophecies will give him status, and as a patriot, wants to wall England round with brass (compare *Faustus* A 1.1.90). The play's nationalism makes him beat the German magus, Vandermast, returning him to Germany, transported by the Hercules whom he has raised up. Faustus' pupil is Friar Bungay, his comic servant Miles, who lets him down over the appearance of the brazen head, for which he goes to hell, on the devil's back (but Miles wears the spurs, so the devil is put to it). However, Friar Bacon breaks the glass, renouncing his magic.

Friar Bungay tells Vandermast, who is surely a reply to Doctor Faustus, that 'magic haunts the grounds' (*Friar Bacon and Friar Bungay* 9.46). For Empson, that is a claim for 'the value of matter', which he takes to be:

> the essential novelty of the Renaissance. (Matter is not evil and made from nothing but part of God from which God willingly removed his will: one can therefore put [more] trust in the flesh, the sciences, the natural man . . .) (Empson 1965: 33–34).

Empson supports this via his own anti-Augustinianism, and anti-Manicheism. He almost equates the double plot, which he says English drama up to 1642 did not outlive, with the devil. *Doctor Faustus* shows the double plot with Robin the Ostler (a Miles figure) and Rafe, not coincidentally the fool's name in *Friar Bacon and Friar Bungay*; and their attempts to conjure the Devil.

1 Doctor Faustus: The Good Angel and the Spirit

Empson accounts for the differences between *Doctor Faustus* A and B by arguing for a censorship affecting all published editions of the play, turning it towards an orthodoxy which Marlowe lacked. He notes the reference to 'infernal, middle and supreme powers' (Jones 1994: 99) who witness the bargain that Faustus seals with Mephistopheles (Mephostophiles in the *Faust Book*: the name's meaning is given as 'no friend to light', or 'the light is not a friend': Empson 1965: 203). Jones annotates powers as 'nature spirits, e.g. nymphs, goblins, salamanders, etc.' (Jones 1994: 193, compare; Empson 1987: 98–106). As Oberon distinguishes himself from damned spirits of the night, saying 'But we are spirits of a different sort; / I with the morning's love have oft made sport' (*A Midsummer Night's Dream* 3.2.388–389), so here. The powers fit Valdes' simile, when, alluding to Mexico, and Peru, he says: as 'Indian Moors obey their Spanish lords,/So shall the subjects of every element / Be always serviceable to us three' (*Doctor Faustus* 1.1.123–125). Although Faustus has said that 'necromantic books are heavenly' (1.1.52), so claiming black magic, the Evil Angel tempts him less to 'evil' than to Tamburlaine-like exploration and dominion:

> Go forward, Faustus, in that famous art
> Wherein all nature's treasury is contained.
> Be thou on earth as Jove is in the sky,
> Lord and commander of these elements.
> (*Doctor Faustus* 1.1.76–79)

For Empson, Faustus compacts not with the devil, but middle spirits, another example of whom might be Ariel, in *The Tempest*, servant of Prospero, whose name translates as Faustus (fortunate). These 'middle spirits' are fairies; in Empson's plotting, 'Marlowe supposes a Middle Spirit who is a quisling or rather a double agent, professing to work for the devils, and actually inducing them to grant their powers to Faust, but on condition that Faust gives his immortal soul beforehand to the quisling' (Empson 1987: 121). This is lost in censorship. Reading Empson's view allegorically, rather than literally, might allow thinking that Marlowe revised the moralistic *Faust Book* to admit white magic, and affirm the presence of something other than the opposites present in Augustine; the play makes magic wonderful, and non-Christian, as well as diabolical.

In A, apart from the Iago-like 'aside', 'O what will I not do to obtain his soul?' (*Doctor Faustus* 2.1.73), the strategy revealed of the Tempter, the devil (Matthew 4:3), Mephistopheles is less active than melancholic, aware of his own loss, repeating endlessly 'Lucifer' (*Doctor Faustus* 1.3.41–100), who, as a son 'most dearly loved of God' lost heaven 'by aspiring pride and insolence', and who is eroticised in the lines: 'as beautiful / As was bright Lucifer before his fall' (2.1.160–161). Lucifer is 'Lightborne' in *Edward the Second*: he sodomises the king with a red-hot spit. The B text turns Beelzebub, an Old Testament god (2 Kings 1:2) into Lucifer's 'dam'

(*Doctor Faustus*, B.2.3.95), and makes Mephistopheles, the 'familiar spirit' (A. 4.1.4) more malicious:

> 'Twas I, that, when thou wert i' the way to heaven
> Damned up thy passage. When thou took'st the book
> To view the Scriptures, then I turned the leaves
> And led thine eye.
>
> (B.5.2.95–101)

Mephistopheles says Faustus 'begets a world of idle fantasies/To overreach the devil' (B.5.2.14, 15). Hyperbole is the figure for overreaching (*OED* 1579 citation); Feste calls the Malvolio's demon 'hyperbolical fiend' (*Twelfth Night* 4.2.22), though 'to overreach' may also mean to defraud, by language (*OED* vb.5b), so that diabolism works by hyperbole and by guile. Faustus as 'overreacher', like the base-born Tamburlaine (see Levin 1954), would also exceed God:

> Excelling all whose sweet delight disputes
> In heavenly matters of theology;
> Till, swoll'n with cunning of a self-conceit.
> His waxen [cp. 'waxing'] wings did mount above his reach
> And melting heavens conspired his overthrow[.]
>
> (A Prologue 18–23)

Theology's danger is disputing over texts which circle around what cannot be known, the mastery of which, creating pride (hence 'swollen'), becomes apparent when it seems the heavens have 'conspired' (but with whom? Hell?) to destroy him; the Icarus imagery makes him Luciferian.

The Chorus' narrative of his fall (is all up with Faustus before his soliloquy?) is difficult to correlate with what opens with 'the man that in his study sits'. Is his 'study', his location, or his occupation? Faustus says 'settle thy studies, Faustus', as if they were unsettled. And to make a comparison, Macbeth says 'I am settled' (1.7.80) when resolved to murder Duncan. Which is diabolical, an unsettled state (the devil among the books), or a settled one? Following Benjamin, 'the Renaissance explores the universe; the baroque explores libraries. Its meditations are devoted to books' (Benjamin 1977: 140), Faustus is melancholic, baroque; like Prospero, who thought his library was dukedom enough (*The Tempest* 1.2.109–110). Faustus has exceeded and rejected the university faculties: philosophy (logic), medicine, law, and theology, to pursue magic, since 'a sound magician is a mighty god' (A1.1.64), but he is self-divided, introspective, of the baroque, as Benjamin (1977: 152, 179), claims Agrippa of Nettesheim to be saturnine, melancholic.

Faustus starts with a 'self-discourse' (Williams 1983: 48), addressing the self as an other, a second person, as if looking at himself (as every speaker of a soliloquy must know s/he is being looked at: the question is by whom). There may be three people present in Faustus' speech to Mephistopheles:

> I charge thee wait upon me whilst I live,
> To do whatever Faustus shall command....
> (1.3.37–38)

In *The Jew of Malta* (*c.*1590), Barabas, who speaks half the lines in the play, many in soliloquy form, starts with a sentence in mid-flow. *Richard the Third* also starts with a soliloquy (uniquely in Shakespeare – as though the Machevill speaking the Prologue in *The Jew of Malta* becomes, in Shakespeare's tragedy, Richard the Machiavel speaking his own prologue). Richard passes from 'our', to 'I' and then, addressing as 'Thoughts' the other which, as inside him, makes him speak, he says: 'Dive, thoughts, down to my soul, here Clarence comes' (*Richard the Third* 1.1.41). This address to a named part of the self, such as the faculty of Thought, C.S. Lewis associates with late Latin literature, specifically Prudentius, in *Psychomachia* (*c.* CE 400), where different qualities fight for possession of the soul. So Lewis writes:

> to fight against 'Temptation' is also to explore the inner world; and it is scarcely less plain that to do so is to be already on the verge of allegory. We cannot speak, perhaps we can hardly think, of an 'inner conflict' without a metaphor. (Lewis 1936: 60)

He connects such metaphorising with allegory. The 'inner world' is that of soliloquy. The *Confessions* noticed Ambrose's private reading:

> when he was reading, his eye ran over the page and his heart perceived the sense, but his voice and tongue were silent... Very often when we were there, we saw him silently reading and never otherwise. (Augustine 1992: 92–93)

Desire for selfhood defined by its own silent thoughts, not reading aloud to a community, so not defined by other people, restraining his own language, was fundamental for Augustine; the desire has deepened ever since. Augustine wrote *Soliloquies*, i.e. dialogues; his invention, described in the *Confessions* (Augustine 1992: 9.4, 159) where he tells God: 'the books that I wrote [in retirement a year after converting from Manicheism] were indeed now written in your service, and attest my discussions with those present and with myself alone before you'. In these, Reason begins with Augustine, 'What then do you want to know?' Augustine replies that he wants to know his soul. But that is impossible, for the soul contains the unknown. And what is the Reason that speaks? Is he or she inside, or outside him? If inside, who is the 'Augustine' who answers? It is an Augustine who responds to Reason, so that it is no more than a single aspect of Augustine. And Augustine's form of utterance, throughout the *Confessions*, is to speak of 'I', unified, like Ambrose. But that 'I' of the narrative exists at a temporal distance from the 'I' that writes, and, following the linguist Emile Benveniste, the speaker, the subject of the enunciation, may be present, but his 'I' exceeds the 'I' within what he says, which saying is a creation of rhetoric, and a dramatization of that 'I'. The 'I' who speaks knows, and is, much more than the 'I' who emerges in their speech (Belsey 1985: 42–54). Hegel says 'I' is a universal: that is, when I say 'I' I am only saying what everyone else can also enter into. I can say nothing unique about my 'I' which is unique to myself; 'I' becomes a conventional rhetorical term, and reveals nothing that is not a universal statement. Paul de Man (1996: 98) quotes Hegel's *Encyclopaedia of the Philosophical Sciences* paragraph 20:

> When I say 'I', I *mean* myself as *this* I to the exclusion of all others; but what I say, I, is precisely anyone; any I, as that which excludes all others from itself. (Hegel, in de Man 1996: 98)

The context is Hegel's previous sentence, 'Since language states only what is general, I cannot say what is only my opinion' to be saying that '*I* cannot say I'; which would mean that an attempt to say 'I' does not actually succeed in reaching the identity of the speaker.

All naming – I, you – is catachresis. Personification allegory, calling an aspect of the self 'Thought', or, in medieval literature, splitting the self into parts (Love,/Reason/Fear/Idleness) reifies categories by creating them in the names. If the devil is 'the original allegorical figure', non-real but potent, that is because allegory assigns a mask to categories which have no objective existence. But the non-existence of qualities or thoughts does not prevent them from controlling. Kierkegaard, for example, defines anxiety – which is already halfway towards being a personification – in terms of fascination, as 'a sympathetic antipathy and an antipathetic sympathy' (Kierkegaard 1980: 42). Anxiety, allegorical so unreal and diabolical together, is something which the subject is drawn to and away from simultaneously. If I am fascinated, I am held by something neither inside nor outside, putting subjectivity and rationalism into question; both real, and nothing, like the equally allegorical Worry, which can keep a person awake all night. Kierkegaard's editors gloss his definition of anxiety from his journals as 'an alien power which grips the individual, and yet he cannot tear himself free from it and does not want to, for one fears, but what he fears he desires' (235). Anxiety is the nothing which holds power which seems to be addictive.

Benjamin calls the devil 'allegorical', when discussing the devil on stage, instancing *Richard the Third.* Richard's plotting in his first soliloquy is nothing – words – yet it produces something, for immediately Clarence enters, going to prison, and then Hastings, leaving it, but also, indirectly, on his way to death; and then Lady Anne enters, whom Richard will woo and destroy. The soliloquy as nothing starts something. It comes not necessarily from a confident person taking an audience into their confidence; it relates to two concepts which C.S. Lewis pairs, temptation and allegory: these, which may be the names of nothing, invoke the devil. In Marlowe, then, as Faustus thinks on necromancy, self-observation takes over:

> How am I glutted with conceit of this . . .
> (*Doctor Faustus* A.1.1.80)

In the excess which craves absolute knowledge, he wants spirits to 'Resolve me of all ambiguities' (82). But the devil sides with ambiguity. Hence Benjamin notes Richard's alliance to the devil in his mastery of double language: as he says, 'Thus, like the formal Vice, Iniquity, / I moralise two meanings in one word' (*Richard the Third* 3.1.82–83).

During Faustus' soliloquy, others are on-looking, tempting, increasing ambiguities: the Good and Evil Angels (B: 1.1.68: 'Enter Angel and Spirit'). What is the difference between these? (The *Faust Book* calls Mephistopheles a spirit: Faustus asks him, as 'the spirit', how God made the world – he does not answer (Jones 1994: 116). They are implicit in the second act's initial soliloquy (2.1.1–14):

> Now Faustus, must thou needs be damned,
> And canst thou not be saved.

What boots it then to think of God or heaven?
Despair in God and trust in Beelzebub.
Now go not backward. No, Faustus, be resolute.
Why waverest thou? O something soundeth in mine ears:
'Abjure this magic, turn to God again!'
Ay, and Faustus will turn to God again.
To God? He loves thee not.
The god thou servest is thine own appetite
Wherein is fixed the love of Beelzebub.

(A.2.1.1–12)

The first six sentences give plural voices, urging 'resolution' (compare 'resolved'), a keyword for Marlowe and the play (McAlindon 1981: 129–140). This breakup into separate sentences does not appear to make Faustus irresolute; rather, 'resolution' would complete his damnation, in ending irresolvable 'ambiguities'. The first set of voices are answered by another ('O something soundeth . . . '), its exhortation quoted: 'Abjure . . . '. It leads into another voice, agreeing, which is succeeded by another ('To God?'). Is that diabolical, or the protest of another voice, which feels unloved by God? Faustus, saying that something sounds in his ear, does so though no external voice has been heard; whereas in Act 2 Scene 3, he contemplates repenting, and immediately the angels appear:

GOOD ANGEL: Faustus, repent yet, God will pity thee.
EVIL ANGEL: Thou art a spirit [i.e. a devil]. God cannot pity thee.
FAUSTUS: Who buzzeth in mine ears I am a spirit?
Be I a devil, yet God may pity me.
Ay, God will pity me if I repent.
EVIL ANGEL: Ay, but Faustus never shall repent.
FAUSTUS: My heart's so hardened I cannot repent.
Scarce can I name salvation, faith or heaven
But fearful echoes thunder in mine ears:
'Faustus, thou art damned!'. . . .

(2.3.12–21)

Faustus does not identify these voices with the angels; they seem part of a plurality, interior *and* exterior, contradicting each other; yet, since the Good Angel here is reduced to a single line, they imply a hostility towards the man who is being induced towards suicidal despair, or, more simply, and less dramatically, driven more and more towards seeing himself as a single subject. The point is often made that any loving heaven is excluded from the play. Apart from the Good Angel, and the Old Man (5.1.36), there is no evidence of God in the play, no expression of a loving God. If Faustus' first soliloquy reads out, as a sample text, from Justinian's *Institutes*, '*Exhaereditare filium non potest pater nisi –*' (1.1.31): 'a father cannot disinherit his son unless – ', the ambiguity of the father comes out: why *would* a father be expected to disinherit his son – unless that father is diabolical? The challenge to God becomes necessary, but it is, Mephistopheles points out, the devil's opportunity (1.3.47–52).

What happens in that first soliloquy, when Faustus reads Jerome's Bible selectively? He is not alone, for the Angel and Spirit beside him continue, or expand his dialogue/soliloquy (there is hardly any difference between these terms here), as both internal and external. And how would an audience know which is good and which is evil? – though presumably the Good Angel stands on the right-hand side, as happens in the morality play *The Castle of Perseverance* (see Chapter 2). What distinguishing marks would resolve the ambiguities implicit in their speeches into different identities? Who is giving good advice? Remembering Shakespeare's two 'angels' in Sonnet 144, who are apparently male and female, are they gendered? If so, how? Faustus, who does not respond to the Evil Angel till he is gone, answers the Good Angel: 'Contrition, prayer, repentance – what of them?'

GOOD ANGEL: O they are means to bring thee unto heaven.
EVIL ANGEL: Rather illusions, fruits of lunacy,
That makes men foolish that do trust them most.
(A.2.1.17–19: B 2.1.19: 'that makes them foolish that do use them most')

'Trusting' is dismissed: the Evil Angel is Machevill (i.e. Machiavelli, as interpreted by the French Protestant commentator Gentillet), saying in the Prologue to *The Jew of Malta*:

I hold religion but a childish toy,
And hold there is no sin but ignorance.
(*Doctor Faustus* 248)

'Religion: O *Diabole*' the Duke of Guise said, in Marlowe's longest soliloquy in *The Massacre at Paris* (2.66: 515). Machevill announces that the Guise, a Machiavellian, who was assassinated 23 December 1588, is dead: time for an alternative overreacher: the Jew of Malta (1.2220–225), his devilish methodology being 'policy' (the word is used thirteen times).

When Faustus wonders if it is too late to repent, the angels return, echoing him, and there seems a strange equivocation in the Good Angel:

> EVIL ANGEL: Too late.
> GOOD ANGEL: Never too late, if Faustus can [will – B] repent.
> (A.2.3.78–79, B.2.3.80)

'Can' leaves open the question whether he has resolved and can undo that. Hamlet knows how resolution unravels:

> Thus conscience does make cowards of us all
> And thus the native hue of resolution
> Is sicklied o'er with the pale cast of thought....
> (*Hamlet* 3.1.85–87)

This soliloquy equates 'conscience' with 'thought', preventing resolution, being negative. Macbeth, too, desires, and thinks he has, 'resolution'; 'Resolve yourselves apart....We are resolv'd my Lord' (*Macbeth* 3.1.136, 137); and so the apparition tempts him: 'Be bloody, bold, and resolute' (4.1.79). But later Macbeth must say: 'I pull in resolution, and begin / To doubt th'equivocation of the fiend / That lies like truth' (5.5.43–44). This 'fiend' – meaning devil or foe, as in 'friend or fiend' (*OED* gives a first citation of this from 1175) may be the 'apparition', who was one of the 'masters' of the witches (4.1.63); but 'And be these juggling fiends no more believ'd / That palter with us in a double sense' (5.8.19–20) makes him plural. *OED* defines 'palter', 'to mumble or babble', and 'to shift, equivocate, or prevaricate in action or speech; to act or deal evasively, esp. for treacherous ends; to use trickery' (verb 2a). The equivocation between the singular and the plural voices /presences in the terms 'masters'/'angel'/'fiend' never resolves into a thought establishing their identity. Neither *Doctor Faustus* nor *Macbeth* nor perhaps *Hamlet* let 'resolution' be other than a deceptive commitment, caught up in equivocation. If resolution is the devil's work, much in *Doctor Faustus* makes it also the work of an angry heaven. A soliloquy, always open to other, unattributable voices ('Who buzzeth in mine ears I am a spirit?'), tempting and not tempting, and with these voices urging resolution and freedom from ambiguities, while perpetuating them by what is said, is the devil's sphere, even if Augustine thought it a means towards God.

Shakespeare owes much to Marlowe, but is not quite his heir in the sense that T.S. Eliot said Jonson was, in that Jonson followed the farcical 'savage comic humour' within the Marlovian hero's hyperbole (Eliot 1951: 123), itself owing something to Rabelais. Faustus as magician, trickster, playing games with vanities of the Pope and Benvolio, is unlike Macbeth. Faustus' aspirations are humanist, sheerly material and comic, as in his enjoyment of the Seven Deadly Sins. He is open to the sexual, with Helen of Troy, as Macbeth is not. Nor is Richard Marlovian; he never approaches the comic indignities of the Jew of Malta, for example even when gulling his victims. If *Doctor Faustus* shows how Calvinism imposes dread (Stachniewski 1991: 243–331), that applies only to the play's general dislike of God, as conspiring against Faustus. Calvinism is not the play's main emphasis, for Faustus is tricked by voices emanating from a magic which his 'fantasy' (1.1.105), deceptive and devilish, or not, wants. The magus is done and undone by necromancy more devilish and elusive than even Mephistopheles, and it discomfits all around him in the B text. Selling the soul to the devil needs no Calvinist prompting: Wagner, Faustus' servant, shows that, as he, like Robin, ostler and clown, is fascinated by magic and the devil (2.2, 3.2). Poverty or hunger is likely to compact with the devil: Wagner knows Robin 'would give his soul to the devil for a shoulder of mutton, though it were blood raw' (A.1.4.9–10); Marlowe's version of selling one's birthright for a mess of pottage (Genesis 25:34). The devil is too intimate a familiar and too much part of a farce to make it other than likely that the poor should sell themselves to him every day: that produces a comedy destabilizing all certainties, even until Act 5.

2 IAGO'S SOLILOQUIES

Though Shakespeare hardly ever shows devil-possession and the devil, his soliloquies explore diabolism, as in those of Richard, Iago, Angelo, and Macbeth. Soliloquy and comedy coincide with Lancelot Gobbo, the Clown in *The Merchant of Venice*. He is like Marlowe's Wagner and Robin; divided between his conscience, which giving an awareness of evil, tells him not to run away, while his sensible desire to escape Shylock's service, he (mis-) interprets as the voice of the devil:

> Certainly my conscience will serve me to run from this Jew my master. The fiend is at my elbow and tempts me... 'Budge!' says the fiend, 'Budge not', says my conscience. 'Conscience', says I, 'you counsel well'; 'Fiend', say I, 'you counsel well'. To be ruled by my conscience I should stay with the Jew my master who, God bless the mark, is a kind of devil; and to run away from the Jew I should be ruled by the fiend who, saving your reverence, is the devil himself... (2.2. 1–3, 15–21)

Conscience, like the 'devil incarnation' (2.2.25: the red devil inhabits Gobbo's comprehensive malapropism), seems on both sides of the argument, but eventually advises adherence to the devil one knows; the devil advises adherence to the devil one doesn't. 'Gobbo' is Italian for 'hunchback', which associates Lancelot with Richard the Third, and the devil, through Pulcinella, in the *commedia dell'arte*, who becomes Punch (see Chapter 5). Film criticism can add a connection to Marty Feldman's hunchback in Mel Brooks' *Young Frankenstein* (1974), and cultural studies recall Benjamin writing about Kafka, on the hunchback as the 'prototype of distortion' (*SW*2.811). Gobbo's reactiveness compares with how Richard the Third's murderous 'thoughts' reappear as ghosts before Bosworth Field, in the form of what his soliloquy (*Richard the Third*, 5.5.131–160) calls 'coward conscience', making resolution be lost:

> Richard loves Richard; that is, I and I.
> (5.3.184 *Q1* reading)[1]

Adding I and I, as if 'I' was both a number (one) and a pronoun, as Richard does, does not arrive at the answer one, nor make an I; it is not a question of adding bits to each other and achieving a unity. Shakespeare's Sonnet 136.8 says 'Among a number one is reckoned none'; that is, one is not a number, as when we say 'a number of people'; a number implies plurality, but it seems too that a number cannot allow for a unity of one, meaning that it is impossible to be one. A soliloquy, which in any case, has the devil in it, cannot be the expression of a unified self; any talk about 'character' must understand that character is more than one. (And if 'among a number one is reckoned none', one is unimportant, it does not count: it means nothing.) The Richard who loves Richard does not constitute a unity; but the line is not tautological, for the 'I' then adds and adds, never reaching completeness. 'Myself', eleven times repeated, further divides: 'I myself/Find in my self no pity to myself' (as his own evil angel), just as 'conscience' multiplies into different tongues, which further multiply. Yet it multiplies from nothing. Everything mocks the words 'there's none else by': there is no unity of self, no 'I' who can speak; only multiplicity, or the devil as the 'original allegorical figure'; and if Richard gives way to conscience, as though that was a truthful aspect of self, he later dismisses it: 'a word that cowards use/Devis'd at first to keep the strong in awe' (5.6.39, 40).

Richard, according to Benjamin (1977: 125), may be the 'intriguer', alongside Iago, or Polonius – scheming, calculating; any Machiavellian, or diabolic figure. The intriguer introduces comedy into 'mourning plays', or 'more precisely, the pure joke' as the inner side of mourning. Benjamin notes:

> the affinity of the strict joke and the cruel. Who has not seen children laugh where adults are shocked? The alternation of the sadist between such childlike laughter and such adult shock can be seen in the intriguer. (Benjamin 1977: 126)

The 'strict joke' differs from the carnivalesque festive or holiday joke, which loosens everything up: the strict joke finds humour in tightening, and pulling, exposing inadequacy. Richard is outsmarted when the child, his nephew Richard, who also 'moralises two meanings in one word', mocks his uncle as a hunchback and as the Fool carrying the monkey (*Richard the Third* 3.1.128–131; see Hammond's note). The joke mocks human pride, as Benjamin points out, and the rogue/jester/intriguer is 'part of the devil' (ibid). At the end of the *Trauerspiel* study, Benjamin returns to the 'devilish jocularity of the intriguer, his intellectuality' (1977: 227) via a history of how the medieval church allegorised classical pagan gods as devils, and demonised matter, which was seen as negative, and which was created in order to absorb everything of Hell (Tartar). The virtuous allegorist, however, separated from matter, which has been spiritualised away, is in for a shock:

> Scorning all emblematic disguise, the undisguised visage of the devil can raise itself up from out of the depths of the earth into the view of the allegorist, in triumphant vitality and nakedness. (Benjamin 1977: 227)

Allegorical mournfulness, which spiritualises everything, and therefore leaves out what matter signifies, is confronted by 'devilish mirth' and 'the triumph of matter', which cannot be made a symbol of something spiritual. The devil, a Manichee, cannot allow that. The hunchback's body demonstrates the triumph of matter which evades spiritualising. The 'scornful laughter of hell' greets whoever would mute matter through allegorising; laughter takes over reality, showing mind embraced by matter. That describes Satan as the derided allegorical figure, returning as all-encompassing matter in Satan's avatar, Richard. Benjamin sees Satan tempting, as Richard does, with knowledge, which is in excess; similarly, Faustus is so tempted. Satan causing 'terror in mourning' (229), as happens, ultimately, to Faustus, and Richard – but not Iago.

Mourning is 'the mother of allegories, and their content' (230). It creates the devil as a figure of loss to account for it. Benjamin reconsiders his earlier essay 'On Language as Such and the Languages of Man' (1916), from which he quotes:

> Evil as such, which is cherished as enduring profundity, exists only in allegory, is nothing other than allegory, and means something different from what it is. It means precisely the non-existence of what it represents. By its allegorical form evil as such reveals itself to be a subjective phenomenon... The Bible introduces evil in the concept of knowledge. The serpent's promise... was to make them 'knowing both good and evil'. But it is said of God after his creation, 'And God saw everything that he had made, and behold, it was very good'. Knowledge of evil therefore has no object. There is no evil in the world. It arises in man himself, with the desire for knowledge, or rather for judgment. (233, compare *SW1* 71–72)

Benjamin argues that if God created everything good, there can be *no* knowledge of evil; to know evil is only to know an abstraction because there is nothing there. Those who talk about evil literally do not know what they are talking about; they are interested in a spurious knowledge, which gives space for accusing and condemning others to guilt. Evil and the devil belong to allegorical thinking, and to a melancholia wanting 'resolution', to fix something where there is nothing fixable.

Such negativity also inscribes Iago within *Othello*, whose Venice uses its black mercenary who trustingly works for it, but secretly despises him. That is evident with Brabantio, whose reaction to Desdemona's marriage to Othello is his own death, in the defeat of his own possessive instincts over his daughter and property. And had Brabantio seen Desdemona's murder, his brother Gratiano muses, he would have done 'a desperate turn' (which implies suicide), 'Yea, curse his better angel from his side / And fall to reprobance' (*Othello* 5.2.205–207). Brabantio seems a Faustus, with a willingness for self-defeat, in his inability to accept less than the absolute for himself, jealous over his daughter and envious of Othello, and he anticipates a strange willingness in Othello to do something analogou with Desdemona. Nonetheless the principal agency of temptation of Othello is that 'demi-devil' who, Machiavellian like the Duke of Guise, swears '*diablo*', uniquely in Shakespeare (*Othello* 5.2.298, 2.3.157). Iago has several asides and seven soliloquies, a greater number than Othello (who learns to soliloquise during the play), perhaps the largest number of any character in Shakespeare's tragedies. In the first of these (1.3.382–403), Coleridge noted 'the motive-hunting of motiveless malignity' (Honigmann 1997: 33).[2] These soliloquies assemble pseudo-motives, justifying and spurring on his hatred of 'the Moor', including a spreading jealousy (*Othello* 1.386–387, 2.1293–295), for Iago is of the 'tribe of hell' (1.3.358) – i.e. one characterised by jealousy (3.3.178). Yet he is more envious than jealous: envy evincing fear of not being in possession of something, producing soliloquy as a desire for possession. Apparently conscienceless – unlike Richard – he also differs from Richard in speaking not only a flexible verse but an inventive prose, the best in Shakespeare, marvellously indefinite, as with 'put money in thy purse' (1.3.340), a phrase whose precise meaning within its various repetitions would puzzle any auditor. Its literal sense, to Roderigo: get money so that I can have it, is scandalous enough not to be interpretable literally. It generates meanings to be guessed at, its literality appearing in the bluntness of the soliloquy following: 'thus do I ever make my fool my purse' (1.3.382): said to *someone*, as the interrogative 'How? How' implies: this is certainly 'double knavery' (1.3.393).

Iago's verbal universe – 'thou know'st we work by wit and not by witchcraft / And wit depends on dilatory time' (2.3.367–368) – contrasts with the rhetorical 'Othello music' heard in the Moor's speeches, as with: 'This only is the witchcraft I have used' – (1.3.170), whose seductiveness, devil-like, it parodies. Something is learned about Othello in his falling for Iago's unspecified temptation (to do what? – is to murder Othello's idea?). There is a knowledge of him possible within that magnificent uncomprehending narcissism (Leavis 1952: 136–159). But Iago, securing Desdemona's, Roderigo's and Emilia's deaths; Cassio's nearly, and indirectly; and perhaps hypnotically, Othello's suicide, keeps everyone guessing. Concealed, he observes and shapes the world. Depending on action, he tells Roderigo, it is only indulged 'for my sport and profit' (1.3.385). And 'pleasure and action makes the hours seem short' (2.3.374) – dismissively lightweight terms work against hours otherwise 'dilatory': slow, postponing. The line describes, justifies, what he has just achieved as a beginning: (a) making Cassio drunk, (b) engineering a fight, (c) having Montano wounded, and (d) Cassio cashiered, (e) spoiling Othello and Desdemona's wedding night, and (f) keeping Roderigo on side. Sexual paranoia, often advanced as a theory for his malignity, explains little in Iago. Wherever a putative sexual reason for anger is stated – Othello, or Cassio taking Emilia, his own love for Desdemona – it is raised and dropped as probably only provisional. There is an endless pouring out of improvisatory language, obscene on and beyond occasion, enjoying obscenity's potential to slander others: Desdemona, Emilia, or Cassio. His rationality undoes Othello's romanticism: he stands for the disenchantment of the world: but while anticipating or displaying Enlightenment instrumental reason (Grady 1996: 101), his wit is too pronouncedly fantastic, heterogeneous, for that to convince fully. He needs action; cannot bear the 'dilatory', as Othello – 'to be once in doubt/Is once to be resolved' (3.3.182–183) – also cannot.

'Resolution' – that word from *Doctor Faustus* – resonates in Othello's intolerance of ambiguity: he must make things that may seem nothing, something. Yet to 'dilate', which overlaps with 'delate', and implies opening up, and amplifying, as well as accusing, informing, implies also the exposure, the 'showing', of the woman's 'secret place' (Parker and Hartman 1985: 54–74, 1993: 60–95), as the nothing which may beget Iago's 'wit'. For 'Nothing' works as a familiar pun, as in Hamlet's obscenity towards Ophelia's 'lap' (*Hamlet* 3.2.101–110): it is that fantasised absence ('some monster in thy thought / Too hideous to be shown' (*Othello* 3.3.111–112)) which, for Freud, compels masculine thinking to become fetishistic (*SE* 21.149–158). From Augustine onwards, the devil operates inside the ambiguity of 'nothing': accusing it, drawing attention to it, obsessively in this play: 'oft my jealousy/Shapes faults that are not' (3.3.150–151). While that statement is a literal declaration of what he does, a 'fault', as an absence, a gap (*OED sb.*4) had the slang meaning implying the vagina (Astington 1985: 330–334). The obscenity becomes a matter of negation: a fault that is not a fault, or a fault which is a nothing.

Iago, at the end of Act 3 Scene 3, the 'temptation' scene, telling heaven to witness what he will do for 'wronged Othello' (*Othello* 3.3.468, 470), names himself, for only a second time, in self-identification with Othello: 'I am your own for ever' (3.3.482), as if wanting to inhabit Othello. Equally strangely, Othello follows him above all the others who could tell him the truth about Desdemona (and Cassio); as if possessed by him. That reflects back on Iago's first self-naming: 'Were I the Moor, I would not be Iago' (1.1. 56). In this quibble, if he was the Moor, he would still be Iago: a double: Othello/Iago. But either he would not wish to be Iago (losing half that doubleness), or he would not actually be Iago since no identity as Iago would remain. Finishing this early speech, which has virtually become a soliloquy, for all Roderigo's attention to it, he enters into disavowal: 'I am not what I am' (1.1.64): the hypocrite, the white devil; negating YHWH's name (Exodus 3:14). The will to be Othello/Iago or not to be Iago reappears when Lodovico, who has witnessed Othello strike Desdemona – crying 'devil' – asks if Othello is mad. Iago replies in words not enlarged on, yet they are not an aside:

> He's that he is: I may not breathe my censure
> What he might be; if what he might, he is not,
> I would to heaven he were!
> (*Othello* 4.1.270–272)

Iago seems to intimate that Othello may become a murderer, and even endorses that wish, but also implies that he may become mad, or dead, certainly 'not', as in the language of Genesis 37:30: 'the child is not', meaning the child is dead. 'He's that he is' inverts 'I am not what I am'; it teases Lodovico in riddling on what a person is. It resumes from 'Men should be what they seem,/Or those that be not, would they might seem none' (3.3.129–130), a line to be commented on later.

In the next scene (4.1), Othello's accusing questioning of Emilia is in Iago's language: he echoes him, as earlier, Iago echoed Othello, not just literally (3.3.109), but in bringing on action. We can compare Othello's 'Look where she comes' (Folio reading, 3.3.281) which is echoed in Iago's 'Look where he comes' (3.3.333): and, incidentally, to which angel or spirit are these gestural demands to 'look' directed? Iago's last riddle to Othello: 'Demand me nothing. What you know, you know,/From this time forth I never will speak word' (5.2.300–301) ends dilation/delation, while remaining accusatory; he knows there is no more to be got from Othello, no point in possessing him further; similarly, there was never anything to be got from Iago. His soliloquies respond to other voices, hence: 'And what's he then that says I play the villain...?' (2.3.331); they address himself as other:

'Dull not device by coldness and delay!' (2.3.368, 383), delay/dilatoriness/absence being his temptation and fear, and perhaps, including a sexual fear. His Othello must speak to his Iago; he must be double or nothing.

3 Angelo, Iago, Macbeth

For he who tempts, though in vain, at least asperses
The tempted with dishonour foul, supposed
Not incorruptible of faith, not proof
Against temptation.
(*Paradise Lost* 9: 296–299)

Adam's words to Eve in Milton, before she is fatally tempted, indicate how the tempter morally degrades the tempted person. Those words 'at least' convey a danger. Lancelot Gobbo's 'conscience' tempting him not only makes temptation soliloquy's subject, it indicates that the tempted part of the subject addressed has been reduced, thought of reductively. Angelo, the duke's deputy in *Measure for Measure* (perhaps written just after *Othello*, in 1604) agonises when confronted with sexual temptation – which he will then practise – after seeing the virtuous nun Isabella, and promising to see her again; his soliloquy concluding the scene with questions, the main one:

The tempter or the tempted, who sins most, ha?
(*Measure for Measure* 2.2.167)

Since Isabella was urged to make an 'attempt' at Angelo (1.4.79), i.e. an 'essay, or 'try' (so *OED*, giving this example), and since 'attempt', from Latin 'tendere', to 'stretch', is the verbal form of 'temptation', it seems she *has* been tempting him. He blames her, as though she had superior power over him, but then turns to self-hating blame: 'What dost thou, or what art thou Angelo?' where his naming self-accuses. The Devil is 'an accuser' (*diabolos*), though the New Testament word calling Satan 'the accuser' (Revelation 12:10) is *kategoros*: to 'categorise' someone is to accuse them: a Foucaultian point. Angelo becomes his own devil, degrading himself before degrading Isabella. Legal language is the instrument of temptation: it works by accusation. It contains both the sexual voice (in Isabel) and the psychoanalytic, forbidding Law of the

Father. Yet Angelo also thinks the devil may be the 'enemy' tempting with Isabella, personified as 'virtue':

> O cunning enemy, that to catch a saint
> With saints dost bait thy hook!
> (*Measure for Measure* 2.2.183–184)

That resembles Iago:

> Divinity of hell!
> When devils will the blackest sins put on,
> They do suggest at first with heavenly shows
> As I do now.
> (*Othello* 2.3.345–348)

Devils work by 'suggestion', meaning 'prompting or incitement to evil; an instance of a temptation of the evil one' (*OED*). 'Suggestion', in that sense, survives in the tempting word 'suggestive'. Iago's temptations are obscenely suggestive: the divinity (theology) of hell, or its ruler, gives the cue to devilish action, as, similarly, Angelo – now come to life from his earlier frigidity – momentarily thinks of Isabella as diabolically tempting, though his next soliloquy identifies the devil with himself:

> When I would pray and think, I think and pray
> To several subjects: Heaven hath my empty words
> Whilst my invention, hearing not my tongue,
> Fastens on Isabel: Heaven in my mouth,
> As if I did but only chew his name,
> And in my heart the strong and swelling evil
> Of my conception. The state whereon I studied
> Is, like a good thing being often read,
> Grown sere and tedious; yea, my gravity,
> Wherein – let no man hear me – I take pride,
> Could I with boot change for an idle plume
> Which the air beats for vain. O place, O form,
> How often dost thou with thy case, thy habit,
> Wrench awe from fools, and tie the wiser souls
> To thy false seeming! Blood, thou art blood.
> Let's write good angel on the devil's horn –
> 'Tis not [*F*] the devil's crest.
> (*Measure for Measure* 2.4.1–17)

Angelo, like Claudius (*Hamlet* 3.3.41), is 'to double business bound', the victim of 'thought', like Richard, or Hamlet. Thinking dominates, hollowing out the prayer, which becomes directed to who knows whom? – 'to several subjects' (addressees), anyway. The soliloquy arises from noting that everything is split: mouth and heart are separate. While praying, Angelo is controlled by his 'invention' (imagination), but that leads to something else; 'the strong and swelling evil/Of my conception', recalling Faustus' 'swollen with cunning'. This is sexual, also invoking pregnancy (thoughts are pregnant, and may lead to a literal conception). As another Angelo-figure, Malheureux in Marston's *The Dutch Courtesan* (1605) is told, '*Diaboli virtus in lumbis est*' – which is St Jerome's statement as quoted by Montaigne and translated as 'the strength of the devil is in our loins' (2.1.89, Marston 1997: 27). Or else 'conception' means Angelo's own: i.e. born in sin (Psalm 51:5): what theologians call 'original sin', though it is baffling to consider how sin, if taken in Augustine's sense, as a negative, can be an origin. Feeling he is bringing forth evil, Angelo hates how the appearance of rank and formality ('false seeming') wrenches awe from fools and wise. 'Seeming' may be inherently false, as Angelo thinks; a 'seemer' (1.3.54) being a hypocrite, probably a Puritan. We can recall Iago's attack, specifically in the context of Cassio being 'honest', on hypocrisy: 'men should be what they seem,/Or those that be not, would they might seem none' ('would they might seem (not be) nothing of the sort', i.e. would they might not seem to be honest. And 'honest' is a clue-word for Iago (Empson 1951: 218–249). 'Honest' means something else for a woman than it does for a man (*Hamlet* 3.1.103), hence Claudio, the deceived bridegroom in *Much Ado About Nothing*, virtually calls Hero, the woman he thinks not honest, 'seeming' (4.1.56), responding to how she 'seemed' to be, which was how she was. And Isabella will similarly attack Angelo for 'seeming' (*Measure for Measure* 2.4.151) when the nature of his temptation becomes apparent.

It seems there is a new emergent impossibility registered within Shakespeare of 'being' *without* seeming, requiring doubleness, acting (compare *Hamlet* 1.2.175–186): that being a fertile source and product of diabolism. Angelo ends his soliloquy with the tautology of 'blood, thou art blood': this acknowledges 'blood' as sexual passion, and puns on his name, as if the (fallen) angel's fortunes exactly describe him, in that way getting out of doubleness, making being what he is a consequence of naming. In the last comments, where puns enforce the being/seeming distinction, a horn is for blowing, but 'horn' puns: a horned angel makes the human dual: the horn should be inscribed 'good angel' to recall Lucifer, and to indicate that absolute ambiguity characterises the devil. It is Lucifer's 'crest', heraldic marker of pride (so *OED* 1b, and compare 'crestfallen'): but it is not the devil's crest if he is crestfallen. Angelo confesses to 'swelling' pride, perhaps visualised in 'idle plumes' (appropriate for a 'seemer' but *not* what Angelo would wear: he is losing objective control); the plume being synonymous with 'horn' and 'crest'. Angelo convicts himself of pride and sexual faults together, hating in himself that aspect of an Iago in himself aiming 'to plume up my will' (*Othello* Folio, 1.3.392), in a fantasy of male sexual supremacy, in which 'the will', an expression of diabolism in the person since Augustine, gives permission to love (1.3.336).

Macbeth recalls Angelo's temptation when he 'fears' what he hears the witches prophesy for the 'hereafter': temptation in this play is called 'this supernatural soliciting', (*Macbeth* 1.3.130), where to solicit, as Derrida (1978: 6) shows, means 'to shake'. The temptation shakes, and may be sexual. Iago hopes Othello will see Cassio 'soliciting his wife' (*Othello* 2.3.382), where to what extent sexual temptation is intended is in question. The person tempted is shaken, as Macbeth is physically in this third scene. He breaks into a soliloquy or aside, where 'two truths' told seem 'happy prologues to the swelling act/Of the imperial theme'. The future as certain, undelayed, opens up, with 'earnest of success / Commencing in a truth', but it accompanies 'that suggestion / Whose horrid image doth unfix my hair' (*Macbeth* 1.3.127–128): where dread from soliciting becomes sensible, bodily:

> Present fears
> Are less than horrible imaginings.
> My thought, whose murther yet is but fantastical
> Shakes so my single state of man,
> That function is smother'd in surmise,
> And nothing is, but what is not.
> (*Macbeth* 1.3.127–142)

The 'suggestion' is a creation of the future, annihilating the present, but it is the thought of murder – which will murder his thought – which already shakes with 'surmise', which means that 'nothing is' (the present is gone) except 'what is not': the future, an imagined state, the sphere of unreality, the loss of 'being' into seeming, an Iago condition, supplementing L.C. Knights' (1964: 29) description of the play as 'a statement of evil', infecting everything; nothing, everywhere. The witches were fantastical (*Macbeth* 1.3.53); the future, like that for Faustus, is also fantasy. Macbeth's soliciting excites, as the word 'swelling' – Angelo's word, and the Chorus' word for Faustus – indicates (he will also be 'shaken' by nightly terrible dreams (*Macbeth* 3.2.19)). The temptation intimates Macbeth to be a result of the thinking that has produced *Doctor Faustus*, and differentiates him from Banquo, who is untempted by murder, and in any case, is not the subject of the witches' meeting. Macbeth fears Banquo's 'royalty of nature': 'under him/My genius is rebuked, as it is said,/Mark Antony's was by Caesar' (3.1.55–58).

The 'genius' recalls the Roman tutelary spirit accompanying a person from birth, Socrates' *daimon*. In *Julius Caesar* Brutus evokes the dispute between 'the genius and the mortal instruments' (2.1.66) in a moment of crisis before enacting murder, that 'dreadful thing'. Within his soliloquy, later, Caesar's Ghost haunts him (a revision of Richard before Bosworth), as 'thy evil spirit, Brutus' (*Julius Caesar* 4.2.333). The spirit recalls *Doctor Faustus*; it was the genius Brutus murdered. *OED* relates 'genius', etymologically, to 'beget', to the genital; hence the double significance of Macbeth's 'barren sceptre' (*Macbeth* 3.1.63). *OED* on 'malus genius' includes melancholy, that baroque state which affects Brutus, and Milton's Samson Agonistes: 'my genial spirits droop' (Milton 1998: 481, line 594). The 'genial', the 'genital', and 'genius' relate, as an 'other' in and outside the body, not possessed but possessing; quoting Rabelais: 'some Platonists say that whoever can see his Genius can know his destiny' (Rabelais 2006: 502). So with Brutus before Philippi.

Leonora, the mother in love in Webster's *The Devil's Law-Case* (1616) thinks she is not alone in her soliloquy:

> I do talk to somewhat, methinks; it may be
> My evil genius.
> (3.3.268–269, Webster 1972: 362)

The 'genius', spoken to and speaking in soliloquy, remains ambiguous. In the same way as St Paul, Augustine, opposed to paganism, would not have tolerated the 'daemon' or demon as meaning anything other than the diabolic. Macbeth's witches – including Hecate – seem to express Macbeth's 'genius', which he considers rebuked by Banquo, just as Banquo 'chid the sisters' (*Macbeth* 3.1.55, 56). The witches called Banquo's destiny 'happier' than Macbeth's. Is Banquo's Ghost Macbeth's genius? Like Caesar's Ghost? If so, Banquo and Macbeth have a strangely symbiotic relationship: Fleance becomes the son Macbeth lacks. If the genius is 'the angel whom thou still hast served' (5.10.14), in equivocal (singular and plural) relationship to the 'juggling fiends', then it sides with and against Macbeth simultaneously, like Faustus' good angel/evil spirit. Soliloquy engages with the genius, who may be the fiend at Lancelot Gobbo's elbow, like Gloucester's 'worser spirit' who 'tempts' to suicide (*Lear* 4.6.213); or Hamlet's 'father's spirit' who may tempt towards desperation and the flood (*Hamlet* 1.4.69). This Ghost stands in strange relationship to the Shakespearian soliloquy; with Hamlet, it even incites the question whether the spirit seen was the devil (2.2.594–599). In *Doctor Faustus*, inside a tradition which is then given to Shakespeare, soliloquy and the spirit-world coexist as forces of temptation, which has no origin, as an unattributable state in the divided subject-state of tempter and tempted.

In the next two chapters, I will approach Shakespeare again – especially *Macbeth* again, and the Falstaff plays, and *King Lear* – through other traditions which are given to him: Chapter 2 considers how the devil in his plays owes something to the devil in medieval texts. It is not just the devil as having the power of temptation, and so inhabiting soliloquy, but as an insistent other, whose mode may be comic. And the power of comedy, and carnival, is the subject of Chapter 3.

Notes

1. Differences between the Quarto readings (of plays issued usually within Shakespeare's life, but not with his authorisation) and the Folio (1623) should be noted, but are only commented on here where relevant: see Wells and Taylor (1997) for textual aid, and various editions of the plays. In the case of *Othello*, the Quarto is of 1622, so posthumous, and its differences from the Folio are always interesting.
2. See *Othello* but see also 2.1.284–310; 2.3.330–357 and 377–383; 3.3.324–336, where soliloquy becomes an aside, though aimed at Othello; and 4.1.44–47, and 5.1.11–22. I discuss Coleridge's formula, Tambling 2003: 101–124.

Chapter 2: Medieval and Early Modern Devils: Names and Images

Robert Muchembled, arguing for the presence of devils in modern popular culture, with a large filmography making his point (Muchembled 2003: 227–270, 322–331), thinks of the devil as a product of religious thinking which started in the twelfth century, when there was an assertion of new forms of church control and discipline. The Gothic begins in that century, and produces demons enough in the grotesque forms visible in the exteriors of Gothic cathedrals. The twelfth century, which had its own Renaissance of thought, and belief in mystical thinking (Bernard of Clairvaux), also saw, in Joachim of Fiore (*c.*1135–1203) a new stress on interpreting the Apocalypse literally, so portraying such figures as the Antichrist and the Dragon, historical figures, as soon to arrive in reality, not simply as allegorical abstractions, as Augustine had done (McGinn 1985: 51–97). The devil becomes more visible, part of a religious imagination extending into Dürer, Luther, and Protestantism, which personalises him in the name of an individualising theology, and makes the nature or identity of spirit beings less ambiguous; whereas the latter, and demons, were not necessarily so specified as to identity and function as particularised anti-Christian devils, certainly not in medieval gargoyles and architectural decorations. This tendency is apparent from the texts I consider here, from Chaucer (1340–1400), Dante (1265–1321), and Langland's *Piers Plowman*, broadly contemporary with Chaucer, and from late medieval drama.

In another study, Alain Boureau finds demonology and the devil's relationship to heresy stressed between 1280 and 1330, roughly the time

J. Tambling, *Histories of the Devil*,
DOI 10.1057/978-1-137-51832-3_3

of Dante's *Commedia* and the Papacy of John XXII (1316–1334), who conducted consultations about magical practices, saying that they were heretical. An increasing sense that humans and devils could be bound together by possession, by invocation, and by pact caused agitation against witchcraft in the fifteenth century, as with the Dominican John Nider's *Formicarius* (1435) and the 'Hammer Against Women who carry out Malefice or Harm', the *Malleus Maleficarum* (1486) of the Dominican Henry Institutoris. The period produced the belief that the human could have a 'familiar double', an angel or demon: thus the Catalonian Dominican Raymond of Penafort (1175–1275) had a 'familiar angel of God' who woke him before the matins bell, while Boniface VIII (1294–1303), had, according to a rival – i.e. the cardinal Pietro Colonna – an individual demon, called Boniface (Boureau 2006: 162).

Aquinas downplayed the significance of the devil, unlike the Franciscans, such as Peter Olivi, a follower of the thinker of Apocalypse Joachim of Fiore, who believed that 'the creation of humans was desired by God in order to replace the same number of fallen angels' (Boureau 2006: 115). One tenth of the angelic orders had fallen. Aquinas found disturbing the implications of the angels having complete, intellective knowledge, as opposed to man's 'rational' or 'discursive' knowledge, which reasons things out from a position of ignorance. For then, 'how could an incorporeal creature with perfect intellect sin with full knowledge? How could it "want the impossible", that is, equality with God?' He had to accept that the fall of the angels was immediate, a point of some controversy; referring to the text 'the devil sinneth from the beginning' (1 John 3:8) Augustine had accepted that, and the implication of the statement that the devil goes on sinning. He referred to the verse: 'the evening and the morning were the first day' (Genesis 1:5), which comes after the creation of light but before the creation of the sun and moon on the fourth day. It meant that some angels, the majority, passed from twilight to morning knowledge. Others would not wait for light, but fell; twilight and dawn (equivalent moments at the equinox, when the heaven and earth were created) distinguished the angels who, in the same moment, received illumination or passed into darkness (Cornish 2000: 119–141; *City of God* 11.9). For Aquinas, following Augustine, the angels who sinned would not recognise, in the sense of acknowledge, the light from whence they came (Aquinas 2003: 458–467). They made an instantaneous decision; Satan could not have deliberated, for that action belongs to rational knowledge. The angels that sinned failed to acknowledge the source of their power, i.e. in divine light, and so, according to Dante, there could not have been a count to twenty before they fell (*Paradiso* 29.49–51). Counting to twenty means passing from one complete, immediately recognised unity (ten fingers) to another; before the hands could unclasp and clasp, they were gone. The Devil sinned then, virtually in the instant of creation if it was not to be assumed that some angels were created sinful from the beginning. That was the Cathars' Manicheism, condemned as heretical by the University of Paris in 1241. Catharism, if it could be said to exist as a unity of thought, implied that there was a bad development within the creation, which would put responsibility for the Fall onto God (Boureau 2006: 94–104); this was at a time when it was much questioned whether all demons were fallen, or whether there were daimonic forces outside this cosmology of the Fall. A Manichee would oppose matter and materiality to the spirit; the devil's fault was not that he was material, for angels are spirit beings, lacking bodies save those they assume. The duality proposed in the concept of fallen angels makes the spirit itself divisible, with a refusal of the will inside a spiritual being itself.

1 Chaucer's Devil in Green

In Chaucer, such theological absolutism relative to the devil yields to something else from popular culture: fairies and devils coexist, without allowing for strict differences. But Chaucer is fascinated with what the devil might mean inside culture. Many of *The Canterbury Tales* (*c.*1390–1400), that collection of tales told by vividly described pilgrims, on the course of their journey to Canterbury, turn on a failed recognition of the devil, or of a recognition that comes too late, while the tales themselves depend on knowing that he exists as a (non-) possibility. The Wife of Bath's Tale succeeds her Prologue, but not immediately, because a quarrel breaks out between the Friar and the Summoner, whose nature gives character to her tale, and to the Friar's and the Summoner's tales which follow (Szittya 1986: 386–394). Her tale, when it comes, begins by evoking the time of King Arthur, when this land was full of 'fayerye', when the 'elf-queene' and company 'daunced ful ofte in many a grene mede' (Fragment III.857–861). Now, no one can see fairies, only 'lymytours' and 'friars'; they now comprise the only 'incubus' potentially dangerous to a woman (880).

In the Wife of Bath's Tale, where a knight who has raped a woman has a year's reprieve to discover what women desire most of all, 'ladyes foure and twenty and yet mo' (992) are seen dancing 'under a forest syde'.

The knight approaches this fairy-ring, which vanishes; in its place is an 'olde wyf' who can supply the answer he lacks (women desire sovereignty) but who also holds him to a promise of marriage. He loathes her, but when they are in bed, she speaks to him of 'gentilesse', and when he conforms to her desire for sovereignty and gives it her, he finds he has won: she transforms into a young woman.

The Friar, listening in the company, objects to the Wife's preaching, both in her Prologue, and in the speech recommending 'gentilesse', but says he will tell a tale against the Summoner (the official who summoned people to face the ecclesiastical courts, run by the Archdeacon, under the Bishop). 'The Friar's Tale' shows a mean-minded Archdeacon, an anticipation of Shakespeare's Angelo, punishing all sins, especially fornication. The Summoner spares lechers, however, so that they can lead him to further women (twenty-four are mentioned (l.1326) like the Wife of Bath's fairies), and so he undercuts the Archdeacon's justice. In so making money, he is compared with Judas Iscariot, called a devil (*diabolos*) in John's Gospel (6:70–71), and a traitor: 'the devil having now put into the heart of Judas Iscariot, Simon's son, to betray him' (13:2), so that when he has received the 'sop' from Christ, 'Satan entered into him' (13:27). He goes out 'and it was night' (13:30).

The 'The Friar's Tale' opens with the Summoner, 'ever waiting on his pray' (l. 1376) going out to arrest an old woman on a feigned cause, meaning to extract money from her:

> And happed that he saugh bifore hym ryde
> A gay yeman, under a forest syde.
> A bowe he bar, and arwes brighte and kene;
> He hadde upon a courtepy [short jacket] of grene,
> An hat upon his heed with frenges blakke.
> (ll. 1379–1383)

The Summoner greets him; he takes the first step. This 'bailly' (bailiff), whose dwelling is in the north country (Lucifer's territory), to where he hopes the Summoner will come, and who becomes his 'brother', with the several meanings that implies (of betrayal, of rivalry, and of spiritual kinship), warns with stories of his 'wages' which are 'ful streit and ful smale' (l. 1426) and how he takes everything that is offered to him. Asked his name, he replies, smiling: 'I am a feend, my dwelling is in helle' (l. 1447) – no name appears. The Summoner reacts without seeing any implications for his own safety. Devilish himself (later he even calls himself a 'yeoman' (l.1524)), he is blind to that, but asks questions of this yeoman in green: does he have a single shape? Why does he go about in different shapes? For what reason does he have all this labour? Do devils make themselves new bodies out of the elements? (Devils being angels, they have no bodies.)

The Yeoman does not answer why he wears green, yet the fairy colouring, recalling 'The Wife of Bath's Tale' is significant, like the hunting-implication which associates with the 'grene-wode shawe' (wood) (1386, 1455), like the outlaws, the 'merry men' of *As You Like It* (1.1,111, 2.5,1): 'under the greenwood tree', like 'old Robin Hood of England'. Robin Hood rhymes were familiar to Sloth, one of the Seven Deadly Sins in Langland's *Piers Plowman* (CVII.11); perhaps Robin Hood is remembered in 'Robert the ruflare' (robber) in *Piers Plowman* C.VI.316, as a proverbial name. The yeoman, historically, had some status. If a 'forester' could include both the outlaw, and the law-enforcement officer of the forest, i.e. the place outside (*foris*) the common law, which was subject to a special law that safeguarded the king's hunting, then this helps with the ambiguity of this yeoman-devil's identity. The greenness evokes, for comparison, the Green Knight, a nature god in *Sir Gawain and the Green Knight*; in his other form, as Sir Bertilak, the Green Knight is a hunter. Such folk memories include the name Robin Goodfellow, 'that shrewd and knavish sprite'. In Middleton's *A Trick to Catch the Old One*, 2.1.20–21, a 'good fellow' means a thief. 'Robin' is also 'Hobgoblin or sweet Puck' (*A Midsummer Night's Dream* 1.3.33, 40). *OED* notes the prevalence of place names with 'Puck' or forms of it, especially in southern England, adding 'it seems that to the Anglo-Saxons, streams, springs, pools, hollows, fields, hills – in fact topographical features of any kind – might be seen as the home of evil spirits'. Puck, like Rob, or Hob, names a devil, or goblin (Briggs 1959: 44–55, 71–81). Langland uses 'Gobelyne' as a name for the devil (*Piers Plowman* C.XX.323), when claiming that he tempted Christ in the wilderness.

If the devil in 'The Friar's Tale' can say 'a lowsy jogelour kan deceive thee' (l. 1467), it is unsurprising that he is a shape-changer. He labours, he says, because sometimes, devils are God's instruments, and do his commandments; without him, they have no power (l. 1487), an Augustinian conclusion. Sometimes, devils serve man (as he serves the widow, later in the Tale). They certainly served the apostles (Acts 19:11–17). They can 'feign' by entering into dead bodies, as happened with Samuel (I Samuel 28:7–20). But after a speech, which should have warned the Summoner, this forester, this devil, says that the Summoner will, by his own experience, be able to lecture from a professorial chair more about these matters than Virgil, who described the underworld in *Aeneid* 6, and who was considered a magus; or Dante, whom the Yeoman accounts encyclopaedic in his knowledge of anything concerning hell.

The Tale resolves itself with the Summoner noting how a carter has cursed and invoked the fiend. He invokes the letter of the law (like the Archdeacon) to damn him; but the yeoman-devil is more just. Mere speech means nothing necessarily: 'the carl spak oo thing, but he thoghte another' (l. 1568). But then they reach the old woman, with whom the Summoner shows himself an extortioner, so provoking her into cursing him, giving him over 'unto the devel blak and rough of hewe' (l. 1622 – 'black' was anticipated by the fringes on the yeoman's hat). The devil learns that she means the curse in earnest, and accordingly, he tells the Summoner that he is going to hell that night, 'Where thou shalt knowen of our privetee/ Moore than a maister of dyvnytee' (ll. 1637–1638). And the Summoner goes to hell, body and soul, leaving the Friar to conclude by moralising about 'the temptour Sathanas' and biblical admonitions (Psalms 10:8–9, I Peter 5:8–9, I Corinthians 10:13). The devil has done no tempting: rather, he has been a force checking the Summoner, and if the last twenty lines of the poem are the Friar's preaching, that is his blindness, like that of his fictional Summoner. What may be learned of hell's 'privetee' appears in what follows immediately: 'The Summoner's Prologue', telling of a Friar visiting hell and seeing no friars there, but being told there are millions. Upon this, Satan lifts his tail, and, like bees from a hive, 'Out of the develes ers ther gonne dryve/ Twenty thousand freres on a route' (ll. 1694–1695), buzzing about before they disappear into his 'ers'. Hell is the very body and 'privetee' of Satan, and Chaucer recollects the depiction of Lucifer, given the classical name Dis, in *Inferno* 34.117, at the base of the ninth circle of hell. Satan has three mouths and slowly chomps on Judas Iscariot, and on Brutus and Cassius, traitors against the Roman Empire in its nascent state. In neither Chaucer nor Dante, however, is there any inversion of the orifice implied: mouth and 'ers' are separate, not reversible, as in Bosch, or Rabelais.

2 Dante: The Devil a Logician

Dante, in *Inferno*, encounters devils after journeying through Hell's upper parts, and arriving at the gates of the City of Dis, where he is confronted by a thousand fallen angels (see 2 Peter 4:6). They will not let Dante pass, even after Virgil has spoken to them (*Inferno* 8.67–130). Virgil, an old inhabitant of Hell (he is confined to Limbo), remembers their opposition to Christ entering in when he harrowed Hell (8.124–126), of which event he speaks in covert terms, never mentioning Christ: as the classical pagan, he cannot. Dante's Inferno is both Christian and classical, for it is also staffed by the female Furies, who call for Medusa to come to turn Dante into stone, which, if it happened, would stop Dante and the poem. Medusa now has the attributes of the diabolical, as well as the castrating woman (9.37–57; Freccero 1986: 119–135). Hell is full of male fantasies. As Dante journeys deeper through *Inferno*, guided by Virgil, the relationship with demons becomes tricky; in the eighth circle, given to fraudsters, issues of identity become more difficult to disentangle. In canto 20, the fourth of the ten bolgias (pockets) of this circle, Dante encounters diviners, mythical and real (Gilson 2001). This is Virgil's canto: he speaks in the tone of one proving he never was a magus. Pagan wisdom comes only from reason. In the fifth bolgia, there are barrators, i.e. those who used public office to make money; these are kept in and under boiling pitch by demons called 'Malebranche' ('evil claws') with hooks. A black devil ('*diavol* nero', *Inferno* 21.29; in the collective they are '*angeli* neri', *Inferno* 23.131) says he is returning to Lucca to fetch more barrators, the place being full of them. Dante and Virgil are escorted by ten demons, the principal, Barbariccia ('Curlybeard') leading the military parade by making his 'cul', his arse, a trumpet (21.139).

Much in these cantos reads like medieval comic drama of the marketplace, to be discussed below, with these demons and sinners, who are indistinguishable from each other and play carnivalesque tricks upon each other (Spitzer 1944: 83–88). Canto 23 ends with Virgil realising that the demons have tricked them by giving false directions, and Friar Catalano, a hypocrite from Bologna occupying the next bolgia replies:

> 'Io udi' già dire a Bolgona
> del diavol vizi assai, tra' quali udi'
> ch'elli è bugiardo, e padre di menzogna'.
> (*Inferno* 23.142–144)

(I heard once at Bologna many of the devil's vices told, amongst which I heard that he is a liar, and the father of lies.)

Friars, and Christians, know more and differently from classical poets such as Virgil, who are outside Christianity. Remembering Chaucer, it should be said a friar should know. An 'anti-fraternal' tradition identified friars with hypocrisy and with a belief that they were above the rules applying to the clergy. Marlowe's Faustus demands that Mephistopheles appears to him as a Franciscan friar (*Doctor Faustus* 1.3.26); Robert Greene's magus was Friar Bacon. Catalano, one of the Frati Gaudenti (the Jovial Friars, supposed to be creating peace in Florence, but giving themselves over to a complete city-based laxity of rule), quotes the Gospel: the devil 'was a murderer from the beginning, and abode not in the truth, because there is no truth in him. When he speaketh a lie, he speaketh of his own: for he is a liar, and the father of it' (John 8:44). He speaks casually, as if that was the word on the street, but addresses Virgil, who must get street news from a modern, about a deceptiveness which was hardly addressed by classical texts and their high style. There seems little distinction between the barrators and the Frati Gaudenti and the black devils, save in degree.

Canto 27 shows the damnation of another friar, in a bolgia assigned to false counsellors (Havely 2004: 61–70). Guido da Montefeltro, dead by 1298, had been a Ghibelline (pro-Empire) politician within Romagna, partaking of its civil wars with the Guelphs (who were pro-Papacy, and the more pro-French party within the various Italian cities); in old age he had become, out of policy, a Franciscan. In *Purgatorio* 5, his son Buonconte da Montefeltro, also a Ghibelline, recalls his own salvation at the point of death, running wounded from the battlefield at Campaldino (1289). Because his repentance was so late, his soul is fought over by an angel and a devil (*Purgatorio* 5.103–108), who refers contemptuously to the 'lagrimetta' (tiny little tear) that he shed before dying. The body falls; the devil loses but has power to call up a storm which causes torrents that sweep the body into the Archiano River and then into the Arno, so that it is never found.

Guido, the father, describes his own activities as works not of the lion, but of the fox (*Inferno* 27.74–75), both characteristically, but differently, diabolical (see Luke 13:32). The phrase becomes Machiavelli's, whose Prince (chapter 18) must be lion *and* fox. In *Inferno* the evil counsellors are invisible, swathed in flames, like Pentecostal tongues of fire, pointing to their powers of persuasion, and Guido approaches Dante and Virgil, wanting passionately to know what is happening politically in the Romagna, from which territory he brings his guilt. Dante, who at that moment of encounter (fictionally, the year 1300) is yet to be exiled from Florence (in 1302), and who is writing some time before 1314, replies, telling him that the territory is not without war in the hearts of its tyrants (the potential for fraud is always there), but there is, superficially, peace. Asked who he is, Guido replies that if he thought his words would be carried up to the world, he would stay silent, but since he assumes Dante is damned – evasions and fraud are correlatives of urban political life – he will tell, without fear of infamy. Sinners in *Inferno* desire their fame to survive them. The fraudulent evil counsellor is deceived but does not know it, and has not learned to keep silent. The infamy he fears is that the true report of his death as a sinner, not a repentant Franciscan, will get out. Never naming himself, he is identifiable by his narrative. The fox-like politician, now a friar is then corrupted by the Papacy, Boniface VIII (Pope 1294 to 1303) being more fox-like than him. He is called a Pharisee, hence a hypocrite (see Matthew 23:13–36).

Boniface wars against the Colonna family, who take refuge in the castle of Penestrino (Palestrina). He wants Guido's advice, regarding neither his Franciscan office, nor the peace it commands. Guido, who as a Ghibelline, was of the same political party as the Colonna, and should have mistrusted the Guelph-leaning Pope, his own political enemy, remains silent when asked what Boniface should do, and the Pope's reply recalls the devil as the deceiver, as he twisted Christ's words on giving St Peter the keys of the kingdom of heaven (Matthew 16:18–19):

> 'Tuo cor non sospetti;
> finor t'assolvo, e tu m'insegna fare
> sì come Penestrino in terra getti.
> Lo ciel poss' io serrare e diserrare,
> come tu sai; però son due le chiavi
> che' l mio antecessor non ebbe care'.
> (*Inferno* 27.100–105)

(don't have suspicion in your heart, first I will absolve you, and you can teach me how to throw Penestrino to the ground. I can open and close heaven, as you know; for there are two keys which my predecessor did not hold dear.)

The 'predecessor' was Celestine V, the Franciscan Pope, who abdicated within a year of his appointment (1294) under pressure put on him by Boniface, who deceiving him, subsequently held him prisoner. Guido accepts Boniface's sophistry, even though it comes from an opposing Guelph-identified figure. He tells him to offer an amnesty to the Colonna, but to break it. The advice is proto-Machiavellian in the Marlovian sense of

The Massacre at Paris, while in Shakespeare this specific figure can be identified with Alencon (1555–1584), 'that notorious Machiavel' (*I Henry VI*.5.4.74), the historical dedicatee of Gentillet's version of Machiavelli, and who is known as the Duke of Anjou in Marlowe's play. In Shakespeare, Alencon counsels the French King:

> To say the truth, it is your policy
> To save your subjects from such massacre
> And ruthless slaughters as are daily seen
> By our proceedings in hostility;
> And therefore take this compact of a truce,
> Although you break it when your pleasure serves.
> (*I Henry VI* 5.4.159–164)

Alencon speaks post-Marlowe's *The Massacre at Paris*, 'massacre', as the devil's work, being then a new word, indicating that the work of religion is not to unite but to destroy all others. And Dante's Guido knows that, but he passes over the massacre he superintended to consider Boniface's pride (called 'fever', 27.97). Guido's words that the broken promise 'ti farà trïunfar ne l'alto seggio' (111; 'will make Boniface triumph in the high seat') make Boniface Luciferian, the 'high seat' being the Papal, and the heavenly throne. After the advice is given, the text remains silent over what follows, turning instead to Guido's death, historically occurring in the same year as this destruction:

> 'Francesco venne poi, com' io fu' morto,
> per me; ma un d'i neri Cherubini
> li disse: 'Non portar; non mi far torto.
> Venir se ne dee giù tra' miei meschini
> perché diede' l consiglio frodolente,
> dal quale in qua stato li sono a' crini;
> ch'assolver non si può chi non si pente,
> né pentere e volere insieme puossi
> per la contradizion che nol consente'.
> Oh me dolente! Come mi riscossi
> quando mi prese dicendomi: 'Forse
> tu non pensavi ch'io löico fossi!'
> A Minòs mi portò; e quelli attorse
> otto volte la coda al dosso duro;
> e poi che per gran rabbia la si morse,

disse: 'Questi è d'i rei del foco furo';
per ch'io là dove vedi son perduto,
e sì vestito, andando, mi rancuro'.
(*Inferno* 27.112–129)

(Francis came then for me, after I was dead, but one of the black Cherubim said to him: 'Do not take him, do not do me wrong. He must come below amongst my slaves, because he gave the fraudulent counsel, since which I have stood fast by his hair, for it is not possible to be absolved if there is no penitence, nor to repent and to will at the same time, for the contradiction does not allow it'. Oh me, unhappy! How I awakened with a start when he took me, saying to me, 'Perhaps you did not think that I was a logician!' He bore me to Minos [classical judge of the underworld; seen in *Inferno* 5], and that one twisted his tail eight times round his hard back, and after biting it with great rage, said, 'This is a sinner for the thievish fire!' so that I, where you see me, am lost, and so clothed, going, embitter myself.)

Francis cannot claim this Franciscan, who believed the Papal fraudulent counsel and gave counsel to defraud (make many promises, but with no fulfilment), undermining the future, as Boniface's words to Guido undermine *his* future. The black cherub points out Boniface's illogic in what was said, and what Guido chose to believe. You cannot be absolved without repentance, nor be penitent and simultaneously want to do the very thing of which one repents. This is Aristotelian – you cannot do two contradictory things at the same time – interpreted here in terms of what is done on the surface and what in reality. Even Francis could only see the hypocritical outward appearance. The black cherub, of the second rank of angels, marked as an order, by 'fulness of knowledge', sees the penitence of this Franciscan servant as empty. An Aristotelian logician: the devil condemns Guido not for his theology, but his illogic. Fraudulence involves self-contradiction. Minos the judge is unambiguous; his biting his tail may symbolise Guido's remorse. The black cherub is the most sophisticatedly humanist of Dante's devils, sharper than the tyrants ruling Romagna, by whose hair he obviously stands, waiting, and sharper than Boniface, whose imminent damnation was foretold in *Inferno* canto 19, dedicated to followers of Simon Magus. Following the poem's narrative, rather than chronological order, Boniface, Guido's tempter, is already damned, though still alive.

There are two further bolgias in the eighth circle. In the ninth circle Mahomet is mangled as a sower of discord, a schismatic within Christianity, ritually and mechanically split by an impassive devil – but the wound heals again (*Inferno* 28.22–63), so that the wounding can be repeated (Frank 2007). It is as if the radical difference between Islam and Christianity has not yet appeared; the two have a strange coexistence. The tenth bolgia contains various falsifiers, including Griffolino of Arezzo, burned at Siena for fooling its ruler by saying he could teach him to fly, but assigned to his place in hell by Minos because he was, secretly, an alchemist. One fraudulence covers a deeper, which Hell, where a discourse of truth prevails, uncovers. The last sinner in canto 29 is a Florentine or Siennese, burned alive for alchemy in 1293. He calls himself Capocchio:

> che falsai li metalli con l'alchìmia;
> e te dee ricordar, se ben t'adocchio,
> com'io fui di natura buona scimia.
> (*Inferno* 29.137–139)

(who falsified metals with alchemy, and you must remember, if I see you well, how I was a good ape by nature [or, of nature].)

The ape, as mimic, is another figure for the devil, and this characterisation of alchemy will lead to Chaucer (see below), but another moment in *Inferno* must be noted, in the ice-bound ninth circle of Hell ('in thrilling region of thick-ribbed ice' – *Measure for Measure* 3.1.126), where fraud involves multiple forms of treachery. This ninth circle is formed from the frozen river Cocytus. The ice thickens over four zones: Caina, Antenora, Tolomea, and Giudecca (Sinclair 1939: 418). Tolomea is a pendant to the episode of Ugolino, where mutual political betrayal takes place, and Ugolino reports how he and his sons were starved to death. In Tolomea, hosts murder guests. Dante finds Friar Alberigo of Faenza, one of the Frati Gaudenti, who murdered his brother in 1285. Alberigo tells him that sometimes the soul falls down to Hell before the body has died, and the soul's place is taken by the demon who thereafter rules it. This idea follows the already noted increased interest in demonology at the end of the thirteenth century. But Dante describes not demon possession, but a substitution of demon for soul, making death otiose, in the spirit of Psalm 55:15 (which Cowper applied to himself in his despair – see Introduction): 'Let death seize upon them, and let them go down quick into hell'.

Friar Alberigo gives another instance (the damned often point to someone worse than themselves): Ser Branco d'Oria who, he says, 'winters' ('verna', 33.135, the playfulness is icy too) behind him. Branco d'Oria, a Genovese Ghibelline, who seems to have died in 1325, after Dante, murdered his father-in-law, Michel Zanche, governor of Logoduro (in Sardinia) in 1290, helped by his nephew. Michel Zanche was earlier mentioned (but not seen nor heard to speak), as keeping company with another friar, Gomita, in the bolgia of the barrators (*Inferno* 22.88). Branco d'Oria does not speak in this episode:

> 'Io credo', diss'io lui, 'che tu m'inganni;
> ché Branco Doria non morì unquanche,
> e mangia e bee e dorme e veste panni'.
> 'Nel fosso sù', diss'el, 'de Malebranche,
> là dove bolle la tenace pece,
> non era ancora giunto Michel Zanche,
> che questi lasciò il diavolo in sua vece
> nel corpo suo, ed un suo prossimano
> che'l tradimento insieme con lui fece.
> (*Inferno* 33.139–147)

('I believe', I said to him, 'that you deceive me, for Branco D'Oria never yet died, and eats and drinks and sleeps and puts on clothes'. 'Up in the ditch', he said, 'of Malebranche, where the tenacious pitch boils, Michel Zanche had not yet arrived, when this one left a devil in his place in his body, and in that of his nearest [i.e. his relative] who did the treachery along with him.')

This periphrasis intimates that the devils performed the murder, as Satan entered into Judas *before* the betrayal of Christ. Branco d'Oria is worse than Frate Alberigo, who had his soul replaced *after* betrayal. Dante will not commit himself to any humanism about what people are, especially his then contemporary Italians. Just because a person lives and eats and drinks (these betrayals and murders seem both to be associated with festive eating) and sleeps and puts on clothes does not imply any 'human' quality in them. These two sinners with their bodies inhabited by devils, seem unconscious that things could be different; obviously, there was to be no chance for repentance for either of them. If so, the devil has power to pre-empt such a chance: the most disturbing thought to take from the canto.

3 The Pardoner's and Canon's Yeoman's Tales

Returning to Chaucer from this Dantean thought entails wondering if there are figures in his writings who are already devils, whose soul has gone before their body died. After 'The Friar's Tale', Chaucer deepens the sense of ambiguity about who people are; for example, the status of the Old Man encountered in 'The Pardoner's Tale', who cannot die, and yet seems to be in his shroud, is puzzlingly ambiguous, and not just to the riotous youths who meet him. Perhaps he mirrors the Pardoner, if the Pardoner – a figure of hypocrisy, except that his character is not explained by that description – is the pilgrim who is dead while he speaks (Purdon 1992). Certainly the Old Man exceeds explanations, like the Pardoner, who by his tale's end will have overreached himself, suffering absolute verbal and sexual degradation from the Host's ribaldry, as if some uncanny power – not inseparable from his drunkenness – possessed him, making him destroy himself. After, at the start, confessing in vivid manner to his avarice and trickery in preaching in churches in order to get money for himself, the Pardoner tells a moral example of three young rioters who are looking for Death, this 'privee theef' ('The Pardoner's Tale', l.675) in order to destroy it. These rioters, examples of gluttony, gambling, and swearing, do 'the devil sacrifise' within 'the develes temple' (ll. 469–470); the carnival entertainers in these taverns are 'the verray develes officeres' (l. 480). As they climb over a stile – stiles are crooked, in the nursery rhyme, and their shape evokes a cross – they find the 'oold man and a povre'. This strange figure of vagrancy directs them to go 'up this croked wey' into a grove, where Death will be found under the oak tree: there they find gold.

The youngest rioter, who poisons the other two to gain sole possession of the gold guarded by the other two, is singled out:

> And atte laste the feend, oure enemy,
> Putte in his thought that he sholde poison beye [buy]
> With which he myghte sleen his felawes tweye:
> For-why the feend foond him in swich lyvnge
> That he hadde leve him to sorwe brynge. [permission to bring him to sorrow]
> For this was outrely his fulle entente,
> To sleen hem bothe, and never to repente.
>
> (844–850)

The other rioters kill the youngest, before drinking the poison he has prepared for them. Death is indeed found under the tree, as in Genesis 3:

the gold, mocking their quest, keeps them from remembering either what they came for, or the implicit warning of the Old Man whose incapacity to find his own death makes Death an 'other' force, whose strange attracting power moves everything along in the text, as the devil leads the youngest rioter to death. Death and the devil as goat-like, consort in Dürer's print, *Knight, Death and the Devil* (1513), as here they exist in ambiguous relationship and death here is everywhere and nowhere.

In *The Canterbury Tales* Fragment G, the Second Nun gives a hagiographical account of St Cecilia. Afterwards, a Canon (so Chaucer guesses him to be) rides up towards the pilgrims, both him and his horse displaying signs of frenzy and agitation, and haste. The Host notes his filthy clothes. His Yeoman, following, wants to tell stories about them both, yet not to reveal things, associating, and distancing himself, from the Canon, whom he reveals, indirectly, to be an alchemist (ll. G.620–626). Pursuit of gold, then, links this with 'The Pardoner's Tale'. Asked about his red face, the Yeoman says it comes from blowing to stoke up the fires in their experiments: a contrast with the martyring fires for burning St Cecilia, which do not cause her to sweat (G.522). Stanton Linden calls alchemy 'the idea that metals were living substances, that natural gold was the end result of long "gestation" within earth's womb; and adopting the metaphor of human and divine sexual differentiation and conjunction, that sulphur and mercury were the "reproductive fluids" from which metals arose' (Linden 2003: 7). Alchemy exalts art over nature, makes nature that which the processes of art imitate; this comprised its conceit (Linden 2003: 12–15). But alchemy in this Canon's Yeoman's telling, is shabby: alchemists 'doon illusioun' to people, taking money and saying they will make double from it, but they do not have the secret of turning all to gold:

> Yet is it fals, but ay we han good hope
> It for to doon, and after it we grope.
> But that science is so fer us biforn,
> We mowen nat [cannot], although we hadden it sworn,
> It overtake, it slit awey so faste.
> ('The Canon's Yeoman's Tale' ll. 678–682)

In this haste, hope is illusory, the men are self-deluding. Alchemy is 'that slidynge science' (l. 732: deceptive, snake-like, moving fast like quicksilver); they are 'never the neer' (no nearer to catching up with it, l. 721), always in a state of desire. The Yeoman's words make the Canon vanish, under fear of being slandered, and the Yeoman, saying 'the foule feend hym quelle' (l. 705) – the first of many devil images throughout the tale (compare ll. 782, 861) – says he will speak of the Canon and how he came into that 'game'. This confession comprises the tale's following first part. It displays the Yeoman's complicity, desire for respectability, and conceit: his pride in 'our elvysshe craft' (l. 751, compare 842). He needs no audience, since his divided subjectivity pours forth in self-revelatory speech, expounding alchemy's mysteries as fascinated by them. The 'elixir', the 'philosopher's stone' is aspired to, but this, as an illusion, and significantly called 'him' in the following quotation, reads like part of a hope to raise and control the devil:

> He hath ymaad us spenden muchel good,
> For sorwe of which almoost we wexen wood, [mad]
> But that good hope crepeth in oure herte, [another snake-like image]
> Supposynge evere, though we sore smerte,
> To be releeved by hym afterward.
> Swich supposing and hope is sharp and hard;
> I warne yow wel, it is to seken evere.
> That future temps hath maad men to dissevere [to take leave]
> In trust therof, from al that ever they hadde . . . (ll. 868–876)

We may compare Langland's *Piers Plowman* A text, XI.159–161 (*c.*1350) on alchemy (I modernise the orthography):

> Yet arn there febicchis in forellis of many manis wittes,
> Experimentis of alkenemy of Albertis making,
> Perimansie and nigromancie the pouke to reisen . . .
> (Schmidt 2011, 1.417)

(Yet there are alchemical manipulations or tricks in hidden away in boxes, from many men's wits, experiments in alchemy made by Albert the Great [(*c.*1193–1280); see Linden 2003: 99–110 for this], divinations by looking at the flames of a fire, black magic in order to raise the Puck [Schmidt 2011, 2. part 2: 589 notes *negro* (black) magic as a corruption of *necro* (dead): necromancy is 'the raising of demons and the spirits of the dead'].)

'Puck' (Shakespeare's Puck: the devil in *Piers Plowman* C.XVIII. 50, 278), surfaces from alchemical experiments, which Langland calls black magic. The Canon's Yeoman passes to the disasters caused in burning off the metals, when 'the pot tobreketh, and farewell, al is go!' ('The Canon's

Yeoman's Tale' l.907), a line comparable with 'al our revel was ago' in 'The Franklin's Tale' (see Introduction):

> Withouten doute,
> Though that the feend noght in oure sighte hym shewe,
> I trowe he with us be, that ilke shrewe! [same]
> In helle, where that he lord is and sire,
> Nis ther moore wo, ne moore rancour, ne ire. [there is not]
> (ll. 916–919)

The laboratory seems like another Hell. The experiment crashes; participants are maddened; the wisest looks the most foolish, while 'he that semeth trewest is a theef' (l. 969), in a combination of folly and fraud. Whereas 'The Friar's Tale' and Guido da Montefeltro illustrate the devil's logic within language, as the logician, here he, as 'a 'shrew' (*OED* notes this as an example of 'shrew' meaning 'devil') is more elusive, inside chemical processes impossible to tame. The Yeoman proceeds to his Tale (the *pars secunda*); here, the devil is a Canon, outsmarting any deal made with him; not now attempting alchemy, but cheating:

> Ther is a chanonoun of religioun
> Amonges us, woulde infecte al a town . . .
> (ll. 972–973)

This opening claims the tale as documentary realism, not a past fictional narrative, so differentiating it from all the others, though putting it into a curious relationship with St Cecilia, also presented as historical. It implies the devil's supernatural power within a city setting, and introduces a religious hypocrisy with power to deceive the Priest, like the devil with Faustus. The Canon misuses his wit (l. 649). The Yeoman's audience can take the description naturalistically (the tale is about a Canon), or see the Canon as a presiding devil (Gardner 1967; Linden 1991: 42–53). The Yeoman makes the comparison with Judas Iscariot (ll. 1003, 1007). As those who pursue alchemy smell of brimstone (l. 885), so intimations of the devil coruscate throughout.[1] The Yeoman's denial that the tale's Canon is the one who rides off (ll. 1088–1095), if it convinces – which it may not – only suggests a hierarchy of evil which makes his position ambiguous: how much is this over-talkative Yeoman implicated? At the end he condemns alchemy (ll. 1388–1425), but cites four alchemical authorities: Arnold of Villanova, a French alchemist (1235–1311), who in his turn is made to quote Hermes Trismegistus; then Aristotle, as a disciple of Plato; this source, called 'Senior', comes from a tenth-century Arab alchemist, Senior (Muhammad ibn Umail). Plato gets the last word, saying that Christ wished to keep secret the quintessence that makes up the philosopher's stone, called here, 'Magnasia', and revealed them only to those he chose. So the Canon's Yeoman ends piously. God does not wish that philosophers unveil how a person can reach the philosopher's stone: it can only be revealed by Christ. Pursue the knowledge, and you go against what is the gift of God, and become victim of the devil's hoax, like the priest fooled by the Canon. The danger exists in *ignotum per ignocius*, i.e. explaining the unknown by the even more unknown. Yet that is the Faustian method, of course: use hell to explain heaven, or the irrational to explain the rational. And perhaps it is the only method: certainly, you cannot explain the unknown by the known.

The Canon's Yeoman may be sincere here (Schmidt 1974: 40–41), but what in his dramatic voice has been offered is an instability, apparent in his love of making a story out of the Canon. While full of protestation about the perils of being 'blinded' by the Canon, his development of the story to the full attaches him to the world of the 'falsehede' (l. 1173). Nor, significantly, will he join the pilgrimage (l. 970).

4 The Harrowing of Hell

The devil is the efficient cause of plays.
(Stephen Gosson, *Plays Confuted in Five Actions*, 1582) (Chambers 1923: 215)

Demons appeared in popular forms in pageant-plays performed in European towns, and in England by the town craft guilds, performed to accompany the annual Corpus Christi liturgical processions, or else, following E.K. Chambers, they attached themselves to that procession, whose official ecclesiastical status was not confirmed until 1311 (Chambers 1903: 2.95). Of several cycles of plays, whose compass is the Creation to the Last Judgment, I take examples from the Towneley cycle comprising thirty-two plays (the name is that of the Burnley family who owned the manuscript). These took shape in Wakefield, during the fifteenth century (Pollard 1897) following material from the parallel York plays. Some eight plays are by one identifiable, anonymous hand, including 'The Second Shepherds' Play' (XIII), which parodies the birth of Christ with a stolen sheep being placed in a crib for the shepherds to admire: he is a 'horned lad' (Cawley 1959: 59, l. 601).[2] The sheep, like a changeling, has been stolen from the shepherds by Mak, the 'shrew' (l. 453), trickster and buffoon, whom Chambers identifies with the Antichrist, the 'horned and blackened devil' who is 'the same personage, with the same vague tradition of the ancient heathen festival about him, whether he riots it through the cathedral aisles in the Feast of Fools [in carnival], or hales the Fathers to limbo and harries the forward spectators in the market-place of Beverley or Wakefield' (Chambers 2.148, compare 2.91).

On this reading, developed in related ways by John Speirs (1957: 335–348) and Robert Weimann (1978: 85–97), devils and demons evoke a folk culture whose irrepressibility and comedy involves a subversiveness which the more official and orthodox culture cannot quite control. This view is challenged by impeccably scholarly American scholarship in John D. Cox's rejection of 'Chambers and his socialist heirs' (Cox 2000: 18); he would rather affirm the plays' orthodoxy, and see the 'demonic' threat coming from the court. Thus he thinks the point about Mak is that he apes courtliness (Cox 2000: 80). Perhaps, but if he is a yeoman from the king (201) he is in Herod's service anyway, and more relevant is Mak as magus, casting a spell on the shepherds by his magic circle (278). Stressing devils as features of drama which sanction a reaffirmation of the sacred in relation to church authority, and which use the devil to emphasise his rejection and defeat, only underscores that there is a politics involved in considering the devil; orthodoxy and the right need him. Socialism must wrest the demonic from a conservatism which stands for authority.

The devil appears by implication throughout the Towneley pageant-plays: as Garcio, the boy (shrew, l. 30), who is Cain's servant (the 'thrall of Satan', as he says, II. 464), and is known as Pikharnes (stealer of armour). This 'merry lad' (II. 2) comes in blowing his horn, to rough up the audience, being both for and against Cain, another 'shrew' (l. 380). Virtually the same boy appears as Jack Garcio in the First Shepherds' Play (XII. 179–190) as a contrast of youth to age, seeing these figures of winter as fools, and saying that their sheep have been found not dead or famished, but in grass to the knee (a spring miracle anticipating the birth of Christ). He reappears as serving Christ's torturers, called Froward, 'ever curst' (XXI. 379): the only one named. Froward, 'the opposite of toward' (*OED*), appears in translation of an Erasmus paraphrase of Matthew 6:13 – deliver us from evil [the evil one] as 'the forward temptour' (*OED*). And the devil also appears as

Herod, the tyrant (XVI), whose play is a study in self-delusion. And he reappears as Pilate, who has a huge and vivid part in this cycle (see XX, XXII, XXIII, XXIV, XXVI) (Williams 1950: 37–51).

Devils appear in the first play, and in the Last Judgment (XXX) and in the Harrowing of Hell, no. XXV (Woolf 1972: 269–275), where three devils are named: Ribald, Beelzebub, and Satan. No. XXX, following the York cycle, uses two demons, plus Tutivillus: the demon bearing a sack on his back which contains the records of idle words spoken in church; so making Tutivillus an agent of slander (Jennings 1975). These demons say that if Judgment Day had not happened they would have had to build an extension to hell (XXX. 179–180) while the Second Demon says:

> Our porter at hell gate
> Is haldyn [guarding] so straite,
> Up erly and downe late,
> He rystys [rests] never.
> (XXX. 373–376)

Truly, 'if a man were Porter of Hell Gate, he should have old turning the key' (*Macbeth* 2.3.1–3). 'Ribald', with which *OED* compares 'rebel' – it includes the meaning 'a jester', as one speaking offensively and dissolutely – pairs with Tutivillus in the Last Judgment plays (Stevens 1987: 163–165, Cox 2000: 28–29). And M.D. Anderson (1963: 171–177) surmises that Sir Toby Belch's 'Tillyvally, lady' (*Twelfth Night* 2.3.72–73) and Mistress Quickly's 'Tilly-vally Sir John' (*2 Henry IV* 2.4.81) are both corruptions of this devil's name, as ongoingly popular.

'The Harrowing of Hell' refers to the events of Holy Saturday when, according to the apocryphal Gospel of Nicodemus, Christ – in spirit, not in body – descended into hell, specifically Limbo, to free the souls of the Old Testament righteous. This Gospel, popular in the medieval period, dates from the fifth century, and purports to contain the separate, identical, testimonies of the sons of Simeon (Luke 2:25), Karinus and Leucis, who have risen from the dead with Jesus after the harrowing of hell (Elliott 1993: 190–198, Tamburr 2007). They disappear in glory after writing. The episode also receives extended treatment in *Piers Plowman* (BXVIII.110–443, CXX.113–478), as the militaristic triumph of Christ over the devil, in a form which suggests the Apocalypse (Bertz 1985). In this episode of *Piers Plowman*, the dreamer, whose marginalisation as a wanderer, a holy fool, and as one who is near madness is key to the C version of the poem, descends into deep darkness in hell.

He hears and sees the arrival of the four daughters of God, Mercy (west), Truth (east), Righteousness (north) and Peace (south), coming from the four points of the compass, to debate and mark the encounter of Christ's arrival. He demands that the gates of hell, which is a castle, be opened. In the grotesque comedy of the response, Satan addresses a personified Hell and calls to Ragamoffyn (*Piers Plowman* 281), a name for a worthless person (*OED*). 'Ragged' seems to be an adjective evoking the devil; 'ragman' is a name for the devil at CXVIII.122, in a passage which shows how the devil has taken all the Old Testament saints into Limbo, and which has 'affinities with (and possibly influence from) the way in which this episode was treated in the earliest Miracle Plays' (Schmidt 2011: 2.2.693). Ragamoffyn is Belial's grandson, and his mother (name not given), is mentioned: Satan wants him to stop the light coming in. Other devils mentioned are Astaroth, also named in the Towneley Play, and Colting, possibly for the association of a colt with wantonness and lechery (Pearsall 1994: 332). And there is Mahond, and Mahomet, one of many misnamings, by whom the Towneley Herod swears.

The Towneley play (XXV) begins with Christ's words after his death, declaring he must now rescue the Old Testament saints from hell. To warn of his coming, he sends a light, which is beheld by the Limbo inhabitants: Adam, Eve, Isaiah, Simeon, John the Baptist, and Moses, all those who died in faith before the crucifixion of Christ. This light is followed up by an alarmed Rybald, and by Belzabub calling up Astaroth (2 Kings 23:13) and Anaball (unidentified, Happé 1975: 688); also Bell, Berith (Baal-berith, Judges 8:33) and Belial. The last of these (Hebrew: 'worthlessness', hence 'sons of Belial' (1 Kings 21:13)) is a devil's name (2 Corinthians 6:15). They bid them warn Satan and Lucifer – differentiated here – before Christ is heard calling for the gates of hell (again, a castle) to be raised, in the language of Psalm 24:7. Satan appears indignant and Belzabub tells him they are besieged. Satan begins bluffing but Christ outside bursts the bars, to Ribald's dismay, and confronts Satan, who tells him he cannot be God's son because he is the holy fool: 'thou has lyffyd ay lyke a lad/In sorrow and as a sympill knaue [knave]' (XXV. 257–258).

When Satan begins to lose the contest, Jesus tells him he can keep some souls, such as those of Cain, Judas and Achitophel, and Satan thinks about how he will go out and make men sin, but he is bound – this is the apocalyptic note of the Harrowing of Hell (Revelation 20:2, compare

Piers Plowman CXX.446) – and sinks further down into hell. The play ends with the souls thanking Christ as they pass out of hell. As with *Piers Plowman*, the other devils remain unbound, sources of comedy in their inadequacy and quarrelsomeness among themselves, as with Ribald reviling Satan ('now shall thou have a fytt' (l. 362). The devil may be contained, but there are others left over beyond him.

5 Goodman Devil

In the morality play *Mankind*, probably from the Benedictine Abbey at Bury St Edmunds, Suffolk, *c*.1471, a piece of popular theatre perhaps performed at Shrovetide, i.e. at the end of the Carnival season (Bruster and Rasmussen 2009: 12, 33), Tutivillus becomes Titivillus. *Mankind* opens with Mercy, a priest-like figure, speaking to the audience in a highly elaborate, aureate language, which is immediately mocked by Mischief, who has qualities of the Fool, and by the devil, who probably also doubled as Titivillus. Mischief introduces three characters: Newguise, Nowadays, and Nought, two wasters and a fool (l. 275), brought together in Nowadays' line to Mercy: 'Say nought again [against] the new guise nowadays' (l. 107). Mercy warns Mankind, who is here a farmer, like Adam the delver, about Titivillus ('all vile', or 'evil'):

> Ye have three adversaries and he is master of them all: [compare l. 304]
> That is to say, the Devil, the World, the Flesh, and the Fell.
> The New-Guise, Nowadays, Nought, 'the World' we may them call,
> And properly Titivillus signifieth the fiend of hell.
>
> (ll. 882–886)

The Flesh and Fell signify the body and the trinity of evil also appears in the slightly earlier morality play *The Castle of Perseverance* (see below). It may also be said that all the characters, apart from Mercy and Mankind, embody devilish features, which are highly theatrical and entertaining if also ominous and anarchic, while they are also on both sides of the law and likely to be hanged (l. 520). As figures of the world they are funny, and dance, and mock Mercy in 'idle language' (l. 147) which is the key to how the devil works in the play; the three involve the audience in their speeches as when they sing the Christmas song (l. 333), so pushing the audience (the 'yeomanry', l. 334), involuntarily, onto the devil's side in the comic release that the song produces. The meaning of 'morality', in 'morality play' expands beyond the point where it can be said to yield a single, edifying message. This idle language is only one of many defecatory moments in the play (see ll. 778–785), which have the effect of not allowing the audience to consider themselves higher, more ideal, less bodily present, than these figures, biblical 'sons of Belial'. A similar point holds for *Macbeth*, which as one of Shakespeare's tragedies, is notable for being almost entirely bawdy-free (the classical tragedies, *Julius Caesar* and *Coriolanus* are similar). The only exception in the play being the drunken Porter, who is a reverse of the Harrowing of Hell: not letting souls out, but welcoming them in. The price for noting this piece of morality is that of experiencing the play's only bawdiness and defecatory detail.

Audience involvement is required when Newguise, Nowadays, and Nought are on stage alone with Mischief, and collect money from the audience for the privilege of seeing Titivillus (l. 460). This devil figure, who acts as a conjuror, sends them off by blessing them with his left – the devil's – hand (l. 522); he places a board in the earth to prevent Mankind digging. Later he tricks Mankind while the latter is sleeping by pouring deceitful words into his ear, which Mankind takes as a terrible dream. The three jokers, plus Mischief, reappear, and draw Mankind towards the seven deadly sins, until Mercy returns looking for Mankind. Mischief's last temptation is to suggest that Mankind should hang himself (ll.791–804), as though that spirit which induces suicide is the chief characteristic of 'mischief'. For strictly speaking, Mischief is extra to that theological ordering of the trinity of the world/the flesh/the devil; in this he is like the Towneley devils, those unabsorbable remainders, outside all order. *Mankind* concludes with Mercy's mercy towards Mankind, and his wish to the audience that they may be 'play-feres' (companions) with the angels above (l. 912). That defines everything in the play as a divine comedy.

This play's mobility, between farce and a seriousness which is parodied when it appears in Mercy's speeches, exceeds that of *The Castle of Perseverance* (written *c.*1400–1425). These plays, together with those in which the Vice appears, such as *Respublica* and *Like Will to Like* have in common a life as 'morality plays', or 'interludes': terms interchangeable; certainly parallel (Bevington 1962: 8–18). *The Castle of Perseverance*, like *Mankind*, was a touring play. As its opening announcements (called 'Banns') show, it seems to have required performance in an open-air circle. It needs a castle centre stage, its interior visible, and five scaffolds around the circle. In the north, that of Belial, armed with gunpowder; in the north-east, Covetousness, or Avarice; in the east, God; in the south, the Flesh; in the west, the world (Happé 1979: 78–79). Richard Southern, describing the play's staging, stresses a kinship he makes between it and Brecht's epic theatre. He sees it as a 'social play', belonging to that form of society 'where the smallest social unit is not one man but two men' (Southern 1975: xx). He assumes an audience situated *inside* the circle, and so actively involved, moving about (Southern 1975: 138), and the castle on stilts, to ensure visibility of its interior episodes. Southern's controversial reconstruction of the staging has been defended by Catherine Belsey, even if her argument that the audience is offered a 'single, stable position from which to understand the nature of human life' (Belsey 1985: 22) seems perverse. An audience moving about, with its back to at least one scaffold at any one time, only sees things relatively, incompletely; no single view is to be had, no one sense of human life. That associates the play with a psychomachia, with a movement to and fro between different interested parties, where not even the presiding opening figures, the World, 'Belial the blake' (*The Castle of Perseverance* l. 199) and the Flesh, are unified, even though they all announce an ability to destroy Mankind from his birth, which is then witnessed (compare *Doctor Faustus*, Prologue line 11: 'Now is he born . . .').

Mankind, in the midst of all, has a pre-Marlovian Good and Bad Angel. While the seven deadly divide between Belial (Pride, Anger, and Envy) and the Flesh (Gluttony, Lechery, and Sloth), Avarice, the only one from these scaffolds to move about, possesses a single space as apart from the other six, which makes him the principal vice, as in *Respublica*. He gives the play a less abstract quality. And Avarice's servant is an extra, i.e. Backbiter, the figure of detraction, which is indeed his name: he is Detraction, an allegorical name (persisting into Falstaff's 'Detraction will not suffer it', *I Henry IV* 5.1.138). Diller comments on Detraction as an early version of the Vice (Diller 1992: 150–151). Adding to the spilling-over which spoils neat allegorical categorisations, the World has extra tendencies, or vices: Lust-liking, and Folly; while at the end of life, the Boy, the page of the World (l. 2961), calling himself 'I-Wot-Nevere-Whoo' (l. 2991), takes everything.

The play shows Mankind tempted and, aged forty, saved, through the agency of Confession and Penitence, and then by Charity, Abstinence, Solicitude, and Generosity, Meekness, Patience and Chastity (seven virtues), escorting him to the Castle of Perseverance. In Happé's 1979 edition, which divides the play into parts, the Second Part shows the Bad Angel calling up Backbiter, called Flypyrgebet, a name to be returned to in the next chapter, and meaning 'a chattering or gossiping person' (*OED*, first citation 1549, alongside 'flatterer'). Backbiter tells Belial, the Flesh, and the World of this bad news, but the successful seducer of Mankind's old age is Avarice (2501). Part Three shows the triumph of death; though Mankind dies with 'mercy' as his last word (l. 3031), the Bad Angel carries his soul on his back to hell which is Belial's dwelling. In Part Four, a debate occurs, between the four daughters of God, noted in discussing *Piers Plowman*. Eventually they embrace, and take Mankind from the fiend – in what looks like a reprise of the Harrowing of Hell, as though that deliverance was always a present possibility – and to the scaffold where God dwells. God finishes the play with a reference to 'our games', so that 'God's great role is laid aside, and the Poor Player speaks' (Southern 1975: 216).

Everything, including Belial and his associates, has become theatre; evil is acting, part of a 'good game' for Backbiter when Gluttony, Sloth, and Lechery are beaten by Flesh (l. 1832), and like everything else in the drama, dependent on an audience whom it has enticed to believe in it, in that shared flat space Southern and Weimann name the *platea* (Weimann 1978: 79). There, hierarchies are impossible, since it is the territory of intimacy between actor/fool and audience. It is also the acting space for the mad Herod: Harold Jenkins' edition of *Hamlet* quotes, at 3.2.14, from the medieval Coventry Play: '*Erode ragis in the pagond and in the strete also*' (see also Diller 1992: 33–45, Weimann 1978: 64–72). Herod rages on the stage, and in the street; comedy and terror combine, as Benjamin confirms. This allegorical drama, the theatre of the world, a play of masks, presents history as allegory, not as it literally is, but in complex image-forms.

Herod's comic fury compares with the significance of the torturers of Christ (Towneley Play XXII), who come in via the audience, shouting to them to 'make room' (l. 62) (Diller 1992: 98–99, 131). These torturers are A.P. Rossiter's subject. His posthumous volume of essays on Shakespeare, *Angel with Horns*, partially referencing *Measure for Measure*, instantiates the angel and the devil together as an essential ambiguity within Shakespearian drama, and before Shakespeare, *Doctor Faustus*.

Here, noting a double tone in the 'Buffeting' play (Towneley XXI), Rossiter compares it with paintings by Bosch (*c*.1450–1516) of Christ crowned with thorns (Gibson 1973: 125, 126):

> in both, two spirits are at variance: *one* focuses on the pathos, emphasised by the simplicity of the Christ: *the other* takes a cruelly humorous delight in the different epitomes of derision in the hard and mocking faces which imprison

> Him. . . . A fiendish delight in the inflicting of savage pain appears throughout . . . yet the fiends are heartless comedians. (Rossiter 1950)

Referring to the Crucifixion, Rossiter finds 'two rituals at once, of which the one is the negation of the faith to which the piece is ostensibly devoted. The very values of martyrdom – of *any* suffering as significant – are implicitly denied by thus making game of it'. The comic devilish, which is given room, exists as 'the inversion, reversal, or parody of the divine' (Rossiter 1950: 69–72). The 'uncombinable antimonies' relate to two discourses, one Christian, the other, the more-than-traces of 'primitive paganism' (i.e. folk religion) in these dramas, creating an 'unholy zest'. For Rossiter, 'a ritual of defamation, sometimes reaching an adumbration of the undermining negatives which threaten all human values and respects, regards and venerations' (73, 74) descends from medieval drama. Reverting to the Buffeting, it is impossible not to assume that the pleasure the torturers feel in buffeting Christ is real and shared by the audience (Diller 1992: 225).

Laughter cannot be recuperated and made ecclesiastically acceptable, which V.A. Kolve argues is the function of this comedy in medieval drama: 'God is in control, the evil and the demonic behave stupidly because that is in their nature, and the proper reaction to this example of the rightness of things is laughter' (Kolve 1966: 140). Disagreement with Kolve's sober logocentrism, and agreement with Rossiter entails theorising laughter and the demonic together while thinking that these antimonies are also shaped by class differences between the church and the people, though this is not a clean division. There is something essential in the Towneley torturers, which in Bosch makes their personalities so vivid, irreducible to an allegory of evil.

6 The Porter in Macbeth

The Castle of Perseverance makes the Vices, the Bad Angel, Backbiter, Lust-liking, and the Fool figures of Belial. The Vice emerges in moralities and interludes as 'homiletic showman, intriguer extraordinary and master of dramatic ceremonies' (Spivack 1968: 151); 'the part for the leading comedian' (Wilson 1969: 62). Peter Happé finds the Vice isolated first as a separate figure first in *Respublica* (*c.*1553) (Happé 1972:14–15). The interlude *Like Will to Like*, by Ulpian Filwell (*c.*1568) calls him Nichol Newfangle (compare Nowadays or Newguise). He is the devil's son, who carries the devil to hell when he has done his work of stimulating vice in others *and* seeing it punished. The Vice is of the generation preceding Shakespeare, but Richard the Third – 'Thus, like the formal Vice (3.1.82–83) – maintains the methods of that comic role (see Spivack 1968: 394, noting the self-consciousness within Richard's word 'thus'). 'Old Iniquity', perhaps the source for 'Old Nick' (the devil), is a Vice in Jonson's *The Devil is an Ass* (1616), where he ends by carrying the devil to hell, on his back (Act 5 Scene 6) (Happé 1994: 28–31). Falstaff calls Shallow 'a Vice's dagger' (*2 Henry IV* 3.2.313); in *Henry V*, the Boy compares Pistol's braggadocio to 'this roaring devil i' the old play, that everyone may pare his nails with a wooden dagger' (4.4.73–74). Feste is 'the old Vice . . . with dagger of lath' but says 'Adieu, goodman devil' after calling him 'mad lad' (*Twelfth Night* 4.2.131, 132). Claudius is 'a vice of kings' (*Hamlet* 3.4.98): villain and clown and grotesque, 'a King of shreds and patches', which is how the Vice might have appeared disguised. Indeed 'There is no vice so simple but assumes/Some mark of virtue on his outward parts' (*Merchant of Venice* 3.2.81–82: Craik 1958: 137).

Hal – another 'mad lad', so now acting as his own father – calls Falstaff the 'reverend Vice, that grey iniquity, that father ruffian, that vanity in years' (*I Henry IV* 2.4. 453–454), though Hal might be considered a newer Vice in his calculated politicking (Spivack 1968: 202–204). Playing and deceiving with language is a familiar kind of work. In *Two Gentlemen of Verona*, Speed tells Launce, the clown, that he is the 'old vice still: mistake the word' (3.1.284). The Vice: actor, intriguer, tempter, and clown, all forms of the devil, rejoins Benjamin's stress on Iago and the intriguer as practising the 'strict joke', and informs *Measure for Measure*, which uses 'vice' twelve times, the most of any play in Shakespeare. Angelo would put down 'vice', but it becomes inseparable – almost essential – in all human activities.

Since the Vice is the clown, I finish this chapter with comedy's alliance with the devil, via *Macbeth*'s Porter, who derives from medieval drama (Wickham 1966: 68–74). Empson, discussing the double plot, quotes from Middleton's *Hengist, King of Kent, or, The Mayor of Quenborough*, where Simon the Mayor is greeted by two Cheaters and a clown, and other actors. He asks 'Now sirs, are you comedians?' (5.1.70), which, when Olivia asks it of Viola, 'Are you a comedian' (*Twelfth Night* 1.5.183) means 'are you an actor?' Comedian and actor are synonymous; all acting is comic acting, even in tragedy. The Second Cheater replies 'we are anything sir: comedians, tragedians, comi-tragedians, pastoralists, humourists, clownists, and satirists' and names some plays including *The Cheater and the Clown*. Simon, a clown, though not knowing it, thinks of the clowns he has seen:

> Here was a merry world, my masters! Some talk of things of state, of puling stuff, there's nothing in a play to a clown's part, if he have the grace to hit on't, that's the thing indeed. The king shows well, but he sets off the king. (*Hengist, King of Kent, or, The Mayor of Quenborough* 5.1.130–134)

The clown, for Empson, may be the 'foil' to 'set off' the king, 'not to parody the heroes, but to stop you from doing so: "if you want to laugh at this sort of thing laugh now and get it over"' (Empson 1965: 31), or else, as the Oxford Middleton suggests, to 'put the king out of consideration'. But king and clown form an indispensable unity, and this makes for a different sense of comedy within tragedy from that of comedy as 'comic relief', a term to be buried, as patronising, and as marginalising the clown and his diabolism. The Porter letting sinners into hell is usually seen as unconsciously moralising the play, showing how Macbeth's castle has become a hell. But perhaps better: he relativises what is happening (the Macbeths must leave to give room to him), and acts as the antinomy of the play's more sacral aspects, in the representation of Duncan's qualities: as meek, as clear, as virtuous. He admits three types to hell: the farmer who hanged himself on the expectation of plenty, not waiting for the harvest.[3] Then the equivocator:

> that could swear in both the scales against either scale; who committed treason enough for God's sake, yet could not equivocate to heaven (*Macbeth* 2.1.10–14)

and the English tailor stealing out of a French hose, which includes the physicality of urinating, each is caught by something they cannot quite master. The weather changes; words change; fashions change. After his request for money, as in *Mankind*, the Porter continues in a different vein, debating with Macduff on the three things that drink provokes: three being, naturally, an uncannily dangerous number in this play. Macduff as the comic's 'feed', asks what drink provokes, as if catechising the Porter. He did not need to ask, but having done so, he is caught, and must listen to a nine-line speech, which enumerates the three things drink provokes: nose-painting, sleep, and urine. But then comes an unsettling fourth:

lechery, which drink provokes *and unprovokes*, which is its strange equi*voc*ation (a related word); thus doubling the problem:

> It pro*vok*es the desire but it takes away the performance. Therefore much drink may be said to be an equi*voc*ator with lechery: it makes him, and it mars him; it sets him on, and it takes him off; it persuades him and disheartens him; makes him stand to, and not stand to; in conclusion, equi*voc*ates him in a sleep, and giving him the lie, leaves him. (*Macbeth* 2.3.30–35)

Drink plays Puck-like tricks in creating an ambiguity each time, where contrary effects happen simultaneously, and in sequence. Drink is devilish, priapic (as in Boccaccio's *Decameron* 3.10, which is the story of a monk initiating a girl into sex by telling her that he is 'putting the devil into hell'), and also non-priapic. Its nature is to equivocate with lechery, while, when 'equivocates' is used transitively, it implies 'insinuates' or 'evades'. What has the power of equivocation equivocates; it has double effects in sleep, and both tricks or deceives the person (giving him the lie) and lays him out, in sleep. Macduff says that drink gave the Porter the lie: i.e. it made him a liar (aware only of one truth in an equivoque, tricked by the other), it made him impotent, and made him lie too long, and made him urinate, from another sense of 'lye'. If equivocation is lying, the key example of equivocation, the uncanny part of the word, is that the word 'lie' is virtually what it means:

> That it did Sir, on [Folio reading] the very throat of me [drink has him *by*, and *on*, the throat, in a wrestling image, which compares with the choking swimmers (1.2.8–9); it cannot be got out, or vomited upward, just as Macbeth's 'Amen' stuck in his throat (2.2.31–32); it convicts the Porter of lying at a level deeper than a slip of the tongue: see *Hamlet* 3.2.569]: but I requited him for his lie [third use of this word]; and (I think) being too strong for him, though he took up my legs sometime, yet I made a shift to cast him [vomit, wrestle him to the ground]

Equivocation must be responded to by further violence, and double meanings; but there is nothing outside equivocation. Hamlet notes that the Gravedigger equivocates with him (*Hamlet* 5.1.134) which means that he gets the better of him (Kaula 1975: 105–112). Parolles (words) is an 'equivocal companion' in *All's Well that Ends Well* (5.3.247); Brabantio, in *Othello*, finds all 'sentences' equivocal (1.3.218), while for the Porter, equivocation is a means of avoiding justice. Words mean double; while, in the body, everything is equivocal; the lecher falls asleep, which is what is meant by 'I requited him [drink] for his lie'. He lies down; detumescence (not the 'swelling act') gives him the lie. Nothing can be established, however, for if drink gives the man the lie (as equivocation is a form of lying), the man returns. Rather than letting the drink leave him, as he says in his second speech, he says, in his third, that he actively lays the devil out when he comes in the form of drink. But the Porter is also the devil, and the comic devil wins. But he wins within the body, which, outside any idealising system, is also the devil's part. If we finish with the alliance of comedy and the devil, it will be seen they operate in both words and body. Drink is the source of comedy and folly, as in Rabelais, the subject of the next chapter, or in *Twelfth Night*; drink is also paradigmatic of the devil's work, reducing comedy to folly. The Porter shows the universal folly by which people go to hell; his own status being that of comic fool and an accuser. The following chapter will give material enough for tracing folly's constrained movement from devilish comedy to becoming more fully the instrument of accusation, and being itself accused of madness and subjected to exclusion: though there will never be the time to not 'remember the Porter' (24).

Notes

1. See 'The Canon's Yeoman's Tale' lines 886, in the reference to the goat; and 984, 1159, 1172–1174, 1238, 1273, 1301–1303.
2. The so-called Towneley Master is credited with parts of plays II (Cain), III (Noah), XII, XIII, (the two Shepherds' Plays), XVI (Herod), XXI (the Buffeting), XXII (the Scourging), XXIV (a Pilate play).
3. In Middleton's satirical pamphlet, *The Black Book* (1604), the devil makes his will as 'Lawrence Lucifer, . . . alias Dick Devil-barn, the griping farmer of Kent' (Middleton 2007: 2.215). The farmer is already diabolical. The name Lawrence is presumably on account of his griddling: saint and devil experience the same burning.

Chapter 3: From Carnival to *King Lear*: Ships, Dogs, Fools, and the *Picaro*

> My husband, Tim Tattle (God rest his poor soul) was wont to say, there was no play without a fool and a devil in't; he was for the devil still, God bless him. The devil for his money, would he say, 'I would fain see the devil'. 'And why would you so fain see the devil?' would I say. 'Because he has horns, wife, and may be a cuckold as well as a devil', he would answer. 'You are even such another, husband', quoth I; 'was the devil ever married? Where do you read the devil was ever so honourable as to commit matrimony? 'The play will tell us that', says he. 'We'll go see't tomorrow: *The Devil is an Ass*'.
>
> (*The Staple of News* Act 1 Intermean 30–40; Jonson 1988: 109–110)

So, from Ben Jonson's joke in one play about an earlier play he had written, we learn that Devils, fools, and cuckoldry go together: a point also from Rabelais, Shakespeare's *The Merry Wives of Windsor*, and *Othello*. The devil appears as conjuror, trickster; fool or mad, or holy fool, but this chapter, whose scope is texts of the sixteenth century, from its beginning to its end, witnesses the value and meaning of folly subtly changing under historical processes which it also helped to modify. The subtitle of Foucault's *Folie et déraison: Histoire de la folieà l'age classique* (1961), translates as the 'history', or 'story' – even 'allegories', or, using de Certeau's term, from *Le Fable Mystique*, 'fables' – of madness, or of folly. 'Folly' has rich polyvalent implications in Erasmus in 1509 and Shakespeare in 1700 (Empson 1951: 105–124), and these meanings even include the meaning of wickedness, as when

J. Tambling, *Histories of the Devil*,
DOI 10.1057/978-1-137-51832-3_4

Othello says about Desdemona 'she turned to folly and she was a whore' (*Othello* 5.2.130). Foucault's *folie* means madness and folly: the terms being interchangeable in *King Lear* (written *c.* 1607–1608), in the line 'Be Kent unmannerly/When Lear is *mad*... to plainness honour's bound/When majesty stoops to *folly*' (1.1.134–135, 137–138; Shakespeare 1997).[1] Kent, not distinguishing between madness and folly, follows order in a conservative mode, while the play shows a new world taking shape, where it is more dangerous to be accounted mad, and while folly, in the form of the Fool, disappears as inadequate halfway through. Foucault considers a new discourse of 'folly' to be at work prior to Cartesianism and *l'age classique*; 'fool' not being, earlier, a wholly negative term, but undergoing changes. Similarly, 'clown', which *OED* associates etymologically with 'clod', and so with the peasant, begins to mean the stage fool. *OED* gives 1600 for a first citation of that. Madness gains a newer intensity, becoming more the basis for exclusion.[2] The Alsatian humanist Sebastian Brant, in *Narrenschiff* (*The Ship of Fools*, 1494), writes poems upbraiding sin as folly, using the trope of the ship as the church (still implicit in the word 'nave', from Latin 'navis'), or the ship going down rivers such as the Rhine; an image of exclusion, or of utopia, which Foucault thinks could have been literal. Brant influences Dürer's apocalypticism, and also Bosch, who is discussed here, alongside Pieter Bruegel the Elder (*c.* 1527–1569). Erasmus' *Ecomium Moriae* (*The Praise of Folly*, 1509–1511) was used by Rabelais (*c.* 1485–1552), in the four volumes of *Gargantua and Pantagruel* (1532–1552), whose giants take the main stress in this chapter, so prompting discussion of carnival as the place for the devil. Rabelais, however exceptional, is difficult, and the text runs into difficulties with its own carnival, facing growing signs of opposition which it has to deal with, by accusing the accusers of the way it writes the body of diabolical hypocrisy. Rabelais certainly gave something to English drama in the 1590s and 1600s, hence this chapter comes to an end with Shakespeare, discussed through Falstaff as Rabelaisian, and a reaction to the Rabelaisian body and its folly, and *King Lear.* This play is analysed for its awareness of exorcism, and for the names of devils which emerge from this, and for its sense of the poor as poor devils, to be accorded no mercy by the state.

1 Bosch, Bruegel, and Dulle Griet

Commentaries on Bosch stress that his *Seven Deadly Sins* (Gibson 1973: 36) show sins as *follies*: folly to be the woman who is looking in the mirror when the devil holds it, as in Pride (Superbia). Two jesters are seen with Lust, one dressed as a monk; the other's bare bottom is exposed, to be beaten with a long wooden spoon (Linfert 1972: 44). In *The Conjuror* (Gibson 1973: 27), an over-credulous spectator leaning forward has her purse cut from behind while she looks at the conjuror. The cutpurse's accomplice, in front, has, apparently, magicked a frog from her mouth, as if exorcising an unclean spirit (as in Revelation 16:13). Frogs, and toads alike, are associated with witches ('paddock calls' – *Macbeth* 1.1.8) and with satanic metamorphoses (*Paradise Lost* 4.800–802). The strangely misshapen conjuror, a dog in a jester's cap at his feet, has an owl in his basket. It is hard to know in the variety of forms of deception working in the picture where to find the centre; perhaps nowhere, since this is like Ephesus in Shakespeare's *Comedy of Errors:*

> They say this town is full of cozenage,
> As nimble jugglers that deceive the eye,
> Dark-working sorcerers that change the mind,
> Soul-killing witches that deform the body,
> Disguised cheaters, prating mountebanks . . .
> (1.2.97–101)

The comic fear is of transformation, demonic metamorphosis, and doubling. When the twin Antipholuses of Syracuse and Ephesus meet as each other's double: 'one of these men is genius to the other' (5.1.332). Chapter 1's discussion of the daemonic will be recalled – but Pinch, the play's schoolmaster, trying exorcism to limit the carnivalesque happenings, wants to make folly simply demonic, so worsening confusion.

Folly's incurability (folly to mend a fool) marks Bosch's *The Stone Operation*, or *The Cure of Folly* where the doctor – a funnel on his head, as an improvised fool's cap – removes a 'stone' – a flower – from the seated man's forehead. He is also attended by a priest with a flagon, and a nun with a book on her head. The inscription around the circular work reads 'Meester snijt die Key eras,/Myne name Is lubbert das'. It translates as 'Master, cut out the stone – my name is Tricked Cuckolded Impertinent Hound' (so Linfert 1972: 46, who finds in the picture 'lunacy and sheer malignancy'). *The Ship of Fools* (Gibson 1973: 39, 42 the title is controversial) pairs gluttony with folly. Bosch's boat floats with its crazy craft of ten, the jester to the side the sanest, and two others begging while swimming alongside. Growing up like a mast is a hazel tree: Baldass (1960: 220) quoted earlier commentators, D.T. Enklaar and Dirk Bax, for the view that this was associated with carnival (certainly with magical charms). A roast goose is attached to it, which a robber, issuing forth from the bush is cutting down, while an owl's, or man's head peers from the top amidst the foliage, above the sign of the moon. A similar bush appears on top of hay piled up in *The Haywain* (Gibson 1973: 70), an apparently early triptych – but uncertainty marks everything of Bosch scholarship – whose central panel shows an exaggeratedly gigantic hay cart being pulled by demons. Perhaps a carnival wagon: that associates with the jester in blue, with bagpipes in the foreground.

Hybrid demons people Bosch's pictures, as in *Death and the Miser* (Gibson 1973: 43); and in the folly of the rich man being linked with Midas and his ass's ears in *Narrenschiff*, chapter 17; the illustration is of the rich man and Lazarus (Luke 16:19–31). And that will provide a leitmotif for this chapter. The death scene of the usurious miser recalls, for the contest of demons and angels for the soul, the death of Dante's Guido da Montefeltro; as does the roundel depicting a death scene – the first of the Four Last Things circling round the Seven Deadly Sins. Perhaps these demons fuse with the strangely heterogeneous figure of Antichrist in the centre of the Prado *Adoration of the Magi* (Philip 1953: 267–293): unless he is Herod, or a fourth Magus, from the New World, i.e. not Africa, Asia, or Europe. Linfert (1989: 116–123) notes the strange hybrid, bird-demonic designs associated with these Magi. 'Antichrist' (I John 2:18), as an associate of the devil, suggests the parodic (he is mocking Christ, as much as being antagonistic to him), and his appearance evokes the apocalyptic. In Bosch, times are synchronous, and conflictual, climactic, and the number of different scenes in the Adoration of the Magi makes several chronologies coexist. Antichrist appears in a Dürer woodcut for Brant's *Of the Antichrist* (Brant 1944: 331, chapter 103), seated on the keel of a wrecked ship of fools, at the apocalyptic moment when a third of the ships are destroyed (Revelation 8:9). Satan blows into his ear (slander is evoked here, as in Brant's chapter 101). With a bag of money (like the grey devil in *Death and the Miser*) for an orb and a scourge for a sceptre, Antichrist is indifferent to fools, who, with jesters' caps, are drowning amidst books – versions of the devils in the Gadarene swine, who were drowned (Luke 8:33), in a story which immediately follows that of the storm on Galilee threatening the ship with Christ and the holy fools with him, the storm being as irrational as them (Luke 8:22–25). In the front of the picture, St Peter, who had his own experience of storms (Matthew 14:22–33) hauls in another vessel of the saved, using his key.

As with the Lisbon *Temptation of St Anthony*, conflict, evident with the presence of devils, comes from temptation, resulting from fantasies; ambiguous since these are signs of delight and creativity (Linfert 1972: 74–86). The omnipresence of temptation disallows separation between the saint and the forces working for or against him. No one is in their private world; there seem no separations or isolation. Hell seems not that different from scenes on earth, especially in the *Last Judgment* triptych (Gibson 1973: 50–51).

That applies with the triptych *The Garden of Earthly Delights*, (Prado, *c.*1490–1510). Closed outer panels show either the third day of creation (vegetal life emerging from the waters) or the world of the Flood (Gombrich 1976: 79–90). At any rate, the world is enclosed in a glass globe. Reading schematically, the central inner panel divides into four horizontal strips, following a perspectival order. In the lowest, nearest to the viewer, nude figures and birds and hybrids dance and embrace, in disparate groups, in mussel-shells, and glass spheres, intertwined by flowers. The strip above shows a cavalcade riding, some on horses, anti-clockwise around a vast pool, in which female figures bathe. Above that, a huge area has been flooded, or forms a lake with four rivers flowing into it, perhaps those which went out of Eden to water its garden, and the Euphrates (Genesis 2:10–14). A central, cracked, round ball floats in it, with the ledge around it sizeable enough for people to balance upon it so as to make love upside down, and capped with fantastic towers, tabernacles, and monstrances exaggeratedly crazy, vegetable and architectural together, organic and inorganic. Four other towers and balls, imaginary architecture, perhaps deriving from the pageants and scaffolds set up in medieval squares, both surround, and are in the water, where figures bathe and make love. While the presence of black people, together with the exotic fruit, and the nudity, may suggest Columbus' first reports of the Caribbean, it, the cavalcade and towers suggest European carnival. The skyline is high in the picture; but in the sky, comprising the fourth strip, are birds and monsters and flying fish, issuing from towers like pollen from flowers.

The left panel (the landscapes of the left and the central seem continuous), shows Eden, with God, dressed in red, giving the woman to man (Genesis 2:22). Unlike the equivalents in the triptychs *The Haywain*, and *The Last Judgment*, giving the fall of the rebellious angels, the creation of Eve, the taking of the fruit and the banishment from Paradise (*two* expulsions pictured), here is neither fall, nor expulsion. Fantastic architectural structures dominate high up in the panel's landscape. Birds swarm out of one hole, and fly through another within these structures, in another origin of life, so like the fountain, and like, also, the creation of the woman. The cactus-like tree, behind Adam, has heavily decorated vegetation and strawberries; the animals in the lower part include at least two which are being eaten, one a toad, and animals which are hybrid, or fantastic. Life comes, and is consumed. The centre, perspectivally above the three heads, shows a pink fountain in a blue lake, a structure with an eye-like porthole in its centre, from which, as if from a mirror, an owl looks at the viewer, the bird of night in this daytime; like the owl to the right in the lowest strip of the central panel, sitting astride, and forming the heads of, two dancing figures.

Much commentary, like Charles de Tolnay's in the 1930s, makes Bosch moralistic and didactic (Baldass 1960: 227–229): everything tending towards the night-time hell of the right-hand panel, which has three horizontal strips. Bosch had portrayed hell in *The Haywain*, where devils, like modern 'developers', are building in hell a tower, an infernal Babel; the *Last Judgment* has hell in the right panel, but the whole earth, in the middle panel, is another hell. In *The Garden of Earthly Delights*, the top of the right panel shows a town besieged, and on fire, soldiers crossing the bridge, and bodies in the water. The middle strip is dominated by a figure looking back at the viewer, his body a broken eggshell, inside which is a tavern scene. The shell's back, anus-like, has a ladder propped against it; an executioner, an arrow in his rear, climbs into it. This shell has tree-like features; the front legs of this figure are tree trunks, planted in boats, an instability matching that of many other precariously balanced objects, like the man on the top of the hurdy-gurdy below, balancing an egg on his back – one of a number of eggs, like the one borne in the cavalcade in the central panel. The egg-man hybrid balances a plate on his head. People walk on its perimeter; it is dominated by a set of bagpipes, which are equally the inn sign, on a flag, above the eggshell. Left of these bagpipes are two ears with a blade cutting between them. They are pierced by a spear going through them both, and a figure squats above the lobe; these ears have gone over bodies like wheels.

This part of the picture's base shows water, but the lowest strip shows dry land, and includes a blue (i.e. melancholic – so *OED*) devil with a cooking-pot on his sparrowhawk's head, and his legs in wine-jugs. Further picturing consumption, he is eating a sinner, while sinners, excreted when eaten, but unchanged, disappear into a further cesspit, a round hole, from his night-stool, or throne (Fränger 1952: 93–96). Perhaps in this cycle, what issues from him may originate the life emerging from the pool in the base of the left-hand panel, in a continuous process. But he initiates nothing. The only figure seeming to control anything is God, creating life divided between the two sexes, and now uniting the sexes together, as in the central panel they come together.

Looking, in Bosch's world is always deceptive: do not believe what you see, especially when images swarm. In the hell of the right-hand panel, a woman looks at the convex mirror which forms the posterior of a half-concealed body before her on its knees, the feet become branches, or roots (man as an uprooted tree). If the anus is her mirror, that makes it an eye, as a mirror is. The anus has plural uses too: next to the woman someone is excreting coins, as above him, the devil excretes sinners, as birds fly as if born (another origin of life) from the anus of the sinner he consumes. Bodies are passages; like all the openings in the triptych, all parts of the body are open, and interchangeable, since all bodies here are inverted, turning, or turned over, or prone; in movement which involves the entire body. Some figures are grotesque, but most, attractive in the uses found for their bodies.

The landscape of the left and central panels is 'demonic' (Bakker 2012: 97), because of the Garden of Eden's ambiguity. Baldass (1960: 33, 34) finds 'misshapen, demoniac forms', assuming that Eve is regarded as having brought evil into the world. That endorses the phallogocentrism which assumes that the figure who gives Eve to Adam is irreproachable; but ambiguity starts with him, as the author of division, inside a world of his creation which, not single, has the potential to further divide itself. Wilhelm Fränger, criticised for the lack of empirical evidence for his historical claims, yet interesting in his specific analyses, argues for the central panel showing innocence, based on a thesis that Bosch painted for a Free Spirits Millenarian sect, which rejected the concept of sin; and that he shows death, in the left-hand panel, as essential to life. That, with the treatment of the body I have just described, would make his work a critique of dualism. Perhaps hell may not be permanent, following instead Origen's belief in *apokatastasis*, belief in the restitution of everything, a view adopted by Anabaptists groups in the Netherlands (Fränger 1952: 82). If so, the painting is absolutely ambiguous, allowing no single reading, being particularly resistant to the 'this equals that' approach to symbolism warned against by Michel de Certeau in *The Mystic Fable*. What is 'fabled' for Certeau is spoken language whose objective truth cannot be assessed; the kind of discourse which the Reformation, as the age of print, with its appeal to the objectivity of Scripture, effectively suppressed: oral fables were changed in the direction of writing and literacy (Certeau 1992: 12). Bosch's picture, as like a 'fable' 'does not know what it is saying'; it 'defies investigation', being 'a place to lose oneself' (Certeau 1992: 12, 13, 29, 49–71). Certeau reads it as exhibiting a strange, unreadable calligraphy, resisting reading (and certainly, then, any form of moralising). It may present a scripturally based Christianity, from Creation to the sinfulness of the days of Noah (so Gombrich) progressing towards the destiny of hell. The central panel may record sinful indulgence; or else it may present the world as one of becoming, and innocent. Or, it implies that sexuality, 'madness and delight' together (Certeau 1992: 29) originates in a God whose creation is separation, indeed, self-separation; creating a theatre of illusion, putting life in the body under the imputation of pleasure as foolish sinful excess. All possibilities are there; only after Bosch and Bruegel did painting have to know what it was saying.

Bosch's *Carnival versus Lent*, surviving only in copy-form, shows an interior with Carnival borne on a table, and playing the bagpipes; Lent, a woman on the right, bearing fish on a platter (Koldeweij et al. 2001: 122–125). The idea of gluttony has returned. Bruegel's version of *Carnival versus Lent* (1559) is village-centred, like an earlier etching by Frans Hogenberg (1558) (Gibson 1977: 79–84). Michael Bristol (1985: 197–223) finds a similar motif of carnival misrule versus Lenten Puritanism pervading *King Lear*. Representations of peasants, and peasants' festivities (the *kermis*) in sixteenth-century German woodcuts associated drunkenness with Lutheranism – which had freed itself from Catholic Lent – and the devil (Stewart 2008: 31, 88–89, 98). Bruegel's Falstaffian Carnival figure sits astride a barrel with roast pork on it, jousting with the thin woman, the allegory of Lent. Her broiling iron bears two fish: more fish are sold at the market fountain behind her. Two worlds confront each other: the left, the carnival world, has an inn, the 'Blaue Schuyt' (Blue Boat), name of an originally Antwerp-based carnivalesque society (Kavaler 1999: 121), perhaps recalling the 'ship of fools'. If so, it may relate to Gluttony on the barrel, which rests on a kind of blue boat, and may evoke too, Bosch's fragment, '*Allegory of Gluttony and Lust*' (Gibson 1973: 45). Perhaps the giant Hurtaly, of Rabelais' *Pantagruel* chapter 1 should be mentioned for support: he survived Noah's flood by sitting astride the ark, being too big to get into it, and propelling it with his feet, while the people inside sent him up food through a funnel (Rabelais 2006: 21). The image, with its biblical parody (the Ark as the type of the church), and its love of life, is a fine introduction to Rabelais, his carnival having even more witty learned references in it than Bosch, or Bruegel. And none of these, nor Brant, are distanced from what they see.

Another inn, the Dragon, gives glimpses of the wild man in green, a feature of the Orson and Valentine romance of two princes, who, in the hell of the world-turned-upside-down described by Epistemon in *Pantagruel*, are 'attendants in the hot-baths of Hell, and scraped clean the face-masks of the women' (Rabelais 2006: 149). Behind Lent stands the church, and the faithful emerging with ashen crosses on their foreheads.

While Lent is satirised, it is however the emergent world which refuses carnival and the peasant, who is becoming the object of ridicule, to be identified with boorishness and folly (Vandenbroeck 1984b: 79–124). Behind the slow and moralising exclusion of the peasant world, where Carnival aligns with Gluttony, lies social and political change. The discourse of folly permits such moralising: folly as sin (not the same as sin as folly) – except that Lent may represent the Catholic church, as the presence of the nuns, and the monk and the nun pulling Lent's cart suggest, and Carnival may stand for Protestantism, which had discarded Lent, but was no more holy than Catholicism (Stridbeck 1956: 96–109). And there is a hint of social superiority in the wealthy Lenten bourgeois giving alms to the blind to the right of the picture: that forms yet another critique.

Perhaps the ambiguity of carnival and Lent shows most in *The Fall of the Rebel Angels* (1560, Gibson 1977: 94, 99) where the world turned upside down is literalised in the positions of the falling angels become animals and hybrids, posteriors prominent (Meganck 2014: 46). Are those alongside St Michael figures of Lent, and does the rebel angels being cast down mean the exclusion of carnival, or is the fall itself carnivalesque, as revealed in the painting's invention, making, then, *both* sides necessary for carnival to appear? The fall of the angels, and the apocalyptic fall of the Antichrist, the dragon, driven out by St Michael (Revelation 12:1–9) are fused in one picture, making time plural, and potentially apocalyptic, if that state is definable as a moment of a radical separating out of contrasting forces (Christian 'good' and 'evil'), which share one another's qualities, in the attempt to cast out the devil.

The thin woman reappears with Dulle Griet (*c.*1562–1564, Gibson 1977: 94). Here, Hell is a fantastic city, with ships' masts, dead trees, signs of war, and burning which illuminates everything with redness. A struggle takes place on the bridge to the right, between beast-like devils and women, with a counter-attack from knights appearing at the far right (the collocation of devils and knights being especially interesting), while Dulle ('mad', or 'angry') Griet

(Margaret – the first of several Margarets in this book) comes off the bridge to invade and loot Hell-mouth. (Certeau (1992: 66) finds in Bosch's bridges a devilish motif.) She wears armour, and carries kitchen utensils, a knife and a sword (Puyvelde 1946; Gibson 1977: 102–108; Sullivan 1977b: 55–66; Graziani 1973: 109–119). Hell-mouth, which Bruegel depicted in the print *Descent of Christ into Limbo* (Orenstein 2001: 210–212), where the doors are smashed and ugly hell gapes open for its harrowing, stands anxiously defenceless before this woman. And Hell-mouth is simultaneously a building and a face, with an owl in one nostril.

Older readings of the picture made the woman an allegory of covetousness (Grossmann 1966: 193). But seen in gender-specific terms, as a *woman*'s assault, it has comic, if not castrating, implications, as have the 'bad women' (poem no. 64) in Brant (Gibson 2006: 124–144). Dulle Griet's thinness is anti-carnival and triumphant; though a peasant, she shows a new order breaking through. This iconography of the woman taking on the devil in the context of Spanish repression of the Netherlands should not be depoliticised, though it is uncertain which side Dulle Griet is on.

But she avoids one temptation: in the picture's centre, on one of the posterns of the bridge a male figure sits dressed in woman's clothes, his back turned, and supporting a ship, the *Narrenschiff*, with four figures in it, one holding up a plate with a roast chicken on it, another, with a glass ball. He is no mere abstract allegorical Folly, for he rains coins from his eggshell-like anus: indeed he ladles them out with a long spoon to be collected by the women, as if buying off their rebellion, making them loot instead. The woman is after greater booty, as if going after the devil. Carnivalesque, the picture signifies the end of carnival, for while mad, she is single-minded, and ignores the grotesques, for instance, the two nudes, one in front of her, and one on a wall above her head, who are both exposing the anus: she means more than they can.

2 Rabelais: Pantagruel and Panurge

Mikhail Bahktin (1895–1975), theorising carnival in his *Rabelais and his World* (1940: unpublished until 1965), says that carnival 'does not know footlights' (Bakhtin 1984a: 7). Carnival differs from theatre in giving no space for the outside individual to watch it as an audience. It opposes what Bakhtin calls 'the profound tragedy of the *individual* life itself, condemned to birth and death', a life whose individualism reflects Aristotelian views of the tragic hero as an isolated figure, with individual responsibility. For this, Bakhtin takes as instance Macbeth, who is not seen as a criminal: that would make him transgressive. But if Macbeth *was* seen as transgressive, disagreeing here with Bakhtin, he would have something of carnival in him. This would follow the logic of Peter Stallybrass and Allon White, who define carnival as transgression, i.e. 'symbolic inversion and cultural negation' (Stallybrass and White 1986: 17). Nietzsche, interestingly, finds Macbeth demonic, hence Dionysian, in crime: 'demonic means here defiance *against* life for the sake of a drive and idea' (Nietzsche 1982: 239). For Bakhtin, more conservative than Nietzsche in this, Macbeth follows 'the logic of all life which is self-asserting and thus hostile to change and renewal'. Macbeth wants his own coronation, whose 'constitutive moment' is:

> violence, suppression, falsehood, the trepidation and fear of the subjected, as well as the complementary, converse fear of the sovereign before those who are subjected. (Hirschkop 1999: 287, quoting Bakhtin's 'Additions and Amendments to "Rabelais"')

Bakhtin's argument, applicable to more examples than *Macbeth*, is that the sovereign holds power in a state of anxiety, knowing that time is not on his side; the single time he lives through allows only loss of power in death. Fear of being cuckolded, pervasive throughout comic drama, and central to the comedy of Book Three of *Gargantua and Pantagruel*, Bakhtin relates to fear of loss of sovereignty. Cuckoldry is 'uncrowning'. The male wants to be eternal king:

> but woman is naturally opposed to eternity and unmasks it as senile presumptuousness. Cuckoldry, thrashing, and mockery, are inevitable (Bakhtin 1984: 242–243).

That, as Rabelais and Ben Jonson knew, makes the woman carnivalesque; indeed, such a threat of non-continuance makes Macbeth, 'in the scene of soothsaying' with the witches (Bakhtin 1984: 244), fearful of a son-less future. Bakhtin's sense of carnival as destroying personal time compares with Adorno's *Minima Moralia*:

> historically, the notion of time is itself formed on the basis of the order of ownership. But the desire to possess reflects time as a fear of losing, of the irrecoverable. Whatever is, is experienced in relation to its possible

> non-being. This alone makes it fully a possession, and, thus petrified, something functional that can be exchanged for other, equivalent possessions. (Adorno 1974: 79).

Desire to possess a person, or time, as a commodity opposes what is released in carnival, and in laughter, and the 'deriding of the whole world'. This last phrase, which describes a feature of the Feast of Fools, and the Feast of the Ass, both elements of carnival, Bakhtin (1984: 41–42) takes from Jean Paul (Richter), saying that the grotesque and laughter cannot be separated, and that 'the greatest humourist of all would be the devil'.

Jean Paul (1763–1825) invokes Rabelais, Shakespeare, and *Tristram Shandy* in his *Pre-School of Aesthetics* (1804), lectures which read Hamlet and others of Shakespeare's mad fools as inducing a 'derision of the world' (Casey 1992: 251). Jean Paul finds earnestness in great humorists: 'in the old German farces, this underlying seriousness manifests itself in the fact that the devil is usually the tomfool' (a word which in the medieval age meant a mentally deficient person, before it described a buffoon, and which compares with *King Lear*'s 'Tom o'Bedlam'). The devil, then, is 'the true inverse of the divine world, the great world shadow, setting off the form of the luminous body, as the greatest humorist and "whimsical man"'. But the devil's laughter is too painful, taking the form of 'arabesques'; or, using Jean Paul's phrase, it appears as 'the *moresque* of a *moresque*'; he adds that this humour 'would be far too unaesthetical; for his laughter would have too much pain in it; it would be like the gaily flowering gown of the guillotined' (253–254). The *moresca* was the sword dance in Venice's Arsenale in Venice on the Shrove Tuesday of carnival. It was a fertility dance performed by dancers with blackened faces, who used swords to simulate a beheading. Dancers mastered demons, or Moors, by impersonating them (Johnson 2001: 173–174). Perhaps that intimates a way of thinking about *Othello*, and the appropriations and expulsions of Othello by that play's Venetians. If so, comedy and tragedy as inseparable, factor into Iago's enjoyment of Othello's discomfiture, and illuminate the idea of the devil as the greatest humorist of all. Rabelais (2006: 22) marks such inseparability of laughter and pain when Babedec dies giving birth to Pantagruel. Gargantua, the father, knows not whether 'to weep out of grief for his wife or laugh out of joy for his son' (25); and that conflict plays out in parodic, sophistic form, mocking medieval scholastic debates which swing from 'pro' to 'contra'. Following Jean Paul and Bakhtin, even tragedy is inside this devil-inspired humour.

It is time to consider Rabelais specifically. Born around Chinon, between 1483 and 1494, this son of a lawyer became a Franciscan, and then a Benedictine, then a physician in Paris, and in Rome in 1534, under the patronage of the Bishop of Paris, Jean du Bellay (1492–1560), who let him become a secular priest. He was also an Erasmus-like Humanist, as well as an admirer of Luther. Francois I (ruled 1515–1547) himself went through a Humanist period when he was sympathetic to reform of the Catholic Church. Rabelais published *Pantagruel* (the name of a devil in French medieval drama), as the first volume of what we call *Gargantua and Pantagruel* in 1532 (Rabelais 2006). *Pantagruel* declares itself 'newly composed by Maître Alcofrybas Nasier': an Arabic-sounding, and alchemy-related anagram of Rabelais. At the end of the Book, he is 'the late' (i.e. posthumous) author, called 'Abstracter of the Quintessence' (164). France was feeling the Reformation's power. Rabelais critiqued the Sorbonne's dismal anti-humanism and Catholic adherence to Scholasticism, which the scholarship of Erasmus, and More, as well as the Protestantism of Luther, were blowing away. The Sorbonne responded with censorship and attacks on Rabelais. His Humanism appears in Gargantua's letter to his son (*Pantagruel* chapter 8). Lucien Febvre stresses that Rabelais inhabited a world of belief. It was impossible in the sixteenth century not to accept a world inhabited by demons (Febvre 1982: 452–454), even if it seems that Febvre as an historian is overanxious not to allow as valid any anachronistic reading of a text, or a sense that it could ever be untimely. Hence he underestimates its unconscious, and something else: the place the body has in the text, inverting all ideal values.

In the first volume, Pantagruel, the thirst-creating devil, outclasses the traditional devil. Of the chains used to bind him as a child, one 'was borne away by devils in order to hold down Lucifer, who was furiously breaking out into madness because of an extraordinarily infuriating belly-ache brought on from having eaten for breakfast a fricassee of law-serjeant's soul' (Rabelais 2006: 28).[3] The devil's body is as physical and subject to internal problems as the human. And being dual, the devil sides negatively with a precious and exclusionary language which despises common usage, as appears with the 'diabolical language' of the student from Limoges (35), who must be forcibly reminded of the body as more tangible and real than words. Pantagruel's tutor is Epistemon; his companion Panurge, is Mephistophelean, but more riotous, and Pantagruel's alter ego. Panurge is met in chapter 9, in Paris, near the Cistercian Abbaye de Saint-Antoine (51), which commemorates Saint

Antony, the hermit who was Bosch's subject matter in works showing his temptations by the devil in the Egyptian deserts (Gibson 1973: 138–152). Panurge, who wields thirteen languages in this chapter, is another devil, this time the *picaro*, the impoverished trickster; his name either meaning 'all energy' (*pan* + *ourgos*), or 'who will do all things' (La Charité 1975: 42–50).[4]

As first seen, Panurge partakes of that vagabond world seen in Bosch's outer panels for *The Haywain*, and in the roundel *The Wayfarer* (Rotterdam), which some Bosch scholars think portrays the Prodigal Son (Gibson 1973: 100, 103), moving away from a brothel as if from temptation. In *The Haywain* he is white-haired. There are signs of violence behind him, and bones before him, and he experiences the world as treacherous. These wayfarers will haunt our thinking about the devil; their backpacks recall the popular associations of the pedlar, as when Richard of Gloucester, who has just been called a 'cacodemon' says 'If I should be [king]? I had rather be a pedlar' (*Richard the Third* 1.3.149), where the pedlar, like Autolycus, and Christopher Sly the tinker in *The Taming of the Shrew* – who is the shrew to be tamed? – associate as 'rogues', which was itself a new word of the 1560s. Richard's unconscious association is demoniacal.

Panurge plays tricks, using the power of language. Embodying a phallic power, which he employs in chapter 14, when he 'abandons all the long preambles and protestations usually made by doleful and contemplative Lenten lovers (the kind who shun flesh)' he attempts the virtue of a married woman, pointing to his 'Maistre Jean Jeudy' (Frame 1991: 203). That gesture and language combines the phallic with the sense that Jeudi, the day after (Ash) Wednesday, when one is sorry for one's sins, is the day for play. His attempts on the lady are like the three temptations in Matthew 4:1–11, which was the reading in church for the first Sunday in Lent, for Panurge approaches the lady three times, the second time in church, and the third after dinner (Freccero 1991: 28–37). The lady's repeated refusal means that a trick is played on her by dogs, who surround Panurge, like the devil (see Psalm 22:20), urinating on her and her holiday finery on Corpus Christi (chapter 22). Panurge is intolerable, like the devil, when he incarnates the extreme version of the impulse to mock whatever keeps itself from the carnival, as the lady's 'haughtiness' keeps her from Panurge. Perhaps the episode can be defended for its farcical qualities, which appear in its deliberately exaggerated language (Hayes 2007: 39–52). Dogs, earlier in *Pantagruel*, are associated with the 'poor devils of Turks' (Rabelais 2006: 75), who invoke other devils (77). These dogs, in common with Turks, like bacon. Turks in this chapter, are reminders of the plural forms a discourse of the devil can take, are the 'other' to the European, since they threatened the gates of Vienna in 1532 (Hampton 1993: 58–82). Pantagruel enjoys the comedy of the lady's humiliation by the dogs (Rabelais 2006: 117), which means that the text will not allow the reader to side umambiguously with her. The 1534 ending to the book speaks about readers as 'good Pantagruelists' – who 'live in peace, joy, and health, always enjoying good cheer' (164). A Pantagruelist, then, can take Panurge, without entering into moralising judgments. To do so means seeing the humiliation of the woman as exaggeration, and the excess of language; diminishing the sense that the episode is more than fiction in a world of words. The lady's gestures – throwing him off a good hundred leagues (111) and talking the language of castration, if not worse, when she wants to have his arms and legs lopped off-further qualify the text's anti-feminism. This is a topic to be returned to later.

Pantagruel is succeeded by *Gargantua* (1535), the account of Pantagruel's father, and it declares 'Laughter's the property of Man' (203): i.e. man is capable of laughter (so Aristotle): though this may be a condition of ideology, so that it can be dangerous, coercive, and persecutory (as also anti-feminist), yet its absence is fearful (see below). The book gives the history of Pantagruel's father, and introduces Friar Jean, who has features of Panurge (who, since the text goes back a generation, has yet to appear, chronologically speaking). It contains the battle against Pichrochole, a victim of choler, which has driven him out of his mind (305). The *Tiers Livre* (1546) appeared under Rabelais' name (but the name is still a mask, like the previous one, under which he was so attacked by the Sorbonne), and it was dedicated to Marguerite of Navarre (1594–1549), the king's sister, and a patroness of Rabelais. This third book gives 'the heroic deeds and sayings of the good Pantagruel' (Frame 1991: 247). Its question is whether a now diminished Panurge, lacking his codpiece, should marry, since he is bound to be cuckolded. A formidable number of authorities are contacted, none giving ultimate assurance (Kaiser 1964: 103–192). Panurge here at least commits himself to being a fool, and as an innocent feels he has many brushes with the devil, as with the Sybil of Panzoust (chapter 16). He seems to have learned about the devil when studying at the University of Toledo, then capital of Castile, from the Faculty of Diabolology (chapter 23, 498).

The *Quart Livre* (1552) describes the sea voyage to find the divine, or saintly bottle, which if found would contain the definitive answer about marriage which Panurge needs. It is a journey around islands. An alternative and parallel sea voyage appears in chapter 18. Here the Catholic 'holy Religious' are sailing to the Council of Chésil (Fools); i.e. voyaging to the Catholic Council of Trent (1545, and then 1551–1552) whose aim was to strengthen the Counter-Reformation against the Protestants, indicating the religious disputes working to such bloody effect within Europe. The enforcement of Lent, at the Council of Trent, produces the satire of *Quart Livre* chapter 32 where these characters, joined with others in Rabelais' invective, are the monstrous products of Antiphysis (anti-nature), which creates them in reaction to the work of *Physis*, who is Nature (761). Immediately afterwards the crew on the ship see the monstrous *Physeter*, 'the blower', i.e. the whale, whom Panurge regards as Job's Leviathan, as 'Satan, Devil' (761, 762); he wants to send it back to the lawyers, the Chicanous (chapters 12–16), because its spouting, like theirs, adds gives no wine, but only water, i.e. what is Lenten.

Chapter 28 shows Pantagruel, Panurge, Epistemon, and Frère Jean arriving at the island of Tapinois (i.e. 'hide', or 'coverup', implying hypocrisy, which is a topic for our next section). Tapinois is ruled by the monstrous Quarêmeprenant, meaning 'taking Lent': this means that 'Lent is on its way', as the destruction of carnival, or else 'carnival [is] pregnant with Lent' (Kinser 1990: 83). Quarêmeprenant personifies the tendency to move from Carnival towards Lent (he is worse when married to Mid-Lent (754)), and is discussed and explained by the navigator Xenomanes ('crazy about foreign things'). His enemies are the Andouilles, i.e., the Chidlings: tripe sausages, on the Ile Farouche (ferocious). But their tendency is to become more like anguilles (eels). Aided by Mardi Gras, they are called women. Becoming an eel is dangerous, because it means tending towards the Lenten state: sausages, which should be carnivalesque, will not stay sausages. If Quarêmeprenant suggests Catholicism, Andouilles suggest Protestantism. They also imply that the carnivalesque seems halfway – as perhaps part of an historical process – to becoming Lenten. Three chapters describe the grotesque and empty, infertile, elements of Quarêmprenant's body, revealing that if he dreams, it is of flying phalluses scrambling up walls (759): the return of the repressed indeed. He represents a desire to enforce Lent, as decreed by the Council of Trent; destroying carnival as it were from the inside. The party arrive at the Ile Farouche in chapter 35, and Xenomanes says how there can be no reconciliation between these two forces (exacerbated by the Council of Chésil, 768). The Chidlings, 'always double and treacherous' (769) fight in carnival spirit, as half-serpents, like the one who tempted Eve. And 'it is still maintained in certain academic circles that the Tempter was a Chidling called Ithyphallus' (775). The woman combines features of the devil and of phallic meaning – for the word 'chidling' had earlier been applied, in phallic mode, to Gargantua (242). The devil is on both sides of a gender divide which he makes impossible to establish; Melusine, from French mythology, was 'either a serpentine Chidling or a chidlingesque Serpent' (*andouille serpentine ou bien serpent andouillesque*): female, and male. The voyagers fight with a Great Sow (a Trojan horse), and war breaks out until a flying pig arrives, which makes the Chidlings fall in worship. Dropping healing mustard on them, he flies off, crying 'Mardi Gras' (786). In the following truce, Niphleseth, Queen of the Chidlings is met: her Hebrew name implies 'dildo'. Anxieties about masculinity recur throughout this comedy, and suggest that such fears operated particularly in terms of, and activated, Carnival/Lent and Catholic/Protestant disputes, rendering uncertain, however, whether the fear was of the male, or of the female, or whether these states can be differentiated.

Pantagruel's party move to the Island of Ruach (wind). Chapter 43 sets off thinking about the winds that course through the human body, as through all bodies. This island, which lives on wind, is threatened by a giant, Bringuenarilles; Frame (1991: 881) annotates the name as 'wide nostrils'. He lives on Tohu (*tohu bohu*: the state of being waste and empty, like the state of chaos in Genesis 1:2) and there is a hint here of him as a figure of Augustinian negativity. Bringuenarilles' religious reaction enforces three or four Lents a year and he swallows up windmills, which are the islanders' lifeblood, but he dies from eating a pat of butter (717): carnival food is not for him. The next island (chapters 45–47) gives the Papefigues (Protestants, perhaps specifically those the Vaudois of Provence, massacred in 1545). They are oppressed by the Papimanes, on a neighbouring island. These are Catholics worshipping the thirteenth-century Papal Decretals – i.e. rulings on points of doctrine, defended for their financial efficacy by Honenaz, i.e. Pope Julius III (chapter 53). One farmer is harried by a little young devil who has obtained permission for such persecution from Lucifer (796), and has secrets of hell to reveal, e.g. that Lucifer's preferred dish is lawyers who pervert justice and rob the poor (799). He and the farmer are near to a contest where he will scratch the farmer but he is outwitted by the farmer's wife, the old woman, who tells the devil her husband has 'scratched' her. She lifts up her skirt and reveals her pudendum. The devil flees, from a panic attack caused by the castration-fear (801), or, from 'voyant l'énorme solution de continuité en toutes dimensions': 'seeing that monstrous solution [i.e. dissolution, break-up] of continuity in all its dimensions'. That, as a reference, derives from the Third Book, chapter 23, where it is said that devils, as spirits, can suffer blows 'in the continuity of their substances, which are both aerial and invisible' (499). Augustine, quoting Apuleius, believed that demons are 'animals in respect of species; in respect of soul, liable to passions; in mind, capable of reason; in body, composed of air; in life-span, eternal' (*City of God* 9.8, Augustine 1972: 352). This scholarly Platonist and Augustinian terminology is now used parodically. The devil, though immaterial, fantasises that his masculine self has suffered a wound, as much as Lucifer can feel the belly-ache. If fetishism in Freud is the male's way of disavowing the castration fear (*SE* 21.149–157), the devil, on this reasoning, needs to be a fetishist. It is tempting to pursue *OED*'s derivation of 'to scratch' from 'scrat' (an hermaphrodite) and to find scratching as devilish, degendering to the point of death, as Mercutio finds with his wound (*Romeo and Juliet* 3.1.94–98). *OED*'s earliest citation for 'Scratch' as a name for the devil is 1734, but the sense may reach back earlier.

Hints of such fears to masculinity have already appeared in *Pantagruel* chapter 11, when announcing a new way to build the walls of Paris, using women's pudenda interlarded with 'as many cocks as were lopped off from wretched Italians at the entry of the Queen into that town' (Rabelais 2006: 82); alluding to the possible fate of prisoners on the entry of Queen Eléanore of Austria, Francois I's second wife, in 1520. That castration joke, later changed to 'with those many stiff tools which, throughout, dwell in claustral codpieces' (82), is followed by 'what devil could ever bring down such walls!' Freud's essay 'Medusa's Head' associates the castration fear with a permanent erection (*SE* 18.273). The joke against genitalia continues with the story, dating from the time when beasts could talk, of the lion with a wound in his thigh – not an innocent place – treated by a carpenter who tells him to keep plugging the wound and swishing it to keep flies off. The lion then sees the pudendum of an old woman, and, getting the attention of a friendly fox, calls it a wound between the legs, which needs similar treatment which can never be sufficient, however; the ribaldry becomes most intense when discovering her other hole 'which stinks like a hundred devils' (84). Lion and fox suggest Pantagruel and Panurge: the chapter closes with Panurge's praise of codpieces (exaggeration praising exaggerative features). Bakhtin associates the imagery for the walls of Paris with a praise of fertility (Bakhtin 1984a, 212–215), while the eulogy of old women in *The Praise of Folly*, still craving sexual love, however grotesque the body, is memorable (Erasmus 1971: 109).

Neither Erasmus nor Rabelais turn away from the body, though there is an implicit sense in the latter of an historical tendency moving towards a more self-consciously Lenten condition, which at the individual level becomes what Julia Kristeva (1981: 56–89) calls the 'abject' state, involving recoil from the mother's body as expressive of the unnameable other which is feared as nothing. The subject will recur in the next chapter, in relation to Luther, and Lacan's comments on him. The 'abject' reverses Rabelais' non-separation from the other, as unidealisable matter, as Kristeva, one of the earliest sources of knowledge of Bakhtin in France in the 1960s, inverts Bakhtin's sense of the carnival body, by showing what is more usually, and dangerously, the case. In *Powers of Horror*, because the 'hard', ultimately Fascist masculinity which fears the mother's body, as the body of the 'other' provokes into being, wills and enforces preservation of borders, it fantasises these borders as contaminated by the 'other', as liquid heterogeneous matter, falling from the body. The 'abject' state represses and de-represses the power of the other, by exposing it, conflictually, in a form which horrifies the male subject. It is an apocalyptic state, producing 'the dramatic convulsions of religious crises', which suddenly cannot contain the 'other' within the spirit of carnival (Kristeva 1981: 209), but must suddenly break out, perhaps to murderous effect. So it happened with the massacre at Paris of 1571, so well dramatised by Marlowe, where on St Bartholomew's Eve – Bartholomew is the patron saint of butchers – butchery broke out against the Protestants. In Rabelais, that incipient fear, which has historically sometimes taken the form of violent crazes of self-flagellation, or punishings of the body, must be compensated for by folly and exaggeration. The danger is of defining the self as that which must put off defilement and pollution from the other's body. It threatens masculine ability to accept either cuckoldry (Othello: 'I will chop her into messes! – cuckold me?' – *Othello* 4.1.197), or the finite nature of its desire. It makes the self to mark its singleness, which at the beginning of this section, I called its 'sovereignty', by, in the case of Iago, a guilefulness, which will be considered in what follows in the next section, on hypocrisy.

3 Rabelais: On Calumny

Rabelais' devils have plural existences. The absence in Rabelais of 'any idea of sin as such, and the emphasis on the intellectual process by which men are impelled to do wrong' means that 'vigilance can always outwit the forces of evil' (Krailsheimer 1963: 112). In Book Three, the devil is the Calumniator, one of whose tricks is to have devised a book on dice, usable for divination purposes, because trapping and deceiving (Rabelais 2006: 450–451). Vigilance must fight against the devil's manifestation as 'the Slanderer from Hell, who often transfigures himself as an angel of light through his ministers, the perverted lawyers . . . ' (583). And the evil angel of temptation leaves a person melancholic: 'perturbed, anxious and perplexed' (466), potentially abject. Rabelais' letter of 1552 to his patron, Odet de Chatillon, as a Preface to the *Quart Livre* declares how his writings have been for the relief of melancholia, and discusses how good doctors must appear to be: how they must act, disguise themselves, be masked (*prosopée*) to enliven and stimulate the patient. The opposite to such acting is the dour truth-telling practised by certain doctors, which is called, specifically, the 'calumny of certain cannibals [i.e. dog men, on the etymology of *canes*, "dog"], misanthropists and agelastes' – monsters who cannot, or will not, laugh. They are of the party of 'the Calumniating Spirit, the *diabolos*' (642). An earlier Prologue (1548) to the same book said 'the Greek for calumny' was '*diabole*' (625). Hypocrisy – compare Satan as the 'angel of light' – pairs with calumny.

By means of an inscription set above the main gate, hypocrites were banned from the utopian Abbey of Thélème. Rabelais writes a set-piece of vituperation (the etymology of this word means 'speaking against vice') against his then contemporary Pharisees, i.e. the New Testament agents of hypocrisy (Matthew 27:23). I cannot fully translate each of these synonyms for empty-headed Goths and the Ostrogoths (vandals before Rome, compare 768); much was expressed in language that was censored – even violently – by French seventeenth-century linguistic policy. Nonetheless, much here communicates before it is understood, and the reader will get the idea:

> Cy n'entrez pas, hypocrites, bigotz,
> Vieux matagotz, marmiteux, borsoufléz,
> Torcoulx, badaux, plus que n'estoient les Gotz
> Ny Ostrogotz, précurseurs des magotz

> Haires, cagotz, caffars empantoufléz,
> Gueux mitoufléz, frapars exorniflez,
> Beffléz, enfléz, fagoteurs de tabus;
> Tirez ailleurs pour vendre vos abus.
> (364, compare Bakhtin 1984: 431,
> Kinser 1990: 89)

Leo Spitzer (1939: 139–150) quotes this to argue – contra Abel Lefranc's thesis that Rabelais is always historically grounded – that Rabelais' language is in excess of what can be historicised. Vulgar insults are Rabelais' mode throughout: this, heaping up some eighteen synonyms and inventing words, comprehensively, deliberately, exaggerates, and is echoed in the 1548 Prologue to the *Quart Livre* (Rabelais 2006: 625).

Hypocrites are actors, as the meaning of the Greek word indicates, good words covering their self-serving baseness. A hypocrite is a mask, so cannot be unmasked: as a *persona* only, the hypocrite is an allegorical figure, diabolical. Calumny, or slander, subject of one of Lucian's *Dialogues*, is hypocrisy's weapon, coming from people who 'peer through a hole' (*Pantagruel* (1534) 164), 'spying into abuses', as Iago affirms he does (*Othello* 3.3.150).[5] Those included in Rabelais' vituperations are monks with cowls (Agrippa's comments on monks will be recalled), censors, who found *Pantagruel* obscene, and voyeurs – as Iago would make Othello a voyeur (*Othello* 3.3.397–399) – are included. Hypocrites advertise their goodness, but since they have none, it takes the form of calumniating others, the hypocrites declaring themselves only interested in truth. The calumniator disparages Rabelais' method of acting as a good doctor; i.e. seductively, acting, in a liberal spirit which will cure a patient from melancholia. Siding with restraint makes calumniators Lenten: the worst devil induces melancholia in the name of truth.

Hypocrisy is denounced at the close of the Prologue to the *Tiers Livre* (Rabelais 2006 411), which is a key to much in Rabelais. It starts with Diogenes, the Cynic Philosopher, full of mirth and given an honourable place in Epistemon's upside-down underworld (150), unlike Alexander (147). Rabelais likens his 'Pantagruelic Sentences' (409) to the spirit of Diogenes: Pantagruelism being that by which people 'will never take in bad part anything they know to flow from a good, frank and loyal heart' (410), endorsing the comedy of the body, and the spirit of Panurge. Such cynicism becomes truth-telling; open, spontaneous, undoing the pretensions of idealistic thought which gain impetus from hatred of the body (Szbari 2005b: S84–S123). 'Black beetle hypocrites' (*caphards* – compare 'calumniators and black-beetles', called devils (210)) contrast with Rabelais who is like Diogenes, in telling them to get 'out of my sunshine'. Diogenes bid Alexander the Great do as much, the cynic cutting the imperialist down to size (Sloterdijk 1988: 156–169).

Rabelais derives 'agelast' from Erasmus' *Adages* (1500–1515) which speaks of 'the laughless rock', which applies to 'anything very sad and painful':

> In old days, a rock used to be shown to visitors in Attica, on which tradition had it that Ceres sat, when she abandoned heaven and sought with lighted torches for Proserpine who had been carried off by Pluto. When in the course of this she reached Eleusis, she took her seat sadly on a certain rock, which they call the Laughless Rock for that very reason. Zenodotus [Zenobius] is the authority. It will be suitable for severe and gloomy characters, for whom Greek uses the same word *agelastos*, laughless... (Erasmus 1991: 268–269).

The agelast misses what carnival represents as 'the feast of becoming, change, and renewal...hostile to all that was immortalized and completed' (Bakhtin 1984: 10). That latter phrase critiques the classical body of the Renaissance, 'a strictly completed, finished product' (29). 'Openness to the future' in the 'grotesque body', 'in the act of becoming, never finished, never completed' (317), makes carnival utopian. Some Rabelaisian criticism, especially North American, shows a hostility to Bakhtinian readings; Donald Frame (1977: 104–110) being an exception. Disliking Bakhtin's 'Marxist populism' ([*sic*], Schwartz 1990: 7), it compensates by finding what he writes about popular culture 'patently ahistorical' (Hampton 1993: 82, citing Richard Berrong, and Walter Stephens, who places Rabelais' giants outside popular culture). This 'specialist' put-down appeared in *Representations*, the 'new historicist' journal committed to revaluation of what topoi were judged 'historical' within history's claims to be a discourse of truth! The hostility diminishes Rabelais' carnival in favour of the Christian/Humanist, as if these stood necessarily opposed. Berrong strips out the carnival and the sexual from Book Three – as if discussion of cuckoldry was anything else! – saying how few 'only slightly off-color remarks' appear in the banquet of the *Tiers Livre* (Berrong 1986: 83). The devilry challenging that intellectual order of things is ignored, to which, of course, Rabelais is committed, parody emphasising his love for it. Just so, cuckoldry as a motif stresses the absolute claims of the body – which is urged on to marry – as comic and unknowable at once, and intrusive on the world of ideas, which would like separation from the body. The devil acts within that world too: he has, as Krailsheimer noted, an *intellectual* nature as calumniator. Panurge asks: 'is there any man as learned as the devils are?' And 'this devil Pantagruel' replies, 'Indeed not, except by the special grace of God' (Rabelais 2006: 101–102). (Panurge responds by drinking all night.) Berrong (1986: 27–28) thinks *Gargantua* chapter 12 (Rabelais 2006: 250), where Gargantua tells his father the plural ways he has found to wipe himself – the best way being a young goose – is an illustration of him cleansing himself from carnival ways; but there seem to be wittier lessons to be learned.[6] The chapter is never outside the carnivalesque (that includes its excess): it is – to take an example from a text which shows how Rabelaisianism was lost in the early modern period – quite unlike Iago, looking on at the courtesy of Cassio talking to Desdemona, putting his fingers to his lips, Iago fantasising these as 'clyster pipes' (enema tubes, *Othello* 2.1.176) anally applied, of course. Cassio, the non-drinker, is not Rabelaisian; nor is Shakespeare's Venice, and nor is Iago; but Bakhtin (1984: 370–377) can read the Rabelaisian episode as inverting the face and 'lower body stratum'. The face equally needs wiping after much talking, which is itself a bodily process, though post-Rabelais, as in *Othello*, talk has become self-consciously idealised, separated from the body ('Keep up your bright swords, for the dew will rust them' – *Othello* 1.2.60). And Cassio, the Lieutenant in Venice's state, where the unyielding Brabantio is a worthy senator, reserves his laughter (his bodily reactions) for his association with Bianca. But Rabelais' Humanism, and learned culture does not separate itself from the body; and characters and language, as grotesque, part of giant bodies, are not part of single complete subjects, but 'unfinished' (Bakhtin 1984: 29), so open towards Utopia, place of further possibilities.

4 Carnival Time

Like Bakhtin, Walter Benjamin theorised carnival, in a short story, 'Conversation above the Corso' (1935, *SW3*: 25–31)), set in Nice, on a Shrove Tuesday. Benjamin masked his identity by publishing this in the *Frankfurter Zeitung* under a pseudonym, which begins the carnival theme. Descartes had said of himself: 'as actors, to avoid their shame appearing on their faces wear masks, so I, about to ascend the stage of this world, in which, till now I have appeared as a spectator, go masked ('*larvatus prodeo*') (Browne 1977: 272). A philosophical statement, or position, cannot be simply 'true'; it must, like language itself, dissimulate (pretend not to be what it is) or simulate (pretend to be what it is not), and 'larva' means both 'ghost' and 'mask': the verb 'larvare' meaning 'to bewitch, to enchant'. The philosopher comes forward as a ghost and as a mask: both having devilish features; masking relating to 'transition, metamorphoses, the violation of natural boundaries, to mockery and familiar nick-names. It contains the playful element of life . . . it reveals the essence of the grotesque' (Bakhtin 1984: 40).

In Benjamin's story, the 'I', a doctor, is daydreaming at the harbour, as ships come and go. A friend wants him to meet an unnamed Danish sculptor, who likes living only on islands: perhaps a compliment to Brecht, who lived on Funen, a Danish island. The sculptor works huge figures directly from rocks in mountainous regions; in Rhodes, one of the islands he has visited, he is called 'the sorcerer'. He says that carnival has been combined, wrongly, with the circus. But 'the carnival is an exceptional state (*Ausnahmezustand*). A descendant of the ancient saturnalia, when everything was turned upside down and the lords waited on the slaves'. The circus, in contrast, is not exceptional. Commenting on the processional carts in the Place Masséna, the Dane thinks of the cart as 'something that comes from far off', upon which the 'I' thinks of carriages and carts being like ships. He links the *carrus navalis* ('nautical cart') to the etymology of 'carnival', when boats were reconsecrated and relaunched after winter storms. Refusing the etymology where 'carnival' means 'farewell to meat' (*carne, vale*), so emphasising less the opposition to Lent, he thinks of ships as carts (as with the boat on the barrel in Bruegel's *Carnival versus Lent*, where 'anything from far off must have something special about it'. The Ship of Fools supports the *carrus navalis* etymology; the ship on the dry Corso is an image of madness, indistinguishable from carnival folly in cart-like-ships. The Carnival Prince in one has a lion-tamer's uniform, while the lion's toothy smile is called 'exaggerated'. The Dane contends that 'what is exaggerated sometimes repels us only because we aren't strong enough to take it in. Actually, I ought to say: not innocent enough'. And 'exaggeration lies in the nature of things themselves . . . just as there is a world of colour beyond the visible spectrum, there's a world of creatures beyond those familiar in nature. Every folktale knows of them':

> There are two spheres of complete innocence, and they are found on the two boundaries where our normal human nature . . . passes over into the gigantic of the diminutive. Everything human is burdened with guilt. But the gigantic

> creatures are innocent, and the bawdiness of a Gargantua or a Pantagruel – who belong to the dynasty of carnival princes... is just an exuberant proof of this. (*SW3* 29)

The lights come up in the Place Masséna, now seen as a great European ballroom-like public square of the type which originated in Italy, and illustrated, for instance, by an artist who will be discussed in the next chapter, the Lorraine-born Jacques Callot (1502–1635) who worked for the Medici in Florence, as with a sequence called the *Guerra d'Amore* (1616) (Daniel 1974: plate 3). The Dane comments on children's books, praising less their renderings of 'tiny delicate creatures' than their dwarfs and giants and 'the uncouth inhuman side'. 'Children, who may be shy with grown-ups, feel totally at home down there among the giants. Yet for us adults the carnival should be an opportunity... to behave in a slightly giant-like way – at once more freely and more decently than we do in our everyday lives' (*SW3* 30). Giant-like behaviour, as in Rabelais, means that the monstrous appears as less hypocritical than in ordinary life. And parodic. Benjamin's 'The World of Children's Books' (1926) notes children's puzzle pictures, in fantasy books inspired by the likes of Jean Paul, where figures are in a 'masquerade: exuberant, impromptu games in which people walk upside down, stick their arms and legs between tree branches, and use a house roof as a coat'. The 'unmasking', the 'Ash Wednesday of this carnival of words and letters', comes with the 'motto', i.e. the wise words which 'gaze out' in the picture as the gaunt figure of reason' – like an allegorical *rebus*, a visual puzzle carrying a message, which Benjamin notes was once derived etymologically with *rever*, to dream. Even in the motto, masquerade is never wholly avoided; it only lightly bears the markers of Baroque melancholic allegory (Benjamin 1977: 169, 176). Colour, the Dane says, has to do with fantasy, being more primal, less willed than what is associated with the creative imagination (*SW1*, 436–437, 442).

Carnival implies, then (a) an exceptional state (b) freedom from guilt, and innocence, and (c) a time for exaggeration. Exceptionalism makes carnival time a revolutionary moment, a state of emergency, breaking with history as a 'temporal continuum' (*SW4* 407), 'homogeneous, empty time' (*SW4* 395). If Bakhtin's descriptions of carnival are challenged as ahistorical, so is carnival, outside, and questioning, what an historical continuum can record; carnival being, as noted with Bruegel, a plural time. The French Revolution introduced a new calendar, whose initial day recurs 'in the guise of holidays, which are days of remembrance... calendars do not measure time the way clocks do' (*SW4* 395). The holiday, like the carnival, is an initial day, belonging to a state of 'exception' in requiring a transition to a new way of numbering days; hence in the July Revolution (1830) people fired at clock-faces 'pour arrêter le jour' (to bring the day to a standstill). Carnival holds in abeyance the normal progress of the year. The initial day of the calendar it works with 'presents history in a time-lapse mode', which means that the first day incorporates into it all preceding time, so that nothing is lost. This is Benjamin's interest in *apokatastasis*, belief in the salvation of all souls at the Last Judgment (Löwy 2005: 35). His desire, or his 'will to apokatastasis' is 'the resolve to gather again, in revolutionary action and in revolutionary thinking, precisely the elements of the "too early" and the "too late", of the first beginning and the final decay'(Benjamin 1999: 698). Nothing can be allowed to be lost to history: that utopian idea fires carnival, and licenses its folly: its incorporation of the heterogeneous makes its loss, or exorcism, dangerous.

Exaggeration is hyperbole, whose overreaching is diabolical; as piling up, accumulating (Latin *agger*, a heap). *OED* gives it three senses: in the first two, exaggeration legitimately accumulates detail for emphasis, perhaps for vituperation. Its third meaning is: 'to magnify beyond the limits of truth; to represent something as greater than it really is'. Exaggerating is ambiguous, calling into question where any statement ends, and what may be said to be its limits. I may exaggerate when bringing out, by emphasis, what is the truth, in which case I may not go over the limit; or, I may exaggerate by going beyond the truth. So Adorno writes: 'in psychoanalysis, nothing is true except the exaggerations' (Adorno 1974: 29.49). The same is true of Rabelais' world. Exaggeration as demonic, at home with lies, transgresses limits, which assume we can have a prior sense of what the truth is, and what is exaggerated. Not to exaggerate:

> denies itself by its very caution the experience of its limit, to think which is, according to Hegel's superb insight, the same as to cross it. Thus the relativists are the real – the bad – absolutists, and moreover, the bourgeois, who need to make sure of their knowledge as of a possession, only to lose it the more thoroughly. The claim to the absolute that overleaps its own shadow alone does justice to the relative. By taking untruth upon itself, it leads to the threshold of truth in its concrete awareness of the conditionality of human knowledge. (Adorno 1974: 82.128)

It is the devil's spirit of story-telling that we find in Rabelais, surviving, for example, in Carpentier, and Marquez, and Borges.

5 Falstaff and Melancholia

POINS: What says Monsieur Remorse? What says Sir John, Sack-and-Sugar Jack? How agrees the devil and thee about thy soul which thou soldest him on Good Friday last for a cup of Madeira and a cold capon's leg?

PRINCE: Sir John stands to his word, the devil shall have his bargain, for he was never yet a breaker of proverbs; he will give the devil his due.

POINS: Then art thou damned for keeping thy word with the devil.

PRINCE: Else he had been damned for cozening the devil.

(*1 Henry IV* 1.2.106–117)

And so to Shakespeare, again. David Bevington, Oxford editor of *I Henry IV*, notes that 'devil' appears more times here than in any other Shakespeare play. We can add other diabolical allusions: Hal telling Falstaff 'these lies are like the father that begets them' (2.4.218–219). Falstaff is like Faustus, or the starved clown, Robin, since, on Good Friday, the climax of Lent and the strictest of fast-days, this fat man would sell his soul to the devil. In *2 Henry IV*, the devil gets his due, when Falstaff is excluded from Hal's sight. Not just the devil but Falstaff, embodiment of something of what carnival means, is cozened, since he fools for the benefit of the Prince whom he only partially understands, and who is fooling him. When he goes, heterogeneity is lost, as *Henry V* knows (Hall 1995: 215–234).

In *I Henry IV*, the enduring conflict, partly mock, between Hal and Falstaff, opposes the fat knight and the thin prince (2.4.218–240), Carnival versus Lent. In their flyting (ritual exchange of insults), and in the mock-play of the interviews between father and son, where the world is turned upside down, since the state is taken for a joint-stool, the golden sceptre for a leaden dagger, and the precious rich crown (here, a cushion on Falstaff's head) for a pitiful bald crown (2.4.367–369), Hal, speaking as his father to the son, played by Falstaff, says he has been 'carried away from grace' (like Faustus), 'a devil haunts thee in the likeness of a fat old man' (430–433). The contempt produces Hal's carnivalesque exaggeration of the fat man's qualities, since Falstaff's wit is the cause that wit is in other men (*2 Henry IV* 1.2.5–9):

> ...that trunk of humours, that bolting-hutch of beastliness, that swollen parcel of dropsies, that huge bombard [leather bottle, like a cannon] of sack, that stuffed cloak-bag of guts, that roasted Manningtree ox with the

> pudding [i.e. stuffing of sausage-meat] in his belly, that reverend Vice, that grey iniquity, that father ruffian, that vanity of years?.... That villainous abominable misleader of youth, Falstaff, that old white-bearded Satan. (2.4. 432–438, 445–446)

Hal's vituperation connects an anti-Carnival spirit with contempt of the devil and with a sense of Carnival tipping into old age, and so into its opposite. 'Ruffian' relates to 'Ruffin', a devil's name in the Chester mystery plays (*OED*). Vice – (compare Falstaff's 'dagger of lath' (2.4.131) – Iniquity, Ruffian, and Vanity constitute four allegorical, demonic names, personifying what morality establishes itself to be by its disdaining them. In a fat/thin contest, in *2 Henry IV*, Falstaff thinks of the Bolingbrokes as thin politicians. Falstaff is in service with Prince John of Lancaster, Hal's younger brother, tight-lipped and Machiavellian: annihilating rebellion by promise-breaking, in the spirit of Guido da Montefeltro (*Inferno* 27). Falstaff's soliloquy notes: 'this same young sober boy doth not love me, not a man cannot make him laugh, but that's no marvel, he drinks no wine' (*2 Henry IV* 4.3.83–85). This produces praise of 'good sherris sack', source of 'excellent wit' (100). The 'cold blood' that Prince Harry 'did naturally inherit of his father, he hath, like lean, sterile, and bare land manured, husbanded and tilled, with excellent endeavour of drinking good and good store of fertile sherries':

> if I had a thousand sons, the first human principle I would teach them should be to forswear thin potations, and to addict themselves to sack (115–123).

So Gargantua, who hardly needs to teach Pantagruel, the 'thirsty devil'. He calls for drink at Pantagruel's birth (Rabelais 2006: 25), to banish melancholy.

But Falstaff is double: 'one of those fat men in whom a thin man is struggling to get out' (Salingar 1986: 41). As the Roman Saturnalia (recalled in Saturday) means festivity, so it recalls Saturn, the melancholy god. Carnival and melancholia are inseparable. Falstaff thinks in 'thin' terms: 'hang me up by the heels for a rabbit-sucker [young rabbit] or a poulter's hare' (*2 Henry IV* 2.4.420–421); or a 'shotten herring' (2.4.124): herring, as in Bruegel's 'Carnival and lent' being Lenten (the astrological sign for February). He is a 'bunch of radish' (2.4.179), like the lean Justice Shallow, a 'forked radish' (*2 Henry IV* 3.2.305). He is a 'peppercorn' (3.3.8, small and dry); a 'soused gurnet' (4.2.11–12), with the most soliloquies, as when told, on Shrewsbury battlefield, 'thou owest God a death':

> 'Tis not due yet. I would be loath to pay him before his day. What need I be so forward with him that calls not on me? Well, 'tis no matter; honour pricks me on. Yea, but how if honour prick me off [i.e. selects me to die] when I come on? How then? Can honour set to a leg? No. Or an arm? No. Or take away the grief of a wound? No. Honour hath no skill in surgery then? No. What is honour? A word. What is in that word 'honour'? What is that 'honour'? Air. A trim reckoning. Who hath it? He that died o' Wednesday. Doth he feel it? No. Doth he hear it? No. 'Tis insensible then? Yea, to the dead. But will it not live with the living? No. Why? Detraction will not suffer it. Therefore I'll none of it. Honour is a mere scutcheon. And so ends my catechism. (5.1.127–139)

The actor in Falstaff, always presenting himself to an imaginary audience, does more than debate. He acts out disingenuous arguments, taking both sides, revealing his temptation: to back out of fighting altogether, in a fear of the future, fear of death. One part of the self tempts another. He is Carnival in rejecting the idealism of honour as 'air' – 'a mere scutcheon' – and Lent, since prizing only bare life, and replying consistently negatively. The speech thinks allegorically, as when thinking about 'Detraction', a demonic character in *The Castle of Perseverance*. It works diabolically in overturning the concept of 'honour', which Hotspur advocates, carnivalesque in his disregard for prudence. Falstaff's braggadocio in 'A plague of all cowards, I say' (2.5.104), echoing Hotspur's attitude throughout, makes his own carnivalesque survival impossible, since he endorses *only* survival. His soliloquy shows him the split subject: good angel, bad spirit, conscious of time, remembering the death's head, or memento mori, as also in *2 Henry IV* 2.4.224–225. He is Benjamin's melancholic, thinking allegorically, when he tells Bardolph, whose red face he compares to the emblematic salamander (see Dürer's *Knight, Death, and the Devil*), living in fire (3.3.44):

> I never see thy face but I think upon hell-fire and Dives that lived in purple, for there he is in his robes, burning, burning. If thou wert any way given to virtue, I would swear by thy face; my oath should be, 'By this fire, that's God's angel'. But thou art altogether given over, and wert, indeed, but for the light in thy face, the son of utter darkness. (3.3.28–35).

The biblical narrative (Luke 16:16–31) returns in Falstaff's guilt about his soldiers, 'as ragged as Lazarus in the painted cloth, where the glutton's dogs licked his sores' (4.2.24–25). The biblical parable of hell seems to have been vivid, then, in early modern visual culture, for example, in wall-hangings in domestic surroundings. Moralising and the devil are Falstaff's reference points. Dives, the rich man is himself, an allegory of gluttony (this is not carnival language), who, tormented in hell, sees the beggar Lazarus in Abraham's bosom. Falstaff's soliloquy calls his conscripted men 'a hundred and fifty tattered prodigals, lately come from swine-feeding, from eating draffs and husks' (4.2.33–34). Notably, Falstaff's room is 'painted about with the story of the Prodigal' (*The Merry Wives of Windsor* 4.5.6–7). The Prodigal Son began carnivalesque, wasting his substance with riotous living (Luke 15:13), but returned, the Lenten repentant like 'Monsieur Remorse', a common subject, judging from *2 Henry IV* 2.1.142, where this minatory allegorical image becomes part of a commodity, linked with a 'drollery' (a Dutch comic painting) and a 'German hunt' in imitation tapestry on the walls.

The Merry Wives of Windsor uses the phrase 'Jack o' Lent' twice, meaning a figure of abstinence, or of Judas Iscariot; or a puppet made to have things thrown at it. It is said of Robin, the page (3.3.23), but Falstaff applies it to himself, after trying to seduce two women at once, while crowned with horns, like a monstrous stag, a fertility god. He then realises that he is no more than a cuckold, as Master Ford points out (5.5.110), knowing now how 'wit may be made a Jack-a-Lent' (5.5.128) (Jonassen 1991: 46–68). If Falstaff, dressed as the widow of Brainford, was treated as a witch (4.2), at the end of *The Merry Wives of Windsor*, a play probably just predating *2 Henry IV*, he is cuckolded, a strange angel with horns, outclassed and exorcised in a carnivalesque but calculated moment, because the play's context is more bourgeois. The ending of *2 Henry IV*, where he is banished by Hal, exorcises him finally, completely.

6 KING LEAR: EXORCISM

> No exorciser harm thee
> *Cymbeline* 4.2.276.

Exorcism, remembered from *The Comedy of Errors*, takes hold within Catholicism and Protestantism alike. Clark notes that apocalyptic thinking in the sixteenth century stressed the text: 'the devil is come down to you having great wrath, because he knoweth he hath but a short time' (Revelation 12:12). This justified popular thinking that there might be a spike of cases of devil-possession in the short time left before the Last Judgment (Clark 1997: 404). The practice of exorcism, for instance in Protestant northern Germany after 1560 as well as in Catholic countries, made the divine, George Gifford (1540–1620), pronounce: 'daylie it is seene, that the devil is driven out of some possessed, that where he did vexe and torment men in their bodies and in their cattle, they have remedie against him'. Clark called the seventeenth century 'the golden age of the demoniac' (Clark 1997: 389–390).

In *The Discoverie of Witchcraft* (1584), Reginald Scot argued against witchcraft's existence, declaring that miracles had ceased. James VI of Scotland's *Daemonologie* (1597) wanted the state, not exorcists, to handle witchcraft (Dijkhuzen 2007: 135–137). Samuel Harsnett (1561–1631), the Bishop of London's chaplain, wrote against Catholic exorcism in *A Declaration of Egregious Popish Impostures, to with-draw the harts of her Majesties Subjects from their allegiance, and from the truth of Christian Religion professed in England, under the pretence of casting out Devils* (1603). This Shakespeare used in *King Lear* (Muir 1951: 11–21; Brownlow 1993), especially for Edgar's language. Harsnett aimed at the Jesuit William Weston (*c.*1549–1615), self-styled Friar Edmonds, in a recall of Edmund Campion, the Jesuit executed at Tyburn in 1581. Weston came to England in the 1580s, practising exorcism, including on a girl, one Sara Williams. Imprisoned at Wisbech, he clashed in the so-called 'Wisbech stirs' with other, 'secular' Catholic priests, figures from before the Reformation. He was exiled in 1603.

The anonymous *True Relation* (1601) of the riotous events at Wisbech gives examples for the language of *King Lear*'s Goneril and the name Edmund – both derived from Weston's behaviour in Wisbech (Kaula 1975: 1–29). Harsnett aimed too at Anglican/Puritan attempts at dispossession, in *A Discovery of the Fraudulent practises of Iohn Darrel, Bacheler of Artes, in his proceedings concerning the Pretended Possession and dispossession of William Somers at Nottingham; of Thomas Darling, the boy of Burton at Caldwell; and of Katherine Wright at Mansfield, & Whittlington; and of his dealings with one Mary Couper at Nottingham, detecting in some sort the deceitfull trade in these latter dayes of casting out Deuils* (1599). John Darrell (*c.*1562–*c.*1617) was an Anglican/Puritan preacher who was imprisoned as an impostor in 1599 and mocked in Jonson's *The Devil is* *an Ass* by the confidence-trickster Merecraft who recalls 'little Darrel's tricks' (5.3.6). Darrell, however, was capable of responding to Harsnett's rhetoric as duplicitous in its turn.

Stephen Greenblatt (1989: 94–128) notes the fictionality of Edgar's Harsnett-derived language; how Harsnett thought of exorcism as a theatrical performance, played for spectators, as Edgar acts. Nonetheless, it is too easy to follow Greenblatt's implication that Harsnett's rationalist voice was hegemonic and that Shakespeare agreed with him as regarding either the Catholic or the Puritan exorcisms (Gibson 2006: 151–160). It could be said that Harsnett sided with those who would silence, or marginalise others. Darrell the exorcist could be seen as giving something to Malvolio in *Twelfth Night* (Hamilton 1992: 86–110). This agelast, near to misanthropy in his self-love, can be fooled into what he wants to believe, that Olivia loves him. But that turns sour, becoming different when Sir Toby and Maria treat him as possessed – as the devil, since his fall, was supposed to be mad. Comedy takes its cue from the devil, whom it also mocks, following the medieval sense that the devil could be overcome by man's laughter (Hornback 2009: 34). Malvolio is subjected to 'exorcism' by Feste, playing the parson ('I would I were the first that ever dissembled in such a gown' (*Twelfth Night* 4.2.5–6)), but he thinks, and speaks, nobly of the soul. Who is the deceiver; who is the deceived, and where is Darrell in this interchange? Is Malvolio's last line: 'I'll be reveng'd on the whole pack of you' (5.1.377) misanthropic, the agelast's voice, unable to see how he has put himself outside anything festive? Or does it point to a crisis which Harsnett unwittingly produces: that dismissal and theatrical parody of demon-possession will not do, because it releases worse devils in those who are silenced, like Malvolio? Certainly, revenge threatens the end of Carnival.

7 KING LEAR 'I CANNOT DANCE IT FURTHER'

> PUG: Your best song's 'Tom o' Bedlam'
> *The Devil is an Ass*, 5.2.35

In *King Lear*, Edgar becomes the ultimate excluded wayfarer, *picaro*, vagabond, resembling 'Bedlam beggars':

> who with roaring voices,
> Strike in their numbed and mortified bare arms

> Pins, wooden pricks, nails, sprigs of rosemary,
> And with this horrible object from low farms,
> Poor pelting villages, sheepcotes and mills
> Sometime with lunatic bans, sometimes with prayers
> Enforce their charity. Poor Turlygod, poor Tom,
> That's something yet; Edgar I nothing am.
> (*King Lear* 2.3.14–21)

Tom o' Bedlam, imitated by Edmund (1.2.135–136), the vagabond who has his own songs (Wells 1961b: 311–315), wounds himself, which is, again, like Edmund (2.1.34). He becomes a wild man, cheating, as the unintelligibly named 'Tuelygod' (Q – see Wells and Taylor 1997: 515–516), who is perhaps the upside-down god, poor Tom; a bare 'something' ('the thing itself' – 3.4.104). *King Lear* is the most socially conscious of Shakespeare's tragedies. Bedlam, London's madhouse, like Bridewell, is where the mad were whipped and exorcised, and defines the world outside the court. Edgar in the hovel acts the Bedlam, who was also called the 'Abraham's man' (MacDonald 1983: 127), since, recalling Luke 15:16–31, the rich man in hell saw the beggar in Abraham's bosom. Edgar exceeds Lear's Fool in heterogeneity of language and behaviour. Indeed, the Fool seems readier to accommodate himself to the behaviour which had excluded him and Lear.

Having said he will 'elf his hair' – (2.3.181) – as if devils tangled it – Edgar speaks, on the heath, as if the 'foul fiend' or 'madness' ('mad Tom', 'madman, and beggar too' (4.1.28, 32)), and not folly, drives him everywhere, in a nightmare version of fairies wandering everywhere (*A Midsummer Night's Dream* 1.3.1–6). Edgar/Tom is obsessed with temptation towards suicide, suicide being the devil's work (compare *Doctor Faustus* 2.3.21–25). He blames or punishes himself for others' underhand actions (for example, *King Lear* 3.4.83–98 applies to Oswald's, and Edmund's deeds: they are his 'others', and he kills both). He must act more intensely when his father appears:

> This is the foul fiend Flibbertigibbet. He begins at curfew and walks till the first cock. He gives the web and the pin [eye-diseases, like cataracts], squinies the eye and makes the harelip, mildews the white wheat and hurts the poor creature of earth.
> Swithold footed thrice the wold [old, *Q, F*];
> He met the nightmare and her nine foal, [fold, *Q, F*]

Bid her alight, and her troth plight,
And aroint thee, witch, aroint thee.
(3.4.112–120)

Calling his father – blind in not recognising him – Flibbertigibbet, resonates in several ways. It sounds like a female devil, with the added *gibbet* no coincidence. 'Flibbertigibbet', as a night spirit, names every kind of punishing accident which needs a cause, leading to the hurtings – devils hurt, humans punish – which Tom evokes. There follows the rhyme about Swithold/old/fold. The 'nightmare' being the goblin and night melancholia ('mare', *OED, sb2* 1.b), appears in a dance which leads to a crisis encounter ending with the triumphant woman cursed as a *Macbeth*-like witch. Another devil's name follows: Smulkin, a mouse in Harsnett (*OED*: a farthing; the smallest coin); Edgar's 'study' being 'how to prevent the fiend and to kill vermin' (*King Lear* 3.4.155). The exorcist Richard Napier noted of one 'possessed' woman: 'she thinketh that she seeth a mouse running about her head' (MacDonald 1983: 213). Mouse-likeness contrasts with: 'The prince of darkness is a gentleman. Modo he's called, and Mahu' (*King Lear* 3.4.139–140), again from Harsnett. Names were apparently taken from inscriptions on wall-hangings which Sara Williams had seen, and evoked while exorcised. Names proliferate:

> Frateretto calls me and tells me Nero is an angler in the lake of darkness (3.6.6–7)

> the foul fiend haunts Poor Tom in the voice of a nightingale. Hoppedance cries in Tom's belly for two white herring. Croak not, black angel . . . (3.6.29–31)

Harsnett adds that Hoppidence appeared as a whirlwind (Brownlow 1993: 312). The raven-like '*black* angel', though 'croaking' also means 'rumbling', ask, as though starving, for two *white* herring, i.e. Lenten food, so making that season, the time of Pisces, and hunger, alike diabolical, though goodness is also to be swallowed up.

These allusions suggest being haunted by music playing, making for hopping/hobbling/dancing, like Bruegel's cripples (Gibson 1977: 184). 'Hoberdidance' (compare Edgar's 'I cannot dance it further' (*King Lear* 4.1.55 *Q*)) – comes from Harsnett; the name implies a demon of the morris dance, like Frateretto and Flibbertigibbet, as if the devil compels an involuntary universal St Vitus's dance. The poet John Skelton (1463–1529) said that Fortune took him by the hand and 'led him a dance',

OED's first citation (1545) for that phrase. Behind it stands the dance of death. The language in the list becomes more nonsensical: incantatory, as if internally rhyming names, babbling (Babel-like) comprise the devil:

> Five fiends have been in Poor Tom at once, of lust, as Obidicut, Hobbididence, prince of dumbness, Mahu, of stealing, Modo, of murder, Flibbertigibbet [Q: Stilberdigebit] of mopping [Q: mobing] and mowing, who since possesses chambermaids and waiting-women. (*King Lear* 4.1.61–66, compare Brownlow 1993: 172–174).

Here Hobbididence stands for dumbness, perhaps fatal, as Cordelia's silence is to her, or he represents (compare 3.6.113–115), what causes defects. Perhaps the significance of the devil having the voice of the nightingale is to act as a parodic voice testifying to the rape of women, of violence done to them, as Cordelia suffers hanging. The women's mowing (grimacing: almost involuntary behaviour), behind the backs of their mistresses, becomes a sign of possession, a marker of punishment, which means acting as a devil in consuming everything filthy (3.4. 125–129). This, worse than beggars' fare, worse than Lenten food, joins with common exclusion: 'whipped from tithing to tithing, and stocked, punished and imprisoned' (3.4.130–131) and with the vagrant implications of: 'come, march to wakes and fairs and market towns' (3.6.71–72). That 'marching' implies an endless dance, which the poor must perform. It is the worse for them that the devil driving them on, is a 'gentleman'. We have noted several examples of houselessness, as when the Prodigal Son (Luke 15:16) is echoed in Cordelia's:

> And wast thou fain, poor father
> To hovel thee with swine and rogues forlorn
> In short and musty straw?
> (*King Lear* 4.7.38–40)

All these implicitly summon up thoughts of the excluded criminal as devil. The material causes of the Bedlam's poverty, and the injustice the poor suffer are implied in:

> Thou hast seen a farmer's dog bark at a beggar? ... And the creature run from the cur? There thou mightst behold the great image of authority: a dog's obeyed in office. (4.6.153–155)

The dog barks at the *picaro* in Bosch's *Wayfarer*; then the image, which punishes the *picaro*, modulates into quasi-carnivalesque satire.

Lapdogs – bitches, by their names – bark at Lear, he says. Tom responds by fantasising dogs fleeing him (3.6.60–70) but the reality is other, and the dogs and hounds which chase Caliban and his friends, who are 'diverse spirits', also called 'goblins' (*The Tempest* 4.1.253, 258) are equally disturbing. Hunting includes hunting humans. The gender of suffering appears in:

> Thou rascal beadle, hold thy bloody hand
> Why dost thou lash that whore?
> (*King Lear* 4.6.150–151,156–157)

Lashing recalls Tom on whipping; the Fool is threatened twice with the whip (1.4.108, 172). The beggar reappears in: 'through tottered rags small vices do appear' (4.6.150–151, 156, 160 *Q*), which the Folio reads as 'through tattered rags great vices do appear'. Doubtless, beggars' rags were 'tattered', but *OED* annotates 'to totter' as 'to swing to and fro, esp. at the end of a rope'. This, another form of dancing, relates to Lear's previous line: 'the usurer hangs the cozener': the usurer having gained enough status to do so, since his trade was legalised in 1571. This point is noted in *Measure for Measure* (3.1.274–276). The avaricious – the usurer, the rich man of the *Narrenschiff* – is no longer estimated the fool. He seems to be on the 'right' side.

Rags – lack of clothes means that 'Tom's a-cold', and cannot 'dance it further' – are a metonymy for the hanged beggar. The Folio's 'great' allows the thought that displaying the beggar's hanged body magnifies the vices marked on the body, whereas 'robes and furred gowns hides all'. But those hanged have 'small vices' in comparison to the usurers. The play is aware of a culture condemning the vagabond, victim of the enclosure acts that More's *Utopia* had critiqued (which had created rich farmers with dogs) and legislated against in various Poor Law Acts, which silenced the carnivalesque in judging wandering lunatics as punishable for feigning madness. Or they were treated as mad, and confined (Beier 1985: 9, 115–116). Harsnett emphasised the theatricality of Catholic or Puritan exorcisms but he neither accounted for the exorcists' motivations, nor – more critically – attended to what was going on with those who claimed devil-possession or were accused of it. Edgar's 'I cannot dance it further' summons up a world of coldness, being led a dance, and being at the end of one's rope, as the normative conditions for poverty.

NOTES

1. This is the reading of the 1608 Quarto version, for the play exists with significant differences in the Folio edition (1623); I note these, while citing Foakes (1997) whose edition tries to integrate the changes. The Norton Shakespeare (1997) prints both Quarto (Q) and Folio (F).
2. The debate with Derrida's reading of Foucault, and especially the latter's criticism of Descartes (Derrida 1978: 31–63, 169–195) and Foucault's responses, (Foucault 2006: 541–590) is one of the most important exchanges about the relationship of madness to the logos which permits speech: the speech of madness and that which speaks about madness, or writes (his)stories about it. The dispute, an indication of the haunting of Derrida by Foucault, does not bear directly on this book, and the histories need supplementing, for instance by Benjamin, and Adorno, but it is worth noting how Derrida considers that a 'demonic hyperbole' (hyperbole being demonic excess, and including madness) launches Descartes, beyond the 'historic structures' which Foucault points to (Derrida 1978: 57–61); philosophy, then, which should exclude the devil, is produced by it; as Descartes feared, with his belief in the *malin genie* (see below). See Johnson 1993: 45–52.
3. The editions of Donald Frame (1991); and of M.A. Screech (Rabelais 2006), both of which embody separate lifetimes' study of Rabelais, have both been drawn on: they have excellent annotations. *Gargantua and Pantagruel* runs to five volumes; the fifth, because it is of questionable authenticity, is not discussed here.
4. The etymology of the Spanish *picaro* is uncertain; it may come from a phrase meaning a boy serving in the kitchen for leftovers. As a *picaro*, Panurge may recall the German prankster Till Eulenspiegel: his life and death were written up in 1515; 'Till Eulenspiegel', i.e. 'owl mirror', associates with folly unable to see its own folly (Richardson 1974: 182–188).
5. 'Abuse' and its cognates appears the most times in Shakespeare in this play. Brabantio virtually calls Othello a devil in the phrase 'an abuser of the world' (1.2.78) i.e. as a magician. Iago's moral high tone of spying into abuses includes spying out temptations, and sexual excess, as in Judges 19:25: see *OED* 'abuse' *vb*4, citing this example.
6. For the integration of this idea into *Gargantua*, see Conley 1992: 41–69; his chapter on Rabelais draws out the calligraphic puns, and plays with language at the level of the letter in the text.

Chapter 4: Fallen Fire: Job, Milton, and Blake

To the Accuser who is The God of This World.

Truly my Satan thou art but a Dunce
And dost not know the Garment from the Man
Every Harlot was a Virgin once
Nor canst thou ever change Kate into Nan

Tho thou art worshipd by the Names Divine
Of Jesus & Jehovah: thou art still
The Son of Morn in weary Nights decline
The lost Travellers Dream under the Hill
(Blake (1755–1827): *E* 269)

So runs Blake's 'Epilogue' to *For the Sexes: The Gates of Paradise*, a book of text and pictures engraved around 1818, showing a growing entrapment of the soul in matter. Both are rendered melancholic and are looking for a possible reversal out of that. In the picture here, a serpent with thirteen coils sleeps width-wise above; beneath, the 'traveller' sleeps, staff in hand (Erdman 1975: 279). Above him, back turned, black batwings outstretched, the devil flies off, like Moloch in Blake's watercolours to Milton's 'On the Morn of Christ's Nativity' (Butlin 1981: cat. 538.5) or 'Morning Chasing away the Phantoms' for *Paradise Regained* (cat. 544.9). His wings shine with stars and sun and moon. Another sun rises on the horizon, behind a hill.

Satan is another name for Blake's 'Spectre', his torturing, dominating negative genius, speaking only to restrain: 'I in my Selfhood am that Satan!

J. Tambling, *Histories of the Devil*,
DOI 10.1057/978-1-137-51832-3_5

I am that evil one! He is my Spectre!' (*E* 108). For 'the Negation is the Spectre; the Reasoning Power in Man' (*E* 142). The Spectre is the darkly reasoning superego; *my* Satan, acknowledged as inside the self, and as rational, a 'dunce' in thinking the garment is the man, and his accusations are in the sexual sphere, pronouncing, like Lear's 'rascal beadle', on the woman as harlot. Though having the divine names, Blake playing on Lucifer's name, 'the son of morn in weary night's decline', the light-bearer who must give way to another, different, day; 'the lost traveller's dream under the hill', a nightmare agitating the lonely wanderer, like Satan appearing in Eve's dream in Eden in *Paradise Lost* (hereafter cited as *PL*: 5.28–93), or in 'Christ's Troubled Dream' in *Paradise Regained*: (Butlin 1981: cat. 544.8). If 'the hill' suggests Mount Sinai, where the law was given, that also connects to Bunyan's *Pilgrim's Progress* (1678), when Christian swerves from the pathway, directed by Mr Worldly Wiseman.

While Blake's illustration makes the devil only an illusion, the poem is more complex, indeed non-paraphrasable, wistful, even affectionate in mourning Satan's inadequacy, as little more than a shadow under the authority he bears. And why is he a 'dunce', a word quoted from the rationalism of Young's *Night Thoughts*? He has done something stupid. His reign implies Pope's *Dunciad*; something is missing that should be there in him: something lost from the devil. A confusion exists between God and devil. The devil has the wrong name, or there may be no difference between God and the devil, possibilities turned over in this chapter, which moves from Luther towards Milton, and *Paradise Lost*, and dwells equally on Blake: his Milton, his Bunyan, and his conception of Job. In other words, the chapter dwells on the plural senses of Satan.

1 Poor Devil

I start again with the sixteenth century, and one of the contexts for *Dr Faustus*: commenting on Martin Luther (1483–1546), who marks a crisis in and for the self. This, thrown onto its own resources and unable to trust either ecclesiastical authority (the Catholic church) or its own senses, must exclude reason and the power of human choice, since these are corrupt, to free itself from bondage to the devil. So Luther believes. Subsequent attempts to exclude this crisis in the self through a rationality which would disown the self as being so entrapped, appear in Milton (1608–1674), whose *Paradise Lost* (1667) attempts, like his rationalising of Christianity throughout *De Doctrina Christiana*, unpublished in his lifetime, to keep separate God the rationalist and the devil, so protecting reason and liberty as the sphere of the first.

For Luther in the Reformation it was no longer possible to trust the outward senses. Certainty must come from within, from faith, not from guaranteed authority, such as the church. Hence the fear that the self, which must rely on its own convictions, might be possessed and not able to be its own warrant for truth. Its dearest convictions might even be the work of an evil genius (*malin genie*). So Descartes thought, wanting to put reason beyond doubt. He feared that his certainties might be the work of 'some malicious demon of the utmost power and cunning' (Descartes 1988: 79).

The 'evil genius' persists in a seventeenth-century archive which Freud discussed, concerning a Catholic Bavarian painter, Christoph Haizmann: 'A Seventeenth-Century Demonological Neurosis' (1923). Haizmann signed a Faustian nine-year bond with the devil in 1669 (Freud makes much of the various nines concerned in this case), to free himself from a depression, which Freud deduces was occasioned by the death of the father. In 1677 Haizmann suffered convulsions and sought help from the Church, and was exorcised at the shrine at Mariazell (in Styria, a famous place of pilgrimage). On 8 September (the Nativity of the Virgin Mary), the devil appeared in the church as a winged dragon, returning him the bond, signed in blood. Apparently cured, Haizmann went to live with his sister in Vienna, but suffered convulsions and repeated visions of being oppressed by the devil, and by Christ, and Mary. He returned to Mariazell in May 1678, alleging that there was an earlier bond with the devil which had to be reclaimed, written in ink. After he had the bond returned to him, he entered the Order of the Brothers Hospitallers, and stayed there, with occasional convulsions, until his death in 1700.

Haizmann illustrated the devil's appearances to him in eight paintings, plus a frontispiece, perhaps, Freud thinks, during his second visit to Mariazell (Thurn 1993: 873). Copies were kept within an archive of the 'case', the *Trophaeum Mariano-Cellense*, held in a law library in Vienna. They are reproduced in the commentary by Ida Macalpine and Richard Hunter (1956). The archive contained an account of the case, and of Haizmann's life by a cleric, and other documents, including Haizmann's diary (1677 to January 1688), which described his attacks (see *SE* 19.100–102). The whole dossier, Freud deduces, was assembled around 1714.

Freud's analysis resembles the one written on Schreber (*SE* 12.3–82, compare 19.91–92), since both cases relied solely on documents, as with

Schreber's *Denkwürdigkeiten eines Nervenkranken* (1903) ('Memoirs of my Nervous Illness'). Schreber, a high-court judge in nineteenth-century Germany, believed that his body was being taken over by God as a diabolically driven father figure, to be transformed into a female body, to be handed over for sexual abuse and then 'given over to corruption' (*SE* 12.19). Left to rot, while he suffered bird-like souls to speak about him in a made-up language which, Freud guessed, implied fear of the voluptuousness of girls. Freud noted that Haizmann wanted to sign a bond with Satan in order to 'be his bounden son' (*SE* 19.82). He wanted a father, the lack of which caused melancholia. He ensured, in and after his exorcisms, that he kept a father figure via the church. This point Michel de Certeau comments on, noting how Freud's reading of a case history allows him to think in terms of a larger history repeating itself, since comprising different manifestations of differently inflected needs which nonetheless all construct a father (Certeau 1988: 287–307). Haizmann fled from one father to another. The devil is a father-substitute, reflecting the ambivalence with which the father is regarded; both longed for and feared, as in 'Totem and Taboo' (1913), where the father, murdered by the sons because of the imposition of law, becomes the sacred object guaranteeing the rule of law. Freud contends that 'God and the devil were originally identical – were a single figure which was later split into two figures with opposite attributes'. An idea with a contradictory, ambivalent content becomes divided, in rationalising thought, into contrasted opposites (*SE* 19.85, 86).

The triptych-like frontispiece to Haizmann's account puts the Mariazell shrine at the centre. Four monks are kneeling, backs turned, Haizmann just visible. Above, in flames, appears the Virgin and child, and a devil, a winged, tailed dragon, red and green, bearing the pact written in red, which he yields to Haizmann. While the devil and Haizmann are visible in the side panels, everything of safety is enwombed within the classical shrine's triumphal arch with – inset within Gothic vaulting – the Virgin, the child, and the devil, below Mary. His red colour matches hers: his phallic is subordinate to the virginal maternal. The shrine's base is protected by a red balustrade, enfolding a space which reinforces Freud's sense that Haizmann 'wanted to make his life secure', that as an 'eternal suckling', he could not 'tear himself away from the blissful situation at the mother's breast', one of those who, 'through all their lives persist in a demand to be nourished by someone else'. Here, there is even the sense that the devil portraits are portraits of the painter, as 'a poor devil' (*SE* 19.104); self-representations of the luckless, who both hates and loves the father.

That 'poor devil' sense also appeared in Daniel Defoe's *A Political History of the Devil* (1726), an essential document in rationalising belief and excluding superstition, and cutting arguments about the devil down to size. Defoe needs such rationalisation when Man Friday can gravel Robinson Crusoe by asking: '*if God much strong, much might as the Devil, why God no kill the Devil, so make him no more do wicked?*' (Defoe 1972: 218). In Defoe's *History of the Devil*, which criticises *Paradise Lost* for its poetic excess and Arianism (i.e. its sense that Christ was not originally divine, that he had a subordinate position), Satan is 'confin'd to a vagabond, wandring, unsettl'd Condition'. Defoe cites the Book of Job's opening, where Satan comes before God, opposing his boasting about Job's righteousness, by saying that if Job's 'Estate was taken away, and he was expos'd as he was, to be a Beggar and a Vagabond, going *to and fro in the Earth, and walking up and down therein*, he would be a very Devil too, like himself, and curse God to his Face' (Defoe 2005: 86, 98).

Haizmann's triptych's left-side panel places the devil as a bourgeois older figure, like Mr Worldly Wiseman (Bunyan 1987: 18–20). The devil is a complacent hypocrite, who, in *The Pilgrim's Progress* would return Christian via the hill, Mount Sinai, to the Old Testament patriarchal law, and to the town of Morality. The devil has a black dog by his side. *OED* gives no earlier citation than Doctor Johnson for the 'black dog' meaning melancholy, but the dog recalls Agrippa, as it accompanies Goethe's Faust, as Mephisto; so this, in Haizmann's picture is a doubling figure. Haizmann appears sitting at the devil's feet, his vulnerability implicit in his open collar. On the right panel, the devil reappears, with a stick, as if like Asmodeus, *le diable boiteux*, as Le Sage's novel (1707) calls him, but this time, animal-like, with horns, on spindly legs which end in bird's claws, and his chest exposed to reveal multiple women's breasts. He is in front of Haizmann, as if walking off with the pact which he holds aloft. The frontispiece is followed by eight pictures, showing the devil by himself in a rocky and desolate landscape. The first makes him the confident older, bearded, bourgeois, with stick and dog, the second in the form he has in the right hand of the triptych; save that he looks as if he is narcissistically posing. The third adds bat's wings, and a tail, which forks; he bears a book, which Haizmann said was full of sorcery and black magic. The fourth clearly shows the multiple breasts, while the tail ends with an arrow; in his right hand he bears a ducat for Haizmann to spend. The fifth makes him adversarial; his hands are webbed, and the penis seems to be a serpent. Macalpine and Hunter (1956: 102) dispute this Freudian reading. Freud uses it to emphasise that the devil is male (*SE* 19.90). In the sixth, his red tongue lolls, like the dog's, and his eyes are wide open, as if myopic. This picture has been found feminine (Thurn 1993: 864). The seventh, derived from the visions at Pottebrun, where Haizmann went first for help, show the tail more divided, and the hair streaming behind. In the eighth, similar but not identical to the triptych, he is the winged dragon, mainly green, and bearing the pact. The paintings show an aggressive attitude to the father, and, in the breasts, a feminine disposition towards him.

Freud's analysis of Haizmann implies that relationships between the devil and God are closer than close. That intimacy is this chapter's subject matter, which started with emergent changes of thought in Luther's sixteenth-century. A new modernity becomes aware of an imminent crisis in the self, now forced into depending on its own subjective feelings and to find directions for itself. Luther's writings produced in Jacques Lacan insights informing his seminar *The Ethics of Psychoanalysis* (Westerink 2012). We may begin on these by saying that Lacan, like Freud, refuses to think ethics can be founded on a basis of rationality or duty, or by appeal to the greatest happiness of the greatest number. Neither self-interest nor rationality – they may be the same thing – can become the basis for how people should behave. The sexual, which conduces to the death drive, and the death drive itself, are stronger, and counter all forms of socially constructive behaviour. People do not act according to their 'best', 'rational' interests. Further, working towards such an ethical good is undesirable, since it is underwritten by a coercive sadism; a repressive desire to control.

2 LUTHER, LACAN, LOUDUN

Diabolus: Monachas super latrinam
Non debes meger primam!
Monachus: Purgo meum ventrem,
Et colo Deum omnipotentem:
Tibi quae infra,
Deo omnipotenti, quod supra!

(Devil: You monk on the latrine, you may not read the Matins [Prime] here! Monk: I am cleansing my bowls and worshipping God Almighty: You deserve what descends and God what ascends.) (Oberman 1989: 338–339)

The theological underpinning which associates God and the devil comes from Luther's 'Table-talk', citing a popular rhyme about the 'lower body', whose vituperative Rabelaisianism reverses the very spirit of Rabelais, making the body's excrement not only the expression of what the body is, but an object of fascination and hatred. Luther, a monk until 1524, used such language to address the people, and if he said of his inspiration 'the Spiritus Sanctus gave me this realisation in the cloaca' (Oberman 1989: 155), then this symbolises the powerlessness, or abject state of man. The association of physical purgation, and relief, symbolises divine awareness, makes the body the place of a contest between filth (the devil) and God as spirit: materiality versus the spirit. Fascination with filth may be necessary for spiritual vision. The devil tempts towards a theology of material, visible good works, but Luther's doctrine, 'justification by faith' begins with the self as radically corrupt, in reason and will, with no freedom to choose to serve God, since it is in bondage to Satan.

God's Law proves that salvation comes as the gift of God, which must be received by faith. Yet it is not God's nature simply to give freely. Contending with Erasmus defending the freedom of the will, Luther's *On the Bondage of the Will* (1525) cites God: 'I will harden Pharaoh's heart' (Exodus 4:21). Luther says that means exactly what it says, quoting St Paul: 'Therefore hath he mercy on whom he will have mercy, and whom he will he hardeneth' (Romans 9:17–18). And *Isaiah* 63:17: 'why hast thou made us to err from thy ways and hardened our heart from thy fear?' (Luther 1969: 223–239).

Justification by faith before God, therefore, relates to a God beyond reason, a God who is arbitrary. Luther rejects the consolations and optimism which appear within a humanist and rationalist framework, where Erasmus could agree with Origen who was condemned in CE 400 for the doctrine of *apokatastasis*. Luther's God, in hardening Pharaoh's heart, was the author of sin (Walker 1964: 57), *more* responsible than the devil, who was a created being incapable of free will. And God does nothing contingently: what he does he wills (Luther 1969: 120). Luther quoted St Paul (Galatians 3:19) on the law of God, conceding it was good, saying that it was given to increase transgressions; so that as good, it had a deliberately perverse effect (Luther 1969: 306). That compares with what Lacan feels about an ethical guide being the basis of any goodness. On one reading, modernity begins with Luther's refusal of a rational, progressive prevailing over Erasmus' Humanism and optimism (Gillespie 2008: 101–128).

Lutheran faith, unlike 'good works', commits the self to the unseeable; squatting in the latrine shows the self vainly discharging itself of all relationship to the material. The historian Heiko Oberman notes Luther's scatology; the devil, as real to Luther as Christ, becomes a personal foe, in his rooms, seen and heard physically, and a slanderer, to be met with equal physically charged venom, telling the devil to indulge in coprophagia, particularly Luther's own excrement. The slanderer (the backbiter; an expression the language below literalises, and recalling Rabelais' hatred of the hypocrite), is characterised excrementally:

> A slanderer does nothing but ruminate the filth of others with his own teeth, and wallow like a pig with his nose in the dirt. That is also why his droppings stink most, surpassed only by the Devil's... And though man drops his excrements in private, the slanderer does not respect this privacy, He gluts on the pleasure of wallowing in it, and he does not deserve better according to God's righteous judgment. When the slanderer whispers: Look how he has shit on himself, the best answer is: You go eat it. (Oberman 1989: 107–108)

Oberman (1989: 109) quotes Luther in 1515 saying that the Devil drags God's name and his works of justification through the mud, making him the authority figure to be contested. Luther links him, the Papacy, and the imminent Antichrist, the ultimate liar and corruptor of the church in the Last Days, in such ragings as: 'Great Swine', 'Papal Ass', 'Antichrist'. Lacan (1992: 92) discusses this invective against authority, noting, via the Haizmann analysis, how Freud associated the *diabolus* with the prince of this world; 'the symbolic [order] here is united with the diabolic'. The Lacanian 'symbolic order' – language as the Law of the Father, theological order, sides with good works, public good, and, in *The Pilgrim's Progress*, Bunyan's town Morality, inhabited by Legality and Civility, epitomes of hypocrisy. The devil can quote the Scriptures and debate with Luther, who responds to his ecclesiastical piety scatologically. Like Judge Schreber whose schizophrenia divides God into upper and lower halves, possessed with the Zoroastrian names of Ormuzd and Ahriman, and who thinks of the lower as performing a 'soul murder' on him via Flechsig, his psychiatrist (*SE* 12.44), so God seems split, attracted to the body he wills to destroy.

Lacan, unlike Freud, was interested in mystical thought, and he sees the 'symbolic order', the devil's power as father, as replacing, sublimating, *das Ding*, 'the thing'. And what is 'the thing'? It is the strange other, which refuses to enter definition, the no thing, which intrudes constantly, and which Augustine's theology sees as evil. Put another way, it is what makes any other person, however well known, different, and strange, while still familiar. Excluded, 'the thing' must 'be posited as exterior, as the prehistoric Other that it is impossible to forget – the Other whose primacy of position Freud affirms in the form of something *entrefremdet*, something strange to me although it is at the heart of me' (Lacan 1992: 71). Fear of 'the thing' produces Kristeva's 'abject' state. As unnameable matter, nothing and something, Lacan relates it to the Christian-Judaic model of creation *ex nihilo* (Lacan 1992: 121–122, 213–214). As the 'lost object', associated, psychoanalytically, with the mother's breast, it is feminine, the lost object of desire, needing to be refound.

Mysticism invests in the corporeal presence of Christ (Certeau 1986: 59). Clinging to the body, and matter, the mystic wants *das Ding*, resisting the abstraction of the *logos*, the language of the 'symbolic order', which is masculine, of the Father. Mystical speech emanates not from what becomes the rational Cartesian self, but from the 'other', about whom all that can be said is that 'it speaks' (Lacan 2002: 344), perhaps as the *malin genie*. It 'insists' in the speech of the self. Heidegger quotes Novalis' essay 'Monologue': 'the peculiar property of language, namely that language is concerned exclusively with itself – precisely that is known to no one' (Heidegger 1971: 111). A Shakespearian soliloquy, a Novalis-like 'monologue', comes not from a single centred subject, but from the unconscious within discourse. Its ambiguity is to be the organising speech of the symbolic order, *and* what interrupts, *and* insists in that. Mystical speech comes not from the publicly endorsable God of the logos but from 'it'. Nonetheless, if it came from that God, it would still be ambiguous, or diabolical. Who speaks in mysticism: the devil, or a hidden God?

Michel de Certeau noted Lacan's interest in Luther, testing the *logos*'s orthodoxy with statements such as 'you are that waste matter which falls into the world from the devil's anus' (Lacan 1992: 93). Lacan contrasts Whitman's affirmation of the body – knowing no limits to its oneness with the world – with Luther, who was focused on waste matter. And Lacan contends for Luther's superiority over Whitman: matter cannot all be so assimilated nor waste so sublimated (the devil is that which believes in the possibility of the sublimation of matter). This comes in the context of Lacan noting Freud's, and Luther's, rejection of the idea of the self knowing that Sovereign Good, such as happiness, which it must, and does, pursue. Erasmus, Lacan says, had written on free will:

> to remind the excitable mad man from Wittenberg that the authentic Christian tradition... led one to believe that works, good works, were not nothing, and... that the tradition of the philosophers on the subject of the Sovereign Good was not to be just thrown out.

Luther, however 'madly', insists there is something unassimilable to such rationalism, and his *Bondage of the Will*, answering Erasmus, places something undefinable, irremovable, and spoiling rational human relationships: 'at the heart of man's destiny'. It is Lacan's '*Ding*... the *cause* of the most fundamental human passion' ('cause' puns on 'la chose' – the thing: so the 'cause' is something indefinable, obscure, outside definition). Luther sees God's eternal hatred of men as existing 'even before the world was created'. That hatred is 'the correlative of the relationship that exists between a certain influence of the law as such and a certain conception of *das Ding* as the fundamental problem, and, in a word, as the problem of evil'.

To attempt to clarify here: who is this hating God/Father? He is Freud's 'tyrant of the primitive horde, against whom 'the original crime was committed, and who for that reason introduced the order, essence, and foundation of the domain of law' (Lacan 1992: 97, making reference to Freud's *Totem and Taboo*). Law, as a hate-full reaction, then, to the materiality of the self, indeed to the body, which includes *das Ding*, further incites murder and makes 'evil' the name for what is unassimilable to the order and system which it legislates into being, before and after the father's murder – 'the original crime' – by his sons. 'Evil', therefore, instantiates law, but law, which has the function of naming, cannot name it, since it cannot be ascribed a definite entity, but remains outside naming, as waste matter, *das Ding*. Perhaps it is named most in comedy, certainly in carnival. Luther stressed its existence as waste matter, but any attempt to impose progress or a gradual ascent for humanity, such as evolution, in a belief in progress, must reject it (Lacan 1992: 213).

Luther's wrestling with the devil is a 'thinking with demons' which became concurrent with a new science (Cartesianism) which tried to assert a rational identity which would absolutely exclude the devil. The contest – rationality versus the demonic – produces reactionary behaviours: for example, in France, a contest between Catholicism and the Reformed Religion (the Protestants, the Huguenots) was fought on several fronts:

sometimes in direct conflict, but also in witchcraft trials, and in exorcisms, two of the most famous of these being those at Loudun (1634), and before that with the Ursuline nuns in Aix-in-Provence, Madeleine Demandols and Louise Capeau (1609–1611). In this latter case, when exorcised for demon-possession by the Dominican inquisitor Sébastien Michaelis, these nuns accused the priest Louis Gaufridy, who was executed on 30 April 1611. The demons announced that they could only be exorcised by Gaufridy's death since he had practised on them with witchcraft. Yet Madeleine Demandols was herself, in 1653, ultimately convicted of witchcraft (Ferber 2004: 70–78).

Michaelis wished to assert Catholic authority through the testimony of demons, hence the place he gave to exorcism. He had to work round a problem for any such testimony: that the devil only speaks lies. Behind his, and other exorcists' discourse compelling truth, is the desire to assert a single authority, one which will rout heresy, by having the power to define it. The devil could be used by either persuasion, Catholic or Protestant, to demonise the other in asserting 'the truth'. The devils at Loudun, a town to the south-west of Paris, were used, both politically, and by Catholicism, to undermine the town's numerically stronger Huguenots. Loudun's priest, Urbain Grandier, was set up and burned as a sorcerer, for supposedly causing the members of the local Ursuline convent to be possessed.

'Obsession' refers to the devil attacking from outside, as Job was obsessed. 'Possession' applies to the devil being inside the self, as in the case of the New Testament demoniac who says his name is Legion. Seeing Christ, who is commanding the spirit to leave him, the spirit who is Legion says, 'I adjure thee by God that thou torment me not' (Mark 5:7). D.P. Walker says that exorcism comes from a Greek word implying an oath, translated into Latin as *adjuro* or *conjuro*, meaning, putting the devil upon oath (Walker 1981: 5–6). The superior power has the ability of adjuration, of invoking the authority of God, of compelling the devil to speak the truth, which is what exorcism implies. 'Obsession' implies that the devil has more than the power of tempting a person. This further power defined witchcraft, as the idea that someone might be able to make some kind of pact with the devil (Midelfort 1972: 56). The nuns at Loudun, whose testimony, like that of the women at Aix, indicates secret hatred of patriarchal church structures which confine them so narrowly, were not considered witches, but as possessed, under Grandier the sorcerer's influence (it should be remembered that they had not seen Grandier, though they might have heard of him, and even known he was a womaniser).

Local and national politics interwove to destroy Grandier, but the case was not closed. It would not disappear with his execution. Apart from the multiplication of documents that began circulating after the event, a series of symptomatic coincidences followed. Lactance, the exorcist, died exactly a month later than Grandier in delirium, like Mannoury, the surgeon, and Chauvet, the lieutenant-general, who had supported Grandier. Another exorcist, Tranquille, died in convulsions in 1638. And others involved died, or suffered (Rapley 1998: 198–208). Michel de Certeau examines the case of the Jesuit Father Jean-Joseph Surin (1600–1665) as a melancholic. Surin was tasked to exorcise the nuns after Grandier's death, especially Jeanne des Anges (1605–1665), mother superior, and leading accuser of Grandier (Certeau 1986: 101–115). Within a month, Surin felt he was obsessed and possessed. Lying in bed:

> he began to feel the presence of the demon, who first began to walk on him as would an animal, and, from on top of the covers, to press down on him at different points on his head and body, as would a cat with his paws. This did not surprise him much. But after that, he felt on his skin as if a snake had crawled in and wrapped himself around, and by its bites, more poisonous than painful, gave him much suffering. (Certeau 2000: 206–207)

Surin, an intellectual who rejected Humanist and Renaissance reason, in that way paralleling Luther, deteriorated as Jeanne improved. He felt he had two souls within him, which showed itself in an ambivalence towards God; the devils were making sport of him. In September 1635, he wrote to Laubardemont, Grandier's chief persecutor: 'we who treat what is most important, we know something entirely different about it than the spectators of the exorcisms' (Certeau 2000: 210). Jeanne des Anges and Surin became close friends, dying the same year. Surin believed that he was damned, which he refused to see as an evidence of madness. He thought he was accepting the Father's wrath against him. Certeau (1986: 109) reads damnation as exiling the speaker from the realm of verisimilitude, from statements discussable as true or false. The damned, or the mad, is stripped of authority for any statement or pronouncement; but such comes, neither from the 'I', or the logos, but from the other, from that strange non-being which speaks, which Lacan calls *das Ding*.

And what of the Loudun women? After 1637, Jeanne des Anges toured France displaying her hand which had, apparently been 'sculpted by the devil', since the demons, on leaving her body had inscribed the names of Jesus, Mary, and François de Sales on it, as testimonies of their triumph over them (Certeau 2000: 213–226). Her autobiography (1644) modelled itself on the life of St Teresa, the arch feminine mystic. This solves nothing: it increases the ambivalence if not hatred and fear which mystic spirituality excited, since mysticism also appealed, like exorcistic practices, to the immediate, immanent presence of spiritual forces, whether God or the devil, beyond the symbolic order. Grandier had been trained as a Jesuit. He was a man who loved women, and was a supporter of the governor, d'Armagnac, who wanted Loudun's walls preserved, against Richelieu's centralising ambition to pull them down to reduce the town's autonomy. Grandier suffered from Loudun's attempt to restore its order and cohesion. The symptoms of what it suffered from, including the plague – which demoniacal possession might seem to symbolise – continued after Grandier's death to take other forms, demanding the expulsion of the 'other'. In Foucault's terms, which Certeau accepts, this entails a madness which tries to expel the irrational. This was just when, as *The History of Madness* emphasises, France, influenced by Descartes's belief in a single rationality, which while individual was also general, entered the 'classical period' wherein madness was liable to 'the great confinement'. In such anxiety to establish a single firm identity, excluding *das Ding*, and attempting to solve then contemporary civic, social and theological splits, 'unreason' was intolerable. Grandier could be implicated as a libertine, as a form of unreason, since libertinism included intellectual free thinking. Grandier's trial brought out, for example, how he was a reader of Cornelius Agrippa (Foucault 2006: 99; Certeau 2000: 165).

Richard Popkin, tracing a history of scepticism from Luther to Henri Bayle, thinks the scepticism induced by the Grandier case – i.e. how could anything to do with demons be proved valid? – might have influenced Descartes' fear of the *malin genie* (Popkin 2003: 149). H.C. Erik Midelfort believes that sixteenth-century witchcraft trials fell off in the seventeenth century because though people might believe in witches, secular courts were dysfunctional in detecting, or proving witchcraft. If the devil is a liar, can any testimony under oath be accepted? And as another example of how rationalism was impelled to assert itself, Milton argued not for creation *ex nihilo*, which might include matter extraneous to God, i.e. *das Ding*: rather, God created the world out of himself (Sewell 1939: 124–134; Patrides 1966: 26–53).

3 The Vagabond God – and *The Pilgrim's Progress*

English Protestantism excluded the Nonconformist John Bunyan, a tinker, which could have made him a poor devil, imprisoned in 1660 for preaching without a licence. He refused the Act of Uniformity, which re-established the authority of the Episcopalian Church of England. Released in 1672, he was re-imprisoned in 1676, but published *The Pilgrim's Progress from this World from that which is to Come: Delivered under the Similitude of a Dream, Wherein is Discovered The manner of his setting out, His Dangerous Journey; and safe Arrival at the Desired Country*. Christian, first called Graceless, carrying a burden on his back, like a Bosch wayfarer, must leave wife and children and the City of Destruction to travel to the Celestial City. On the way, he undergoes crises of melancholia: facing the Slough of Despond, whose mire might tempt thoughts of the 'abject'; the Valley of the Shadow of Death; and Giant Despair, and the pangs of death in crossing the river. Encountering the diabolical figure Apollyon:

> the monster was hideous to behold, he was clothed with scales like a fish (and they are his pride) he had wings like a dragon, feet like a bear, and out of his belly came fire and smoke, and his mouth was as the mouth of a lion. When he was come up to Christian he beheld him with a disdainful countenance and thus began to question with him. (Bunyan 1987: 51)

Apollyon means 'the destroyer'. In Revelation 9:11 the locusts 'had a king over them, which is the angel of the bottomless pit, whose name in the Hebrew tongue is Abaddon, but in the Greek tongue hath his name Apollyon'. So Christian calls him 'O thou destroying Apollyon' (52). The Book of Job says of God, in the Revised Version, 'They that are deceased [mg: the shades, the *Rephaim*] tremble beneath the waters, and the inhabitants thereof. Sheol (mg: the grave, KJV: "Hell"] is naked before him, and Abaddon [mg: Destruction] hath no covering' (Job 26:5, 6). We can compare Bunyan's visualisation of Apollyon with Haizmann's; and to do this I will look at Blake's Apollyon, in the sketches – only one coloured – he made for *The Pilgrim's Progress* (Bentley 2001: 429–430; Butlin 1981: cat. 829, Plate 976).

Apollyon's scales like a fish derive from Leviathan in Job 41:15: 'his scales are his pride, shut up together as with a close seal'. These scales, 'courses of shields' or 'channels of shields' (Revised Version), help personify Pride, but the dragon's wings, unvisualisable, are not allegorised, nor are the feet like a bear, though the brown bear was identified with the devil in medieval Europe (Pastoureau 2011: 113–134). Nor is what he breathes out from his 'belly', which is an image of hell, nor is his mouth. Pride has a 'disdainful countenance': Apollyon is a feudal lord – 'I perceive thou art one of my subjects, for all that country is mine; and I am the prince and god of it' – when arguing with Christian about his 'service and wages'. Jeremy Taylor (1613–1667), in *The Rules of Exercises of Holy Dying* (1651) called 'Sin' 'the Apollyon, the Destroyer' (Bunyan 1987: 283): and 'the wages of sin is death' (Romans 6:20). Milton, in *Paradise Lost* (2.647–814) literalises the relationship within that last quotation by making Sin the goddess, who springs from Satan's head while he is still in heaven. When Satan couples incestuously with her, her offspring is Death, who repeats the incest with Sin to produce 'yelling monsters' which retire into her womb, reappearing at will. Milton and Bunyan differ in how they gender Sin: Bunyan makes Sin masculine, as Apollyon, contending against the 'Prince' whom Christian serves.

Eventually, after trying flattery, Apollyon 'broke out into a grievous rage, saying, I am an enemy to this Prince: I hate his person, his laws, and people: I am come out on purpose to withstand thee'. Language is at the heart of things, for the fight resolves itself in Christian's words after he has refound his sword, '"Rejoice not against me, O mine enemy! when I fall I shall arise", and with that gave him a deadly thrust which made him give back'. The 'that' refers to the sword, 'the sword of the spirit, which is the Word of God' (Ephesians 6:7), and to Christian's words, a quotation from Micah 7:8. St Paul made an allegory out of the sword, which has a double force: as magic charm, and something well found, as word and sword both are.

Everything in Apollyon's body is separable, non-unified. He is less a symbol than an allegory, i.e. a collection of signs standing in relation to, perhaps quoting, previously given signs, like Haizmann's images. One Russian scholar, Alexander Makhov, traces an analogy, in medieval literature, between rhetorical tropes and figures, and visual distortions of the body's order, finding that a connection can be made between this and the devil's extraneity to the world's order, which is as remote from that order as a rhetorical figure is remote from the natural order of speech. 'The devil's image may be regarded as a kind of embellished... "visual speech"' (Makhov 2011: 34). Four types of alterations embellish this speech:

(1) addition of some new elements to the 'natural utterances', like – using an architectural image – adding new stones to the edifice of speech.

(2) Removing some elements from the natural order of speech.
(3) Transposing one element from its proper place to an improper place.
(4) Replacing a certain element by some new element taken from outside the given speech, from some hypothetical stock of words.

Each of these appear in medieval constructions of the devil's visual image. With (1), we can think of examples of multiplication – extra eyes, extra horns, and compare with Freud's essay 'The Uncanny'. For Freud, the multiplication of symbols are a desired 'preservation against extinction', an attempt thwarted since the 'language of dreams' is 'fond of representing castration by a doubling or multiplication of the genital symbol' (*SE* 17.235). The impulse to multiply 'is to be regarded as a warding-off of castration' (*SE* 5.357), but it threatens to destroy uniqueness. It multiplies anxiety, then, about the male self, as Rabelais' devil was anxious (*SE* 18. 274). Examples of (2) are where the devil is one-eyed, or rendered blind. Origen connected evil with blindness (Mahkov 2011: 44). For (3), alteration by transposition comes in images which, for instance, place the eyes in the centre of the body. Alteration by substitution (4) appears where animal parts replace human parts, as with Apollyon.

Mahhov (2011: 42) is interested in duplication, and multiplication, calling the text, 'My name is Legion, for we are many' (Mark 5:9), 'the devil's confession of his own nature'. And as a nice comment on that, Roland Barthes in his essay 'From Work to Text' sees plurality as 'the demoniacal texture' which makes any literary work multiple, not single, and therefore not subject to any 'law' which talks in terms of genres, or which takes it upon itself to name a text in monolingual fashion (Barthes 1977: 160). All genres are mixed, which means that there are no genres worth talking about; a multiple text is devilish. As a way of signifying the devil, in *Macbeth* 1.2.9–12, 'the multiplying villainies of nature' 'swarm' upon the rebel Macdonald. He attracts 'gallowgrosses' (Folio), a word intensifying the thought of multiplication; or 'gallowglasses' (Second Folio: gallowglasses are horsemen with axes). If the devil is many, he splits continually. If the demonic presents us with visual riddle-like metaphors, Kierkegaard, in *The Concept of Anxiety*, noting that 'the demonic' appears when approached by Christ, as with Legion, defines it as 'anxiety about the good' (Kierkegaard 1980: 119). If the good is single, monological, the demonic pluralises itself, and its activities.

Blake's picture of Christian fighting Apollyon (cat. 829.21) shows Christian beaten down but not back, turned away, not kneeling to

Apollyon, but rather in the space formed by Apollyon's almost enclosing legs. Apollyon 'stroddled quite over the whole breadth of the way' (Bunyan 1987: 53–54), and Blake shows his arms held upwards, making the body a gigantic X, a chiasmic shape. His darts in either hand are ready to rain down on Christian, who bears the shield, and whose right arm reaches for the sword between Apollyon's paw-like feet. Apollyon's scales, which cover everything, including his gender, make him completely armoured. His wings are bat-like, black and jagged. Three forks of lightning come from his mouth. His eyes are prominent in their stare. His hair stands upright in points. His halo enforces his privilege. Yet this is the moment before the defeat of a figure whose scaly costume, outline and belted-in masculinity constitute what Lacan calls 'the armour of an alienating identity' (Lacan 2002: 78). I will return to the significance of armour later in the chapter, with Hobbes. While Christian, in bare feet and flowing robe, looks feminine, Apollyon's staring anger – with multiple spikes and bristles, and fires, which, according to Nordvig (1993: 182–189) threaten homosexually – makes him a victim of his own muscularity. He threatens to collapse into nothingness, indeed, 'Apollyon spread forth his dragon's wings and sped him away, that Christian saw him no more' (Bunyan 1987: 54).

The same collapse into embellishment which removes reality infects Haizmann's pictures. Perhaps Blake knows that such determinate shapes with a hard surrounding line, as Apollyon has, finally diminish his truth and interest. They contrast, in any case with the affirmative, even optimistic rationality implied in the title *The Pilgrim's Progress.* Not surprisingly, Bunyan has been seen as a novelist, for his social observation is shrewd, comic, and as neat as that of Jane Austen, as T.F. Powys intuited. Hypocrisy is Bunyan's theme, as with Mr Worldly Wiseman's 'good works'. Bunyan contrasts with de Certeau in *The Mystic Fable, by* writing with a certainty which contrasts with those 'fables' of mysticism discussed in the last chapter, stories which are not reducible to rationalist truth statements. A last 'fable' in de Certeau describes 'Labadie the Nomad' (1610–1680), moving from position to position: from 'Jesuit, Jansenist, Calvinist, Pietist, Chiliast or Millenarian, and finally Labadist' (Certeau 1992: 271; Popkin 2003: 186–187). Labadie wanders, and walks, like a vagabond God:

> [in] a struggle to the death with his disappointing creation, a god outside of himself, on the boundary where he is exiled both from himself and from the world, furious with a desire lacking an object. (Certeau 1992: 285)

Bunyan's pilgrim travels surely, direction known. Blake's 'lost traveller', outside certainty, fears a more uncertain devil than Christian: this devil was inside, as the dream.

4 MILTON: 'MAN'S FIRST DISOBEDIENCE'

> We spoke of the Devil, and I observed that when a child I thought the Manichaean doctrine, or that of two principles, a rational one. Blake assented to this and in confirmation asserted that he did not believe in the omnipotence of God – the language of the Bible on that subject is only poetical or allegorical. Yet soon after he denied that the natural world is anything. 'It is all nothing, and Satan's empire is the empire of nothing'.... I saw Milton in imagination and he told me to beware of being misled by his *Paradise Lost*. In particular he wished me to show the falsehood of his doctrine that the pleasures of sex arose from the Fall. The Fall could not produce any pleasure'. I answered the Fall produced a state of evil in which there was a mixture of good or pleasure, and in that sense the Fall may be said to produce the pleasure. But he answered that the Fall produced only generation and death and then he went off upon a rambling statement of a union of sexes in man as in God – an androgynous state in which I could not follow him. (Morley 1938: 1.330)

So Crabb Robinson talking with Blake in 1825. Their mutual interest in the Manichees recalls how Voltaire, Blake's antithesis, and in *Candide* (1759) critical of Milton's 'extravagant absurdities', makes his scholar Martin declare himself a Manichee (Voltaire 1990: 82–83, 58). That testimony was partly prompted by the Lisbon earthquake of 1755, which killed some 100,000 people, and fairly tested belief in God's providence (Lamb 1995: 91–95). What justice could there be if everything depended on general laws operating throughout nature which took no account of the specific? Lisbon ended the possibility of a Leibniz-like *Theodicy* (1710), a defence of God's justice. A theodicy only worsened matters, by implicating God, as Bayle noted, when he argued that the universe could be considered as Manichean, and virtually identified God and the devil (Walker 1964: 56–58, 178–201; Popkin 2003: 283–302).

The Book of Job was commonly read as a theodicy in the eighteenth century. Jonathan Lamb's study of its then reputation shows that it could be quarrelled over, because of the tension it raised between general law which depends upon precedent, and exceptional and singular cases which cannot be justified within general law, but which test the idea of the validity of a general justice. The Middle Ages, since Gregory the Great, had made Job a Christ-like example of patience, the man who sang in his sorrows, and 'alle his sorwe to solace thorw that song turnede' (*Piers Plowman* C18.18) (Besserman 1979; Astell 1994: 71–96). If the eighteenth century tested God's justice, it found in Job's complaints a troubling self-righteousness. Blake illustrated Job, and one comment must be made at once. Whereas the eighteenth century used Job for justifications for God and law, and the presence of evil, or the lack of such justifications, Blake, calling the Lisbon earthquake 'the Natural result of Sin' (Erdman 1982: *E* 615), as if implying that nature was under a curse, needed no theodicy. Throughout, as Crabb Robinson's record implies, he assumes that there is something wrong with God, and therefore, something wrong with Satan, to say nothing of Nature.

Milton warned Blake about being 'misled' by *Paradise Lost*, but the poem often works by misleading and then correcting, and the correction is less pleasant than what preceded. An instance comes with the Fall of one of the rebel angels, Mulciber, who has set up Pandaemonium, the palace in hell. As in Ovid's *Metamorphoses* 2.1–8, he, as the Roman version of Hephaistos, also Vulcan in Latin, built the Palace of the Sun. The account of Hephaistos' fall comes from *Iliad* 1.1591–595. Milton's poetic project, to 'soar' with 'no middle flight' (1.14), intends to outdo Homer. He says that this angel, whose heavenly name is withheld (Leonard 1990: 84–146), was known in heaven for 'many a towered structure high':

> Nor was his name unheard, or unadorned
> In ancient Greece; and in Ausonian land
> Men called him Mulciber; and how he fell
> From Heav'n, they fabled, thrown by angry Jove
> Sheer o'er the crystal battlements: from morn
> To noon he fell, from noon to dewy eve
> A summer's day: and with the setting sun
> Dropped from the zenith like a falling star
> On Lemnos th'Aegean isle: thus they relate,
> Erring, for he with this rebellious rout
> Fell long before; nor aught availed him now
> To have built in Heav'n high towers...
> (*PL* 1.738–749)

The excited imagining of his fall, to Lemnos, the volcanic island, so implying interest in how a mythology is formed (similarly, Mulciber resembles a falling star: Milton naturalises the fallen angel image) is made a 'fable'. But fabling, unlike with Certeau, is said to be 'erring', in a complete and jarring dismissal (Leavis 1964: 44–45; Forsyth 2003: 105–107; Hartman 1970: 113–123). Rather than respecting other mythologies and experiences, Milton asserts the truth, and so implicitly aligns Mulciber, art, and architecture – Assyrian and Egyptian ruins, and classical and Renaissance temples, all of them – with the false. And the word 'rout' associates later, in the Proem to Book 7, with the restored Cavalier court of Charles II, in an allusion to the 'barbarous dissonance/Of Bacchus and his revellers, the race/Of that wild rout....' (7.32–34). Since the writing must disavow or dismiss the imaginative vision, it assumes a melancholic, or mourning character (Rapaport 1983: 23–58). Its solution to the question of the value of the classical gods is negative. It makes them demons, as with the twelve devils who are enumerated and given brief CVs in Book 1.376–505. Christ tells Satan in *Paradise Regained* (1671) that the 'oracles are ceased'. Satan is equated therefore with Apollo, and will no more be asked for in Delphi (1.456, 458). Christ becomes wholly Hebraic, in Matthew Arnold's sense of the term, since he opposes anything Hellenistic in classical learning (4.286–364). Anxiety not to be contaminated corrects one error by affirming something more narrow, making sure, in a theodicy viable for the Age of Reason, that God and devil will never be confused with one another.

Blake repositioned Milton's emphases in his prophetic work *Milton* (1804), indeed throughout his poetry, and illustrations. A set of *Paradise Lost* watercolours appeared for the Rev. Joseph Thomas (1807, the 'Huntingdon' set), then, modified and revised, for Thomas Butts (1808, the 'Boston' set). Between 1816 and 1820, Blake illustrated *Paradise Regained* for John Linnell, and began a third *Paradise Lost*, based on Butts. The sequence for the first two series runs:

1) Satan Arousing the Rebel Angels
2) Satan, Sin, and Death: Satan comes to the Gates of Hell
3) Christ Offers to Redeem Man
4) Satan Watching the Endearments of Adam and Eve
5) Adam and Eve Asleep (replacing Thomas: Satan spying on Adam and Eve, and Raphael's Descent into Paradise, which is no. 4 there)
6) Raphael Warns Adam and Eve (revised from the Thomas set)

7) The Rout of the Rebel Angels
8) The Creation of Eve
9) The Temptation and Fall of Eve
10) The Judgment of Adam and Eve: 'So Judged he Man'
11) Michael Foretells the Crucifixion
12) The Expulsion of Adam and Eve from the Garden of Eden.

(Butlin cat. 529, 536)

God is almost excluded, only half seen in no. 3; and replaced by Christ elsewhere, even with the creation of Eve (the Father creates her in an 1803–1895 watercolour of the same, Butlin cat. 435). Something of Urizen's face appears in the four riders, the Cherubim (*PL* 12.628), shadowing Adam and Eve as they leave Paradise (no. 12); this scene is more negative than Milton's writing. But Blake emphasises Satan, the serpent, and the woman. In no. 2, Satan is wingless, and nude, and associated with serpents with multiple coils and heads, consorting with Sin and Death; as he is also in nos. 4, and 4 in the Thomas set. The serpent without Satan appears in nos. 6, 9, 10, 11 and 12; reduced in the last three. As the 'infernal serpent' (*PL* 1.34), which is the poem's 'first' name for Satan and one whose significance will be developed throughout, or as 'the great dragon ... that old serpent, called the Devil, and Satan, which deceiveth the whole world' (Revelation 12:9, compare *Isaiah* 27:1: 'in that day the Lord with his sore and great and strong sword shall punish leviathan the piercing [RV: swift] serpent, even leviathan that crooked serpent, and he shall slay the dragon that is in the sea'), Satan appears in at least nine of either set. In Butts no. 5 he is the toad at the ear of Eve (*PL* 4.800). He appears in Butts no. 6; in no. 9, he coils round Eve, as if replacing Adam's endearments, making her take the fruit from his mouth. Hybrid snakes, with hellhounds, reappear with Sin in no. 10, putting snakes above and beneath in that plate (Sin and Death are dead, outstretched beneath the tree in no. 11). Snakes are only not associated with Satan in nos. 1, and 7, in the latter of which the rebel angels fall in a space bisected by Christ's bow; above is clarity, and Christ enclosed in a nimbus; below, with fire, the angels fall in ways that recall the Michelangelo *Last Judgment* (Figs. 1 and 2).

As for the woman, she is represented as Sin in no. 2. Object of Satan's attention in 'Adam and Eve asleep', Eve is central in no. 6, in front of the tree to which Raphael points, while she regards Adam, who looks away from her and the tree, as if attending to Raphael. She is central, too, in the

Fig. 1 Lucas Cranach, *Adam and Eve at the Fateful Moment of the Temptation*. ACTIVE MUSEUM /Alamy Stock Photo

Fig. 2 Hans Baldung Grien, *Eve, the Serpent, and Death*, classicpaintings/Alamy Stock Photo

depiction of her creation (Adam seems more central in cat. 435), and again in 9, where Adam has his back turned. Adam only appears singly when paired with the crucified Christ, the example of 'filial obedience' (*PL* 3.269) in no. 11, succumbing to a legalistic demand of an angry God, who calls Adam 'ingrate' (3.97), and wants 'satisfaction' for man's sin: 'Die he, or Justice must' (3.210, 212). But what is this Justice, which God speaks of as separate from himself?

In no. 5, watching Adam and Eve's 'endearments', the snake coils round Satan (as in Thomas no. 4) and he soliloquises, as he does in all three occasions on which he enters the new world.[1] If we have analysed soliloquies in relation to temptation, whose force is the devil, soliloquy now shows the devil, as a divided subject, speaking with himself, when Iago-like, he watches the 'conjugal love', so Adam calls it, saying that Satan envies it (9.263–264). Indeed:

> aside the devil turned
> For envy, yet with jealous leer malign
> Eyed them askance and to himself thus plained.
> (4.502–504)

There seem heavy repetitions here. Envy and jealousy are conflated while 'leer' and 'askance' repeat each other, and 'malign' seems unnecessary. Blake dramatises that complex look by the double figure of snake and Satan, who also corresponds to Adam. Satan is a cross between the snake and the man. The lovers are 'imparadised' (4.506): 'Paradise Lost' means loss of sexual bliss. What does that imply?

In *The Marriage of Heaven and Hell*, Plates 5 and 6, Blake aligned Job with Milton (Erdman 1975: 102–103). Plate 4 gave the 'voice of the Devil' saying that Bibles are dualistic, separating the body from the soul; the voice affirmed 'that Energy. calld Evil. is alone from the Body. & that Reason calld Good. is alone from the soul'. The devil declares the body the soul, and that 'Energy is the only life and is from the Body and Reason is the bound or outward circumference of Energy'. Then:

> Those who restrain desire, do so because theirs is weak enough to be restrained; and the restrainer or reason usurps its place & governs the unwilling.
>
> And being restraind it by degrees becomes passive, till it is only the shadow of desire.

> The history of this is written in Paradise Lost. & the Governor or Reason is calld Messiah.
>
> And the original Archangel, or possessor of the command of the heavenly host is calld the Devil or Satan and his children are calld Sin & Death.
>
> But in the Book of Job, Milton's Messiah is call'd Satan.
>
> For this history has been adopted by both parties
>
> It indeed appeard to Reason as if Desire was cast out. but the Devils account is, that the Messiah fell. & formed a heaven of what he stole from the abyss.
>
> This is shewn in the Gospel, where he prays to the Father to send the comforter or Desire, that Reason may have ideas to build on; the Jehovah of the Bible being no other than [the Devil – *del.*] he who dwells in flaming fire.
>
> Know that after Christs death, he became Jehovah.
>
> But in Milton; the Father is Destiny, the Son, a Ratio of the five senses. & the Holy-ghost, Vacuum!
>
> Note: The reason Milton wrote in fetters when he wrote of Angels & God, and at liberty when of Devils & Hell, is that he was a true Poet and of the Devil's party without knowing it (*E* 34–35)

Energy, in the 'Voice of the devil' has become 'desire', whose history, as having failed, follows. 'Those who restrain desire' do so in themselves and for others, because theirs is weak enough to be restrained. The restrainer, or reason (aligning repressive rule and reason) usurps its 'place'. Since the restrainer or reason governs the unwilling, it usurps the 'place' of the unwilling. Do they lack will? Is their desire weak? Are the others, oppressed and unwilling to be so, smouldering with revolution? They will be politically 'unwilling' if they see that reason and restraint are identifical, and that government is reactive.

The opening implies that the conflict between reason and desire comes because something within desire wills repression, or restraint. Desire and reason are not opposites. Psychoanalytically, desire appears as displeasurable, and repression appears as desire. If something in desire retards it, making it double, then desire, restrained, made unwilling, is indeed 'passive', the shadow of desire. But Adam and Eve transgressed God's will 'for one restraint, lords of the world besides' (*PL* 1.32). Restraint seems needed to provoke desire, as it provokes rebellion. And restraint is what the 'infernal serpent' uses and challenges, though God as restrainer set it in place. Restraint becomes key to everything: even rebellious desire includes a repressive reason, which governed it; hence 'desire', sexuality, in *Paradise Lost* takes on an embarrassing faux innocence, the tone of prurient desire, aware of restraint, as with Eve's 'conjugal attraction':

> half her swelling breast
> Naked met his under the flowing gold
> Of her loose tresses
>
> (*PL* 4.495–497)

The ambiguity of 'loose' (wanton) is the point. Eve yields the pleasures of fallen desire in the guise of it being unfallen. Satan's envy of this, a few lines after, is not that different from the desire /restraint created in the reader-made-voyeur.

The Marriage of Heaven and Hell gives a 'history' of this desire turned self-conscious. The Governor, governing the unwilling, or Reason, is called Messiah. In Blake, he is Urizen, Ur-reason. His task, in *Paradise Lost*, is to deal with the consequences of desire. The other, original governor, 'possessor of the command of the heavenly host', is now called the Devil (accuser) or 'Satan' (the adversary); titles making him a figure of reaction, and not 'original'. Who does this 'calling', which includes calling Satan's children Sin and Death? If Satan was the original Archangel, then Reason (Messiah) has usurped his place. It reverses the idea of Lucifer having fallen from Heaven, having tried usurpation. Blake's text makes Lucifer the 'original', and not the usurping second. If Reason is now where Desire was, that may imply a failure of desire. Otherwise the Restrainer could not have succeeded; making Desire now become the accuser, the adversary, or envious, as Satan becomes.

A different version of the Fall comes from the Book of Job. But here, names are incorrectly assigned, unlike in Milton: his rationalist Messiah becomes here Satan, the rationalist. If 'the true name of the figure who torments Job is not Satan, but Messiah or Governor' (Shock 1993: 460), this is terrifying, because the only difference between God and Satan is how much rationality they claim. Milton's Messiah – Job's Satan – is a rationalist, asking God 'Does Job fear God for naught' (Job 1:9): as though accusing Job of utilitarianism, like himself. In England's revolutionary politics of 1790–1793, the time of composition, the Bible is made to seem to suggest that there is no alternative to repressive rule, while Satan is like reason, adversarial, accusatory. Milton conceals Reason's repressive nature, calling it Messiah, but in Job, Satan is no better. He is talking to someone much like Urizen. Blake follows a strain in Job, which makes God the oppressor, complaining to Satan, 'thou movedst me against him, to destroy him without cause' (Job 2:3).

The Marriage of Heaven and Hell reports the account of both parties, Reason and Desire. According to Reason, it seems as if 'Desire was cast out'. As heterogeneous, desire has been excluded, leaving only the rational. 'But the Devil's account is, that the Messiah fell. & formed a heaven of what he stole from the abyss'. Here, reason steals desire, a contrast to Prometheus (desire) who stole fire from heaven. Reason has stolen, or usurped, from the devil's abyss, creating an antithesis between the abyssal (literally utopic: no bottom), and heaven, as a place. For Reason, there is the fall of desire, as not subservient to it; for the Devil, the fall, as an upwards flight from the abyssal utopia, attempts to escape the sexual body, but since Reason takes fire with him from the abyss, he knows – repeating the point – that law only works with desire as its weapon.

This Devil's account is demonstrated by his diabolical biblical reading (the Devil or Angel, who lives in a flame of fire, and who spurns the Ten Commandments, 'is my [Blake's] particular friend: we often read the Bible together in its infernal or diabolical sense' (*E* 44)). According to him:

> This [i.e. that the Messiah has fallen and taken fire with him] is shewn in the Gospel, where he [Messiah] prays to the Father to send the comforter or Desire that Reason may have ideas to build on, the Jehovah of the Bible being no other than he, who dwells in flaming fire.

Erdman (1982: 801) notes that 'he, who', was in an earlier draft 'the Devil who'. And the Holy Spirit came as tongues of fire (Acts 2:3). Reason must pray to the Father to send Desire, for inspiration, and imagination. That prayer identifies Jehovah with desire, Promethean fire, and with the devil, and Messiah with patriarchy, as the Governor or Reason. Reason disguises God's nature as being identifiable with fire, concealing how God and Desire, or the Devil, are the same. Reason can only become anything else by undergoing its own death: 'Know that after Christ's death, he became Jehovah': the Devil who dwells in fire. The name 'Christ' is non-Miltonic. Christ is 'Messiah' in *Paradise Lost*, and it seems from Blake that Milton has missed something, supporting Reason as in Book Three, and making the Father Destiny, as a form of reason, determinism, and pessimism; the Son, humanity, enclosed and limited within its five senses. Milton's Arian tendency, if the criticism is valid, is seen not as anti-Christian, but as making Christ a creature confined to the limits of

Lockean empiricism. Finally, the Holy Ghost is not fiery desire, but emptiness. Milton takes his place within seventeenth-century empiricism, but the famous 'note' which follows makes him a 'true poet': he glimpsed desire, and his poetry gives a vision of this. Writing of God he becomes unwilling, fettered, but writing of devils, and of hell, where the devils are chained, 'free'. But if so, the poem keeps disparaging Satan, as when Gabriel calls his behaviour in heaven that of a 'sly hypocrite' and asks 'who more than thou/Once fawned, and cringed, and servilely adored/ Heaven's awful monarchy?' (*PL* 4.957, 958–960). Not only is Satan not allowed heroic rebellion, but it seems as if Heaven tolerates – even encourages – hypocrisy. Was it worth being there then? And is not hypocrisy at the centre of the text?

Describing prelapsarian sexuality, Adam says that the unfallen Eve possesses 'virgin modesty' so that Adam must lead her 'blushing' to the bridal bed (8.501,511). Blake asks 'Infancy' and 'Innocence', in *Visions of the Daughters of Albion* (1793) 'Who taught thee modesty, subtil modesty!' – a word which associates with hypocrisy, in Blake's valuations. Quoting Empson:

> Modest applies to dissembling; *if* a narrative of a fall from innocence is sustainable, then Eve is already fallen, and her modesty is even required in order to incite Adam to take her. So no less unsympathetic to Blake a critic as C.S. Lewis points out. (Empson 1981: 104).

Milton's language of love and innocence, which Satan envies, making it in origin not from the poet who is the devil's party, but inspired by the rationalistic and hypocritical Satan, comes contaminated with a suspiciousness noticeable in Raphael, whose advice to Adam bids him control Eve so that she will 'to realities yield all her shows' (8.575), as though her innocent naked appearings were only 'shows', and so potentially hypocritical. The line can but recall 'shows of seeming pure' (4.315), which accompany, lubriciously, fallen shame. In the poem the innocence derives not from any enlightened sense; rather, the blushing includes the restraint which is upon desire. That law speaks in Eve, and there may be the sense that the sexual works when it takes a transgressive form. Milton in Blake's *Milton* must realise that not innocence speaks, but law, so that 'I in my Selfhood am that Satan: I am that Evil One!/He is my Spectre' (*E* 108); giving three synonyms for 'Urizen'. He is the force of repression that contaminates desire: the figure addressed in 'To the Accuser, who is the God of this World'.

The sexual in Eden works by creating envy, having accusatory force, making the concept of Satan both the force of desire, *and* the force restraining it, speaking in the language of religion and innocence. This may help with Blake on postlapsarian sex, the account of which may have suffered from Crabb Robinson's puzzled recollection of it. Blake, opposing all absolutes, may be saying that the 'pleasures of sex', definable in 'Earth's Answer' from *Songs of Experience* as those of secrecy, and of 'delight / Chained in night' and liable to 'cruel, jealous selfish fear' (*E* 18–19), are precisely those which were given in the Fall. Postlapsarian sexual delight is experienced in Book Nine, *PL* 1027–1066, after which Adam feels the 'newcomer', 'shame' (9.1079). Yet it seems, on the basis of Eve's blushing modesty and Adam's actions, that such shame was implicit before the Fall, when 'pleasure' was inside the rule of 'modesty'. Why else does Raphael blush when angelic sex is mentioned (8.619)?

The Fall seems less an event than a continuous falling, as if falling was the only possible state.[2] Millicent Bell quotes Augustine that, in Adam's transgression, 'the evil will preceded the evil act'; Adam had already sinned before taking the apple, in that the matter of being asked to obey made the will rise up, opposing the constraint;

> thus the evil act, the transgression of eating the forbidden fruit, was committed only when those who did it were already evil; that bad fruit could only have come from a bad tree... but only a nature created out of nothing could have been distorted by a fault. Consequently, although the will derives its existence, as a nature, from its creation by God, its falling away from its true being is due to its creation out of nothing. (Augustine 1972: 571–572; Bell 1955: 1194)

That 'nothing' refers to prime matter, out of which creation took place.

Two conclusions follow: first, that Adam's creation makes the narrative of 'before' and 'after' the Fall meaningless, because his will had already given way to temptation (Angelo's fall in *Measure for Measure* repeats this Augustinian view of Adam), and the will's liability is to stray in resistance to restraint. Second, in Augustine's terms, God is responsible for the sin (a) because of the materials he used in creation, (b) because to place any constraint upon someone is to compel a wrong choice, an exercise of the will in opposition. Free will, which God insists on (*PL* 3.80–134) in a way expecting obedience, loosens allegiance. This freedom is the Fall already, as Augustine notes. God cannot offer a gift (Paradise) on the basis of a condition, and when the condition is not met, offer another gift (salvation from damnation) on the basis of the human accepting it. Each case convicts God of a secret imposition of forcing obedience, cancelling out the will, a point recognised in Calvinism, which does not even allow mankind the choice of salvation or damnation.

Everything in Adam and Eve's prelapsarian language is couched in terms presupposing it. Milton concedes the Fall may be slow in its final coming since, unlike Aquinas' timetable, discussed in Chapter 2, Satan stays in heaven long enough for Sin to become pregnant. Whereas Dante thought that Adam only lasted in Paradise less than six hours (*Paradiso* 26.109–142), Milton's Adam and Eve sin on the ninth day (*PL* 9.48–69). For Kierkegaard (1980: 42), the key to Adam in Eden is anxiety, fascination generated by the prohibition of 'that forbidden Tree' (*PL* 1.2). Anxiety precedes but stands in no necessary cause-and-effect relationship to the 'qualitative *leap*' which is the '*Fall*'. Similarly, Sin 'sprung' from Satan (2.758). Sin is 'the sudden', 'the leap' as 'the demonic is the sudden' (Kierkegaard 1980: 32, 129–130). The demonic knows neither continuity of time, nor place – hence the devil is always pictured as flying. And 'the moment' around which anxiety forms itself (Kierkegaard 1980: 81) is potentially traumatic, a series of shocks.

Such a 'leap' emanates from a self-tempting: Kierkegaard insists, from James 1:13–15, that temptation does not come from outside (1980: 48; Tanner 1992: 68–105). Kierkegaard cannot maintain a distinction between pre- and postlapsarian anxiety. Anxiety is 'dizziness' before the abyss (before nothing) which causes a succumbing, and, he says, 'in that very moment everything is changed, and freedom, when it again rises, sees that it is guilty. Between these two moments lies the leap, which no science has explained, and which no science can explain'. Anxiety, in the afterwards, then becomes more reflective; 'the nothing that is the object of anxiety becomes . . . more and more a something' (Kierkegaard 1980: 61).

Kierkegaard, unlike Milton, but like Augustine, did not think that there was a sexual relationship before the Fall (49); but afterwards, sensuousness became sexuality. Blake's comments to Crabb Robinson identify the Fall with the prior separation of the sexes, which conferred separate identities upon them – male/female, which they fight to maintain, instead of seeing male and female as inseparable qualities within gender. Adam, who is laden with requirements from Raphael, as for example to keep knowledge 'within bounds' (*PL* 7.120), is given a second condition, i.e. of not eating from the tree. This second was concealed within the first condition. God has not played fair. The first condition was imposed *before* the woman was given to him (Genesis 2:15–25). In the second condition, he is constituted inside the sexual relation as attracted to the woman (so passionate) but required to be obedient (rational). As Christ says: kingship belongs to him 'who reigns within himself, and rules / Passions, desires, and fears' (*Paradise Regained* 2.466–467). Adam's sin is in hearkening unto the voice of his wife (Genesis 3:17), failing proper obedience to God (*PL* 10.145–156). Specifically, 'fondly overcome with female charm' (9.999), he resigns his 'manhood' (10.148), as humanity continues that feminising in 'effeminate slackness' (11.634). The will, itself sexual, is inherently divided. The woman is the temptation which Adam did not realise was the real thing. The history of Paradise requires seeing woman in patriarchal terms, inscribing 'rule' (10.155) and making her the object of control. *Paradise Regained* becomes the narrative of regaining masculine rule, called 'reason', separate from either the woman, or Satan.

Kierkegaard's thesis about anxiety cannot accommodate the serpent, as he admits (1980: 48). With him 'anxiety' loses a psychoanalytic sexual dimension. But in contrast, Blake stressed the serpent in his illustrations, as did Freud with Haizmann's paintings. And the art of the Fall, some of which Milton must have known, shows up the problems in Genesis which his reading must negotiate. Cranach's *Adam and Eve* (1526, Courtauld Institute, see Fig. 1) places the Fall in a woodland, with animals framing Adam and Eve, an episode within a series of hunts, which Cranach delights to paint. Any interaction inside nature implies a hunt: hence, 'The Friar's Tale' made the devil a forester. Nature growing round Adam and Eve in the form of vine leaves supplies their genitals, rather than being what conceals them, while a stag's horns additionally supplement Adam, as they adorned Falstaff, by being significantly placed before him. The Fall becomes an episode within the relationships of the human and nature, the latter being both for and against man. Man has been told to have dominion over nature, but nature destabilises first through the serpent. Hunting attempts to reverse the Fall by perpetuating the death which it introduces. The snake is part of that nature, the highest visible creature in the Courtauld picture, and central, above the artist's signature, which is a winged serpent inscribed in the trunk. Cranach signs himself as devilish, confusing distinctions between art and nature; repeating such a confusion in the Fall, since there, the serpent (nature), speaks, as art.

In another Cranach painting, the snake has a woman's head, and coils round the tree's trunk (1530, Vienna Kunsthistoriches Museum), while in a Cranach woodcut she leans against the trunk, as Eve's mirror image (Campbell 2007: cat. 1, cat. 5 fig. 37, cat. 15). The twelfth-century theologian Peter Comestor attributed to the serpent a maiden's face (Evans 1968: 170). In the Harrowing of Hell, Christ accuses Satan:

> ylik a lusard [lizard] with a lady visage,
> Thefliche thow me robbedst
> (*Piers Plowman* B.18.338–339;
> Schmidt 2011: 1.682, 2.2.696).

The woman's deceptiveness doubles when Satan becomes a woman, making the phallic feminine.

In Cranach's contemporary, Hans Baldung Grien's *Eve, the Serpent, and Death* (see Koch 1974), Eve, an apple hidden behind her in her right hand, moves her right leg forward temptingly, her left hand on the serpent's coil (Fig. 2). Her outstretched arm is held by the left hand of Death, partially behind the tree, with another apple held aloft warningly in his other, right hand. The serpent, who defines and owns, and *is* the 'forbidden tree', also coils also round him, biting his left wrist, like another coil (the etymology of 'wrist' connects it with 'writhe'). Cornelius Agrippa, in *De originali peccato* (1518–1529) connected the word 'serpent' with swelling, so phallicising it. Eve's hand is excitatory; the erection, silently evoked in 'they knew they were naked' (Genesis 3:6) symbolises guilt and shame. It is St Paul's thorn in the flesh, 'the messenger of Satan' (2 Corinthians 12:7). For Agrippa, Eve's reason overcame Adam's faith, and sexual intercourse caused the Fall, a view Augustine had writhed against in *City of God* 14.23. Agrippa said Eve was not forbidden the fruit but Adam was; hence Baldung's Adam, bitten by the serpent, appears as Death (Death arresting the maiden is one sense of the picture). Eve seduces, witch-like, so perhaps causing the erection, but the serpent's presence eliminates any first time. Hence Adam independently holds the apple, and since Adam and Death are allegories of each other, lasciviousness causes the Fall, and sex equals death: a Manichean idea (Koch 1974; Marrow and Shestack 1981: 55; Hieatt 1980, 1983). The devil is the forbidden tree *and* forbidden fruit; Angelo's 'the tempter and the tempted'.

In another Baldung 'Fall of Man' (1511, Marrow and Shestack 1981: 120–123), the apple and Eve's breast relate to each other, as the man's dual temptation, while the snake encircles another tree, watching, hissing, an envious Iago. Yet another (Marrow and Shestack 1981: 174–177), gives a crest to the serpent, looking at Adam, suggesting Angelo's 'devil's crest'. So too, in Jan Gossart's *Adam and Eve* drawing (*c.*1525). There, Eve holds the apple in her left hand while her right hand is about to grasp Adam's genitals. Adam's right hand is about to reach out to her breast, rather than the apple, while his left hand holds a branch of the tree which projects in metonymic nearness to the snake. In Gossart's painting, the serpent bites the apple (not the wrist, as in Baldung) as Eve proffers it to Adam (Ainsworth 2010: 316–317, 114–115). The drawing is reprinted by James Turner (1987: 293), who outlines Manichean and Gnostic accounts of the Fall which are inescapable contexts for Milton, and which make the Genesis 3 narrative the record of conflicts of interpretation which have not been resolved, but remain as marks of repression, secondary revisions, in Freud's terms. Adam has fallen from androgyny, and his genitals are the cause of the Fall, and must be considered together with the object of desire: i.e. Eve, who is also the apple. Eve's desire for the fruit, incited by the serpent, is for the phallic, perhaps, under the devil's influence, to destroy this, as in popular representations of witchcraft, as in Baldung. The conclusion must be that the devil inhabits every separable object of representation: forbidden tree; branch; forbidden fruit, whether apple, male or female sexual parts, or serpent. The enmity between the serpent's seed and that of the woman (Genesis 3:15) sexualises the serpent, and suggests inherent division within and between male and female sexuality.

Eve copulating with the serpent appears in a later passage, recording Milton's allegorical awareness behind the devils' fabling:

> how the serpent, whom they called
> Ophion, with Eurynome, the wide-
> Encroaching Eve, perhaps, had first the rule
> Of high Olympus....
>
> (*PL* 10.580–583)

Leonard's edition gives the necessary annotation. 'Ophion' means 'serpent', and Eurynome 'wide-ruling', or, in the context of Eve, what Milton translates as her 'wide encroaching' goes 'wide of the law'. The fable means that the serpent and the woman have had prior rule before the Olympians. They are usurping unnatural figures needing to be overthrown in order to instantiate the non-diabolical nature of the sexual. Fables indicate repressed knowledge, but Milton is aware that allegories are real (5.574–576) and however repressed, they tell a truth about the need to diabolise, and criminalise: pagan gods becoming demons in Christianity. Unacceptable knowledge must be dumped, though it still finds its way into the text, perhaps indicating something divided in the poet, and recalling Blake's judgment on him as of the devil's party without knowing it.

All of this only indicates how much Milton must resist to order to articulate 'man's first disobedience' (1.1); to be sure of what is first, or to be able to give a single narrative. That implies order: 'say *first*', 1.27, repeated 1.28. That second 'first' puts the first one inside a pattern of repetition. Something has already been said, so that the 'first' is already displaced. And to say anything *first* is impossible since the devil – not Milton's devil, but something more insidious – has already inhabited Genesis, spoiling Milton's text which would further rationalise this pattern of repetition, and indicating that the man who must rule has already been subverted, whether he was a spiritual being brought low, or sexually fallen before the Fall.

Paradise Lost would like to be read as a political history of the Commonwealth's failure and the monarchy's restoration: so Christopher Hill (1979: 354–412) reads it, and the tone is certainly a warning to kings. In Book 1, Satan appears as 'the excess of glory obscured':

> as when the sun new ris'n
> Looks through the horizontal misty air
> Shorn of his beams, or from behind the moon
> In dim eclipse disastrous twilight sheds
> On half the nations, and with fear of change
> Perplexes monarchs.
>
> (1.593–599)

The lines compare Satan to the sun in mist, and then concealed in an eclipse, so that it sheds only 'disastrous twilight' (a *double* light, then, in that 'twi') which makes monarchs fear – as, apparently, an eclipse on 26 May 1630, when Charles II was born, provoked such fear (see Milton 1998: 724). Satan's state – his eclipse – warns monarchs. To that republican sense, which justifies Hill's will to read Milton as a proto-Marxist, it must be added that Milton sees the loss of liberty in the Fall revealing only a series of abuses of power, productive only of tyranny (*PL* 12.95). Such tyranny is already inside the poem. If the reaction the poem enforces against Satan makes him a tyrant (4.393–394), yet he first moved against despotic power. If God wishes to abdicate power to the Son, as Empson argues (1961: 130–146), that is on the basis of the Son assuming equal power. Adam falls by not exerting power over the woman and over himself; in *Paradise Regained* Christ assumes that power on the basis of near nihilistic self-sacrificings of art and life. A single narrative effacing its 'other', which lies concealed in the assertion of eternal Providence, constructs the republican Milton as thinking inside single patriarchally expressed power. Its oppressiveness shows in the verse's prevalent heaviness. Its single narrative strives for a rationalism subverted by the text's unconscious, and its diabolism.

5 BLAKE'S JOB AND MILTON

Hear the voice of the Bard!
Who Present, Past, & Future sees
Whose ears have heard,
The Holy Word,
That walk'd among the ancient trees.

Calling the lapsed Soul
And weeping in the evening dew:
That night control,
The starry pole;
And fallen fallen light renew!

O Earth O Earth return!
Arise from out the dewy grass;
Night is worn
And the morn
Rises from the slumberous mass.

Turn away no more:
Why wilt thou turn away
The starry floor
The watry shore
Is giv'n thee till the break of day.

(*E* 18)

'Introduction' to 'Songs of Experience' gives Blake's 'intuition of evil, disharmony, and a general fall' (Leavis 1964: 119), freely invoking, not conforming to, terms from Druidism, Christianity, and Milton, another 'Bard', whose account of Mulciber's fall returns in Blake's 'evening dew' and 'fallen light'. Milton resisted the mythologically historical fall of Mulciber though he alluded to it, by placing his fall before all history; Mulciber has always fallen; the fall is continuous, endlessly repeated and can never complete itself, falling being life's nature. Whoever in this poem calls to Earth to return does so in what is both the evening and the morning, the 'disastrous' twilight, which, following Augustine, was the time of the fall of the rebellious angels, and which may be a single moment, as Lucifer's 'host' is 'innumerable as the stars of *night* / Or stars of *morning*, dewdrops . . . ' (*PL* 5.745–746). The morning dew is equivalent to the night stars: the starry floor and watery shore may be reversible, turning constantly or falling into each other (Tambling 2005a: 40–42).

'Falling' illuminates the Job illustrations: nineteen watercolours for Thomas Butts, painted around 1805–1806 (Butlin 1981: cat. 550. nos. 1–21); and a second and third set for John Linnell in 1821, who then commissioned twenty-one engravings from the watercolours (1825). Blake had worked on Job since, in 1785, a version of Plate 10, *Job Rebuked by his Friends* (1785) appeared as a pen-and-wash drawing (Butlin 1981: cat. 162). Job's wife sits left, her hands over her knees, with Job in the centre, knees up, and hands held up, in protestation. The 'comforters', blaming Job for his sufferings, kneel in profile to the right, the one in the downstage position holding his left hand to point, accusingly. Another similar drawing of 1786 (Keynes 1971: 176, Butlin cat. 164, 165, 166) is inscribed: *The Complaint of Job: 'What is Man that Thou shouldst Try him every Moment?'* (Job 7:17). 'What is Man' is an inscription for the emblem-book *For Children: The Gates of Paradise* (1793) (*E* 32–33). This was revised with the new title of *For the Sexes: The Gates of Paradise*, and I quoted its Epilogue at the start of the chapter. That it evokes Job in surveying human life shows in the emblem-book's last picture: the soul saying: 'I have said to the Worm, Thou art my mother & my sister' (Job 17:14, *E* 267). Blake did further work on *Job and his Daughters* and a watercolour for Butts: *Job Confessing his Presumption to God who Answers from the Whirlwind* (Butlin 1981: cat. 394, 461). The whirlwind, containing the eyes of God, is as vortex-like as anything in Turner. But Blake has no sense of Job needing to be ashamed and confessing in the Butts, or Linnell watercolours (Butlin 1981: cat. 550.13, 551.13).

Blake reduces the Job/friends dialogue to six pictures, emphasising rather Job, Satan, and God; Job's ending, Job chapter 42, receives five pictures. Each engraving has a double frame, one leaving a space around the picture, and then another outside that, containing marginal figures, and biblical texts, drawn from the entire Bible. Whereas Blake's *Night Thoughts* illustrations, or those for the illuminated books put the text at the centre, with the artwork surrounding, here, the words surrounding the illustrations form designs themselves: 'visionary forms dramatic' (*J* 98.28, *E* 257). Whereas Milton's text is inherently conflictual, Job, as argued already, seems more repressive; its theodicy proclaims the dominance of reason, and Blake's engravings critique it actively.

A letter to George Cumberland (12 April 1827), four months before Blake's death, helps get to this:

> I have been very near the Gates of Death & have returned very weak & an Old Man feeble & tottering, but not in Spirit & Life, not in The Real Man The Imagination which Liveth for Ever. In that I am stronger & stronger as this Foolish Body decays. I thank you for the Pains you have taken with Poor Job. I know too well that a great majority of Englishmen are fond of The Indefinite which they Measure by Newton's Doctrine of the Fluxions of an Atom, A Thing that does not exist. These are Politicians, & think that Republican Art is Inimical to their Atom. For a Line or Lineament is not formed by Chance: a Line is a Line in its Minutest Subdivisions: Strait or Crooked It is Itself & not Intermeasurable with or by any Thing Else. Such is Job, but since the French Revolution Englishmen are all Intermeasurable One by Another, Certainly a happy state of Agreement to which I for One do not Agree. God keep me from the Divinity of Yes & No too, the Yea Nay Creeping Jesus, from supposing Up & Down to be the same Thing as all Experimentalists must suppose. (*E* 783)

Blake seems both King Lear, ruler of Albion, and Job (compare: 'naked we came here [to Felpham] naked of Natural things & naked we shall return' (Job 1:21, letter to Butts 10 January 1803, *E* 725). Job and Lear fuse in the early prophecy *Tiriel* (1789) (Bate 1989: 132–156; Stieg 1990: 273–296). The Job engravings show a gradual retreat in historical time: the first, truly pastoral, with setting sun and rising moon and star, shows a Gothic cathedral: 'Grecian is Mathematic Form: Gothic is Living Form' (*E* 270, see also *E* 559, and Joseph of Arimathea as a Gothic Artist, *E* 671). Loss of Gothic forms, and their replacement with ruined Druidic forms (nos. 4, 5, 6, 7, 8, 10, 11, 13), associate Job with Lear as a study in the

Fall, as with James Barry's *King Lear weeping over the Body of Cordelia*, which shows 'a Druid Temple, similar to Stonehenge' (*E* 545): following the antiquarian William Stukeley's *Stonehenge: A Temple Restored to the Druids* (1740) (Smiles 1994: 75–112).

Blake's letter opposes artists who prefer dots and atoms to lines, contrasting them with himself and Job, and identifying them with the reactionary politics of the 1820s which are anti-'Republican art'. Such reaction has made Englishmen fond of the 'Indefinite'; they think of themselves as intermeasurable (interchangeable) with each other. That means abandoning the 'wiry bounding line' (*E* 550), which constitutes the 'great and golden rule of art, as well as of life'. Blake rejects such conformity, refusal to differentiate between yes and no, up and down: the Illustrations, post-Waterloo, have a revolutionary drive; their subject-matter being 'Job's Captivity' (Keynes 1971: 206).

In the first engraving, Job and his wife sit under the oak tree, the children gathered around, and musical instruments hang in the tree. Commentators stress the passivity, the legalism of the worship, since the musical instruments are not used, in contrast with no. 21. Here, Psalm 137's captivity motif helps:

> By the rivers of Babylon, there we sat down, yea, we wept, when we remembered Zion.
>
> We hanged our harps upon the willows in the midst thereof.
>
> For there they that carried us away captive required of us a song; and they that wasted us required of us mirth, saying, Sing us one of the songs of Zion.

The Psalm is not cited, and there is no weeping in the Illustration, but something of it remains. Blake illustrated Psalm 137, 'By the Waters of Babylon' as a pen and watercolour (1806, Butlin cat. 466). A harp hangs on a willow tree above the head of a group of crouched and manacled captives. Nebuchadnezzar appears in red, crowned and sceptred, with attendant warriors, and a woman points at the harp, commanding that it and the other musical instruments be played; Empire commanding art. Behind, are the rivers of Babylon and its buildings. Lamb (1995: 112) says that William Warburton (1698–1779) read Job as an allegory of the plight of the Jews after the Babylonian captivity. That Job's musical instruments are unplayed suggests an offstage repression at work, implying that captivity is also present. And the line beneath engraving no. 18, 'And my Servant Job shall pray for you', cites Job 42:10: 'And the Lord turned the captivity of Job when he prayed for his Friends'. It echoes Psalm 126:1: 'When the Lord turned again the captivity of Zion, we were like them that dream'. Job, standing, for the first time in these Illustrations, is the visionary; the flame, answering to his hair hanging down, rises up into the sunlight: a parallel to the image of Noah and the Rainbow (1803–1805, Butlin, cat. 437). No God appears from there to the end of the pictures, save one rendered in art (no. 20). Everything yields to art in the last scene, no. 21, displacing the individual and continuing, though Job dies 'old and full of days'. Butlin compares cat. 490, 'The Hymn of Christ and the Apostles' for the musical instruments, and the last of the 'Songs of Experience' for Job as the Bard, while Milton has a harp in Blake's Illustrations to Gray's 'Ode to Music' (cat. 335.93–102).

Perhaps Job is the 'shadow of desire' in no. 1, as being only 'one that feared God and eschewed Evil', if it is argued that that is negative, showing someone 'unwilling', i.e. having no emotional will behind his fear to make the relationship less fearful, or constrained. If so, that implies a politics within the text, and perhaps allows the accusations which make him self-interested. Most commentators have found something to criticise in no. 1, thinking it shows Job as initially self-righteous, undergoing an experience where he moves from being legalistic and pietistic to being chastened and humbled by the Lord in the whirlwind. There is something Urizenic in his features, but the trouble comes from elsewhere, and such criticism simplifies, tending towards being pious itself. It replaces a political by a moral reading; and pairs with the interpretive method which ascribes fixed symbolic meanings to images, such as the symbolism of the left foot and the right. That requires the illustrations to be deciphered rather than finding in them any signs of an excess or freedom which goes beyond saying that one thing in the picture equals something else. The inscriptions 'The Letter killeth The Spirit giveth Life' and 'It is Spiritually Discerned' (in no. 1) invite an allegorical reading which critique the Hebrew inscription of no. 2, which translates as 'Jehovah is King'. In the context of republican art, Job is in captivity.

As with lightning falling in James Barry's aquatint, *Job Reproved by his Friends* (1777) (Pressly 1983: 77–78), and as with the lightning of pictures of Lear in the storm by Romney and West (Sillars 2006: 77–84), Blake's 'fallen, fallen light' has become lightning. Sillars compares Zuccarelli's *Macbeth Meeting the Witches* (1760) where lightning strikes Macbeth's castle, and he reproduces Benjamin Wilson's *David Garrick as King Lear* (1754) (Sillars 2006: Plate 3), complete with lightning. So, in

Blake's no. 2, Satan sits astride fire beneath God, where the faces of Job and his wife appear, as part of the sphere of fire (Butlin 1981). The Butts watercolour of this may be compared with *Enoch walked with God* (Butlin 1981: cat. 550.2; cat. 146).

If God is the usurping Urizen, Satan's ambiguity is to appear as energy, and as light, yet not to be as aspirant as Milton the Marlovian, whose 'advent'rous song, / . . . with no middle flight intends to soar/Above th'Aonian mount' (*PL* 1.13–150). Satan, as said before, speaks rationally. In no. 3, he dominates, surrounded with forked lightning, crouched on columns, destroying everything underneath. Whereas no. 2 makes him athletic, athleticism in no. 3 passes to Job's son, whom he is destroying. A subscript speaks of the 'great wind from the Wilderness', which destroyed, but a superscript says: 'The Fire of God is fallen from Heaven'. Is this God's judgment on Job's family? Or the Fall of Lucifer? Or the Fall of man? When Eve takes the fruit from the serpent's mouth, in the *Paradise Lost* illustrations, lightning falls on both sides (Butlin, cat. 536.9).

Lucifer's fall is the fall of God, since this is the fire of God. If fire is desire, this now is lacking. All that heaven retains is rationalism without desire, passive, 'the shadow of desire' in the God separated from fire whose rationalism sanctions Job's treatment. No. 4 emphasises the messengers running to give the news to Job and his wife, self-dramatising: 'And I only am escaped alone to tell thee'. Yet, that this is not a singular event is shown by two messengers being visible, the second supplying the words written below the picture, from Job 1:16: 'The fire of God is fallen from heaven & hath burned up the flocks & the Young Men & consumed them & I only am escaped alone to tell thee'. The messengers implicitly, accuse Job.

But in 5, 'Then went Satan forth from the presence of the Lord'. He takes fire as he falls, which is in the vial he pours out: as in 6, he pours out fire. The angels who form a half-circle round God's throne while also in fire – for the bottom line of inscription reads: 'Who maketh his Angels Spirits, & his Ministers a Flaming Fire' (Hebrews 1:7) – recoil from him. Fire divides from fire. And God, in his grief ('And it grieved him at his heart') is outside the fire as if it is fallen from him, dividing God. Satan cast down and God downcast are split-off equivalents. The melancholia echoes in Job, visible below, surrounded by angels, and giving alms to the old man. No. 6, which Blake coloured, giving Satan wings (Butlin 1981: cat. 807), shows Job smitten with boils, while his wife – in Blake, unlike in the Bible, not alienated from him – weeps at his feet. The sun is going down in a more intense repetition of the first picture. Fire falls from clouds which are like a cloak around the wings. Fire falls in the pouring out of the pestilential boils, and in the thunderbolts, like those of Apollyon, or by God as Death in the colour print of 1795, 'The House of Death' (Butlin, cat. 320), another picture for *Paradise Lost* (11.477–525), where Death is the intensest form of Urizen.

The painting makes Satan a young, failed ungendered figure of desire. Blake writes in 'The Laocoon' (*c.*1820): 'Art can never exist without naked beauty displayed' (*E* 275). Satan resembles Fire in *For the Sexes: The Gates of Paradise* (*E* 262), drawn from Barry's heroic humanist nude in *Satan and his Legions hurling Defiance towards the Vault of Heaven* (1792–1795; *PL* 1.229–301, Pressly 1983: 154–158). *For the Sexes* makes defiance unheroic; Fire is engendered from melancholy:

> Blind in Fire with shield & spear
> Two Horn'd Reasoning Cloven Fiction
> In Doubt which is Self contradiction
> A dark Hermaphrodite We stood
> Rational Truth Root of Evil & Good
> Round me flew the Flaming Sword
> Round her snowy Whirlwinds roard
> Freezing her Veil the Mundane Shell
> (*E* 268)

Fires of desire and revolution become reasoning, doubt, and rational truth, threatening sexlessness. If the androgyne combines both sexes, the hermaphrodite negates either, and Fire's genitals are covered by scales (Erdman 1975: 271), just as there is 'a lightly-sketched codpiece of scales' on the Satan of no.1 of the Huntingdon *Paradise Lost* set (Dunbar 1980: 46). This gives a clue for Blake's Satan. As he aspires towards desire, though chained, even suffering, he is masculine, and 'my friend'; but as he accepts, becomes rational, he tends to the neuter, to the restrained, the hermaphroditic, and is but a dunce.

Suggestions of fire and of light characterise nos. 7–10, scenes of mourning, threatening incipient madness, including Eliphaz the Temanite, who speaks about his vision (Job 4:12–18). The accuser who stands before Eliphaz in his dream is like God in no. 2. In no. 10, all the comforters point accusingly both hands, the fingers like arrows, more intense than the thunderbolts-as-arrows of no. 6 (Warner 1984: 54–58). That the Illustration displays Job's captivity shows in the manacles outside the margins to left and right, and the inscription's 'The Just Upright Man is laughed to scorn', recalling the word 'upright' from no. 1. Hence Job's kneeling is 'upright'. The next is the central picture (Butlin cat. 550.11), confirming the interrelated nature of God and Satan, complete with cloven hoof, and flaming hair. As the god of rationality, and intensifying the dream-image of no. 9, his right hand points back, like those of the Comforters to tablets of religious law (as if he had written them) as he threatens Job with the hell visible to Job on his couch, or catafalque. It recalls one of the large colour prints of 1795: *Elohim Creating Adam* (Butlin 1981: cat. 289), but is more malevolent. There, Adam's body was engirdled by a serpent; now it is God's, who possesses two heads, his own and a serpent's.

In *Elohim Creating Adam* (Butlin 1981: cat. 289), the serpent encircling Adam associates him with the animal, like the colour print of Nebuchadnezzar (cat. 301). Here, what threatens Job is madness, in a dual image of oppression where he is borne down upon, with lightning above and fire below, and held in captivity to three Apollyonian demons arising, his comforters in dream form, one holding down his feet, another his middle, and with one hand appearing over the genital area, both restraining and provoking the desire which is evident as fire rises from Job's body. The third holds chains: Blakean 'mind forg'd manacles'. The dream-figure covers Job like night, and as though his right hand will come down covering Job like his left hand in an embrace, so that the 'piercing' of the inscription intimates God as both Reason and no. 6's quasi-erotic figure. Job's recoil, with head and hands, indicates that the statement that he 'feared God' (no. 1) is based on an inadequate sense of the power of this God to imprison, and of how reason is brought into being by desire. The engraving is heavily inscribed; the top using Job 30:17 and 30:30; the central inscription raising that issue central to Blake: hypocrisy:

> The triumphing of the wicked is short, the joy of the hypocrite is but for a moment (Job 20:5)
>
> Satan himself is transformed into an Angel of Light & his Ministers into Ministers of Righteousness (2 Corinthians 11:14–15)

Blake pairs hypocrisy with qualities which are excavated in 'A Divine Image', a poem whose form is that of a chiasmus, and whose illustration shows 'a youthful blacksmith hammering a human-faced sun on his anvil' (*E* 800): he is naked, and aggressive:

Cruelty has a Human Heart
And Jealousy a Human Face
Terror, the Human Form Divine
And Secrecy, the Human Dress

The Human Dress is forged Iron
The Human Form, a fiery Forge.
The Human Face, a Furnace seal'd
The Human Heart, its hungry Gorge.
(*E* 32)

Clothes, marking the Fall, do not cover shame but come from secrecy (hypocrisy). They make a bad situation worse. The face is open to view, but conceals jealousy, as inherent to reason, since this builds on the premise of possessive individualism. The youth smashing the sun-like face, extinguishing openness, exhibits the heart's secret cruelty. The second stanza illuminates what the forge means: the satanic figure of desire is creating what he will wear: forged iron (armoured masculinity exceeding Apollyon's scales); the dual figures in the illustration show what the human form means: destroying, repressing its warmth and sunniness, creating a predatory, gorging nature. Hypocrisy in no. 11 suggests that that which is God and that which is Satan has become impossible to decide. The created figure is described in the words at the engraving's base: 'Who opposeth & exalteth himself above all that is called God or is Worshipped' (2 Thessalonians 2:4), echoing Lucifer's self-exaltation, but also implying how far extends the jealousy of a God demanding worship. In the face of that, only the quoted affirmation of Job 19:22–27 is possible, concluding that he will see God 'tho consumed be my wrought image' (Wicksteed 1910: 89; Rowland 2010: 45), as though suggesting that 'a divine image' is but 'wrought', that he has himself been forged, in the work of God-as-devil which has so stretched him out.

No. 12 shows a quieter scene with Elihu's intervention, the 'interpreter', the poet (Hagstrum 1964: 134), with right hand outstretched, and left hand pointing behind him – the reverse of God in no. 11 – to twelve stars in the night sky. They are seen for the first time; as something other than 'fallen, fallen light'. The picture is non-visionary and contrasts with no. 13's whirlwind vision, its inspiration Michelangelo's *Creation of Adam*; the former mantle for God becoming the enwrapping whirlwind. No. 13 condemns the comforters, the power of accusation, and it makes Job and his wife look up. Everyone is in the enveloping whirlwind, which is God, just as it contains Job, and expands outside the frame. If there is something different about this God, it is because he speaks *inside*, not outside, creation. No. 14 enframes him: it places the morning stars, the 'sons of God', above him, diminishing his patriarchy. The cropped picture lets them extend outwards infinitely. God has, beneath his arms, outstretched in 13 and 14, figures of Apollo and Diana, while Job and the others appear below, in a cavernous space.

God's questions about paternity ('Hath the Rain a Father' (No. 13, Job 38:18), and what follows with Leviathan as Satan, counter Satan's claims to eternity:

> We know no time when we were not as now;
> Know none before us, self-begot, self-raised
> By our own quickening power . . .
>
> (*PL* 5.859–861)

and the inscription to 14, 'When the morning Stars sang together. & all the Sons of God shouted for joy' (Job 38:7). It recalls the inscription to no. 2, when the 'sons of God', including Satan (Job 1:6) are present. It implies another possible mythology, outside the contest between God and Satan: other sons of God. Yet there is also, from 'The Tyger':

> When the stars threw down their spears
> And water'd heaven with their tears:
> Did he smile his work to see?
> Did he who made the Lamb make thee?
>
> (*E* 25)

That recalls Adam's repentant return to God, to confess:

> Humbly our faults, and pardon beg, with tears
> Watering the ground.
>
> (*PL* 10.1089–1090)

The smile, Shakespeare's marker of diabolical hypocrisy, implies the duplicity within the loving demand for obedience. It dominates, under the pretence of liberty.

No. 14's inscription, 'Canst thou bind the sweet influences of Pleiades or loose the bands of Orion' (Job 38:31) resembles the question to the

Tyger: what could 'frame' (? bind) it, having let it loose. The five-times-repeated formula 'Let . . . ', in the left and right margins of 14 brings out the significance of 'loosening', as if God's expansion of being took place in letting things happen, not retaining them. Sun and moon move away, to right and left, from the body of God.[3]

Contradictions continue in no. 15's almost cinematic continuance, as though the view was rolling downwards, unfolding life below the cavern where Job exists with the others. The sons of God are now too high for visibility; but for two thirds of the page, the circle of the earth (*PL* 7.224–232) is revealed, containing the rhinoceros-like, tusked Behemoth and the twisting sea serpent Leviathan. *OED* gives 'to twist' as one etymology of Leviathan. The KJV marginal reading for Leviathan is 'a whirlpool'. Leviathan is analogous to the whirlwind in which God appears; an avatar of God, who points downwards. His arm bisects the cavernous space where the humans are. Their deject position wittily makes them look down towards Behemoth, whose ear humanises him, hence the force of the words 'Behold now Behemoth, which I made with thee', and to Leviathan, as if they are witnessing another form of power with which they are kin.

Leviathan, named also in *Isaiah* 27:1, echoes Satan lying on the flood, a moment when the simile's expansiveness and ambiguity allows Milton to write, as Blake says, 'at liberty':

> in bulk as huge
> As whom the fables name of monstrous size,
> Titanian, or Earth-born, that warred on Jove,
> Briarios or Typhon, whom the den
> By ancient Tarsus held, or that sea-beast
> Leviathan, which God of all his works
> Created hugest that swim the ocean stream:
> Him haply slumbering on the Norway foam
> The pilot of some small night-foundered skiff,
> Deeming some island, oft, as seamen tell,
> With fixed anchor in his scaly rind
> Moors by his side under the lee, while night
> Invests the sea, and wished morn delays:
> So stretched out huge in length the arch fiend lay . . .
> (*PL* 1.196–209)

If Leviathan is the great whale (Genesis 1:21), Milton is ambivalent about its nature; is the moored ship safe? Demand for certain knowledge about the whale, as the unknown other, fires *Moby-Dick* and Ahab's demonic quest to make ambiguity cease by destroying the whale as diabolism. Here all meanings are overturned, as D.H. Lawrence reminds readers of classic American literature: 'you *must* look through the surface of American art, and see the inner diabolism of the symbolic meaning' (Lawrence 1956: 347). God's description of Leviathan – 'upon earth there is not his like' (Job 41:33) indicates Leviathan's singularity and incomparability. Leviathan may also be an image of suffering, upturned, looking up towards God. God seems to have been writing (two recording angels appear as caryatids on the top and sides of the frame), and what he has marked, and points to with his left hand, is an image of suffering, in these stationary beings: Behemoth looking downwards, Leviathan upwards.

Earlier, when Job 'cursed his day' (3:1), he said, 'Let them curse it that curse the day, who are ready to raise up Leviathan' (3:1. KJV mg). And he asks if he himself is a sea monster, or a whale (Job 7:12), which implies a Leviathan comparison. Besserman (1979: 21) cites these passages, plus Job 9:13, on the 'helpers of pride', and Job 26:12–13 on God:

> He divideth the sea with his power, and by his understanding he smiteth through the proud. By his spirit he hath garnished the heavens; his hand hath formed the crooked serpent.

Job characterises Behemoth and Leviathan as examples of pride and of strength, so that God is merely quoting Job's words back to him, not really answering them, and silently acknowledging what his hand has formed. Job may have rejected the comparison.

There seems no escape into another mode of thought outside God's dominance. *Jerusalem* shows God as the Spectre, so identifiable with Satan:

> forming Leviathan
> And Behemoth, the War by Sea enormous & the War
> By Land astounding'
>
> (*J* 91.39–41, *E* 251)

The names recall oil paintings of 1808 evoked in the 'Descriptive catalogue':

> The spiritual form of Nelson guiding Leviathan, in whose wreathings are infolded the nations of the earth

meaning that his coils, under Nelson's authority, have entangled them, and:

> The spiritual form of Pitt, guiding Behemoth, he is that Angel who, pleased to perform the Almighty's orders, rides on the whirlwind, directing the storms of war: He is ordering the reaper to reap the Vine of the Earth, and the Plowman to plow up the Cities and Towers. (*E* 530; Blunt 1959: 97–103; Erdman 1977: 448–453, 521–22)

Morton Paley takes these pictorial visions of glory as ironic. Remembering the Old Testament passages about Leviathan, God pointing to the latter and Behemoth suggests something further developed in no. 16. Paley quotes *2 Henry VI* 5. 2. 35, 'O War! thou Son of Hell', copied – perhaps by George Cumberland – onto Plate 8 of *Europe*. This makes Leviathan and Behemoth (a) the creation of God and (b) the creation of hell, marrying these two, and emphasising the responsibility of Job's God for war (Paley 1970: 185; Erdman 1977: 448–453, 521–22). But Blake makes these also tormented figures, like Milton's Satan, destructive and destroyed in battle (Job 41:8).

War is controlled by 'Apotheoses'. Blake's 'Descriptive Catalogue' says that he has been taken in a vision to see the originals of the Cherubim: 'The Artist has endeavoured to emulate the grandeur of those seen in his vision, and to apply it to modern Heroes, on a smaller scale' (*E* 531). Nelson and Pitt are these modern heroes, 'guiding' and 'directing' 'storms of war' (Erdman 1977: 494). Nelson and Pitt were dead by 1808: so the art apotheosises them; but, like the Spectre, they are to be ironised as warmongers. The creation of the enclosed Behemoth and Leviathan troubles: as they are confined, even tormented, it is curious that God says he made them alongside Job, as if emphasising their kinship with him. Whereas 'Reason' and 'Desire' were opposed in *The Marriage of Heaven and Hell*, the Book of Job allows only God to 'answer [for] Job', making the enthroned Urizen (nos 2, 5, 10) accuse the accusers in 'Who is this that darkeneth counsel by words without knowledge?' (no. 13). God has been driven into some action, justifying himself, but unsustainably. Behemoth and Leviathan confirm his ambiguity.

Leviathan's scales, like Apollyon's, and Satan's, are his 'pride', and suggest how 'Leviathan' in the seventeenth century also named the 'artificial man' that was desired in Hobbes' *Leviathan* (1641). That concept is of a commonwealth expressed in a Sovereign, with everyone else his subject: a '*Mortall God*' (Hobbes 1968: 227, 228, compare 81, 362). Milton desired liberty, which 'always with right reason dwells' – the necessity for the qualification says much about the poem's self-doubts – but liberty has been lost (*PL* 12.82–85), and *Leviathan* anticipates that. It reacts from, and against, a commonwealth, it has no room for republicanism. Hobbes' Leviathan is the devil in new form: as an artificial man, outfacing fear and the violence of all against all by surrendering liberty to the sovereign, in exchange for personal independence: the reign of self-interest, 'possessive individualism', as Hobbes' editor, C.B. McPherson, called it. Blake's ironic 'divine image' is forged on the same anvil as the artificial man. There Blake expresses what is meant by belief in such armouring, such protection against fear, which is not so much of Leviathan, the wounded monster, defeated in battle, as it is paranoid fear of the other, expressed in the necessity felt to control other classes – the poor – in society, expressed in such Hobbesian statements as 'Mutual Fear brings peace' ('The Human Abstract', *E* 27). Here, Satan clearly takes negative, reactive forms as the artificial man.

In no. 16, with God as judge, Satan, answering to Behemoth and Leviathan in the previous picture falls, his hands behind his head, like a Michelangelo captive or a figure from the Last Judgment (compare Butlin, cat. 50) as an ungendered and scaly figure, in fire and into fire, along with Job and his wife, also naked. This picture, answering to nothing in the Book of Job, and which is as contradictory as de Certeau finds Bosch, and for similar reasons, inscribes above God:

> Hell is naked before him & Destruction has no covering (Job 26:6)

God is the revealer of shame as Satan plunges down. God's definition seems to be that his secrets are unknown, as in the outer texts to left and right:

> Canst thou by searching find out God Canst thou find out the Almighty to perfection (Job 11:7)
>
> It is higher than Heaven what canst thou do It is deeper than Hell what canst thou know (Job 11:8)

No one can 'find out' the Almighty; but 'finding out' is also detecting: God's criminality goes un-found out.

The inner texts left and right read:

> The Accuser of our Brethren is Cast down who accused them before our God day & night (Revelation 12:10)
>
> The Prince of this World shall be cast out (John 12.31)

Below:

> Thou hast fulfilled the Judgment of the Wicked (Job 36:17: KJV: 'Judgment and justice take hold of thee')
>
> Even the Devils are Subject to Us thro thy Name. Jesus said unto them I saw Satan as lightning fall from Heaven' (Luke 10:17–18).
>
> God hath chosen the foolish things of the World to confound the wise And God hath chosen the weak things of the World to confound the things that are mighty. (I Corinthians 1:27)

'Thou hast fulfilled the Judgment of the Wicked' means (a) you have judged the wicked, and (b) 'you have judged according as the wicked judge'. The equivocation fits the ambivalence of the God who is the 'restrainer or reason' who 'casts' both *out*, and *down*, the force of energy which may also be the restrainer or reason, empowering the reason which excludes it. A downcast state indeed. If this fall like lightning is the triumph of God's reason, and revenge against the accuser, there is sorrow also on the face of the Job watching from below. It perpetuates melancholia, making the picture less than triumphal. Christ's words in Luke 10:18, which are quoted above, recall 'The Fire of God is fallen from Heaven', but his language may be supplemented or contradicted by 'the Messiah fell, & formed a heaven of what he stole from the abyss'. And the falling, naked Job and his wife are not pictures of a legalistic worship which is to be replaced. They suggest the loss of energy in the name of usurping reason. If Plate 16 is how things are to be, there seems to be nothing for it but the artificial man. The text from Corinthians, at the foot, memorialises a holy foolishness discussed in Chapter 3, lacking any place in Milton's, or Hobbes' modernity.

In no. 17, God, still rationalist, stands to bless Job and his wife; but then, strangely, as if he has been found out, he disappears. These last scenes reverse the end of *King Lear*, giving Job three new daughters. In no. 18, God's standing form is replaced by Job's. Job and the others have their backs turned towards the viewer, and Job looks towards the flame which ascends, now not falls, towards the open heaven. He is not seeking forgiveness (compare the inscription of no. 21: 'In burnt Offerings for Sin thou hast had no Pleasure'). Nor is he giving: rather, in no. 19, 'Every one also gave him a piece of Money'. He is rather the source of fire, which, ascending, has not been stolen from the abyss, but comes out of his own excess. The illustrations culminate with art within art, and its praise, not with the equivocations of reason, and desire and the resort to that other Satan, the artificial man.

Notes

1. For these soliloquies, see *PL* 4.33–113; 4.358–392; 4.505–535, and again, two soliloquies in relation to the Fall (9.99–178, 9.473–393).
2. The idea of continuous falling derives from Paul de Man's in *The Resistance to Theory*, ed. Wlad Godzich (Minneapolis: University of Minnesota Press 1997), 16.
3. For this discussion, I disregard the 'signature' in the pencil-drawing of this illustration, for which see Beer 1979: 258–260.

Chapter 5: Masks, Doubles, Nihilism

For Charles Baudelaire (1821–1867), it is unwise not to think of the devil. In 'Au Lecteur', the poem which opens *Les Fleurs du Mal* (*The Flowers of Evil*, 1857), 'c'est le Diable qui tient les fils qui nous remuent': 'it's the devil who pulls the strings that make us dance'. The dancing motif of *King Lear* can be rephrased inside the context of humans as puppets (Baudelaire 1986: 53; Baudelaire 1998: 86–100). We are always on the way down, and amongst the 'ménagerie infâme des nos vices' (the sordid menagerie of our vices) is one which would reduce the world to nothing (a theme for this chapter) – to 'un débris', swallowing everything up in a yawn. That vice is named *Ennui* (boredom, indifference), and many readers will recognise the poem's last lines from their quotation in *The Waste Land*:

> Tu le connais, lecteur, ce monstre délicat –
> Hypocrite lecteur, – mon semblable, – mon frère!
> (You know, reader, this delicate monster – hypocrite reader, my twin, my brother!)
>
> ('Au Lecteur', Baudelaire 1986)

These last lines suggest that the reader is a hypocrite not to acknowledge his or her acquaintance with boredom, and that boredom is itself a hypocritical state. Hypocrisy has been noted in this book, in detail, with regard to a French tradition which Rabelais attacks, and to an English tradition which includes Bunyan, Milton, and Blake, and it will be seen again with Hogg. In each of these cases, it has reference to different forms of religion, especially

J. Tambling, *Histories of the Devil*,
DOI 10.1057/978-1-137-51832-3_6

when, in the British case, this is inseparable from the assertion of class superiority which always requires state religion for its support. Baudelaire, however, thinks of a more striking, more modern form of hypocrisy, which takes the form of denying its indifference, acting a part which it does not feel: this is a definition of sentimentality.

Baudelaire, however, takes further account of the devil in his essay 'On the Essence of Laughter' (1855); of course, in laughter, feeling is revealed, and hypocrisy may be overthrown. At the beginning, Baudelaire gives good, if deeply ironic, reasons for being an agelast: the wise man does not laugh; when he does, it is with trepidation. Christ, 'the sage of all sages, the Incarnate Word, has never laughed. In the eyes of Him who knows and can do all things, the comic does not exist' (Baudelaire 1972: 142). Comedy disappears when a person possesses absolute knowledge and power. Laughter belongs to the Fall; 'the comic is an element of damnation and of diabolic origin'. Baudelaire rethinks the tale of Paul and Virginia, from the novel by Bernardin de Saint-Pierre (1788), of the innocent girl from Mauritius, freshly arrived in Paris – the city, especially the colonising city, is the devil's sphere. By chance, her innocent eye catches sight of a displayed caricature, a picture. As in *Paradise Lost*, that moment is her Fall: 'she is looking at the unknown.... she scarcely understands, either what it means, or what its purpose is ...' (145). The little comic caricature proves to be an abyssal tempting moment and it will ruin her, and she will laugh at it, and 'the comic is one of the clearest marks of Satan in man' (145). For laughter associates with feelings of pride or of superiority. To feel ability to laugh at others means being held by a satanic idea or delusion; for no one is ever 'mentally ill out of humility' (145). The ability to laugh, which may also mark hypocrisy, is a sure sign of believing in one's own superiority. But laughter also associates with a sense, or fear, of weakness. Baudelaire invokes 'satanic' elements in romanticism: in Charles Maturin's novel *Melmoth the Wanderer* (1820), an influence on Dostoevsky (Frank 1977: 128), and in E.T.A. Hoffmann (1776–1822). All damned figures in melodrama laugh: like Melmoth, the 'wanderer', a role which including the 'Wandering Jew', and the devil as wanderer (Job 1:7), succeeds the earlier *picaro*. Melmoth is still living on in a damned state in Ireland in 1816, when the action is set, though he was damned in 1666, in Spain, for the 'great angelic sin – pride and intellectual glorying' (Maturin 2000: 557). Melmoth was permitted a 'posthumous and preternatural existence' (558) to see if in 150 years, anyone would swap with him, but whatever crisis any potential victim is undergoing, however much the temptation, no one will (601). Baudelaire writes:

> [Melmoth] laughs and laughs, as he constantly compares himself with human caterpillars, he so strong, so intelligent, he for who a certain number of the physical and intellectual laws that condition humanity no longer exist! And this laughter is the perpetual explosion of his wrath and suffering . . . the necessary product of his dual and contradictory nature, which is infinitely great in relation to man, infinitely vile and base in relation to absolute truth and righteousness. (1972: 147)

'Melmoth is a living contradiction' for Baudelaire: his laughing is, and responds to, a split in the self, a split which hypocrisy denies, its characteristic behaviour enacting a desire to present a single identity. The point holds too for the agelast, who is related to the hypocrite. Baudelaire argues that laughter betrays anxiety; for example, with pagan, non-Christian images, which were revered in primitive times. Christians can laugh at them as grotesque survivals, but that shows culpable superiority and weakness together, a feeling of inadequacy towards such things which in pagan times were taken seriously, and which the Christian cannot feel comfortable about. Laughter is, and expresses, a double or contradictory feeling (150). 'A convulsion occurs', Baudelaire writes, as earlier, he speaks of 'bursting out laughing' (145). The suddenness, and physicality of laughter is the point. Laughter tears the subject apart, and breaks self-control, as is evident with the phrase 'fits of laughter': it threatens madness. Hence in the eighteenth century, the Earl of Chesterfield's advice to his son: 'I would heartily wish that you may often be seen to smile, but never heard to laugh while you live.'[1]

Baudelaire isolates two forms of the comic. One imitates nature; but another, more significant, the grotesque, the 'absolutely comic', recalls what Bakhtin says about the carnivalesque 'grotesque body' which is 'in the act of becoming': it reveals, and brings about, something new (Bakhtin 1984a: 317). This laughter shows not superiority over man (a delusionary danger), but nature:

> laughter excited by the grotesque has in itself something profound, axiomatic and primitive, which comes much closer to the life of innocence and to absolute joy than the laughter aroused from the comic derived from social manners . . . I shall refer to the grotesque as the absolute comic, in contrast to the ordinary comic, which I shall call the significative comic. (Baudelaire 1972: 151–152)

The 'grotesque' is a category within caricature, which, coming from a word meaning 'to load' or 'overload', suggests exaggeration, discussed in Chapter 3.

This 'absolute comic' is innocent, and cannot work when it is aware of an audience: it is 'unconscious of itself' (160). As such, exceeding nature, it produces instantaneous laughter, whereas the 'significative comic' – i.e. jokes which point to and which represent something observably funny in nature – may take some working out. The grotesque, and caricatures, things funny in being outside or beyond nature, provoke unpredictable 'excessive fits and swoonings of laughter'. The dangerous feeling of superiority creates the grotesque (151), and Baudelaire notes its danger when describing the English pantomime, whose distinguishing mark he says is violence (155); later adding that its effects are intoxicating (157). Similarly, E.T.A Hoffmann's 'most supernatural fleeting comic conceptions often resemble the visions of a drunken man' (159): in Nietzsche's terms, there is something Dionysian about such comedy.

In linking ecstasy with the absolute comic, Baudelaire discusses Hoffmann, who was so influential on Pushkin, Gogol, and Dostoevsky (Passage 1954, 1963), and on Poe.[2] Benjamin (1999: 324) quotes Heine on Hoffmann: 'the devil himself could not write such diabolical stuff', and I will consider him in two stages. The first will be through *Princess Brambilla: A Capriccio After Jacques Callot* (Hoffmann 1992: 119), and then, after looking at the diabolical in Molière, going back to him via *The Devil's Elixirs* (*Die Elixiere des Teufels* 1815–1816), which I will compare with James Hogg's *The Private Memoirs and Confessions of a Justified Sinner* (1824).[3]

1 The Comic: The Mark of Satan

Baudelaire's 'absolute comic' artist, not copying nature empirically, exists in another world, and his danger in expressing non-existent possibilities, is madness. *Princess Brambilla* uses Callot's etchings, the *Balli di Sfessania* (*c*.1621), which show dual carnivalesque masked figures from the *commedia dell'arte*, i.e. the improvised street-theatre of professional Italian actors, first recorded in Padua's carnival in 1545, and in England in 1549 (Salingar 1974: 177, 257, 192–193). The *commedia dell'arte* leaves its names behind: the 'zany', from Bergamo's hill country (*OED*), was a comic masked servant. Richard David's old Arden edition of *Love's Labour's Lost* 5.2.463 annotates 'zany' as 'the rustic servant of the pantaloon'. Pantaloon, the old Venetian merchant figure is mentioned in *As You Like It*, 2.7.158; Gremio is a Pantaloon in *The Taming of the Shrew* (s.d. 1.1.47, 3.1.36). In Jonson's *Volpone*, the old Corvino is fearful of being called the *Pantalone di Besogniosi* (2.3.8 – the Pantaloon of the Beggars). Mosca says that the 'true parasite' has his 'zanies' (*Volpone* 3.1.33).

The mask's significance was broached in Chapter 3. The classicist Jean-Pierre Vernant thinks of it, in Greek drama, as a disguise, or as suggesting the presence of the God, smiling while destroying, in *The Bacchae*. Or, the mask was the Gorgon's, threatening death and the breakdown of gender identity; or else that of Artemis, suggesting the need for a perhaps deadly initiation, as for Actaeon (Vernant 1988: 189–206). If comedy needs the potentially bewitching mask, its artificiality shows that expressiveness comes from what never had life; a point which disturbs Freud, writing on the 'uncanny': that the inanimate may precede – and so call into question – the animate (*SE* 17. 230–231). The *commedia dell'arte* had specific masks, such as those for masters: i.e. Pantalone and the Dottore, the Paduan academic; and for servants: Harlequin, Scapin, or Brighella, associated with comedy, and violence (Nicoll 1963: 40), and Pierrot. Harlequin, seen as a devil in *Inferno* 21.118 (Alichino), is 'a character in Italian comedy… in English pantomime a mute character supposed to be invisible to the clown and Pantaloon; he has many attributes of the clown (his rival for Columbine) with the addition of mischievous intrigue' (*OED*: noting also his 'light "bat" of lath as a magic wand'). Further, the *commedia dell'arte* included the *braggadocio*, the Capitano, the braggart soldier in Plautus, and Falstaff in Shakespeare; and Ponchinello, Harlequin's chief rival. He was Neapolitan, hook-nosed, and humpbacked, and must give something to representations of Richard the Third. Ponchinello was associated with puppet theatre, and with Mr Punch: he is 'Pulcinella' in *Princess Brambilla* (157). Marlowe's *Doctor Faustus*, in its comic puppet-play versions, used Harlequin (Wagner) and Scaramouche (the skirmisher, with something of the Capitano) as the Clown: the play becomes a farce when Faustus' scattered limbs' (seen in the B version) come together to dance when the scene changes to Hell. Faustus, and the Punch who defeats the devil, intertwine in popular puppet theatre as a source for Goethe's *Faust* (Butler 1952: 57–68).

Callot's versions of the *commedia dell'arte*, the *Balli di Sfessania*, perhaps from *fesso*, 'cracked', 'split', or mad, shows doubles dancing, duelling and so inter-reacting it is impossible to say which acts first. Baudelaire summarises *Princess Brambilla*, saying it is set in 'the centre of Italy, at the heart of the Southern carnival, in the middle of the bustling Corso' (155): Hoffmann had just read Goethe on the Roman Carnival. Baudelaire writes:

> the character Giglio Fava, the actor [is] a prey to a deep-seated form of schizophrenia [*dualisme chronique*]. This character, one in body, changes from time to time his personality, and under the name of Giglio Fava declares he is the sworn enemy of the Assyrian Prince Cornelio Chiapperi; and when he is the Assyrian Prince, he pours his profoundest and most regal contempt on his rival for the favour of the Princess, a miserable actor by the name of Giglio Fava . . . a creature is comic . . . only on condition that he is unaware of his own nature; just as, by an inverse law, the artist is an artist only on condition that he is dual, and that he is ignorant of none of the phenomena of his dual nature (Baudelaire 1972: 159–160).

Hoffmann's phrase for Giglio's condition is 'chronischer Dualismus' (Hoffmann 1992: 223; Webber 1996: 113–194). Yet it is not that the person is split, and has a double; rather, Celionati, the impresario in the novella, argues that all individuals are Siamese twins (Hoffmann 1992: 223–224). The grotesque body is a preferable mode of thinking of people as having a double, because more friendly than the Freudian double, with his nihilistic potential – it only annihilates the concept of the supreme individual.

Princess Brambilla's lovers, Giacinta and Giglio, become part of a *commedia dell'arte* group in carnival time, orchestrated by Signor Celionati, who may really be running a puppet theatre, so making all the characters, including the lovers, 'only' puppets, part of this world's doubleness (Hoffmann: 1992). When thinking of themselves as single individuals, the lovers experience egotism and unhappiness. When becoming masks and entering the carnival of the *commedia dell'arte*, they become other. Fava ceases to be a strutting tragic actor, feeling heroic, and becomes something in the pantomime world. Celionati enters into discussion with Germans who criticise the carnival's grotesqueness. He says the Germans must make a joke mean something, whereas Italians are happy with the 'pure joke'. The German painter Franz Reinhold concedes this but says that when he sees the humour of the grotesque, he thinks the masks are following something which has become visible to them: a 'primordial image', of which they speak:

> though in an exaggerated manner, because of the effort required. Our jokes are the very language of that primordial image which speaks from deep

> within us and necessarily produces the appropriate gestures by virtue of the inner principle of irony. (Hoffmann (1992: 157))

In irony, one thing is said, another meant. Humour follows a meaning which is unconscious, inaccessible to the comedian. A joke is spontaneously funny and ironic because, unlike Baudelaire's 'significative comic', the meaning only emerges *after* it has been said. In the absolute comic, the comedian is barred from the meaning of the joke. He or she cannot will to be funny. The joke comes suddenly, unplanned. The carnival/*commedia dell'arte* images of the Italians, as opposed to the good humour of the Germans, show 'that frightful, horrible fury of rage, hatred, and despair that drives you to madness and murder' (157). This, Reinhold says, gives him an 'uncanny trembling'; for that 'primordial image' is double, comic, and violent at once, and it has a 'principle of obscenity' which the German lacks; and that principle suggests both carnival and *das Ding*, the unrepresentable, together.[4]

Italian theatrical masks embody 'delicious mockery, the sharpest irony'. Celionati tells a fairy tale which urges seeing the self and the world as upside down (166). Its central symbol, the Fountain of Urdar, Reinhold interprets to mean that what brings happiness to the characters in it:

> is precisely what we Germans call humour, the wondrous power, born from deep intuitive understanding of nature, by which thought creates its own ironic double, whose strange antics [*Faxen*] give delight by revealing the antics... of thought itself and of all sublunary being (167).

It is not just that the 'primordial image' creates something which makes the human speak in humour and in irony. Rather, thought possesses unconscious power to create the 'primordial image' which speaks in the subject, and creates in art, which is the image's double, and it does so through a mask which speaks, so bringing out an uncanny strangeness within thought itself. Thought creates its own fictions, by which it lives, but extravagance and exaggeration appear in the 'strange antics' of humour, which only reveal the antics – the madness ('tomfoolery' in Passage's translation) which makes the world of thought lunatic, ungrounded, crazy from the start. The doubling shows up this grotesque madness, which, of course, puts characteristics of the devil at the very origin; but it is only recognisable when the mimicry of acting, or of a double, exaggerates the distinctive marks of the subject. Only exaggeration (a devilish concept) permits the double to be seen. In Freud, the subject telling a story does not just tell it, but mimes it expressively (*SW* 8.192–193). The double is diabolical: Giglio, freed from the burden of being the genteel tragic actor, casts off his self, and dons the wildest, weirdest masquerade costume, dancing wildly with a girl with a tambourine, the image derived from a Callot etching (Raraty 1972: 202–203). In this carnival-theatre people are 'not only animated by true imagination, true inward humour, but… [are] capable of recognising this state objectively, as though in a mirror, and of introducing it into external life in such a way that it should have the effect of a powerful spell upon the great world which surrounds the little world' (236), responding to a primordial image, which is then created in performance.

2 'He Who Gets Slapped': Molière and the Genius

Benjamin perceives comedy in tragedy with the intriguer, the 'scheming adviser' (1977: 125). The latter is of course diabolical. In Jacques Cazotte's novella, *The Devil in Love* (1772), the devil schemes, even by falling in love, to try to gain his/her victim. Is 'Biondetta', the lovely woman in Cazotte, a Paraceslian spirit, like an undine, who is trying to get a human life? (Cazotte 1991: 70–71). Or, is she Beelzebub? Hoffmann was fascinated by the first possibility, and his opera *Undine* (1816) shows a spirit's attempted coming into life and humanity. But in Cazotte the devil is forever tricking, through gender-doubleness. Benjamin's argument draws on both Baudelaire and on Jean Paul, discussed in Chapter 3, and now to be seen as the theorist of the double, the *Doppelgänger* (Webber 1996: 56–112). While Jean Paul implies that the devil's laughter creates overmuch violence and destruction, he implies that the devil is at the heart of comedy which needs him. Marx knew that, and shows it in *The Eighteenth Brumaire of Louis Bonaparte* (1852 – Benjamin quotes this):

> when the Puritans complained at the Council of Constance about the wicked lives of the popes… Cardinal Pierre d'Ailly thundered at them: 'Only the devil incarnate can save the Catholic church, and you demand angels!' (Marx 1973: 245)

The Council of Constance (1414–1418) was held against the background of the 'heretical' Hussites and Wycliffe, opposing Catholic orthodoxy.

Marx applies the logic, as it appeared on the eve of Louis Bonaparte's right-wing coup in 1851, with which the future Napoleon III had the connivance of the bourgeoisie, who cared more about keeping their property than their political freedom:

> Only the head of the Society of the Tenth of December [Louis Bonaparte's proto-Fascist organisation] can save bourgeois society! Only theft can save property, perjury can save religion, bastardy the family, and disorder order.

Or, in the religious sphere, only the devil can save the Catholic Church, a diabolical structure, as any Cardinal knows, especially when threatened by heresy, which of course always has the devil's finger-marks on it. Comedy depends on diabolical tricks, but Benjamin adds that Baudelaire knew that Satan's ambiguity is that he speaks for 'both the upper crust . . . and the lower classes as well'. Whichever way, he is anti-agelast.

The Roman comic playwright Plautus (254–184 BCE) makes the agelast a hard-headed money-dealer, opposing any spirit in holiday mood. The intriguer-servant is employed against him, as in Molière's *Les Fourberies de Scapin* (1671). A *fourbe* is a deceitful person; *fourberies* are deceptions; 'tricks to catch the old one', quoting Middleton, who was not unaware of the identity of the 'old one'. Molière's farce comes from *Phormio* (*c.*161 BCE), by Plautus' successor, Terence (*c.*190–159 BCE). Set in Naples – classic comedy likes seaports – Molière's young men, Octavio, son of Argante, and Leander, son of Géronte, have found girls to marry – Hyacintha and Zerbinetta – while their fathers are away. These, returning from trading overseas, want them to marry other girls so the sons enlist the aid of Scapin (Italian *scappare* 'to escape'), Leander's trickster servant; a Brighella figure, a companion of Harlequin, with lute or guitar. Silvester, Octavio's servant, is Scapin-lite, while Carlo is a third trickster, but Scapin directs operations as if in the theatre; getting Octavio to practise responding to his disapproving father, Argante, and playing the father himself (a *Henry IV Part I* motif). Argante, arriving, is so obsessed by his son's disobedience that he starts soliloquising, not a good idea when Scapin, this play's devil, is listening. Argante concludes that he will tan Scapin's hide, as the servant whom he suspects is at the bottom of everything.

Scapin derives from two Terence characters, Phormio, the parasite, and Geta, the slave. The slave of Roman comedy would certainly have been whipped if he had been caught in his intrigues. Harry Levin says that the definition of the clown is 'he who gets slapped' (Levin 1967: 137). The comic always includes *violence towards clowns.* 'Slapstick', an American term, describes a European practice of clowns hitting each other: *OED* cites a scholarly source from 1925:

> what has caused the playgoers' sudden callousness? The slapstick. Towards the end of the seventeenth century Arlequin had introduced into England the double-lath of castigation, which made the maximum amount of noise with the minimum of injury.

Hence the theatrical slang 'knockabout', and the Vice's and Harlequin's weapon of the lath. *He Who Gets Slapped* may suggest the characteristic comedy of the Marx brothers, but is the name of a play by Leonid Andreyev (1871–1919), filmed by Victor Sjöström in 1924, starring Lon Chaney. The trickster, clown, or devil is, then, both active, and smart. He is always on the receiving end of blows; masochist and scapegoat, since the blows are often meant for someone else, but land on him as the nearest. Getting slapped, which may be feminising, makes you both a clown and a 'poor devil'.

The Comedy of Errors derives from Plautus' *Menaechmi*, set in the seaport of Epidamnus. Shakespeare makes the port Ephesus, which had gained a crazy reputation from Acts 19:23–41: it is the margin between the sea, as the unknown other, which separates and unites destinies, and the town, where exorcism is carried out (*The Comedy of Errors* 4.4.37–128). Plautus makes one twin brother come looking for his brother on land, who was stolen away in his youth, and who is now stealing a mantle from his wife, to give to his mistress Erotium. He is on holiday, but though he is prosperous, cannot enjoy the holiday mood, being constantly impeded by business in the forum. Meanwhile, the brother from the sea walks in and enjoys the carnival spirit that his twin misses. He gets it because he is the twin, and everyone mistakes his identity and on realising that, he starts acting up. At one point to preserve himself, he must pretend to go mad: only by masquerade, or deception, can he keep his identity and discover his brother's. Both brothers, therefore, use deception as the answer to bad luck (Salingar 1974: 161). Comedy seems a complex interrelationship between Luck/Chance/Fortune, and intrigue/deception. It is no use thinking that craft or trickery must not be employed, via a servant, or woman, or devil.

Comedy faces loss of identity; doubling confuses origins; which twin initiates any action? The twin motif passes into *Twelfth Night*, set in Illyria, another seaport. Both twins, Viola and Sebastian, come from outside, from Messaline, apparently another seaport. The most extreme form of identity confusion comes in Plautus' *Amphitryon*, reworked by Molière, and then by Kleist. Jupiter and Mercury take and take on the identities of the army commander Amphitryon and his servant Sosia, and Jupiter makes love to Alcmena, Amphitryon's wife. She thinks she is making love to her husband, who finds himself locked out, while Sosia (Molière's part) is beaten by Mercury, the other Sosia. The gods can carry out their deception, because they can become duplicates of Amphitryon and Sosia, while the latter, the wise servant, becomes unsure he is Sosia, or perhaps starts to think that being Sosia is only part of what he is, and not the unique bit. No one can be sure that anything s/he does is unique, or that some other devil is not working over one's secret life. *Menaechmi* has one slave, Messenio, who talks about being beaten by his master, the brother from the sea, but Messenio knows how to work things to his advantage, gains his freedom, and has the play's last lines. *The Comedy of Errors* doubles Plautus' twins by giving both brothers slaves, identical twins, both Dromio. They are repeatedly beaten, always because of mistaken identity, always beaten by the wrong master, not knowing he is beating the wrong twin. Nor do the Dromios know that they are talking to the wrong master, because these are also twins. When the wrong master (Antipholus of Ephesus) beats the right Dromio (Dromio of Ephesus), and he calls him an ass, which of course, needs beating, Dromio replies: "I am an ass indeed, you may prove it by my long ears [= years; compare 'donkey's years']. I have served [Antipholus of Syracuse] from the hour of my nativity to this instant, and have nothing at his hands for my service but blows . . . ' (*The Comedy of Errors* 4.4.27–30). Both Dromios are called asses (2.2.199, 3.1.14), and Dromio of Syracuse says that he is 'transformed', like Bottom in *A Midsummer Night's Dream*. If the clown is 'he who gets slapped', slapping confirms the status of the servant/clown as made an ass, but when Bottom becomes an ass, he receives a most rare vision, as in Apuleius' *The Golden Ass*. And the ass has a multivalency, suggesting the body, its slowness, irreducibility, and stupidity: yet, in Carnival, and the Feast of the Ass, he figures humility, even redemption (Bakhtin 1984a: 78, 198–199).

Molière's Scapin is familiar with being slapped, and tells Argante that he has heard a remark from one of the ancients (actually Terence), telling him how to live with the expectation of being beaten. When a father has been away from home:

> he should run his mind over the distressing accidents he may encounter on his return . . . his house burned, his money stolen, his wife dead, his son crippled, his daughter seduced; and whatever he finds has not happened to

> him, impute it to good fortune.... I've always practised this lesson in my little philosophy; and I've never returned home without holding myself ready for the anger of my masters, for reprimands, insults, kicks in the ass, beatings with the stick and strap, and whatever failed to happen to me, I thanked my lucky star for it. (*Les Fourberies de Scapin* 2.5.324)

Argante replies that he is going to law, to free his son from his marriage, and Scapin breaks into a series of speeches about the law as a disaster area (he begins the play by saying how he has been in trouble with the law). But before saying that, in his introductory speech he declared:

> There are few things impossible for me when I decide to get involved in them.... I've received from Heaven a pretty fine genius [*J'ai sans doute reçu du Ciel un genie assez beau*] for the fabrication of all those nice turns of wit, all those ingenious intrigues, to which the ignorant vulgar give the name of mischievous machinations [*fourberies*]; and I may say without vanity that hardly a man has ever been who was an abler artisan of schemes and intrigues, who has acquired more glory than I in that noble profession. (2.5.302)

The comic trickster is saying nothing that need be believed in, but his statement is not egotism. His 'genius' is the daemonic 'it', the double, which possesses him.

Alenka Zupančič (2008: 66) allows for a connection between this 'genius' with Benjamin's essay 'Fate and Character' (1921) (Bontea 2006: 1041–1071). Scapin has 'character', and Benjamin writes: 'where there is character there will, with certainty, not be fate, and in the area of fate, character will not be found' (*SW1* 202). Benjamin identifies Fate – misfortune and guilt – with law, which he calls 'a residue of the demonic stage of human existence, when legal statutes determined not only men's relationships, but also their relation to the gods'. Tragedy challenged both that fixity of relationship, and law, which 'condemns, not to punishment, but to guilt. Fate is the guilt context of the living... it is not... really man who has a fate; rather, the subject of fate is indeterminable' (204). A person may be technically innocent, but the presupposition of guilt remains. Tragedy struggles against the power of law. In contrast, comedy has the power of character, and who has that has no 'fate'. 'Character' demonstrates a 'single trait, which allows no other to remain visible in its proximity' and 'gives this mystical enslavement of the person to the guilt context the answer of genius' (*SW1* 205). That single trait contrasts with what fate brings to light: the immense complexity of the guilty person.

The 'genius', as the double, as character, is the source of comic life which Scapin has, no matter how often he is slapped.

'Physiognomies', which record exaggerative mask-like features in the face, indicate the 'genius', that 'other' in the self which makes the comic character untouchable by law (206). Scapin says getting involved with law 'is to be damned already in this world... the mere thought of a lawsuit would be enough to make me flee to the Indies' (327). 'Genius' both shows and is 'the natural innocence of man'. If comedy shows essential innocence, it is opposite to law, which negates it: law being always the oppressive Lacanian truth-dealing 'law of the father'. No wonder this play has two fathers.

Scapin, and Silvester, coached into playing a *braggadocio* aiming to kill Argante, trick Argante comprehensively, but the miserly Géronte is the worse father, even lecturing Argante on how badly he has trained his son. In Act 2 Scene 7 Scapin tricks him, telling him the Turks have kidnapped his son Leander and want a ransom of 500 crowns, otherwise they will abduct him in their galley to Algiers. Géronte first tells Scapin to tell the Turks he will put the police onto them, to which Scapin replies: 'The police on the open sea? Are you trying to be funny?' (333). Law can only act where it can set boundaries, and the sea knows none. Géronte then tries to get Scapin to take his son's place, as if he was a slave, repeating all the time 'Que diable allait-il faire dans cette galère' – what devil made him get in that galley? – a question showing how incomprehension and comprehension are allied. The devil *is* at work; but he cannot see how. Scapin extracts money from him, for Leander's marriage, and then takes revenge, because Géronte has told lies about him. Under the pretext that enemies are after Géronte, he makes him hide in a sack which Scapin slings onto his back (the miser becomes like a money-bag) and then beats thoroughly (Act 3 Scene 2). Scapin acts in extempore fashion, imitating the voices of first a Gascon ('"What? I won't have the advantage of to kill this Géronte, and somebody out of charity won't tell me where he is?"' (342)), then a Swiss, and then half a dozen soldiers together, all after Géronte, and all beating the sack which contains him. Scapin pretends to Géronte after each beating that the villains were really beating *him* on the back, and that they just hit the sack by accident. Scapin is *all* these imaginary people, *and* the loyal servant who responds to them. Comedy shows him as the deterritorialised schizoid, with no identity at all. The miserly father, the agelast, gets slapped, until he puts his head out of the sack and discovers the trickster's trick. At the end, when the fathers are reconciled to the weddings, Scapin escapes by feigning death, says that he was brained by a stonecutter's hammer, and that he cannot die without Géronte's forgiveness: managing, in asking for this, to announce publicly five times that he had beaten Géronte. When others leave, Scapin snatches off the ultimate mask, his bandages, and sits at the supper, as the parasite.

The trickster/intriguer games with power: if comedies order things hierarchically, as with marriages ending them, tricksters knows that such ordering dissolves itself again, and can only be ensured by a trick, by something else. Nature's order must be supplemented by something else that it cannot recognise, something diabolical. It only works through the trickery of culture. Deconstruction points out this necessity, being, at its best, a diabolical practising, always already at work. More on Derrida in the next section.

3 HAUNTING: HOGG AND HOFFMANN

In 'The Uncanny' ('Das Unheimliche', 1919), Freud shows himself Hoffmann's best commentator, finding in Hoffmann's short story 'The Sandman' (1815) which he analyses, the castration fear, focused (a) in the loss of the eyes (b) and in the idea of the double. He then refers these points to Hoffmann's novel *The Devil's Elixirs*, finding here:

> characters who are to be considered identical because they look alike. This relation is accentuated by mental processes leaping from one of these characters to another – by what we should call telepathy – so that the one possesses knowledge, feelings and experience in common with the other. Or it is marked by the fact that the subject identifies himself with someone else, so that he is in doubt as to which his self is, or substitutes the extraneous self for his own. In other words, there is a doubling, dividing, and interchanging of the self. And finally there is the constant recurrence of the same thing – the repetition of the same features or character-traits or vicissitudes, of the same crimes, or even the same names through several consecutive generations. (*SE* 17.234)

Recurrence, and the appearance of the double, are essential both to Hoffmann and to Hogg, in *The Private Memoirs and Confessions of a Justified Sinner* (Garside 2006). Freud returns to 'recurrence', or repetition, in *Beyond the Pleasure Principle* (1920), describing how, unintentionally, subjects relive unwanted situations and painful emotions, under the sense 'of being pursued by some "daemonic" power' in their 'compulsion to repeat' (*SE* 18.210. Derrida comments:

> The very procedure of the text itself is diabolical. It mimes walking, does not cease walking without advancing, regularly sketching out one step more without gaining an inch of ground. A limping devil, like everything that transgresses the pleasure principle without ever permitting the conclusion of a last step. (Derrida 1987: 269)

Beyond the Pleasure Principle speculates on a death drive motivating the repetition-compulsion, but is silent on how that articulates with the double. Sarah Kofman notes anxieties raised by the uncanny and relates them to the death drive: their proliferating and self-multiplying, multiform force exceeds castration anxiety. She thinks that Hoffmann's intimations of the devil in *The Devil's Elixirs* relate to the ambivalence with which the father is regarded. The devil as father – one of his aspects, as it was for Haizmann – represents an originary 'diabolical principle, the principle of division, the negative principle which Freud calls the death instinct' (Kofman 1991: 157). Beyond that ambivalence lies a more extreme pluralising, which 'Das Unheimliche' calls repetition and doubling, but which is also a splitting of the self, distorting what is living within it:

> Is not the uncanniness of the death instincts, for which the figures of the devil serve as metaphors, the supreme form of *Unheimlichkeit*... and does it not derive from a universal case of repression, a case that is the most resistant of all: the repression of the presence of death within, and at the origin of life itself? (Kofman 1991: 158)

The return of the repressed is diabolical: it shows death to exist inside the organism. What returns is not the demonic: 'the demon is that very thing which *comes back* without having been called by the pleasure principle' (Derrida 1987: 341). Rather, then, inside repetition is the demonic, as the inanimate, the mechanical, inside the organism.

Baudelaire made laughter a satanic realisation of simultaneous strength and weakness, laughter, the 'other' inside the self, being involuntary. The Scapin-like clown and the double support the subject, like a twin, protecting it against death, and being slapped is thus heroic, a marker of passivity which is also creative and genius-inspired. But equally, the double disturbs the self that would think of itself as complete, being, for Freud, an 'uncanny harbinger of death' (*SE* 17.235). As diabolical, he negates the self: before examining *The Devil's Elixirs*, I will show this with Hogg.

The Private Memoirs and Confessions of a Justified Sinner comprises a double text containing the 'Editor's' narrative – presumed to be someone from Edinburgh interested in the Scottish Lowlands – and then Robert Wringhim's confessional autobiography. As a soliloquy, whom does this address? It is followed by the 'Editor's' conclusion, in which Wringhim's body is found. This 'Editor' of the text reprints a letter from Hogg which actually appeared in the Edinburgh *Blackwood's Magazine*, and then quotes J.G. Lockhart, member of the sophisticated Edinburgh set to which the Editor belongs: 'Hogg has imposed . . . ingenious lies upon the public ere now' (Hogg 1969: 246). Hogg, the Ettrick shepherd, and not part of that 'set', is then encountered at work and refuses to search for Wringhim's burial site. However the 'Editor' does search, excavating Wringhim's body, and his manuscript, buried with him, 'written by himself' (253). Who is 'himself'? Wringhim? *OED* says the word is used 'with reference to a particular man, esp. a head of a household or other figure of authority, whose identity is readily understood in a particular context without prior reference or explanation by the speaker'. If so, this may be the devil's account, while the 'other' who is implicitly addressed in Wringhim's 'soliloquy', is the diabolical genius.

The Editor is reconstructing the events of about 150 years earlier, and the century before that. The first page of his narrative lists divers names: Dalcastle/Dalchastel; Colwan/Colquhoun/Cowan/Colwan; and later Wringhim (12), which is the surname of the justified sinner, Robert. Later comes Ault-Righ (236) and Eltrive (241); all these names contain the marks of Derrida's *différance*, in that the rogue letters in the spellings do not affect their pronunciation, yet they mark an uncanny difference complicating identity which is also hinted at when Robert, the 'I' of the narrative, immediately after having had Calvinistic assurance of his own election to grace, meets, at that elated moment, 'the stranger youth', 'the same being as myself' (116). But the word 'same' implies more than one, and makes mockery of another term also applied to him: 'this singular being' (117), 'your brother . . . your second self' (117). This 'singular and unaccountable being' (118), who cannot enter an 'account' (i.e. a narrative), as certain letters of the alphabet cannot be accounted for in pronunciation, has a likeness to the 'I' which is 'quite unaccountable' (119).

Soon implicitly identified in the text as Satan, the stranger calls himself Gil-Martin (129), echoing the name of a boy at Wringhim's school, M'Gill. The letter *l* seems roguish, tautosyllabic, and it has been seen how the names do not sound them out when they are written. Gil-Martin makes M'Gill return, as different, with the silent *l* missing. (The double *ll*, because it repeats, contains the potential to annihilate the uniqueness of the self who bears the name: double letters are diabolical.) When Wringhim is confined to bed, bewitched, he thinks, he conceives himself to be two people, a second self, his companion one and his elder brother George the other, so that he must speak and answer in the character of his brother (154). But that incestuous fantasy may make his brother the devil (compare 188); indeed, the stranger-youth has made that identification (117). And George, in the Editor's narrative, has the feeling of being haunted by his brother (35–36), and beats him soundly when he gets in the way. Later, Robert writes:

> I seemed hardly to be an *accountable* creature; being thus in the habit of executing transactions... without being sensible that I did them. I was a being incomprehensible to myself. Either I had a second self... or else my body was at times possessed by a spirit over which it had no control, and of whose actions my own soul was wholly unconscious. (182)

The text looks over the edge at schizoid behaviour, while playing with the Calvinistic theological hubris which creates a deliberately split subject: one which can do as it wishes because it is convinced that its soul is saved (as happens to Dante's Guido da Montefeltro), and because it needs no good works: a position calculated to maximise hypocrisy.

As in *The Monk*, and in *The Devil's Elixirs* and *Melmoth the Wanderer*, religion is the devil's opportunity, producing delusion, and hypocrisy, as perhaps an essential when religion posits the self as a unitary subject responsible to God, and the self has to so act: it has to create another self, a mask. The devil in Hogg parodies Protestantism:

> sin' the Revolution that the gospel had turned sae rife, [Satan] had been often drive to the shift o' preaching it himsel, for the purpose o' getting some wrang tenets into it, and thereby turning it into blasphemy and ridicule. (196)

Satan's chief pride is to seduce:

> a proud professor [of religious belief], wha has mae than ordinary pretensions to a divine calling, and that reard and prays till the very howlets learn his preambles, *that*'s the man Auld Simmie fixes on to make a dishclout o'. (197)

Perhaps the name relates to 'Sammiel', the devil's name in Weber's *Der Freischütz* (1824). And he is 'Auld', the old one, a primal father. The novel shows his deception, but it also implies Scotland as internally divided, which gives Gil-Martin his opportunity. The devil finds a place within both brothers, and Robert's madness goes beyond him and implicates everyone, especially those in Edinburgh. The text is homely, folkloric; but despite the mysteries to do with his and his brother George's birth, Robert has notably no conventional sexual temptations, which makes it simpler than *The Devil's Elixirs*, where sexuality is the insistent subject. There, Medardus, the young monk, walks away from his monastery, in his 'Initiation into the World' (Pt. 1, chapter 2), avoiding, he thinks, the sexual temptation awakened by the picture of Aurelia/St Rosalia. Exhausted by repression of this desire, he drinks the 'devil's elixir', a potion possessed by the monastery and which was supposed to have tempted St Anthony towards the devil: and now, drinking, 'new strength surged through my limbs'.[5] In this narcissistic state, he encounters on the edge of a ravine a young man in uniform, apparently asleep, as if held by the death drive. As Medardus wakes him, he plunges into the ravine. This is Victor, his unknown half-brother; and Medardus, partly involuntarily, takes over both his identity, and his mistress, Euphemia, at the nearby court. But Victor has not died, and now haunts him as the monk Medardus has ceased to be, as an increasingly mad double; not a double who shows that the subject is mad, as in Hogg. But a mad double only further pluralises the identity of the subject, and shows that the subject is already internally divided.

Drinking, just before seeing Victor, the devil's elixir, of which he knows he only has a limited supply, stimulates Medardus and intimates death. It is the *pharmakon*, medicine and poison together (Derrida 1981: 95–117), and like the *pharmakon*, it destabilises all that is normally identifiable in single terms. The multiplying of identity also divides: Medardus says: 'I am what I seem to be, yet do not seem to be what I am; even to myself I am an insoluble riddle, for my personality has been torn apart' (59, 54). He is divided, being both Medardus and the Victor, whom he thinks 'shattered in the ravine' ('im Abrunde', 60, 55). The double does not stand outside, but is inside, one shattered identity.

Freud's editors note how 'the uncanny' concept emerges from *Totem and Taboo* (1913), where:

> we attribute an 'uncanny' quality to impressions that seem to confirm the omnipotence of thoughts and the animistic mode of thinking in general, after we have reached a stage at which, in our judgment, we have abandoned such beliefs. (*SE* 17.241, *SE* 13.86)

The 'omnipotence of thoughts' emanates from a narcissism which over-values the power of the subject's mental processes to change reality, or make it happen. It rebounds back on the subject, so that it must not be defined as a power putting the subject in control of the environment. Freud derives the 'omnipotence of thoughts' from analysing the 'Rat Man' in 'Notes upon a Case of Obsessional Neurosis' (1909). The Rat Man coined this expression to explain the 'strange and uncanny events' by which he seemed to be pursued: 'if he thought of someone he would be sure to meet that very person immediately afterwards, as though by magic' (*SE* 13.86). Thoughts let the Rat Man down, work against him, doubling another force which brings the other person immediately into view (Tambling 2012a,c: 23–31). The Rat Man and Medardus are similar. Each attempt to conquer belief in the 'omnipotence of thoughts' working against the subject, both confirms such power, and the subject's impotence. The Rat Man's defensive mechanisms are fooled by the repressed mechanisms, demonstrating a principle that when something is to be feared, '*the very thing that is to be warded off invariably finds its way into the very means which is being used for warding it off*' (*SE* 10.225, my emphasis). The cure, the apotropaic, is infected by the very problem needing a solution. Incapable of being outside the problem it must deal with, it doubles it instead. This return of what was repressed is the demonic. This activates *The Devil's Elixirs*. Medardus says how, as a young monk, a woman came to him for confession. She confessed a forbidden love, and then broke out saying that she loved him. The confession closed. He went into the chapel and saw the painting of the martyrdom of St Rosalia. The painting of the saint is an apotropaic against the power of the sexual; a sacred painting should sublimate sexual drives. But when he saw the image, he thought that it depicted the woman at confession. The cure must now be warded off, because Medardus, in the deceptiveness of the 'omnipotence of thoughts', has fantasised Rosalia, the saint, as needing confession, because she is in love with him (35–36). Medardus does not control a situation by his thoughts; rather, his subjectivity is produced by what it attempts to repress.

Having truly jumped into the novel *in medias res*, we must now go back, and attempt an explanation of how the novel works, however baffling it is, and however limited making it a single narrative may leave the baroque folds of its narrative (Daemmirch 1973: 531–546; Passage 1976: 531–546). As in Hogg's novel, everything is framed by an editor who has found 'papers' written by Friar Medardus, in the Capuchin monastery at B-.

The editor reads them in the monastery garden where 'through the dark branches of the plane trees, paintings of the saints – the new frescoes in all their glory on the long wall – look straight at you with bright, living eyes' (Hoffmann 2008: 7, 3). The animistic suggestion means that painted eyes are looking at the reader, giving the same anxiety as in 'The Sandman' or 'Princess Brambilla' in deciding which is the inanimate/animate, which the puppet, which the human. If the line making these distinctions blurs, death exists *within* life (Derrida 1987: 277), rather than life and death being opposed principles. The editor says that the reader may recognise the results of a 'secret union', which later, is shown to be the first Francesco (an ancestor)'s copulation with the devil, in a desire for self-division which is the death drive. He adds:

> After I had with great diligence read through the papers of Medardus . . . I came to feel that what we call simply dream and imagination might represent the secret [*geheimen*] thread that runs through our lives and links its varied facets, and that the man who thinks that because he has perceived this, he has acquired the power to break the thread and challenge the mysterious force which rules us, is to be given up as lost. (8, 4)

The manuscript shows the power of dream and imagination, already implicit in the editor's dreamy writing. These, passive and active together, obscure the existence of a secret [*geheim*] thread which runs through our lives and links them, one which Freud would call sexuality, overcoded by the death drive. The thread may be like that of Ariadne, to guide through the labyrinth of sexuality, but it is also, as a thread, the continuing problem itself, which cannot be escaped from: the guidance which names the problem is itself the problem. The thread and the problem have an intergenerational force, and no power to clarify, and they cannot be escaped from without worse loss. No more is said; the editor transcribes the manuscript.

He later breaks from recording Medardus' confession to give a translation from Italian of the Painter's story, which explains events extending over five generations (Negus 1958: 516–520). Then, after Medardus has recounted his life story, his last words asking how he is to write the confessional narrative which has just been read, the editor gives an appendix from Father Spiridion, Librarian of the Capuchin Monastery in B – which gives an account of Medardus' death as a truly pious man. It is not easy to reconcile the two narratives: it seems from Medardus' account that he goes on living into old age, greying, whereas Spiridion narrates his death as happening exactly a year after the death of the Aurelia he loved. Unless Spiridion is right, and Medardus has gone on writing after his death – which, in view of what follows, is not impossible, as an example of the omnipotence of thoughts, continuing after the death of the author.

Medardus, who adopts his name when as a young man he enters the monastery under the tutelage of Leonardus, the Prior, who seems to possess ironic pre-awareness of him, exceeding his self-awareness (22, 18), undergoes a series of baffling experiences. He both seems to have, and to be, his own double. He is attracted to an ideal woman, whom he identifies with a portrait of St Rosalia. Later she appears as Aurelia; he loves and idealises her, and yet attempts to stab her. At the end, she *is* stabbed, by his double, his brother. But Aurelia is not an ideal, and she writes a confession to the Abbess, addressed as her 'dear good Mother' (182), which Medardus purloins: it confesses her love for Medardus, and that she has been reading Monk Lewis' Gothic novel, *The Monk* (1796). For much of his narrative, Medardus, who it seems became a monk principally out of shame at being discovered kissing the glove of a woman to whom, in his youth, he was sexually attracted, is journeying from B- to Rome: the Painter's book is found in a similar Capuchin monastery outside Rome (212, 229).

Before encountering that book, a Physician gives Medardus an account of past events at the court of Prince Alexander (134, 140) where he was staying. It makes Medardus believe that his father (who, it is said at the beginning, died the moment he was born) was Francesco, and that this Francesco murdered his friend the Duke, and the Prince's brother. He thinks the murder happened on his wedding night, and that the bride, an Italian princess, was his, Medardus', mother. Medardus then realises that he himself used that same knife to kill Hermogenes, who was Aurelia's brother: the son repeats the father's act, making the crucial point that repetition and doubling is intergenerational, historical, exceeding personal subjectivity.

The Physician's partial, and so misleading, explanation, is succeeded by Aurelia's letter, which gives more hints as to an ongoing story affecting her own mother. It precedes the illumination from the Painter's manuscript, from which it seems that this long-dead Painter – who often appears, and who accompanied the Duke and Francesco in the incident recorded by the Physician – returns periodically to the monastery to update the record. When this is read, the editor says, we will understand the narrative's central point. It tells of an Italian family, seen through five generations, from the sixteenth century onwards. The primal father, Camillo, was a Genoese corsair-fighting nobleman. His son, Francesco, paints under Leonardo da Vinci's tutelage, thus having two fathers: the doubling coincidence of the names Leonardo/Leonardus is obvious. Francesco becomes proud of his art, and wants to paint a nude Venus, as St Rosalia. He drinks an elixir from a bottle from St Anthony's cellar: apparently – so it is said – spiked by the devil, in order to turn holy ones towards him. Medardus in *his* monastery also drank of such an elixir, which may have had genuine effects on him, but whose significance is to be, ambivalently, the source of death and of life. The drinking is diabolical, as the power of the death drive, scattering the narcissism and identity it also promotes. The painter Francesco turns from art to the flesh, when copulating with the woman he painted as St Rosalia, but who had the appearance of Venus, and who then appears to him as Venus, though she is in alliance with the devil, as a succuba. She dies as a son is born and he hears voices saying that he will find no rest so long as his stem continues to multiply in sin and wickedness. (The 'stem' then, compares with the idea of the continuing 'thread'.) The future, in other words, will dictate the past. Francesco flees to Prussia to paint in the monastery of the Holy Linden (Medardus will be born there). His original painting is sold to the monastery at B-; a copy being kept in Italy, though which is original and which a simulacrum, with elixir-like powers, remains questionable.

His son, the second Francesco, is brought up as a foundling by Count Filippo. He commits adultery with the Countess, an instance of the near-incest with the mother which runs, thread-like, throughout the narrative. Twins are born (Pietro and Angiola); and then Francesco has a legitimate child, with the name Paolo Francesco (a variant on Dante's Paolo and Francesca, the lovers of *Inferno* 5: the names used jointly here, here disturb gender categories). Paolo Francesco rapes his half-sister Angiola, who goes to Germany and bears a child called Franz, thus pluralising the name Francesco. At the same time, Pietro has committed adultery with Vittoria, the woman whom Paolo Francesco was to marry and a daughter, Giacinta, was born. The half-brothers have, therefore, exchanged a form of rivalrous revenge on each other. Pietro then marries a German lady, by whom he has a daughter, Aurelia.

Prince Theodor, who marries Angiola, brings up Franz, a product, of course, of incest. Theodor himself has two other sons, Alexander and Johann. Alexander, who is met in Part 1 chapter 4, as an artistic dilettante, marries Paolo's second legitimate daughter by Vittoria, whom he meets in

Italy. And Johann in Italy meets Franz, not knowing he is his own half-brother. (The other daughter becomes the Abbess, and the text hints that her desires are equally divided: the sexual 'secret thread' shows in her.) These half-brothers return in friendship to Germany, told in a narrative which the Physician has outlined. As for the Painter who accompanies them, he is the phantom original Francesco, called an Ahasuerus (98, 90) by the barber who is doubly named (Schönfeld and Belcampo), and who is another double of Medardus. Schönfeld presents himself as Medardus' protector, and says he can destroy Medardus' 'adversary through the power of thought' (98–99, 91). The Painter's damnation for allying himself with the Devil means that he must follow the sins of the succeeding generations, inscribing them in the book, so that the book is one in the course of being written, through different generations, all of whom will find it expanded, while, as it continues being written, its emphases must change. Maturin's Melmoth is similar: he is a recurring figure, through history, alive and dead together.

At Alexander's court, as Paolo Francesco fell for Angiola, so Franz, the son, the guiltiest of all in the line, seduces two women, one being Giacinta, the Physician's 'Italian princess', and he fratricidally murders Johann, who is about to marry her. The mother dies. The son is brought up with the name Victor. The second woman Franz seduces is Aurelia. In a distant land, she gives birth to a daughter. Franz also virtually murders her mother. The child is swapped, and brought up as Euphemia, in the house of Baroness S (the dead child, Euphemia with whom she has been swapped, was perhaps murdered by the nurse). Aurelia then marries Baron F (he appears in chapter 2) and has two children with him, Hermogenes and Aurelia. This is the Aurelia whom Medardus loves. The Painter narrates and supplements the incidents in the Physician's tale. He says that Franz, thinking he has committed the unforgivable sin, married a peasant woman, and in continuing remorse, made a pilgrimage to the Holy Linden monastery in 'cold, far distant, Prussia' (11, 7). The son of the union was named Franz: i.e. Medardus. Medardus, at the conclusion of the Physician's tale, thought that he was the son of Franz and Giacinta, and that his real name is Victor, but he is Franz' son by the peasant woman, and has, therefore, Victor as his half-brother. And Victor has had more than an elective affinity for Euphemia, with whom he has been conducting an affair which Medardus must take over when Victor disappears into the abyss, since Euphemia and Victor are half-brother and -sister, as are Medardus and Euphemia.

We can now return to the beginning. In the Painter's genealogy, Medardus (Franz) is the fifth Francesco/Franz, and there has been a migration from Italy to Germany. The first Francesco exists in ghostly, and textual form as the thread inside the generations succeeding him; for example, acting as the double to the Franz who, another double, accompanies Johann (so the Physician's tale). Medardus incarnates in himself the qualities of the previous generations, which is what makes him so self-divided. His actions repeat, and double, the actions of the previous generations. The double extends through history. A double may not be visible simply because it belonged to a previous generation; one person in their life acts the parts of several generations. Yet it seems that the past might be changed through the actions of the present: or better, no past action, because of its ongoing power, can be considered as finished.

Medardus and Victor seem to have a telepathic relationship with each other in how they act out each other's desires. When Medardus first sees the second Aurelia, he identifies her with the woman seen in the confessional (61, 56). So she is also St Rosalia. The reader is sent back to the moment when the woman entered the confessional, but enlightenment comes much later, when Aurelia's letter states that as a girl she saw her mother (the first Aurelia) with a picture of a handsome man (the Franz who seduced her before she married Baron F). Her brother, Hermogenes, identified this portrait with the Devil. So young Aurelia conceives that her mother had an alliance with some demon, that being her idea of the Devil (195, 183). So, following Sarah Kofman on the devil's significance: the love fantasy that the mother, Aurelia has, is death driven; indeed, the mother does die. Because of that, her daughter, the fourteen-year old Aurelia has in her turn – when Hermogenes wants to become a soldier – a fantasy of a handsome Capuchin friar. She reads *The Monk*, which makes her think that this unknown lover-to-be has sold himself to the devil, and intends to lead her into wickedness. Yet she says that she cannot withstand the love that burned within her. She hears of Medardus, decides he may be the unknown lover, and undergoes a night of torture, with demons preying on her, while a monk, whom she calls Medardus, tells her to love him. She then goes to confession, praying to St Rosalia first, and blurts out the words which the woman in the confessional had said to Medardus, at least in his fantasy (41, 35; 199, 187), and which she had previously said in her dream. The episode shows her lack of autonomy. In *neither* account of the episode of the confessional can *either* Medardus or Aurelia control their thoughts. Aurelia is impelled first by the sight of her mother with Franz's portrait, so that in fantasy she transfers the attributes of the painting of Franz onto another figure, Franz's son, by another woman. Second, by the power of *The Monk*, Aurelia prays to Rosalia, and believes that her love for Medardus has gone, and was only the devil's snare. She then sees at the Prince's, Medardus (disguised as a Pole, Leonard von Krczinski). She convinces herself that he is Leonard, *not* the Medardus who has killed Hermogenes. She concludes the account in her letter with the knowledge that she is to be married to Leonard. 'Rosalia' has been, since the time she was painted by Francesco, the figure of one substitution after another, no more than a displacement of what each person wants, yet still binding figure to figure. The power of art is suggested, but at the same time, there is no single signified to the painting. Desire fastens onto it fetish-like, while it has the uncanny power of controlling thoughts. The uncertainty between whether the picture has a real power, or only focuses a divided subject's desire, is the text's diabolism, and uncanniness.

The text offers a parody of a progressive history, but it cannot move forward. Despite the appearance of things happening over five generations, and the bewildering idea of a great precision in these events, if they could only be grasped, they reduce to being no more than a series of repetitions which negate what would be offered in a realist narrative if the latter is premised as depending on the existence of discrete personalities. As the first Francesco set aside the authority of Leonardo da Vinci, so Medardus assumes the name Leonard. These are two unsuccessful attempts to overthrow the father, whose name uncannily returns in the son. While each subject in the Painter's text attempts to be himself or herself, they can only be that by a repetition of incest, followed by attempting to kill either the other, or another. Each subject finds it impossible to assert autonomy, without getting too close or too violent, with the other. Every attempt to come into identity necessitates crime (a Dostoevskian point), or the transgressiveness of a forbidden sexuality. And every attempt at exogamy, to break into a different relationship is negated; for instance when Count Filippo, bringing up Francesco II, unites himself to a poor woman, Francesco seduces her; or, when Angiola marries Prince Theodor, one of the sons of that union, Johann, is killed by Franz, his half-brother.

When Medardus himself reads the Painter's book, he recognises the sketches for the frescoes 'in the Holy Linden' (226) and is unsurprised:

> There was no enigma [*Rätsel*] in this book for me: I had known for a long time what it contained. This ... writing ... described all my dreams and my forebodings.... (226, 212)

Medardus' reaction resembles the editor's, already quoted from the beginning of the book. It is questionable whether Medardus can read the Painter's text, whether he realises that Victor is the brother, not his 'double', though these concepts may uncannily relate, like Shakespearian twins, and whether he can see what the 'thread' running through the characters' lives is. He remains ignorant of what has happened, which is the basis of irony, for he does not know why he does what he does. Staying at the Baron's, he makes incestuous love to Euphemia, who thinks he is Victor, and attempts to seduce the second Aurelia. Double in himself, and Victor's double, he splits his desires between the two women. After that, with the deaths of Euphemia and Hermogenes, both at his hands, he finds himself as Leonard, engaged to Aurelia, at the Prince's. He says Aurelia keeps him from evil thoughts. But before the marriage, he dreams of his mother, whose tears form a protective halo around him, until they are ripped apart by 'a horrible black hand' (204, 191). She asks if he can no longer resist the temptations of Satan, presumably in marrying Aurelia. She says that she has died, but then, that she will deck him with flowers and ribbons, as it is St Bernard's Day, associated with his innocence at the monastery (16, 13). About to sing Bernard's praises, as in his youth, a roar turns the hymn into a howl, drawing black veils between him and the mother, the interdicted love object. The relationship with her is newly sexualised and forbidden, as if she was paralleled by Aurelia, making love to Aurelia quasi-incestuous. There seems no other way than this destructive incestuous mode, the driving force in history.

He then hears that when Victor, thought to be Medardus, heard of Medardus' mother's death, he named his real mother, Giacinta. The mother is double: the 'pure' woman who married Franz and bore Medardus, *and* Giacinta, who bore Victor to Franz. These mothers embody a male projection: the woman as pure, and as sexual. They conduce to equal madnesses: (a) desexualised manhood in the monastery (b) anarchic violence associated with Victor. The next moment Medardus sees Victor about to be hanged for Hermogenes' murder: 'the monk was disfigured by a deathly pallor and an unkempt beard, but the features of my gruesome double [*Doppeltgänger*] were only too plain' (206, 193). If he could have seen that Victor was *not* that impossible thing, the double, but his brother (Victor cannot see it from his reverse position either), that might have ended his madness, his inability to read his situation. He cannot. He stays with the idea of the double, which is his narcissism and belief in the omnipotence of thoughts. Aurelia, seeing Victor, turns to Medardus as Leonard, but he replies in a mad fury as the 'Medardus' about to be hanged, and attempts to stab her, with the sense, expressed in saying he is 'King', of triumphing over his double. But he only acts out the desire of the double that he has not, in fact, got.

Medardus is rescued by the mad and carnivalesque clown Schönfeld, a premodern figure from Foucault's *Histoire de la folie*, who calls himself 'Folly that is always pursuing you in order to assist your power of reason' (213, 199). Only folly will save Medardus, for his reason cannot sustain itself: 'clowning is a protection against madness' (215, 201), an apotropaic, as it is in *Princess Brambilla*. Its folly opposes the reason which believes that a situation can be 'read' completely by the centred subject (who is the only subject who can have a double: if there is no belief in single identity, there cannot be a double). The rationalist desire to know is delusional, declared so by Schönfeld in a passage Freud quotes (217–218, 203, *SE* 17.234). Schönfeld prefers the madness of acting, which, doubling identities, escapes them. His acting in the carnivalesque puppetry, like that in *Princess Brambilla*, is a source of health, opposed by the church (250, 235). He adds that Medardus does not need direction, which assumes a single goal. Medardus sees 'two goals' (218, 204), not knowing which is the right one. The argument assumes, implicitly, that the desire to singularise the self and to have one goal is self-simplifying madness; productive of the diabolical double, or necessitating the doubling that folly gives, as a saving supplement.

Hence, towards the end, Medardus is persuaded against his instincts to let Aurelia become a nun, enforcing on her one identity, seeing her choice as a sacrifice, as an act of violence, like St Rosalia being sacrificed; while wanting both to possess and destroy her, like Victor, whose identity he acts out. Victor has told Leonardus – whom he called St Anthony, saying that the elixirs come from him – thus rooting diabolism in the unconscious of the very father figure who works to save people – that when he searched his heart: 'my secret [*heimlichsten*] thoughts were emerging in human shape as horrible forms of my own self' (274, 258). Having fantasised this 'second self' embodying his secret thoughts, Victor describes how it appeared to throw him into the abyss: double and death drive acting together.

Leonardus' mistake is to think that Victor has died, and that Medardus could be a single, repentant subject, free of any doubling figure. When the ceremony for Aurelia happens, Medardus thinks that she must share his same unconscious impure thoughts (like the Abbess, the half-sister of the father Franz, who must have had incestuous thoughts towards Franz, and him). No illusion of single identity can be sustained. All identities incestuously double others, as all thoughts prove double, in a universal infection. As the vow is pronounced, and Aurelia's hair is cut, in an ecclesiastical attack on eroticism, Victor appears, as the '*Doppeltgänger*' (282, 264). He stabs Aurelia, acting out Medardus' – and the church's – repressed desire, repeating Medardus' stabbing of Aurelia at the wedding. Elizabeth Wright (1978: 170) shows the irony in the fact that when this interruption happens, Medardus is enabled to not accept 'these impulses as springing from his own nature', because he has projected them onto another. Though Wright does not note the church's equal aggressiveness here, it is true that Medardus has been unable to read the Painter's semi-rational account, which would have declared Victor his brother. But negatively, had he been able, that would, confirming Wright's point, have allowed him the fiction of seeing the other, the half-brother, as other, not as expressing his own split subjectivity. Knowing that Victor is a separate being from himself would not allow awareness of his own dualism. He remains unaware of this, which makes ironic Leonardus' demand that Medardus write his autobiography: Medardus cannot know his own life. The text closes with Father Spiridion noting Peter Schönfeld, now a lay brother in the monastery, and his laughter. Leonardus says: 'the irony of fate had turned Peter into a buffoon, and [. . .] through his constant buffoonery, he had lost his reason' (291, 275).

4 Nihilism

> Der Nihilismus steht vor der Thür: woher kommt uns dieser unheimlichste Gäste? (Nietzsche 1999: Vol. 12.125)
>
> [Nihilism stands at the door: whence comes this uncanniest of guests?]

Every diabolical confrontation repeats Nietzsche's question. When Robert Wringhim sees the 'other' approaching, whom he thinks must be Peter the Great, diabolical builder of St Petersburg, he sees Gil-Martin. As the devil within Calvinism's nihilism, its diabolism shown in how it 'sends ane to heaven and ten to hell', as Burns' 'Holy Willie's Prayer' says, he is nihilistic, encompassing both brothers' deaths. In Freud, the double annihilates the identity of the subject; in *The Devil's Elixirs*, belief in the effectivity of any action is dissipated by the sense that the other has worked over and destroyed, the subject's autonomy. The figures of the devil, nihilism, and of the double overlay each other.

For Nietzsche, nihilism is an historical phenomenon. His words of 1885 – misleadingly gathered, as if in a unity, in *The Will to Power*, a tendentiously unreliable text assembled from Nietzsche's *Nachlass* by his sister, who wanted to give a sense of Nietzsche as a philosopher of the Right – suggest something uncanny indeed. The words 'guest' and 'host' being etymologically identical, the question who is within and who without becomes unresolvable. The double indicates a failure in modernity's dream of the self as a single autonomous subject. This 'guest', as double, shows that what awaits is repetition, which undoes the idea of a forwards progressive movement away from the past. The self doubles itself, seeing itself as an object; the self as both subject and its own object, having no sense of an 'other' to itself.

For Heidegger, the 'death of God' spoken of in *Thus Spoke Zarathustra* (Nietzsche 2005: 11) means that 'the highest values devaluate themselves' (Heidegger 1977: 66, quoting *The Will to Power*). In compensation, the self becomes 'self-assertive', promoting itself as its highest value. In 'self-assertion', modern man posits 'the world as the whole of producible objects'. No more and in all his relations to all that is, and thus in his relation to himself as well, he rises up as the producer who puts through, who carries out, his own self. The world and everything in it must reflect, narcissistically, the self that thinks that everything is a producible object (Heidegger 1971: 108–109). The human, wherever it looks, finds its double everywhere, itself the sole source of value, a clue to what produces ennui. The 'other' becomes the object which exists as a source of production for the subject's benefit, and an object of exchange, enframed, and brought into representation (Heidegger 1971: 124). Hoffmann, whose art, and comedy, have nothing to do with realistic representation, is the exception; like Hogg, who stands outside the Edinburgh set which thinks it can master the narrative of the poor devil Wringhim. Objectification, treating everything as a 'resource' for use and for economic 'growth' is not usually considered as nihilistic, since this is more frequently defined as the anarchistic destructiveness of 'Western' consensual values. The devil, the uncanniest of guests, appears as that nihilism which is found when the self lacks an outside, or other: the double looks at the self, though the mirror-gaze is also deceptive.

Heidegger quotes Nietzsche's *The Gay Science*, 'The Madman', section 125: where the madman draws the following conclusion from 'God is dead': 'are we not straying as through an infinite nothing?' Nihilism works to negate the belief that there can be a set of meanings which can be known and brought into representation. It invites the thought that there may be 'no thing', it challenges the idea that the objective world may be considered as consisting of things, as representable entities; that we know what the world is, scientifically, technologically. Heidegger calls such belief in abiding entities 'metaphysics', and he opposes it. To the question 'what is a thing?' comes the response that there are no *things*, that the world cannot be divided on Augustine's lines into 'things' and what is 'nothing'; what is no thing is real; and what is classed as the real thing is part of a logocentric thinking that wants to establish objective reality. Here, in response to that, nihilism knocks on the door. The history that produces this is not recognisable in terms of the discipline of history founded, non-coincidentally, at the same time as Hoffmann's writings, and in his Berlin. Since 'it belongs to the uncanniness of this uncanny guest that it cannot name its own origin', nihilism cannot be explained as part of a history of ideas, with an origin which would explain it (Heidegger 1977: 59–63). If nihilism was explicable, that would end it and whatever it has to offer as a challenge, or provocation. Like the devil, nihilism has no history, which must be a history of things, their development, their progress, their further conceptualisation. Its shadowing that history which it negates is its uncanniness. We cannot talk about origins. And these negations are also an *opportunity*; that ambiguity within the double, and within nihilism, is also part of the devil as the uncanny, and is essential to those texts to be discussed in the following chapters, starting with Goethe, to whom these comments are a prelude.

Notes

1. He continues: 'Frequent and loud laughter is the characteristic of folly and ill-manners; it is the manner in which the mob express their silly joy at silly things; and they call it being merry. In my mind there is nothing so illiberal, and so ill-bred, as audible laughter. I am neither of a melancholy nor a cynical disposition, and am as willing and as apt to be pleased as anybody; but I am sure that since I have had the full use of my reason nobody has ever heard me laugh.' – letter of 9 March 1748 (Chesterfield 1992: 72).
2. His influence ought also to be traced on Offenbach's *Contes de Hoffmann*, which responds to Hoffmann's love of *Don Giovanni* (the trickster of Seville, the diabolical lover). The Powell/Pressburger film *Tales of Hoffmann* (1951) shows acute awareness of Freud's discussion of Hoffmann's story 'The Sandman': the 'uncanny' (*das Unheimliche*) arises from uncertainty about what is living and is automatic, or 'mere' puppetry

and suggests a highly sophisticated diabolism which also works through music as feminine seduction (*SE* 17.233; Tambling 2005b: 22–37).

3. See my previous discussion of this as confessional narrative (Tambling 1990: 122–133). Hogg may have been influenced by Hoffmann: see Garside 2006: xlvii-l.
4. Robertson's note to these German painters implies that Reinhold may evoke the religious painter Peter von Cornelius (1784–1867), one of a group in Rome reviving religious art as the 'Nazarene movement' (Hoffmann 1992: 405).
5. Throughout this discussion, I give two page-references; the first to the German (1969), the second, to the translation by Ronald Taylor (2008): here: Hoffmann 1969: 46; 2008: 42. Further citations are given simply by the two page-references.

Chapter 6: Goethe: *Faust* and Modernity

Faust, which Goethe worked on for over sixty years, was always work in progress. It was begun early, and not completed until just before his death in 1832. Born into a professional and Pietist family in Frankfurt in 1749, the six-year old Goethe was disturbed by the Lisbon earthquake which he says, in *Poetry and Truth*, 'clouded his vision of God' (Boyle 1991: 69). He studied law, first at Leipzig, then at Strasbourg, where he met Herder, the great German literary nationalist, and he felt he had deserted a woman, Friederike von Brion, by returning to Frankfurt. There, on 14 January 1772, he witnessed the public beheading of a servant, Susannah Brandt, for the murder of her child. She, and the previous relationship with Friederike, seem to incite work on *Faust*, alongside two other notable events: first, in Wetzlar in 1772, a disappointment in love with Charlotte Buff, who was engaged to Johann Kestner; and second, the suicide of Carl Wilhelm Jerusalem, a contemporary known to him since Leipzig. Jerusalem killed himself for love in circumstances which Goethe's epistolary novel *The Sorrows of Young Werther* (1774) adopted from Kestner's account (Boyle 1991: 131–136, 168–169; Goethe 2013: 102–194).

Barker Fairley (1953: 50–60), who in the years after 1945 was banned from entering the USA to lecture on *Faust*, argues that *Werther* informs the tragedy of Faust and Margarete, which runs from Scenes 10 to 28 of Part One. This section was written then; Faust is damnable on account of his seduction of Margarete ('Gretchen'), but at the end, is rejected by her and vanishes with Mephistopheles (Boyle 1987: 12–15). The manuscript

J. Tambling, *Histories of the Devil*,
DOI 10.1057/978-1-137-51832-3_7

of those years, called the *Urfaust*, was worked on till Goethe moved to Weimar in 1775 at the invitation of Duke Karl August, to become, effectively, his prime minister: it was only found in 1887. The overlap between *Werther* and the 'Margarete' section suggests that there is something diabolical in the former; for example, in his (Werther's) 'smiling' attack on Albert, whom Lotte marries, he being a rationalist, despising passion, drunkenness, and madness (Goethe 2013: 35). I will return to this letter of 12 August 1770 both later, and in the next chapter. *Faust* was resumed eleven years later, on Goethe's Italian journey (1786–1788), and the result was *Faust: A Fragment* (1790). With Schiller's encouragement, he recommenced work on the text in 1797, splitting the existing material into two; *Faust Eine Tragödie* (i.e. Part One) appeared in 1808. Influenced by Byron's death (1824) and by the persuasions of Eckermann, Part Two then took shape, appearing posthumously in 1832. Unlike Part One, which is structured in 'scenes', it divides as a tragedy into acts; the third, the Helen episode, appearing in 1827; Act One, to line 6306, in 1828. Like Byron with his own influence, Part One in the nineteenth century defined a demonic romanticism, which shows in such nineteenth-century forms as Delacroix's Satan; or Satan as an urban dandy in Baudelaire's prose-poem 'Le Joueur Généroux' (The Generous Gambler). Musically, the *Faust* theme prompted Schubert, Spohr, Schumann, Berlioz, Liszt, Gounod, Boito, and Busoni, all premonitions, for Thomas Mann, that Faust must be a musician. Goethe's material was not taken from Marlowe, whose *Doctor Faustus* was only translated in 1818; but rather from chapbooks which adapted Spiess' *Faustbuch* – he may not have known Spiess – and popular puppet-plays, which made it a popular choice. Part One, for instance, was written mainly in a doggerel-like verse form, *Knittelvers*, derived from the sixteenth century.

The impact of the text has been huge, and its impact will spread over the next two chapters as much as I attempt to convey something of its afterlife in this chapter. Yet despite its afterlife, *Faust* seems anything but popular or easy now. Any account of it must work against its apparent remoteness, and commentary can only hope to get its difficulties right: not the least of these are the extraordinary evidences of Goethe's reading for it. In this chapter, then, I will begin with Part One; then break off for two 'intermezzi', which look at the text's legacy, first in George Eliot, then in Klaus Mann's satirical novel *Mephisto* (1936). I will then turn to the yet more difficult Part Two, and to discussion of the 'modernity' in the plays.[1]

1 Part One: Mephisto and Negation

Before meeting Faust, Part One gives three openings; the first (1797) a 'Dedication' (*Zueignung*), an ode to spirit-figures, i.e. people known to Goethe from the 1770s onwards, and from his earlier versions of *Faust*; these spirits approach as he writes. The opening stanzas address them in terms of their potential to overwhelm and hold him. He might not have been able to possess them, but now they take possession of him. In the third, he compares those who heard his work before with the public who hears it now, which public he wants. In the fourth he notes the spirits' animating power while the present recedes. This power of the imagination recalls *A Midsummer Night's Dream*, and the conversation between Theseus and Hippolyta which opens Act Five. We are already, implicitly in the theatre, which a spirit-realm inhabits, before the second Prologue, the 'Prelude in the Theatre', where the Director, the resident Poet, and the Clown (the Hanswurst, the Harlequin), converse on the play they must write and perform; a work of the future. God may be the Director, wanting to stage a new play for Germany, a complete 'theatre of the world', as in *The Castle of Perseverance*. But in this theatrical world, what can be staged? And how can reality appear, as it does, in spirit form, unbidden, in the 'Dedication'? The Poet, as in the Dedication, creates in figures an ideal world haunted by ghosts; as a Goethe, or a Faust. He despises the requirements of moment; he thinks more about posterity. The clown, the devil, as always, lives in the present and knows that the truth can only be written or performed with 'a charming aimlessness' (209). There can be no will to truth; everything of performance must comprise errings, life itself being erring, labyrinthine, as the Dedication has said (14). The Director knows the performance must be effective, the Poet thinks it should tell the truth, the Clown that it must divert, so that truth is disguised. In this theatre/world, everything appears as other than it is, which is the condition of irony. No resolution between these can be reached, but the Manager calls for 'deeds at last' (215), for the play to be staged, as the medium of theatre is what reality is, as well as the way to show it. For life may be no more than allegorical personifications, but these must pass before the audience, as the spirits approach in the Dedication.

The Third Prelude, set in heaven, replays the Book of Job, in comic mode. Mephisto interrupts the Archangels' theodicy: man fits no sense of order which can be premised on the rhythms of continual ordered change. God points to Faust, a man who wants everything, and can never be satisfied. Mephisto asks to try him and God consents, giving the third statement about erring: 'Es irrt der Mensch, solang' er strebt' (317). Man must err, as long as he strives: 'striving' being a keyword for both plays. God is an eighteenth-century Enlightenment figure: for while erring, man still knows what is right, and God says he has no issues with the devil: of all the spirits that negate (*verneinen*), he does not mind the scoffer ('der Schalk', 339), because the devil causes the human to be active. And God leaves Mephistopheles – the only figure from these Preludes to appear in the tragedy, though he was perhaps also hovering in the Dedication, and was the Clown – reflecting on the old gentleman's civility in talking to the devil, whose ribaldry and comic undercutting of God's Enlightened system is how he performs his negations. Perhaps the Dedication is the Poet's work, the first Prologue the Director's, and the Clown is within the Prologue in Heaven. All qualify what is to come, and point to how the daemonic, and the diabolical appear, before reaching Faust and his bargain.

The first scene, the night before Easter, shows Faust, like Cornelius Agrippa. He was commented upon, as Job was, in the Prologue in Heaven, as the discontented scholar. He has worked his way through the university, but nothing he has done has made him feel he has reached the heart of life: examining the writings of Nostradamus, the French astrologer. He is fascinated. He sees the Sign of the Macrocosm which gives him an intuition of the perfect knowledge to which he strives, with a sense of being godlike (439). Yet he is only the baroque scholar, whose Gothic chamber announces melancholy contemplation, where study leaves him empty. His desire is for action (as throughout these plays). When another page shows the Sign of the Earth Spirit he evokes him (or her: either gender is possible). This Spirit appears but is beyond Faust, representing ceaseless activity: 'ein ewiges Meer, / Ein wechselnd Weben,/Ein glühend Leben' (505–507): a single eternal sea (perhaps a feminine image), a single changing web, a single glowing life, which is the outward expression of God, expressed through time. Such spontaneous, unreflective activity is un-Faustian, and the Spirit vanishes, pronouncing Faust to be like the spirit he can comprehend, not like the Earth Spirit.

Is this a version of Lucifer, with the 'other spirit' as Mephisto? – as when, later, invoking the Earth Spirit, Faust calls Mephisto the negative companion whom he cannot do without (3241–3246)? If so, the text does not distinguish between different forms of magic: Mephisto is not simply to be considered in Christian terms. The devil and hell may be manifestations of the 'productive urge of the deity' (Samuel 1968: xxvi; Mason 1967: 110–178), the living garments in which God is visible.

Faust's parody is Wagner, the scholar, the servant, and the pedant. In the second scene Faust says that two souls are within him ('Zwei Seelen wohnen, ach! in meiner Brust', 1112). In a perception of disunity, he sees himself as double. One soul would separate itself from the other. One in coarse desire for love holds to the world with all its clutching organs ('klammernden Organen', 1115); the other violently elevates itself from the fog ('Duft') towards higher expectations ('Ahnen'). He hopes for one of the spirits in the air who weave and govern between heaven and earth to descend from the golden-scented heights, and lead him away to a new, colourful life (1121): dimly intuiting Gretchen, and Helen of Troy. And then, he notes that a black dog is running round him. Thinking of the double self gives occasion for the devil's emergence. The dog, associated with Cornelius Agrippa (Nauret 1965: 327), follows him into his study: agitating him, like the devil, as he attempts to translate 'In the beginning was the Word' by 'Im Anfang war die Tat' (1237): 'in the beginning was the deed'; so giving precedence to ceaseless action over the word, or language; and to agitation over contemplativeness, and to what Mephisto, who now appears, as 'des Pudels Kern' – the essence of the poodle (1323) – dressed as the scholar, calls appearance and illusion (1329).

Mephisto fulfils what God had said of him in the Prelude (line 338):

> Ich bin der Geist, der stets verneint!
> Und das mit Recht; den alles, was ensteht,
> Ist wert, dass es zugrunde geht;
> Drum besser wär's, dass nichts enstünde.
> (1338–1341)

(I am the spirit that always negates! And that is right, for everything that stands, is worthy to perish, and it would be better that nothing took its place.)

He never names himself. Faust calls him 'Mephisto' (4183). Mephistopheles, the full name, never appears, the name being only a fragment, as Mephisto insists he is only a part (1335) (White 1980: 95–110). Part Two calls him, in English, the 'old Iniquity' (7123) of the old English Moralities (the *Bühnenspiel*) which were discussed in Chapter 2. He is also named Satan (2504, 6950), the second time in a context which implies that the biblical Lucifer, who made his throne in the north, did so because Germany, and Britain, and Nordic countries generally, are those which generate the devil.

That everything deserves to pass away, Nietzsche's Zarathustra virtually quotes as a nihilism which is inherent in Christianity as a paradigm of all religions: and which, as a message of 'madness', man must be redeemed from: that 'everything passes away, therefore everything deserves to pass away' (Nietzsche 2005: 122). Such 'madness', as Zarathustra calls it, comes out of an angry sense of melancholia which cannot bear the impermanence of things; that everything must become 'it was'. The subject lacks control over time, which eventually makes everything into 'it was': hence the spirit of revenge, as 'ill-will' towards 'time and its "it was"', is the ultimate reactive drive: angry sadness at being unable to retain autonomous identity. Brooding on the sense that everything is passing entails an unconscious thought: if nothing can remain, no existence can be justified. If things pass away, they do not deserve to stay, they must have an inherent guilt which makes their passing-away deserved: they must pay the debt (*Schuld*: guilt *and* debt).

Mephisto anticipates Zarathustra's diagnosis that everything may, or should be, negated. The state that Zarathustra thinks mankind must be 'redeemed' from. He adds that he is a part of the power which 'die stets das Böse will und stets das Gute schafft' (1356): which always wills evil but always shapes good. He is part of the part which 'der anfangs alles war' (in the beginning was everything, 1349), the dark of the primeval chaos (1384) which gave birth to the light. Light derives from that darkness: the name 'Helen', so essential to this play, implies light: she is 'the bright one'. Proud Light contends with 'Mutter Nacht' (1351), a phrase associated with Mephisto and his parentage (8811). Night precedes, as the mother, but Light, the upstart son, contests her old status:

> Und doch gelingt's ihm nicht, das es, so viel es strebt,
> Verhaftet an den Körpern klebt.
> Von Körpern strömt's, die Körper macht es schön,
> Ein Körper hemmt's auf seinem Gange,
> So, hoff' ich, dauert es nicht lange,
> Und mit den Körpern wird's zugrunde gehen.
> (1353–1358)

(and it just cannot manage it, for, no matter how hard light strives it remains attached to bodies. It streams out of bodies, it makes bodies beautiful, a body blocks it in its motion, so I hope it will not take long before it will go into destruction with bodies.)

Light depends upon dark material bodies, which it beautifies, and which beautify light, creating colours (the point is developed in Part Two). Bodies also stop the light. Within Mephisto's words lies hatred of the dark human body as material; but these bodies will inevitably go into destruction: and so, he hopes, will light. That pathway suits this spirit whose sphere, he has announced, is that of ruin, and ruining (1349–1358). If bodies, which bring light into colour, could be eliminated, there would be no light. Mephisto would return everything to night, just as Faust, Hamlet-like, contemplated in the first scene how 'not to be' through suicide. Mephisto knows, however, that he cannot achieve nothingness: because of sex, there will always be new blood, new bodies, circulating (1372). Sex raises his contempt, as the 'kalte Teufelsfaust' (1381): the cold devil's fist/Faust. At that, Eckermann's question to Goethe becomes relevant: does not Mephistopheles have daemonic traits? Goethe says no, 'Mephistopheles is much too negative a being. The Demonic manifests itself in a thoroughly active power' (Eckermann 1970: 392). Perhaps, recalling the discussion of the daemonic in the Introduction, it could be said that Mephisto is not daemonic enough. He is overly associated with the conventional and Christian thought which produces nihilism, and which *Faust* critiques throughout. Mephisto cannot quite answer to the devil, or Faust needs something more diabolical.

Mephisto disappears, leaving Faust to fear that he was indeed nothing objective: but in the next scene, he knocks at the door – the uncanniest of guests (1530) – and encounters Faust's own nihilism, which contrasts with Marlovian aspirationalism, unless this is to be taken as also nihilistic. For Faust, nothing proves itself worth itself; and his character of impatient driving on (1606) means that, as the chorus of spirits says, he destroys the world 'mit mächtiger Faust' (with a powerful fist, 1610) as the 'halbgott' (half-god, 1612) he is. One form of nihilism, determined to master everything in its 'striving' (1676), and thus to empty it of sense, meets another. Hence Mephisto offers him a pact which Faust alters from the traditional conditions: Faust will be his if Mephisto can ever get him to settle down, if he will ever say to the moment (*zum Augenblicke*): 'Verweile doch! Du bist so schon' (stay here, you are so beautiful, 1699–1700). At that moment, Faust will assent to go to hell. That bargain Mephisto accepts, making his task to make everything be so irresistible that Faust will cease from restless striving. Two bargains have now been struck: God's with

Mephisto, and Mephisto's with Faust, linking the concepts of Job and of Faust. God is, virtually, heard of no more. Faust makes his pact, of which more in the fifth section, and the two fly off to see the world.

2 Margarete

The scene in Auerbach's cellar in Leipzig, where Goethe had studied, has an autobiographical sense: Goethe's friend E.W. Behrisch (1738–1809), tutor to Count Lindenau of Dresden, seems a partial portrait of Mephisto (Boyle 1992: 66–67). Here Faust is virtually silent, disengaged. In the Witches' Kitchen, he is rejuvenated by thirty years, and catches in a mirror, as if presented with an aesthetic object, an ideal glimpse of a woman: perhaps Eve, or Margarete (2429). Mephisto's cynicism says that with a love potion in him Faust will soon see Helen in every woman, so intimating the presence of Helen in Part Two. He not only quotes the rational Theseus in *A Midsummer Night's Dream* (5.1.10–11), but indicates how women threaten his pact. From line 3605, Part One becomes the tragedy of Margarete, eighteenth-century seduction drama, using Rowe's *The Fair Penitent* (1703), where Calista's seducer, Lothario, is Faustian. There are echoes of seductions from Richardson's *Pamela* and *Clarissa*, and, classically, Goldsmith's *The Vicar of Wakefield*. Margarete receives the emphasis, more than Faust, and Mephisto, whom she detests, is seen as more blameable than Faust, who also blames Mephisto. The latter must ask who ruined her, 'Ich oder du?' (Goethe 2005: 138).

Margarete first appears in the street (line 2605). Her collapse is announced in the Cathedral ('Dom': 3776–3854): an almost operatic scene where the 'Böser Geist' – the Evil Spirit, the voice of conventional religion, which will condemn Margarete, and which Goethe had witnessed in the execution in Frankfurt – says she will never more be 'unguilty' ('Unschuld', 3777). That episode brings to a climax many scenes commented on in her soliloquies (Simpson 1998: 36). A series of lyrical monologues show her as a woman in love: she becomes Desdemona-like as she undresses for bed, singing 'There was a King in Thule' (2759), Goethe's poem, not an actual folk song. In this lyric, the golden cup given (by the dying woman, with echoes of the eroticism of the Song of Songs, 7:2) is the token of life, and the motif of drinking, which combines with tears flowing (2765, 2766), recurs continually. The old drinker (Zecher) drinks the last 'Lebensglut' (life-glow – wine as Dionysian) before throwing the holy cup into the water, which the cup drinks before the water drinks it, and his eyes overflow again. The cup as the gift is outside the restricted economy by which he gives away towns which he possesses to his followers: drinking from it produces an excess (the tears) in himself. It can only be given back to that which has no economic or utilitarian function: i.e. to 'die Flut': the flood. Tears, too, are outside any economic sense: the poem praises coming into subjectivity under the power of the gift, which may be maternal, and which then yields itself up (Wellbery 1996: 233–246). In the gestures of his eyes sinking too, and him not drinking again, repetitions of the images of the cup, the eyes, drinking, water, and sinking, create a logic which values the Dionysian ability to throw away what has been enjoyed at the highest, though that in itself is marked by loss: the cup, as symbol, speaks of something missing. The cup as excess and memory together, outside law (the woman is not a wife) contrasts with how Margarete is being bribed with jewels in that same scene. Woman's excess, in contrast, reflected in tearing the daisies (marguerites) (3177) – the woman giving herself however self-destructively – makes Faust say three times, in the 'Wald und Höhle' scene, that the Earth Spirit, as life, has 'given' something to him (3217, 3220). Goethe, as well as Nietzsche, would have said that 'life is a woman'.

The scene which follows 'Wald und Höhle', 'Gretchen's Room', contrasts her spinning and her spoken soliloquy of desire ('Meine Ruh' kist hin' (3374)) about 'him', so leaving open the question of the addressee, thinking of everything that is 'his' (repeated eight times). Spinning and this poem share a cyclical motion. The poem begins with a refrain, repeated three times, and the scene ends before the fourth refrain can appear. The woman's state is internally split (3384–3385), while, in the last two stanzas, Margarete, or her desire, takes the initiative, again in the language of the Song of Songs. In the following scene, 'Martha's Garden', Faust defers answering a question about God with 'Gefühl ist alles' (feeling is everything, 3456), and saying, in the distrust of language noted before:

> Name ist Schall und Rauch,
> Umnebelnd Himmelsglut.
> (3457–3457)

(Naming is noise and smoke, surrounding heaven's glow [the sun] with cloud.)

Margarete says she has felt that, too. To the question whether Goethe thought of Margarete being seduced before 'Wald und Höhle' (so the 'Fragment'), or after 'Martha's Garden', the ambiguity, or impossibility of an answer may be relevant, destabilising the belief that there can be an original virginity. The point is she gives herself, but is let down by him, and by the conventionality which assumes that what a fallen woman is may be knowable: it runs on in the next four scenes, including her guilt before the Mater Dolorosa. She has poisoned her mother, and, in a duel, set up by Mephisto, arranged like Mercutio's death, she loses her brother, Valentin: a jealous Laertes, his name deriving from one of Ophelia's bawdy folksongs.

At this point, Mephisto and Faust ascend the Harz Mountains, on Walpurgis Night (30 April), the witch-festival with Mephisto attempting to divert him sensually from the implications of his relationship with Margarete. Here are glimpses of women whose sexuality is not in doubt: Baubo, the very portrayal of the obscene; Lilith, Adam's first wife, her name translated as the 'screech owl' in *Isaiah* 34:14; the pregnant Gretchen glimpsed during dances with witches. Mephisto shows Faust a real theatre, where an 'intermezzo' is performed: this is the 'Walpurgisnachtstraum, oder Oberons und Titanias Goldne Hochzeit' (4223–4398). This comic interlude continues fascination with women's sexuality, combining this with fascination for the theatre, opening with a reference to Mieding, stage manager of the Weimar theatre Goethe worked with (4224). It fuses dramatic figures: Ariel from *The Tempest* with the spirits of *A Midsummer Night's Dream* – but Oberon, whose reputation in Germany derived from Shakespeare and Wieland's romance *Oberon* (1780) – is, 'like the gods of Ancient Greece . . . a devil without a doubt' (4273–4274), according to the various travellers and pedants, like the 'Dogmatiker' who forms the audience and thinks he can pronounce on devils. Yet the interlude affirms otherwise: life, and devils, and fairies, as a dream, and the theatre as the place to show what these things mean.

The next two scenes are 'Trüber Tag: Feld' where Mephisto's nihilism says that Margarete is not the first to fall victim to seduction and condemnation, and 'Nacht: Open Feld' where Faust and Mephisto pass the place – the Rabenstein, the 'raven's rock', with echoes of the raven in *Macbeth* 1.5.38, and *Hamlet* 3.2.248 as the bird of death, of revenge, and of misfortune – where Gretchen will be executed. Witches are present, so that the tragedy is combined with the sense of something more primitive, associated with female sexuality and avenging mothers. The culmination is the prison, where Margarete, condemned to decapitation, sings offstage (as if with the power of an echo). Throughout, she has been marked by *Volkslieder*, showing the influence of Percy's *Reliques*, Herder, and Alsatian folk songs Goethe had heard (Willoughby 1943). Her present ballad derives from and expands on a *Volksmärchen* which the Grimm brothers collected as 'Von dem Machandelboom' ('The Juniper Tree', 1812, Grimm 1948: 220–229). This tale's relevance appears in how a little boy is beheaded through the stepmother's agency, as influenced by the devil. It dwells on the significance of red, which as blood and as the juniper-tree berries runs through everything, even, in a Macbeth-like moment (4511–4519) relating to Gretchen and Faust, as though he has blood on his hands. When Gretchen speaks as though she was Medea accusing Jason, Goethe shows that he has turned this episode of child-murder into something else: a play of 'Atreus-like infanticide' (Atkins 1958: 97), whose depth contrasts with the 'Greek tragedy' – an abstract exercise, removed from life – that Wagner supposed his master was reading (523). Goethe rejects the classical rules for drama in *Faust*, and produces this lyric instead:

> Meine Mutter, die Hur,
> Die mich umgebracht hat!
> Mein Vater, der Schelm,
> Der mich gessen hat!
> Mein Schwesterlein klein
> Hub auf die Bein'
> An einem kühlen Ort;
> Da ward ich ein schönes Waldvögelein;
> Fliege fort, fliege fort!
>
> (4412–4420)

(My mother, the whore, she murdered me! My father, the villain, he ate me! My little sister gathered my bones in a cool place. Then I was a pretty bird of the woods. Fly away, fly away!)

These first two lines, heard not seen, accuse Margarete's mother, whose mean Puritanism was noted earlier (3084–3135). Margarete identifies with the boy the mother has killed. Her second two lines implicitly accuse Faust as a figure of the patriarchy. Equally, the dead child accuses mother and father both. Behind the 'sister' stands Margarete's own sister whom she, not her mother, brought up, and who died. As Margarete, thinking of herself as having been killed and eaten, she accuses, in her own right, figures of the past. The boy-become-bird who takes divine revenge, and is resurrected at the end, supplements his song with Margarete's accusations: 'die Hur' and 'der Schelm'. The juniper tree – the place for bones, reappears in Eliot's *Ash-Wednesday*; as in I Kings 19:4, it is made the place for Lenten despair.

Margarete sees herself as the object of songs, and of tales (4448–4449); victim of the 'Avenger' as Mephisto called the forces of law in 'Trüber Tag: Feld' (line 18), victim too of the mother's stone-like power (4566–4571), where the mother also symbolises the church. These, having the negativity of revenge, seem devilish forms, but the play ends combining three voices: Margarete's, Mephisto's nihilistic one 'Sie ist gerichtet' (she is judged – the voice of law), and another, either from Heaven, or the Poet's from the 'Prelude in the Theatre' saying 'Ist gerettet' (she is saved). Theatrical art, or god, corrects Mephisto and the Avenger's word by a subtle changing of letters, marking *différance*. Yet there seems evidence that Goethe supported the execution of Johanna Höhn for infanticide in 1787 (Wilson 2008: 7–32), which increases the ambiguities, and marks yet another form of the demonic within him, and his text.

3 Intermezzo: George Eliot

George Eliot (the pen name of Mary Ann Evans, 1819–1880), following Thomas Carlyle, one of his translators, and G.H. Lewes, who was her partner and wrote the *Life of Goethe* (1855), responded keenly to *Faust* Part One (Röder-Bolton 1998). A first imaginative reaction in *Adam Bede* (1859) concentrates on Arthur Donnithorne, the young squire who sings 'When the heart of man is oppressed by care' from *The Beggar's Opera* (Eliot 1985: 123), a favourite song for the eighteenth-century seducer, which he essentially is. He meets Hetty Sorel, willingly and unwillingly at once, the wood where he encounters her being 'surely... haunted by his evil genius' (137 – cp. lines 3540–3541). Like Margarete, Hetty Sorel kills their baby, and is only just saved from the gallows. Donnithorne cannot, will not, see sufficiently outside his class and situation to think of marrying Hetty, and the text passes a judgment on him for his self-deceptions, noting, in describing his failure, 'our deeds determine us, as much as we determine our deed' (315). Perhaps there is something of 'Im Anfang war die Tat' (*Faust* 1237) in this. The deed precedes everything, as Faust decides. It happens in a way which cannot be prepared for logically (not by 'das Wort', 1224), nor in terms of human understanding ('der Sinn', 1229), and it also happens without pre-knowledge of what power ('die Kraft', 1234) is available. This fascinates Faust, but George Eliot deliberates more on the daimon which predisposes the subject to one deed or another.

Hetty Sorel – and even more Margarete – responds to the letter Werther writes on 12 April 1770, which was mentioned above. The letter is the report of Werther clashing with Albert's rationalism, and defending suicide with reference to the death of a girl who was seduced and abandoned, and found drowned: 'Nature finds no way out of the maze of these tangled and conflicting forces, and the man or woman must die' (Goethe 2013: 37). The woman's tragedy, as a rebellion against a rationalist force of law she cannot resist, anticipates Werther's suicide, and gives that a political dimension. Something of this survives into *Daniel Deronda* (1876), which has as one emphasis a study of Gwendolen Harleth's motivations: it follows fascinatedly her disastrous marriage (Tambling 2012a: 158–170).

Daniel Deronda's first paragraph considers Gwendolen gambling, and asks of 'her glance': 'Was the good or the evil genius dominant in those beams? Probably the latter ... ' (Eliot 1967: 35). Marlowe's Good Angel and Spirit are implicit here. Deronda, looking on, his thoughts being heard, and himself acting as an 'evil eye' (38) because he destroys her luck, thinks that roulette 'brought out something of the demon' in Gwendolen (408). Card-playing attempts to be Mephistophelean in its commitment to the deed. It follows Goethe's illustrator, Moritz Retzsch, in his painting *Die Schachspieler*. This, Eliot says, shows:

> destiny in the shape of Mephistopheles playing at chess with man for his soul, a game in which we may imagine the clever adversary making a feint of unintended moves so as to set the beguiled mortal on carrying his defensive pieces away from the true point of attack. The fiend makes *preparation* his favourite object of mockery that he may fatally persuade us against our best safeguard. (511, my emphasis)

Being prepared is all, and the other word for it is 'safeguard': it will be remembered that the daimon is a safeguard, a restraining force in Goethe. Gwendolen thinks she can best Grandcourt, and also avoid Lydia Glasher, Grandcourt's discarded mistress, and her warnings, but she finds she has no way out, after marrying Grandcourt, whose nihilism – if not diabolism – is signalled in his line 'Most things are bores' (171). She has lost to 'destiny', whose relationship with the 'daimon' of Goethe's 'Urworte – Orphisch' – is complex, and the murder – she has kept a stiletto by her – of Grandcourt on the boat, is her only way out. In the boat with Grandcourt Gwendolen 'was afraid of her own wishes, which were taking shapes possible and impossible, like a cloud of demon-faces' (745–746). What is the status of those demons, for Eliot? Gwendolen is Faust, Mephistopheles, and Margarete simultaneously, but she thinks that a sense of Deronda 'would save her from acting out the evil within'. The divided soul, however, has no defence:

> quick, quick, came images, plans of evil that would come again and seize her in the night like furies *preparing* the deed that they would straightway avenge. (746).

This echoes an earlier moment, when, knowing what Grandcourt is like, but anxious to avoid poverty, she is asked if she will receive him – which means accepting his proposal of marriage. She feels triumph and terror together:

> Quick, quick, like pictures in a book beaten open with a sense of hurry, came back vividly, yet in fragments, all that she had gone through in relation to Grandcourt – the allurements, the vacillation, the resolve to accede, the final repulsion; the incisive face of the dark-eyed lady [Lydia Glasher] with the lovely boy, her own pledge (was it a pledge not to marry him?) – the new disbelief in the worth of men and things for which that scene of disclosure had become a symbol.... Where was the good of choice coming again? What did she wish?.... (337)

Something demonic is at work in Gwendolen. Her daimon and *tyche* (chance) are in opposition, or working together: Eliot is fully aware of how gender inflects decision-making for a man and for a woman, and the passage shows something of a nihilism in Gwendolen – which has already shown itself in her gambling, which was her response to hearing about Grandcourt's past. Eliot does not imply that issues can be simplified into simple clear decisions. On the boat, when the 'plans of evil' return, what has been 'prepared' is a 'dead face and a fleeing figure' (91), a sight she has had in a picture, which, like a palimpsest working in her mind, remains as an unbearable 'dead face' (758) after the drowning.

It cannot be confirmed that she drowns Grandcourt: her confession to Deronda remains incomplete, virtually censored by him because he does not want to hear it. When he first saw her, at the gambling table, he had also seen Mirah, whom he marries. He cannot completely give himself to Gwendolen's case, and thereby causes her confession, in some of the most powerful writing in Victorian literature (56.754–762) to be necessarily edited as he distances himself (759). She accuses herself – 'I have been a cruel woman', then adds: 'I am sinking. Die – die – you are forsaken – go down, go down into darkness' (758), but this utterance cannot be identified with certainty as her response to her situation in the boat before Grandcourt goes overboard, nor to it afterwards. How to divide up, or punctuate that sentence? Grandcourt, too, must *also*, literally, say 'I am sinking'. And who forsakes whom? ('Forsaken' is strong religious language; as with Psalm 22:1: does it imply damnation?) Is this diabolical accusation? Deronda fails to understand the situation's full extent, and he does forsake her. As the concept of a first act is never more than a fiction, as Eliot declares (35), what a first act would be (who destroys whom – husband or wife?) cannot be articulated: yet Deronda convincing himself that 'her murderous thought had had no outward effect' (762), evades, like Goethe's Albert with Werther, a certain diabolism in Gwendolen, who is a Werther; while Deronda is a Charlotte who is also an Albert. This 'Albert' being more inwardly divided between two women cannot wish to hear everything; it is a patriarchy he also bears towards his mother.

4 Intermezzo: Mephisto, and Hannah Arendt

Goethe's *Faust* was staged in Nazi-dominated Berlin in 1932–1933, for the anniversary of Goethe's death. Mephisto was played by Gustav Gründgen (1889–1963). He, who had started as a Communist, and was married to Klaus Mann's sister Erika, until she divorced him in 1929, is portrayed as Hendrik (Gretchen's name for Faust) Höfgen in Klaus Mann's novel *Mephisto* (1936). A black-dressed 'tragic clown, a diabolical Pierrot' (152), he overtakes Faust as the central figure (Rubenstein 2015: 25–70). And God, too, for in the Prelude set in Heaven, God may appear to be an Enlightenment figure, unless, as *Mephisto* suggests in an alternative performance-based reading, his 'euphoric good nature' makes 'an almost simple-minded and senile impression' beside the 'terrible melancholy into which the once favourite angel, the accursed and the dweller in the abyss, fell from time to time, between his bouts of sinister vivacity' (152). Mann ironises Goethe, or draws out a textual possibility, which is increased when the Prime Minister (i.e. Göring) has above him only the Führer: 'like the Lord of heaven, with his archangels, so was the dictator surrounded by his paladins', including Goebbels, cast as a diabolic, 'the agile gnome with the profile of a bird of prey, the deformed prophet' (181–182).

Mephisto fictionalises Gründgens' rise to power and the 'pact with the devil' (the title of his chapter 7) he made by performing for the Nazis. It reads as a moral fable, showing the fate of the man who is throughout an actor, this being what Goethe's Mephisto is (as evidenced by his frequent identity changes). In contrast, Otto Ulrichs, another actor, his parallel, but never renouncing his Marxism, is destroyed by the Nazis. In this novel which has no literal devil, the Faust who sells his soul becomes, by that means, Mephistophelean. The action centres on Mephisto, not on Faust, save that the actor playing Mephisto is the Faust who so acts the devil's part that he wins over Göring, who, Klaus Mann says in his autobiography *Der Wendepunkt* (published posthumously in 1953) was himself infatuated by the stage and by acting: he even married an actress, Emmy Sonnemann. In this performance, the stage Faust is nowhere, but the devil and Faust are the actor and Göring: and which is which remains the undecidable question. Klaus Mann, who gives a close character portrait of Gründgens, virtually suggests that the diabolical performance, of speaking Goethe's lines 'Ich bin der Geist, der stets verneint / Und das mit Recht…' (*Faust* Part One, 1338–1339), quoted above, is a virtual sexual seduction of Göring (Mann 1983: 115–117, 281–282). Perhaps Gründgens' homosexuality was speaking there. At any rate, a 'pact' is made with the Prime Minister, on the basis of an agreement with the nihilism which the actor points up from the stage (153).

For Mann, belief that nothing matters motivated the Nazi. Göring responds to the performance by telling the actor that Mephisto is central:

> He really is splendid! And isn't there a little of him in us all? I mean, hidden in every real German isn't there a bit of Mephistopheles, a bit of the rascal and the ruffian? If we had nothing but the soul of Faust, what would become of us? It would be a push-over for our many enemies.… Mephisto is a German national hero. (Mann 1983: 188)

That is the challenge and boast: that the devil is especially German; a viewpoint which Klaus Mann's father, Thomas Mann, apparently agreed with (Rubenstein 2015: 100–105). In a lecture, 'Germany and the Germans' (1945), Thomas Mann expressed his dislike of Luther, for not having considered political liberty in his Reformation; but adding that neither had Goethe, who was therefore an unpolitical writer.[2] *Faust* had no message for the Nazis, but it was not a text they separated themselves from, hence it could be both produced, and commented on: the Nazi 'ethic of individual striving that culminates in a people's freedom and that trumps all other morals' (Pan 2011: 103), including religion and belief in sacrifice, associates with something in the text, and though not damaging it, contributes to its ambiguity.

Höfgen fails when playing Hamlet, where Ulrichs was supposed to play Guildenstern, but Ulrichs is killed, so that he becomes the Ghost in Höfgen's life. Klaus Mann writes a soliloquy for Höfgen, where Hamlet speaks back to him, reminding him that he is only a 'monkey of power, a clown' (254); Höfgen masculinises the part, and in a production which emphasises the play as Nordic, and with sets appropriate for Wagner, plays him as 'a slightly neurotic Prussian lieutenant'; but 'the deep and mysterious melancholy' that had marked his Mephisto was missing. However, the press regards him as 'embodiment of the tragic conflict between the demands of action and of thought, which so interestingly distinguished the German from other men' (255–256). The writing is ironic, but Faust's self-divided character is made typically German, more so than that of the devil.

Nietzsche admired Goethe, though seeing him as Apollonian rather than Dionysiac (Martin 2008: 115–140). His 'Schopenhauer as Educator' reads Faust as contemplative, Hamlet-like, not a figure of action, and 'when the German ceases to be Faust' he becomes a Philistine; the danger being that he will 'fall into the hands of the devil' (Nietzsche 1995: 202). This would be a worse fate than Goethe's Faust's, to be neither held by the devil, nor invoking him, but to be rather using Mephisto, while seeing through him. The contemplative is the man of action. The danger of being a 'doctor', like Faust, is the cold abstraction and objectifying which produces the Auschwitz doctor, Josef Mengele (1911–1979), the devil in Rolf Hochhuth's play *The Representative* (*Der Stellvertreter*, 1963), which studies the Vatican's complicity in the death camps. Mengele is a nihilist, alongside the play's other devils, Pius XII, and Eichmann, who was hanged in 1962, but who appears in *The Representative*. That was the year that Hannah Arendt (1977: 252) described 'the banality of evil' in relation to Eichmann, who was assessed very differently by Benjamin Murmelstein, the rabbi who was put in charge of the Theresienstadt concentration camp outside Prague. (It is the one visited, and photographed, in Sebald's novel *Austerlitz* (2001).)[3] Murmelstein talked to Claude Lanzmann, in the latter's film, *The Last of the Unjust* (2013), and he noted, instead, Eichmann's determined demonic violence. The 'banality of evil', a phrase which also connotes the nothingness of the person committing it, implies that evil 'has lost the quality by which most people recognise it – the quality of temptation' (Arendt 1977: 150). The world of Angelo has gone, then: everyone now accepts their object-status, and that everything that happens is done in common, everyone doing the same (etymologically, the 'banal' suggests compulsory feudal servitude to a single source). Banality suggests that there is nothing left but stupidity: Nietzsche, in *The Gay Science*, section 328 notes how Christianity has systematically attacked egoism, so benefitting 'the herd instinct', which is banal. In contrast, 'ancient philosophers', with whatever motivations, taught that misfortune began with stupidity: i.e. with living according to the rule. Nietzsche thinks it necessary now to 'deprive stupidity of its good conscience', to harm it (Nietzsche 1974: 258).

Like Nietzsche, Klaus Mann underwrites the view that Faust, like Hamlet, may be a symptom of being German; Germany standing in unique danger of Fascism, as the reference made to a Prussian lieutenant intimates. Lukács, writing on Goethe, connects that danger to the failure of the Peasants' War (1525), when Thomas Müntzer attempted to politicise Lutheranism, to improve, materially, the peasants' conditions. Luther betrayed him. The rebellion was bloodily suppressed. Müntzer was executed. Hence Germany has never had a revolution, and is therefore always liable to a reaction it classes as normative (Lukács 1968: 7–8). While Mephisto negates everything, he is not quite like Hamlet in his negativity and nihilism. Nietzsche thinks of a negating and destroying which desires something else: 'all existence that can be negated deserves to be negated and to be truthful means to believe in an existence that could not possibly be negated' (Nietzsche 1995: 203–204). This, which is a 'completed nihilism' (Heidegger 1977: 67), draws on Goethe, and is a 'philosophising with a hammer', testing whether a wall is hollow, whether there is anything behind the façade. Such nihilism is present in Faust, as it was in Hamlet, but it contrasts with that nihilism of Mephisto.

5 Part Two: Das Ewig-Weibliche

Part Two's adventurousness and reach, which overtops even Part One, begins after Gretchen's execution, with the Ariel figure seen before – Mephisto is absent – who provides a 'sea-change' within the plays' second 'intermezzo', leading Faust to a pleasant place where, speaking in Dantean *terza rima*, he awakens to a rainbow, and to colours. His back to the sun, which he cannot see directly, Faust sees the waterfall with delight, and on rising from it, the rainbow, which comprises colours from light and water meeting and clashing: colours are not inherent in light, which was Goethe's contention with Newton, who claimed that they were (Gray 1952: 101–132; Gearey 1992: 35–37). Light must be darkened to produce colours; colour being the meeting of light with dark objects. In this case this meeting makes the arc's shape and reality an image of 'das menschliche Bestreben' (of human striving, 4725), and affirming that 'am farbigen Abglanz haben wir das Leben' (5727: the colourful reflection is our life). Life comprises two forces meeting in a transitory way, contrastedly; the subject exists as much as it meets its double, as opposite.

This intermezzo gives way to Faust entering the political and imperial world of the Renaissance – again, like Agrippa – where Mephisto is the court intriguer, like Marlowe's Faustus producing illusions. Faust is required to bring up Helen of Troy and Paris. He does this through going down to seek 'the Mothers', who are obscurely discussed in the symbolically named 'Dark Gallery' (6173–6306). 'Mothers', who embody the negativity of dark night, immediately evoke Gretchen, as mother, hence their mention causes Faust to shudder. They also suggest the power of the feminine everywhere intuited in *Faust*, and which Mephisto is uncertain about, since it is not part of the Christianity which he as a demon connects with. The heathen folk, he says, referring to the gods of the classical world, including Helen as the daughter of Zeus, are in their own hell, and no concern of his (6219–6220). He is the northern, Gothic, if not German, Christian devil. The limitation indeed of thinking about the devil is that it can only uneasily comprehend the classical, the non-Christian, to which Goethe was himself closely drawn.

If Mephisto is the spirit of negation, of nothingness, Faust says that he will 'in your Nothing hope to find the All' ('In deinen Nichts hoff'ich das All zu finden', 6256). Helen as the woman is 'the All', and like the Mothers, evokes a polytheism and pantheism first intuited with the Earth Spirit. The key Mephisto gives Faust glows in his hand, as if with the power of imagination, and he 'strives downward' ('strebe nieder', 5303), returning for a performance before the Emperor, as a Prospero-like magus (6436). The theatre's classical columns become keys producing harmonious music, as Paris comes forward in dumb show followed by Helen. Seeing her, Faust breaks into a Petrarchan sonnet praising her (6487–6500), fascinated, before committing himself to find her again in the underworld and to possess her, not as an act of rape, as he replies to the Astrologer, but because his determination is to bring illusion into reality: a point key to Part Two.

This determination, which knocks Faust senseless, returns the action to his study, where he now lies, and to Wagner, who has created an artificial man, the Homunculus, inside a glass container. Homunculus sees what is going on in Faust's dreaming mind: a vision of Leda and the swan, something Mephisto cannot know: and indeed, how can he, asks Homunculus, given his context of northern fog and medieval chivalric Gothic? Homunculus, whose striving is equal to Faust's, wants something else which will give him a body and life: he knows that it is the time for the 'Klassische Walpurgisnacht' (6941): a new, almost oxymoronic concept: the ordered, and the classical combined with the Gothic carnivalesque madness of the witches' celebrations. Homunculus declares that this transcends the Romantic: a real ghost must be classical.

Goethe's writing becomes extraordinary, learned, witty, inventive, as Mephisto and Homunculus head for the Peneus river in Greece in its upper reaches, and the Pharsalian fields and the witch Erichtho. She answers to the witches of Part One, and is the figure presiding over the civil wars between Caesar and Pompey which Lucan (CE 39–65) described, and where Caesar triumphed. Faust is brought along too, asking as he wakes where Helen is. Mephisto is at a loss. Homunculus wants to get a life, and Faust wants Helen. Hence they begin separate journeyings backwards through the classical and mythological worlds – Roman to Greek, and to the pre-Olympian – to find the sources of life. These, for Homunculus, a male flame inside glass, are to be found in water, and when Galatea approaches on her scallop shell – a Venus figure on her dolphins, which will not stay for a moment, and a dramatisation of Raphael's *Triumph of Galatea* in the Roman Villa Farnesina – Homunculus dashes himself against the shell. Fire meets water, in a production of the erotic and the production of life. This classical Walpurgis Night differs from that of Part One in being entirely erotic, and affirmative of the sexual. Mephisto, embarrassed about classical nudity, finds such sexuality hard to keep up with.

In Act Three, Helen appears in Sparta, announcing that she has come from the sea, which makes a link between her and Homunculus. She is about to re-enter her palace at Sparta. Mephisto is disguised throughout this Act as Phorcyas, the woman he was turned into by the blind women, the Phorcides (7969–8033). This 'much loved son of Chaos' (8027) has, in Aristophanic mode, become a hermaphrodite, and also the mendacious wooer, almost a pander, who is to bring Helen, in a dream-state, away from Sparta and from Menelaus, the jealous husband she is about to re-encounter on her return from Troy, and into the protection of Faust. This union of Helen (classical) with Faust (German, Romantic, medieval) is a movement forwards through what Goethe called 3000 years of history, just as Act Two has gone backwards. It has two historical markers, the first of which is revealed in the courtyard scene (line 9127), i.e. the

Frankish-Venetian fortress city of Mistra in Sparta, which the Crusaders held onto. It is as if the medieval was defending the classical (9442–9481). Then comes the birth of Euphorion ('well-favoured': the name echoing the meaning of 'Faustus'). He is Helen and Faust's son, both a Byron and Mozart, an Apollo in miniature (9620). Both *Don Giovanni*, as demonic, and sensual, and *Die Zauberflöte* are present implicitly: the first opera was discussed with Eckermann (12 February 1829). There is something deliberately operatic in the presentation of Phorcyas, the Chorus, Helen, Euphorion, and Faust, as if the rococo of the eighteenth-century has been entered into, until Euphorion, Icarus-like, climbs too high and falls dead (9900 ff.).

This crisis ends the opera which Goethe has worked into this third Act, with the sense that this event commemorates Byron's death at Missolonghi in 1824, in defending Greece. Euphorion's death is the complement to the death of Faust's and Margarete's child in Part One. It ends the dream in tragedy. In a pause, Helen withdraws, and returns to the underworld, the sphere of Persephone (9943), unquestionably one of those the 'mothers' (here Demeter) sought after. The Chorus of women which had accompanied her separates from the deceptiveness of Phorcyas, and either return to Hades, or else become part of nature and the elements, air, earth, water, and, through the last celebration of the vine, fire, in the figure of the god Helios; and, as indicated in the references to Dionysus, Silenus, and cloven hooves, become the force of the demonic in wine. The exuberance of the classical Walpurgis Night has exchanged itself for an acceptance that beauty and happiness cannot coexist, and this prepares for a grimmer *realpolitik* in what follows.

Act Four begins with a glimpse of Juno, Leda, and Helen, and then of Margarete, in clouds, but becomes something more ambitious. It becomes the project of making something of the seas, whose mere repetitiveness in terms of everlasting tides Faust wants to shape, while using their pointless power (10,198–10,233). The element that wishes to dominate cannot be excluded from that ambition (10,187). For this, Mephisto urges him to action, to help the Emperor fight a new anti-Emperor (Napoleon) and so, opportunistically, to acquire the seashore for his purposes. Warfare is the sphere Mephisto especially enjoys, and he has his mighty men to aid him (10,323–10,344), who threaten to act as parodies of what Faust is, especially as they are seen as encompassing all stages of life. The triumph of the Emperor means that the old rule (the *ancien régime*) is reinstated, with added secular power for the church, which virtually blackmails the

Emperor for it, since the latter knows that magic has been at work, propping him up speciously. The completion of Cologne Cathedral seems one of the signs of the church's power (11,004–11,020), but the cynicism with which this is demanded is subordinated to Goethe's admiration for the Gothic (see 9017–9028), as with Strasbourg Cathedral, whose architect he considered demonic and Promethean, and his friendship with Sulpiz Boisserée, enthusiast for Cologne's completion (Robson-Scott 1965: 155–224).

Faust gets little of what he wanted, but in Act Five he is the ancient master-builder of the nineteenth century, working on territory which has been given as his reward for military might, and pursuing dreams of enframing nature's chaos which Goethe intuited as about to happen, as for example, cutting canals, projects like those realised by the Suez and by the Panama. But Faust must carry out his land reclamations even at the cost of killing the old couple Baucis and Philemon, whose cottage stands where he wants to develop. It is first mentioned as associated with linden trees (11043), so significant in German folk song, and evoked throughout the act. Such industrial development as Faust carries out, with intimations of the use of steam engines, is not without the cost of human blood (11,123), and the price of the canal is also its straightness, its mechanical character. Mephisto, now the Benthamite – 'Man hat Gewalt, so hat man Recht/Man fragt ums Was, und nicht ums Wie': since you have power you have right, / You ask not how but what is done (11,184–11185) – acts, with his henchmen, to destroy Baucis and Philemon. He brings about, too, 'Krieg, Handel und Piraterie' (11187) as indissociable aspects of capitalist modernity. There are implications of colonialism in Faust's actions (11,274) as he speaks of his all-commanding will. The song of Lynceus, the man on the watchtower, who loves Nature but who sees the burning of the cottage, is lingered on (11,288–11,337), and the memory that the old couple represent must be repressed.

Yet Faust is nauseated by the magic he employs: he says if he could eradicate necromancy, and face Nature as a man alone, being human would be worth it (11,403–11,407). There are echoes of Prospero's renunciation of magic. If magic is 'a binding of nature', according to Northrop Frye, its renunciation releases Nature (Pelikan 1996: 109–110). As a now old man, he is blinded, and though, unlike Margarete, he is not touched by Guilt (Schuld), nor by Want, or Need, yet he comes under the power of 'Sorge' (Care, or Anxiety), one of these four grey women, like mothers, who come to him. 'Sorge', which has particular reference to the future, unlike the others, which deal with past and present, haunts him, partly as a result of his destructiveness in building. Yet he continues, calling for the use of shovels and spades, to keep digging.

Such digging modulates into the parody of the Gravedigger's song in *Hamlet*, sung by the Lemurs (skeletons) who clown as they dig a grave for Faust. In turn his last speech commits him to permanent revolution, to creating an environment where people are in freedom: in this, the aspiration exceeds what Luther wished for, according to Mann. It may relate to Goethe's interest in the Saint-Simonians. If that change of environment happened, he could say that he enjoyed the highest moment: at such a point, he would have no need to strive more. It is a combination of utopian idealism, seen as practical, and of a highly *dirigiste* approach to others, not especially democratic (Vaget 1994: 43–58). The wish expressed, he drops dead. Mephisto thinks he has won the bargain he made in Part One, and responds to that with customary nihilism (11,579–11,603). The Chorus give one side of an argument: they register that an event has happened – 'Est ist vorbei' – it is over. Mephistopheles tries to refute this, repeating 'vorbei' ('finished') four times: i.e. nothing is over, because nothing started. All has been one long proof of the power of 'Ewig-Leere' (everlasting emptiness, 11,603). To Faust's tragedy must be supplemented Mephisto's: he has the victory over Faust, but it is no victory because it means nothing.

Nor has he quite won, having missed the 'if' in Faust's avowal, which made Faust actually still impose a condition before he would say to 'the moment' that it should linger, as so fair. For things have not yet reached that Utopia he wants. Hence the angels take Faust upwards, and Mephisto is caught by a homosexual fantasy for these boys which means that he loses the contest in losing his concentration, and must acknowledge that he has been caught by his 'Torheit' (foolishness, 11,842). His last words become, then, a strange praise of folly – the devil is more than just his nihilism. He has his moments of madness – as he is left alone.

And Faust is saved through the power of the 'eternal womanly', in the last rhymed chorus:

> Alles Vergängliche
> Ist nur rein Gleichniss;
> Das Unzulängliche,
> Hier wird's Ereignis;
> Das Unbeschreibliche,

Hier ist's getan;
Das Ewig-Weibliche
Zieht uns hinan.
(12,104–12,110)

(All that is transitory is but a metaphor. The inadequate is here the event. The indescribable is here done. The eternal feminine draws us on.)

That everything is only a likeness confirms the dominant image of the theatre, and of Prospero's masque, and of the rainbow. Nothing has its reality in itself, but points to something else, and that potential for finding allegory is the opposite of nihilism. The emphasis falls on the event, i.e. on fulfilled action, and on the indescribable appearing, as it does in this poetry which, as the repeated 'hier' indicates, is the only place where credit can be given to this salvific belief. A final stress falls on the eternal feminine ('womanhood's essence', Atkins 1958: 272). What this means as a concept has been much discussed, not least in relation to Goethe's interest in androgyny (Dye 2001: 95–121, Hamlin 1994: 142–155). The feminine, including Mary, evokes Gretchen, and numerous other women, empowered for life or death: in both Walpurgis Nights, the second including Erichtho, Galatea (Venus, her mother's child, 8386), and Helen, and the unrepresentable mothers themselves, who must include Gretchen's mother.

The feminine cannot be summed up. Helen's eroticism promises an 'other' time, outside time: as Chiron says (7428–7432) when Faust encounters him on his quest to find her. Faust replies: 'So sei auch sie durch keine Zeit gebunden!' (so let her not be bound by time either). Chiron, bearing Faust on his back is, coincidentally, visiting Manto, another daemonic force, or mother, the Sibyl responsible for healing. Faust says he does not want to be healed (7459), meaning that healing would merely normalise him. Chiron makes Faust descend at a temple between Peneus (associated with Rome) and Olympos (Greeks): Pydna, where Roman consuls defeated the Greek monarchy (186 BCE), ending Greece's domination. 'Der König flieht, der Bürger triumpherert' (7468) puts the point in a way which intimates the French Revolution, where the middle class replaces the *ancien régime*.

Chiron says that circling ('kreisen', 7480) within time is his delight. She replies: 'Ich harre, mich umkreist die Zeit': I stand still, time circles round me (7481), including the storm ('strudelnd' – like a whirlpool) which has brought Faust to find Helen. To his desire, Manto replies, 'Den lieb' ich, der Unmögliches begehrt' – 'I love one who wants the impossible' (7488), and leads Faust into Persephone's underworld, as if, like Orpheus, he was a musician. From then on (7494) he is not seen again until he claims Helen as a medieval knight (9182). Two intuitions of time, a subject of increasing prominence to Goethe and his contemporaries, seem intimated (Vincent 1987: 159–174). Manto incarnates the *Ereignis*, the 'event' which 'gives', outside all subjectivity, in the moment. Faust feels that the moment cannot be arrested. But it must be lived, as he tells Helen: 'Dasein ist Pflicht, und wär's ein Augenblick' (were life but for a moment, one's duty is to be; line 9418): yet everything repeats, and Manto's power shows in refusing to go with its whirlpool-like circling character, which returns to violence and wars and disposes of empires.

6 Faust's Wager

What can be said of the despairing pact Faust makes in Part One, his wager that Mephisto would never get him to rest within the moment? Faust is vindicated, though helped by Mephistopheles' lust and the 'Ewig-Weibliche'. He does not rest. The diabolical Faustian idea is to find more and more within time. Marshall Berman comments on the pact via his reading of the *Communist Manifesto* (1847) (Berman 1983: 37–86). He notes how Marx reviews the nineteenth-century bourgeois revolution, its life generated so much by the French Revolution; the changing of everything into the universal exploitation which the bourgeoisie have effected – dismissing feudalism in the name of capitalism – has as its dynamic, Marx says, that 'the bourgeoisie cannot exist without constantly revolutionising the instruments of production, and thereby the relations of production, and with them the whole relations of society' (Marx 1973: 70–71).

This, which is the *locus classicus* for understanding and defining capitalist modernity, may be articulated with how Heidegger, however different his politics, probes 'the question concerning technology'. This, as was seen in the discussion of nihilism in the previous chapter, leaves nothing of nature uncovered or untouched. It opens up spaces for development, enframing them to make them a 'standing reserve', meaning that everything becomes a 'resource' to be drawn on, sometimes a 'human resource'. Everything is for domination, hence Marx writes:

> Everlasting uncertainty and agitation distinguish the bourgeois epoch from all earlier ones. All fixed, fast-frozen relations, with their train of

> ancient and venerable prejudices and opinions, are swept away, all new-formed ones become antiquated before they can ossify. All that is solid melts into air, all that is holy is profaned, and man is at last compelled to face with sober senses, his real conditions of life, and his relations with his kind. (Marx 1973: 70–71)

'Agitation' (including Faust's 'Sorge'), means anxiety, and also implies revolution as 'agitation'. It marks the bourgeois who cannot stop, as 'development' and 'developers' never can. For Marx, the bourgeois revolution undoes all non-modern ideology which would constrain development: naked aggressive exploitation makes people see their *real* conditions of work and their class position. Later Marx argues that this bourgeois modernity presents itself in ideological, phantasmagorical terms, disguising what is happening, representing things to the exploited classes in ways which give their conditions an imaginary consistency or reality. This is the work of ideology. Faust's restlessness, making him suspicious of all ideological constraints, as with his desire that people should be free, makes him continually active, in the sense which Marx describes, and uninterested in what Mephisto offers. But with Mephisto's connivance he passes through a disastrous and exploitative love-experience with Margarete which ends with her death. Parallel to that tragedy, he becomes the architect/engineer, moving land and sea, and destroying, on the way, Baucis and Philemon.

Modernity demands universal exploitation: Faustian man becomes inexhaustible, diabolically prompted by, but outstripping the devil, whose contradictory methodology Mephisto describes in his single soliloquy (1851–1867), when dressed as Faust, as if doubling or caricaturing him. He expresses Iago-like hatred of Faust, acknowledging that he must keep giving Faust stimulants towards a further command of experience, but he will do it all through illusion. He knows that Faust will not stop in his endless striving but he will make Faust stop through the banality of what he provides ('flache Undeutenheit', 1863: flat meaninglessness, or insignificance). Such amusing of the self to death will cause Faust to stop, drugged into a cessation of onward striving. Mephisto – or Faust – seem to be the dynamo of capitalist modernity, part of its disasters, and ambiguous achievements. And Mephisto negates modernity's 'striving', since his spirit is nihilistic, trivial, creating banality, if that means conformist acceptance of everyday reality, and not thinking outside it.

Yet none of this interests Faust: he despises the 'modern' as defined by luxury and comfort (10,176). Another way of defining that complete 'acceptance' of the merely everyday would adopt Arendt's phrase, 'the banality of evil', as emanating from dull unquestioning reactiveness. It associates with how her *The Origins of Totalitarianism* (1951) defines 'radical evil'. This 'evil', which 'has emerged in connection with a system in which all men have become superfluous' – 'utilitarian systems', where everything is a disposable means to an end – wills to 'liquidate all spontaneity, such as the mere existence of individuality will always engender' (Arendt 1968: 459, 456, see also 457, 438). Arendt considers the Nazi death camps as the form of objectifying and enframing that Heidegger should have marked, but failed to do so, to such disastrous effect. But free-market capitalism, 'neoliberalism', may require totalitarianism as a possibility (for example, the nationalism of protectionism and the imposition of tariff-restraints) while its money-power can always control the 'other', buying up its labour power and land. Money is never 'just' a means of exchange: it has, as with the jewels used to seduce Margarete, an unreal pimping and pumping-up power, which is Marx's subject in the *Economic and Philosophical Manuscripts* (1844), when considering money's property. It can buy and appropriate everything as omnipotent: it creates both the need and the desired object. And the commodity fetish makes objects into not those which are needed but those which are desired, which seem to have magical powers; the fetish supplements the desired object, as well as the person who possess it.

David Hawkes considers the Faustian pact as a commitment to the unreal, which he sees as central to capitalism; commitment to death, in transforming humans into objects (Hawkes 2007: 162). Marx quotes Mephisto on money-power as the devil's power (Marx 1975: 375–376):

> Wenn ich sechs Hengste zahlen kann,
> Sind ihre Kräfte nicht die meine?
> Ich renne zu und bin ein rechter Mann,
> Als hätt ich vierundzwanzig Beine.
> (1824–1827)

(When I can buy six horses, is not their power mine? I run along, a proper man, as if I had twenty-four legs.)

Though, unlike Marlowe, Goethe does not specify twenty-four years as Faust's time of controlling the devil, the number is significant. Everything can be credited to the one with money. The imagined number of legs and the added horsepower produces the artificial man, complete in himself, because possessing the secret of money, in modern form. All depends on a new technological/industrial power which expresses itself in the phantasmagoria: what appears for consumption as shining unreality and reality at once, as allegory indeed: so Benjamin quotes the journalist and economist Eugène Buret, writing in 1840, in the very heyday of the expansion of the commodity in Paris: 'the most fantastic creations of fairyland are near to being realised before our very eyes... Every day our factories turn out wonders as great as those produced by Doctor Faustus with his book of magic' (Benjamin 1999: 673, Cohen 1989: 87–107).

Behind Marx's awe at the bourgeois revolution, may be added Nietzsche's sense, which was virtually quoted by Mephisto in his nihilism, that impatience with any existing achievement, and the demand for modernisation, both issue from a sense that no state can justify itself as it is. Everything must pass into ruin, everything must be replaced. The 'law of time, that time must devour its children' (Nietzsche 2005: 122), which was alluded to before, means devaluing the past. Equally, present-day developmental works, in their exploitativeness, will consume the future, laying waste the earth, creating environmental ruin as the future. Faust's onward striving contains that nihilistic potential, responding to something in Mephisto, and as 'collateral damage', self-assertively destroying the other. It remains the question who is more diabolical here, Faust or Mephisto, and it indicates how complex the arguments about modernity must be: driving it on, and restraining its momentum at the same time.

Notes

1. Boyle, Williams, and Jane Brown, have written well on *Faust*, giving both introductory and advanced material. Atkins (1958) gives a useful 'new critical' account of the texts. The translations by Luke and by Constantine are both excellently annotated. I am indebted to all these.
2. Mann's estimate of Goethe was, of course, very high, as seen in the novel *Lotte in Weimar* (1939). See Benjamin for an analysis of Goethe's politics, as feudal and bourgeois together: Benjamin (1999: 160–193).
3. Sebald works from H.G. Adler, *Theresienstadt 1941–1945: Das Antlitz einer Zwangsgemeinschaft; Geschichte, Soziologie, Psychologie* (1955), an eyewitness account of this prison camp.

Chapter 7: Dostoevsky: Murder and Suicide

Dostoevsky's *Demons*, and *The Brothers Karamazov*, the latter text receiving the most attention in this chapter, are central for discussing diabolism – but that as a fantasy extends throughout Dostoevsky (Belknap 1990: 132–137; Leatherbarrow 2005), and through nineteenth-century Russian literature. Pushkin and Lermontov, for example, appropriated *Paradise Lost* before reading Goethe, so that for them, Satan was the Romantic rebel (Boss 1991). More popularly, the devil in Russia appears in folk stories, as when the old landowner Korobochka, in Gogol's *Dead Souls* (1842), says she told her fortune by cards before going to bed just two nights ago, and God sent her the devil as a punishment in a dream: 'he looked so repulsive, and his horns, why, they were longer than a bull's' (Gogol 2004: 58). In 1906, the critic Dmitry Merezhkovsky saw in *The Government Inspector* and *Dead Souls* evidence of the failure of lives to come into being; lives marked by absence. Such an absence pervades Chichikov, the acquisitive materialist in *Dead Souls* (Merezhkovsky 1974: 94). Gogol influences the devil in *The Brothers Karamazov*, when he tells Ivan that he suffers from 'the fantastic'; and that he does not live; i.e. that he is marked by absence: 'I am an "x" in an indeterminate equation. I am some sort of ghost of life, who has lost all beginnings and ends'. He longs to become incarnate (Dostoevsky 2004: 642).

In Gogol, everything is 'the devil knows what', and that vague negative introduces the idea of '*ne to* [not what you suppose, not what you might think]', as 'the concept of negation that transforms seemingly stable reality

J. Tambling, *Histories of the Devil*,
DOI 10.1057/978-1-137-51832-3_8

into the something else that the devil alone knows. Gogol never writes the word devil lightly, for it is he who is ultimately responsible for the undermining and disruption of reality' (de Jonge 1973: 80). For Gogol, the city is especially diabolical territory. In 'Christmas Eve' (1832), from *Evenings on a Farm Near Dikanka*, (Gogol's native Poltava region in the Ukraine), the devil, who is apparently German, carries Vakula the blacksmith to St Petersburg, showing him the fantastic city from an aerial standpoint, and indicating that it belongs to him (Gogol 1985: 1.117, 123–130). In 'Nevsky Prospect' (1835), the warning is to keep away from the lamps at twilight because 'everything breathes deception' – the urban uncanny – most of all:

> when night falls in masses of shadow on it, throwing into relief the white and dun-coloured walls of the houses, when all the town is transformed into noise and brilliance, when myriads of carriages roll off bridges, postilions shout and jump up on their horses, and when the devil himself lights the street lamps to show everything in false colours. (Gogol 1985: 1.238)

Three familiar elements make up the diabolic in Dostoesvksy's Gogolian novella, *The Double* (1846): the city, the negations of Goethe's Mephisto, and the double. The clerk, Mr Golyadkin, is driven towards destruction and the madhouse by encountering his double on a miserable November night after being humiliated when he went uninvited to the dinner party of Clara, daughter of State Councillor Berendeyev. Thrown out, returning home, he notes the potentialities of the canals flooding. This evokes Pushkin's poem *The Bronze Horseman*, and the diabolism of the statue of Peter, emblem of an autocrat sparing no one in constructing St Petersburg, pursuing the maddened Eugene, the peasant who dares 'as if by some black spirit wrenched' (Pushkin 1984: 437) to confront Peter's statue after the disaster of the floods. Golyadkin feels that someone is coming towards him, and going along with him, whom he does and does not know, while 'a miserable wet dog, wet through and shivering' runs alongside him, like the poodle who is Mephisto (Dostoevsky 1972: 171). He feels he has an abyss before him, which he might at last leap into, of his own accord (171). And he envies this double, who is apparently more successful than him.

But the first figure to be looked at in this chapter comes from Turgenev (1818–1883), the Russian who was a European (friend of George Eliot amongst others), and the opposite of Dostoevksy, who detested him, and parodied him in *Demons*.

1 Turgenev: Vera and Bazarov

Turgenev's novella/psychological study 'Faust: A Story in Nine Letters' (1856), derives from both *Faust* and *Werther*. It opens by quoting Faust's wearied statement of what the world believes: that life only exists for Schopenhauerian renunciation, which Faust, of course, resists: – 'Entbehren sollst du, sollst entbehren' (*Faust* 1549: You must forego, you must do without (Turgenev, 1907:104)). It shows Pavel Alexandrovitch B – writing to his friend about resettling, in his late thirties, in 1850, in his house in the provinces, perhaps Turgenev's own Oryol. Yet this latter-day Werther is uneasy: he has got rid of his Petersburg valet at Moscow, because the latter made him feel the superiority of his Petersburg manners (154). He will not be bored, he says: he has books with him, including *Faust* Part One. He meets Priemkov, whom he remembers from his student days, and learns that he is married to Vera Nikolaevna, whom he knew when she was sixteen, between university and going to Berlin in the 1830s. Her father had been accidentally shot. Her mother, who haunts the text, with echoes of the uncanny influence of the old woman, who acts as destructive ghostly mother in Pushkin's short story *The Queen of Spades* (1833), had married Vera's father after running off with him. Vera's grandmother was an Italian peasant girl who had also run away with a man, Ladanov. After giving birth, the man to whom she had been betrothed killed her. Ladanov, back in Russia from Italy, is a reclusive scientist supposed to be a sorcerer, and who has never forgiven his daughter, Vera's mother, for her own elopement: a transgressive, repeating, family history recalling *The Devil's Elixirs*.

Vera's mother responded to this past by shielding her daughter from the town and from novels. And Vera told Pavel, during their first meetings, that 'she was afraid of [life], afraid of those secret forces on which life rests and which rarely, but so suddenly, break out. Woe to him who is their sport!' (166–167). Vera talked in her sleep, saying 'it seems to me that B – is a good person, but there's no relying on him' (168). Though the subject of marriage came up, Vera's mother rejected him, telling him to go to Berlin and be broken by life there (she thinks this is essential, part of the necessity of renunciation): 'you're a good fellow, but it's not a husband like you that's needed for Vera' (169).

Now, re-meeting Vera, a wife and mother, he reads *Faust* to her and its Margarete scenes with virtually diabolical effects. She keeps the book, and says that Mephistopheles terrifies her, 'not as the devil, but "as something which may exist in every man"'; to which he says that this '"something" is what we call reflection' (191), i.e. self-consciousness. She shows him the portraits of her grandparents; the Italian grandmother with vine leaves in her hair; and Pavel sees these signs of abandonment to love in Vera too (202). The catastrophe occurs: Vera tells Pavel she loves him, and asks what he will do. As an 'honest man' he says he will go away (212). She kisses him but sees her mother in imagination (which recalls the significance of Margarete's mother). She says she will go away with him, leaving her husband. But she becomes ill instead and dies, raving about '*Faust* and her mother, whom she sometimes called Martha, and sometimes Gretchen's mother' (220). But she also quotes 'Was will er an dem heiligen Ort' (what does he want in the holy place?, *Faust*, 4603), which shows Margarete's visceral recoil from Mephisto. But if the 'holy place' here is love, it is B- who is Mephisto-like, nihilistic and under accusation, as having failed every test: he has been a Mephisto in tempting her with the book; he has failed as a Faust. Her behaviour, which reverses the pattern of Werther and Charlotte, both points to the demonism which motivates Margarete, and shows that Vera, this woman in love, with an emancipated position, has been failed by his 'honesty'. Her death echoes and comments on *Faust*'s last scene. Though Pavel concludes with the Schopenhauerian belief in renunciation, that nihilism differs from the 'secret forces' which have been produced in Vera.

Turgenev's *Fathers and Children* (1861) described the new radicals or nihilists whom the radical Chernyshevsky, in his novel *What Is to Be Done* (1863) inspired with a political agenda. *Fathers and Children* calls the figure of revolt Bazarov, and shows, in the way Bazarov debates with the previous generation, his attraction towards him. Bazarov's friend Arkady explains: 'a nihilist is a person who does not take any principle for granted, however much that principle may be revered' (Turgenev 1975: 94). Turgenev's novel must, then, identify with Bazarov's position, though when he later falls in love, it seems impossible for him to sustain that intellectual position. As physician and so a materialist, Bazarov dominates *Fathers and Children*, in almost its every scene, dying at the end from virtually self-inflicted causes. This was how the novel began for Turgenev, who said that he was 'out for a walk and thinking about death ... immediately there rose before me the picture of a dying man. This was Bazarov' (quoted, Freeborn 1960: 69).

The nihilists replaced the 1840 radicals, whom they dismissed as Romantics. They evoke a new 'force' of the 1860s; a material quality, which was discussed in the German scientist Ludwig Büchner's *Kraft und Stoff* (*Force and Matter*, 1855). Arkady tells his uncle, Pavel, a 'Romantic', using Mephisto's language, 'we destroy because we are a force . . . a force and therefore not accountable to anyone' (Turgenev 1975: 127). Bazarov, who fights a duel with Pavel, so accepting the risk of death, dies saying 'darkness' (289). So Turgenev wrote to Pauline Viardot in 1849: 'that's what [Nature] is; she's indifferent; the soul is only within us and perhaps a little around us . . . that weak glimmering which eternal night constantly strives to extinguish' (Freeborn 1960: 126, 44). These words cite Mephisto (*Faust* 1349–1358); life is the only light, and for Bazarov, and the nihilists, the darkness overtakes, in a mode which implies a virtual suicide.

2 Demons and Suicide

In Dostoevsky's *Demons* (1871–1872), Stepan Verkhovensky, the 1840s radical, has read *Fathers and Children*, and does not understand the character of Bazarov, whom he identifies with Peter, his own radical son (215) whom he calls a mixture of Nozdryov and Byron.[1] *Demons* was prompted by the 1869 Moscow murder of an ex-nihilist student, Ivan Ivanov, by a nihilist cell, which was led by Sergei Nechaev (1847–1882). In 1873, Dostoevsky discussed this murder in his journalism, *A Writer's Diary*.[2] There, he calls himself an old Nechaevist (Dostoevsky 1994b: 284), since, as a revolutionary, connected to the 'Petrashevsky' group, he had been condemned to the scaffold in January 1849. The sentence was commuted to ten years' exile in Siberia, but it made him the reprieved anarchist, possessed by a wholly ambiguous attitude to the Czar, the Father, who had freed him after putting him through a mock-execution (Frank 2002: 3–66). The group psychology which creates anarchy and murder within the town in *Demons* derives from the Nechaev case, and is seen in the conspirators' ringleader, Peter Verkhovensky, who is a compromiser with nihilism: 'I am a crook, really, not a socialist' (1994: 420). He sees himself as lieutenant to the more complex nihilist, Nicolai Stavrogin. These conspirators create carnivalesque mayhem at the town's fete, including one of them, Lyamshin, walking upside down, which is considered the ultimate insult (510). They murder Ivan Shatov, though others also die in the general anarchy. Peter Verkhovensky wants the murder to be confessed to – in a suicide note – by the innocent Kirillov, an engineer who is fascinated by suicide, apparently having written an article on its increase in Russia, and having also apparently advocated universal destruction, including his own (94). Kirillov, despite believing in essential goodness, and happy in his innocence, agrees, self-contradictorily, to sign the suicide note: an instance of the over-innocent conniving at murder.

Before writing *Demons*, in December 1868, Dostoevsky was planning a novel called *Atheism*. By April 1870 this had become a project of five stories, to be called *The Life-Story of a Great Sinner*. Charles Passage, analysing the material this was to comprise, involving the 'sinner' going into and then leaving a monastery (like Alyosha Karamazov), calls it a version of *The Devil's Elixirs* (Passage 1954: 158), but with the attempt to give it the life-range that marks *Faust*. That would make *The Great Sinner* attempt to conceptualise the absolutely transgressive, the sinner being both Faust and Mephisto. Mikhail Bakunin (1814–1876), the Left Hegelian and later anarchist, finished 'The Reaction in Germany' (1842) with: 'Let us trust the eternal spirit which destroys and annihilates only because it is the unfathomable and eternally creative source of life. The passion for destruction is a creative passion too' (Lehning 1973: 58). Goethe's Earth Spirit and Mephisto fuse in Bakunin, along with Hegel's reliance on the power of negation when an 'eternal spirit' is mentioned: nihilism guarantees freedom: it is essential to 'tarry with the negative'. But Dostoesvky's language of a 'great sinner' makes him less nihilistic than transgressive. The idea of a 'sinner' keeps him within theological bounds, however 'great' his sin. A 'great sinner' is less interesting than the 'great criminal', whom Benjamin finds central in popular culture (Benjamin 1996: 239), since the criminal's violence against law as guilt-making can only be identified with in the earlier novel *Crime and Punishment* (1866), Raskolnikov, who of course murders the pawnbroker (another version of the Queen of Spades) and her sister, is on record as thinking that the 'exceptional' person – who is beyond law – has the power of the 'new word', which is also a 'new law'. He has, apparently, written an article upholding bloodshed as a matter of conscience, and saying that the exceptional man, i.e. a Mahomet, or a Napoleon (the Goethe theme again) can commit crime (Dostoesvky 1964: 220–223, 232). The exceptional man, then, cannot work without establishing law, whose mythic status is to impose guilt: as Benjamin argues in 'Law and Character'. That voice, with its inbuilt contradiction, becomes in *The Brothers Karamazov* that of Ivan Karamazov, who apparently claims that everything is permitted if there is no God.

But between Raskolnikov and Ivan stands Stavrogin, whose predecessors include Nikolai Speshnev (1821–1882), who had been involved with Dostoevsky in the Petrashevsky group: Dostoevsky called him his Mephistopheles (Frank 1977: 258–272; 1995: 466). Kirillov, in dialogue with the narrator, says that pain (always fear of pain!) holds man back, giving him fear of death: the 'new man' will be one for whom it is indifferent whether he lives or dies: 'he who dares kill himself is God' (116). Discussing suicide with Stavrogin, he says time – a law, and a force for division – will be displaced by the 'man-God' who will replace Christ, the 'God-man' (236–238). To time as continuity, denying the self its supremacy, Kirillov opposes 'the moment', which he declares is worth all of time. Shatov tells him that such visionary ecstasy is characteristic of the person about to have an epileptic fit (591): so that the moment of absolute being (possessing the moment) is also that of absolute dispossession, if not death.[3] In his last dialogue with Peter Verkhovensky, Kirillov calls suicide supreme self-will, its fullest point. Verkhovensky replies that self-will would be better displayed in killing someone else, but Kirillov rejects that as less than suicide, which, in affirming the self, destroys it, and with it the myth of God, fear of whom keeps man back from suicide. And 'man has done nothing but invent God, so as to live without killing himself' (617).

Kirillov argues, then, that fear of suicide creates, as a prophylactic against it, God, and it creates theology, with its good/evil distinctions. It creates time, too, as a law that keeps the self displaced from its own full identity, never able to possess the moment. He then instances the Crucifixion, saying that Christ died believing a lie (God's supremacy, and resurrection), but the laws of nature did not spare him. He died fooled, showing that the laws of nature are also mendacious, there to keep the illusion of God in place, making everything 'a devil's vaudeville' (618). The devil's work is to keep things as they are. Suicide would be an escape from that (the devil has *no* interest in breaking with conventional estimates of good and evil). It would be a declaration of the power of self-will (which, it seems, the devil thwarts). Everything waits for someone to kill himself in a demonstration of self-will, as not being under God's will. This self-will is the attribute of divinity and once suicide has happened, as an act of 'insubordination and new fearsome freedom' (619), the complete act of transgression will have happened. The revolution will be ready. Humans will be able to change, even to mutate physically. Suicide, then, is as political a resistance for Kirillov as Werther considered it to be, in the record of his argument with Albert, who as the rationalist, is really the figure suicide rebels against (Goethe 2013: 33–38). Fear of suicide is recoil from taking self-possession, in a fear of the father; whom Kirillov still acknowledges in the word 'insubordination', and by keeping an icon of Christ with its lamp burning.

Further, Kirillov talks like Christ, dying for the people. It is in any case unclear that people can attain this 'freedom' for themselves, without undergoing the same process of self-enlargement, any more than it is clear that Christianity has inherently enlarged people's freedom. In saying 'insubordination', he makes tacit acknowledgement of lacking mastery, since, in *King Lear*, 'Poor Tom' says that the devil incites to suicide, as his work: a point also in Hogg. It seems that diabolism is involved in suicide, or rather, that suicide both does and undoes the devil's work. Kirillov speaks within the discourse of nihilism, but there is a strange demonic possession in his death – suddenly breaking into animal-violence, biting Peter Verkhovensky, as a last act of revenge because he is being forced to kill himself, thus rendering the act pointless, and shooting himself after ten repeated 'terrible shouts' of 'now' (624–625). It is inseparable from the idea of the epileptic fit, which inheres in that repeated 'now' – which sounds like Faust, at midnight, when claimed by Mephistopheles. Or, his 'now' is trying to claim the moment.

Stavrogin always does the opposite of the expected. When violently slapped by Shatov, one of this devil's disciples – and we recall the various valencies, discussed in Chapter 5, that come with being slapped – he does not react (203). But what he does is as violent and sudden as possible, as if dedicated to breaking the thought of identity in his behaviour. Yet he tells the monk Tikhon that he experiences night-time hallucinations, feeling near him some malicious being, scoffing and yet 'reasonable', split into various faces and characters, yet always the same. He wants Tikhon to accept that it is a demon, yet is unsure himself, while Tikhon is even less sure than Stavrogin, who is trying to impress him throughout, just as Tikhon notes the literariness of his 'confession', which, being headed simply 'From Stavrogin', possesses a writer's narcissism. Tikhon thinks the hallucinations may be an illness: Stavrogin may be epileptic, showing that in memory disorders too (Rice 1985: 90, 48, 238–239). Tikhon holds that demons exist, 'but the understanding of them can be limited' (687), and that it is possible to believe in demons without believing in God (688), belief in whom might be an attempt to eliminate demons, to defang them, as it were, by claiming the power of a superior force. Stavrogin is his own devil, and haunted by him, and the plurality of shapes his hallucinations take recalls the New Testament narrative of Legion, 'for we are many' (Luke 8:30). This splitting within the self is rationalised by others as an extraordinary capacity for crime (253), as though Stavrogin was the 'new man', the 'man-God'. Shatov, the ex-serf, the man from below, desires to be tormentor *and* tormented, finding beauty and pleasure in both. He accuses Stavrogin of having married the crazy, crippled, Marya Lebyadkin (still a virgin; she and her brother will be murdered, with Stravrogin's unconscious connivance) 'out of a passion for torture [*nadryv*, self-laceration], out of a passion for remorse, out of moral sensuality' (254). That oxymoron implies Nietzsche's analysis in *The Genealogy of Morals* of the 'ascetic ideal' (Nietzsche 1956): of the sensual, sexual, pleasure that is gained from repression. Stavrogin commits 'crime' to hurt himself, making himself subject and object.

Suicide as an action cannot be pre-programmed: Durkheim can say *how many* people will kill themselves in one year, but not *who*. Suicide breaks a chronological pattern of behaviour, by doing suddenly, in the moment, what cannot have been predicted and in doing so makes the idea of character as single and consistent with itself impossible, which means that it also dissipates belief in self-will: what is willed in suicide is the end of will and of self. When Stavrogin hangs himself – he told Kirillov he would shoot himself: but he perhaps copies, guiltily, the suicide of Matreshka, the child he seduced in Petersburg – an unsigned suicide note reads, 'Blame no one; it was I' (678). But, reverting to the first chapter, 'I' cannot say 'I'. Further, the lack of signature makes this 'I' unattributable, though a signature, remembering Derrida, would not validate anything either, and the temporal gap between writing and acting indicates how self-assertion, self-will fails, especially since in suicide, at some point the 'I' loses the power of agency (Blanchot 1982: 87–107). The 'I' cannot will its own death, and the sense of the note remains indeterminate, though blotting out Stavrogin as the person who wills, as suicide negates the person who says 'I'. If the 'I' is to be established, suicide cannot do it, and Stavrogin's note cannot negate Blanchot's point.

Further, this is the second note, for Stavrogin has already written to Darya Shatov, whom he had seduced, speaking of her as 'magnanimous', and saying of himself: 'what poured out of me was only negation, with no magnanimity, and no force. Or not even negation . . . ' (676). And he says he cannot commit suicide: that would show magnanimity, not Mephistophelian negation. Yet suicide also is negation. The latter note contradicts the former note, making that the suicide note. The notes double and negate each other, leaving Stavrogin still open to interpretation, in an openness which suicide forecloses. 'Blame no one' reifies 'no one', who, or which, gains some status thereby. The diabolical within

Stavrogin indicates that nothing has the power of explanation; but it will be seen that the desire to explain *can* pull suicide down on people's heads.

3 The Meek One

Dostoevsky published *The Meek One: A Fantastic Story* in November 1876 in *A Writer's Diary*; a part of some meditations on suicide which had appeared in May 1876, and October and December of that year (Dostoevsky 1994b: 677–717). Recording the soliloquising fantasies of a pawnbroker consumed by *ressentiment*, and called 'fantastic' because, as said in the October 1876 *Writer's Diary*, 'the end and the beginnings are things that, for human beings, still lie in the realm of the fantastic' (651), the story is of a man whose wife committed suicide: throwing herself out of the window with a Russian icon in her hand. This Dostoevsky had noted factually, as part of city life (a reminder how the devil is part of urban modernity), in that October issue (1994a: 653): the woman absolutely could not get work.

The pawnbroker's soliloquy, or interior monologue, tries to remember 'every little thing... every tiny detail' (*chestochki*: 'little devils', 1994b: 681). He begins noting the sixteen-year old girl whom he marries, as being, he says, one of the 'new generation', i.e., as like the nihilists. To the girl of *The Meek One*, the pawnbroker quotes Mephisto in calling himself 'part of that whole that wills forever evil but does forever good' (682). He implicitly casts her as Margarete. His diabolism – sucking the life out of the other in usurious manner – evokes the old woman pawnbroker, whom Raskolnikov kills in *Crime and Punishment* (1866). This pawnbroker is a Petersburg voice with an injured past. He was an army officer who refused to fight a duel and had to leave the army as a coward, becoming a street beggar before becoming a pawnbroker. The woman was advertising for a post in *The Voice*, a Petersburg paper. The answer, the 'voice' that comes back to her, but which silences hers, is his. He wills to suppress, by silencing her, who is his other. He must make everything reducible to himself; his nihilism being solipsism. The chapter in his narrative, 'A Dreadful Recollection', recalls how she nearly shot him while he was apparently asleep, but refrained. He knew what she was doing, but his silence, in and after this 'duel', silences her, as he now imagines the coroner's court silencing him (716). The woman's muteness now speaks to him but he displaces it onto the law accusing him, while seeing himself the victim of a 'blind immutable force'. His voice continues outpouring his rationalisations for what has happened, trying, failing, to justify himself (Holquist 1977: 148–155). Asking finally: 'what will become of me?' when her body has gone, he knows that without the other, there is no self; rather, nothing.

The earlier October 1876 *Writer's Diary* contains a fine insight for Dostoevsky's fiction: that life exhibits a depth which is not in art, not even in Shakespeare, and that 'the facts of life' require a capacity and vision of the artist, which may not be possible for some. For one person, life passes 'in the most touchingly simple manner' and is never to be examined. For another, these same facts make him/her 'at last incapable of simplifying and making a general conclusion... of drawing them out into a straight line'. Such a person 'resorts to simplification of another sort and *very simply* plants a bullet in his head to quench at one stroke his tormented mind and all its questions' (Dostoevsky 1994b: 651). Perception of the grotesque within life may not be noticed, or may possess the potential to torment the mind towards self-simplification, which is what Derrida means by 'closure'; rejecting contradiction, doubleness, everything meant by the diabolical. Nietzsche has an almost identical analysis of dealing with such torment in 'On the Pale Criminal' in *Thus Spoke Zarathustra*, save that his tormented person called a criminal by the law courts, murders someone rather than commits suicide – but perhaps these actions are the same, ultimately (Peace 1992: 200, 325): suicide as counter-murder.

This alternation between two ways of seeing life fascinates Dostoevsky. He instances a woman's suicide (historically Alexander Herzen's daughter (Paperno 1997: 178–182)), interpreting it as resistance to 'linearity' within life, a 'simplicity' against which she rebels. Her suicide note, thinking about the possibility of her being revived, shows the desire to attain the 'complexity' she cannot find. It is a resistance to life as having a plot, indeed, to narrative as being 'about' a plot. His next example is of the woman who cannot get work, jumping holding the icon. The doubleness and contradictoriness here defy explanation. These things, 'no matter how simple they seem on the surface, one still goes on thinking about it... they surface in one's dreams, and it even seems as if one is somehow to blame for them'. Suicidal meekness may be aggressive: the psychoanalyst Karl Menninger says that the suicide wants to kill, and to be killed, and to die (quoted, Schneidman 1984: 79–87). What is simple is not simple: even Christianity is not free from suicide, as with the tradition which John Donne uses in *Biathanatos*, that Christ's death on the Cross was suicide (as God, Christ could not be killed; he had to will his own death).[4] Dostoevsky follows the suicide of the woman with the imaginary thoughts of a materialist, i.e. a nihilist, committing suicide out of boredom, quarrelling with the 'nature' which like Bazarov, he reads only objectively, scientifically. Dostoevsky writes this as suggesting that the written explanation cannot explain; it relates to the beginning of the whole section called 'Two Suicides': that we can only know surface effects in life, not 'the ends or beginnings of things', which lie 'in the realm of the fantastic'. Suicide as an end, is fantastic; that is, as *tyche*, it can never be predicted (and so silences realist narrative, as being the always present possibility), and returns us to *The Meek One: A Fantastic Story*, which has that subtitle because the pawnbroker is speaking, and the story is taking down his words, which means that it has no sense that an explanation is finally possible. The obviously implicit reasons – his persecution: her silencing – are relevant, but they cannot be confirmed: plots need the fantastical to supplement their failure to clinch explanation, assuming the latter is helpful:

> Perhaps the decision [for suicide] was made just while she was standing by the wall, her head resting against her arm, and smiling. The thought flew into her head, made her dizzy – and she couldn't resist it. (716).

Dostoevsky records a woman in prison saying 'I wanted to do something wicked, but it was as if it wasn't my own will but someone else's' (725). Can suicide have the simplicity of self-will? Can any action fit into a plot? Dostoevsky, confronted with accounts of suicides, and suicide notes passed over to him, cannot explain them (737): 'secret forces' remain at work and they counter the possibility of a narrative – indeed of *any* narrative, certainly, of a 'realist' one.

4 THE KARAMAZOV BROTHERS

With these 'secret forces' defeating narrative explanation, I turn to the devil's presence in *The Brothers Karamazov*. But to begin with a caveat: with all Dostoevsky, one difficulty in reading comes from those approaches to him which discuss the text as a theological argument; some conservative, Christian readings of Dostoevsky find in references to the devil a contest of absolutes in the novel, and an affirmation of theism and Orthodoxy. In Bakhtin's readings, in contrast, the texts are *novels*:

they disallow a single authoritative voice in the sense that they show that a monological discourse represses an inherent 'otherness' which is best expressed in the idea that discourse must happen in the language of the 'other'; the interlocutor, and therefore contains its own 'other' within it, unless this is violently excluded. Bakhtin's readings of Dostoevsky's polyphonic novels are, like his Rabelais, often resisted – even in Joseph Frank's indispensable biography of Dostoevsky – and for reasons already implicitly discussed in relation to Rabelais. The polyphonic and the carnivalesque are alike examples of the 'dialogic', where all utterance is multi-voiced, always containing another voice within it, doubling and parodying it and making it tend towards 'Menippean satire', which Bakhtin (1984a: 156–157) associates with Rabelaisian carnival. It means that all character is unfinished, open, because the 'other' is within it (1984b: 251). The novel disallows – even though Dostoevsky in reactionary moments might wish it – an authorial discourse. The polyphonic or dialogical novel implies the impossibility of getting anything authoritative beyond the second-hand of what 'they say'. As in carnival, no subject position can be maintained, all identities being lost in the carnival-body, so in the polyphonic novel, no opinion can get further than the different voices which contend for authority. Forces speak in this heteroglossia which are impossible to recoup, and assign, or resolve into a system of belief. Assigning the texts literary forms, putting them into genres, are attempts to constrain artificially, but the forces at work in the text disband and parody such limits. Diane Thompson's reading of *The Brothers Karamazov*, which finds within it a cultural memory centred on Christ, is an instance of good insights within a textual reading fatally compromised by an insistence, taken from V.E. Vetlovskaia, that in the novel, 'lack of faith turns into a "catastrophe"'. This in turn assumes that the novel presents only two fundamentally opposed views: again, from Vetlovskaia, 'there is no third way in the novel between good and evil, God and the devil'. *If* something in Dostoevsky wishes to believe that, and an author's intentions – assuming a unitary author – are always problematic – the text's dialogism disallows it, and it is irrelevant to argue that what happens in the novel at the level of plot demonstrates the rightness of these moral judgments. Thompson quotes Bakhtin that 'an idea becomes a *live event* played out at the points of dialogue meeting between two or several consciousnesses'. She says, *contra* this, 'an idea becomes a "live event" because of the way it affects people's lives. That is what stories and plots are for' (Thompson 1991: 58–59). But 'stories' and 'plots' have never been the same since E.M. Forster, and plots should be examined more critically, rather than accepted as controlling, because they impose a way of looking, a linear approach to time. The simplicity of a plot imposes a 'monologic unity' (Bakhtin 1984b: 20). People are not so single in Dostoevsky. Characters voice each other, and there is no necessary relationship between how people think and what happens to them, whether in art or life. To think otherwise – that is what stories are for – is to impose a morality which wants to read one way only. The diabolical, in *some* manifestations, interrupts that. Dostoevsky's texts are full of people engaged in soliloquy, or confession, attempting to say or set down what the 'I' is thinking. These are addresses to the 'other' who is already inside, as well as outside. The devil may be that other, but is not privileged as such. His voice is also relative, for he is not outside the text but inside it, as a figure already represented.

What is apparent is the continuity of *The Brothers Karamazov* with the political nihilism of *Demons*. Its action, said to have taken place thirteen years previously, lasts four days, plus the trial two months later. The Preface indicates that the book will be hagiographic; though this narrator will always be inconsistent. He is giving the life of Alexei (Alyosha), the would-be monk, the youngest of three brothers, his self-divisions deriving from Hoffmann's Medardus (Passage 1954: 162–177). The Preface announces that this is the first of two novels. Alyosha, who has been commented on as hysterical, even epileptic (Rice 2009: 355–375), seems destined to be executed for some political action, perhaps collaborating in the assassination of Alexander II (1855–1881). The Tsar survived several attempts on his life, the first on 4 April 1866, from a shooting by a student, Dmitri Karakazov, who was hanged that September. The details apparently influenced the writing of Raskolnikov (*Crime and Punishment*), and also perhaps, via the name, the idea of Alyosha Karamazov (Verhoeven 2009: 100; Hingley 1967: 25–26). Karakazov was apparently associated with a radical cell named 'Hell', a predecessor to Nechaev's group (Frank 1995: 52, 448). Alexander was killed by a bomb a little over a month after Dostoevsky's death. Dostoevsky's plan suggests that Alyosha would become part of that generation of nihilists with whom Dostovesky's work dialogues constantly.

All three brothers derive from Medardus, whether in sensuality (Dmitri, the eldest, twenty-eight); or, like Alyosha, as a would-be monk who must try the world; or in being radically split in allegiances which produce madness, as with Ivan, aged twenty-four, and with the most to say about the devil. He feels split throughout, between adherence to Russian national identity

(Slavophilia), such as Dmitri feels, and to being Westernised, as an intellectual. One account of *Fathers and Children* and its influence on Dostoevsky says that for him, 'the Westerner, regardless of his age or class, is a nihilist' (Lowe 1983: 136) – including, then, Turgenev. The 'I' narrating intimates that there could be a further novel written about Ivan, perhaps in relation to Katerina Ivanovna (11.6.610), despite his breakdown at the end.

Dmitri was the son of Adelaida, married to Fyodor Pavlovich, the father, the buffoon, (22, 41), a religious sceptic, who parades this in his endless patter. For example, he asks how can there be punishment in hell – e.g. suspending people by hooks – when hell has no ceilings? (24–25). Adelaida shows her contempt for her husband, and deserts him. Her death makes him rejoice and grieve at once, like Gargantua, and that gives a key to the timbre of Dostoevsky's text. Dmitri is abandoned to the care of Grigory, the servant. Sofia, the second wife, the father calls a 'shrieker', i.e. hysterical (22, 137). Ivan was born first to her, followed by Alyosha who 'remembered his mother all his life' (14): a statement which implies that Alyosha has died. In drunken conversation with Alyosha and Ivan, the father remembers his wife as being chased by a handsome man who slapped him in the face: the father is he who gets slapped, and Sofia humiliates him to which he responds by spitting on her icon of the Mother of God. This recollection produces hysteria in Alyosha, and that reaction recalls Sofia, his mother, to Fyodor Pavlovich. He seems to have forgotten that Ivan, to whom he appeals for help – and whose contempt for him is palpable – is also Sofia's son. His mind has gone blank, as if in a form of epilepsy (138). It is part of this novel's fascination with discontinuities in the single subject, as was the case with Stavrogin, which make memory and forgetting so much outside its control. If all that is to be discussed in terms of epilepsy, it makes the point that epilepsy does not *explain*, but points to a problem of which it may be a symptom. It suggests, too, that to discuss memory requires Freud, both for the unconscious, and for the point that memory is blocked and released in repression, whether personal or social. Freud is missing in Diane Thompson's study.

This chapter (1.3.8) ends with Dmitri running in as if to kill his father – the three brothers have different murderous feelings towards the patriarch – his rage caused by the rivalry he has with his father over the woman Grushenka. Dmitri attacks his father, who also attacks him, and Dmitri also threatens Grigory (3.9). This first part, then, establishes the family and the father/son rivalries. In three confessional chapters in which he speaks with Alyosha (3.3, 4, 5), preceding the attack just mentioned, Dmitri is Schillerian in quoting 'An die Freude', and is Nietzschean in being the Silenus, and drunk, and carnivalesque: since, as a Karamazov, he says, he will fall into the abyss head down: the body turned upside -down in true carnival fashion (107). In his attitude to money, Dmitri enjoys what he calls 'depravity' with women, especially the bourgeois Katerina Ivanovna, to whom he must give 3000 roubles, but which his father will not lend him, because that would free Dmitri from his engagement to her, so liberating him to be with Grushenka. (It seems that the father has a packet of exactly the same amount, which he wants to give to Grushenka.) Katerina is also in love with Ivan, but something self-tormenting (*nadryv*), the subject of Book 4, especially chapter 5, binds her to Dmitri, so making her a figure of 'laceration', what Wasiolek calls 'purposeful and pleasurable self-hurt' (Wasiolek 1964: 180). The affect was noted before with Stavrogin: indeed the heart of the novel shows people whose pleasure is in hurting themselves. Ivan is accordingly jealous of his brother, over Katerina, and his relationship with her is equally conflictual. Her sister is Liza, who in Book 11, chapter 3, 'A Little Demon', is so called by Ivan, who seems to have attracted her infatuation. She is also sadistic to herself. James Rice notes the possibility that Alyosha would marry Liza in a future novel.

Karamazov's house contains three servants: first, the old Grigory, and his wife Marfa, substitute parents to Dmitri. Their only child, who died, was born with six fingers, implying something diabolical. Grigor's consolation is reading the Book of Job, and the homilies of the seventh-century monk, Isaac the Syrian – apparently a believer in *apokatastasis* – and becoming interested in the Flagellants (96). The other is Smerdyakov, who is like Ferdka, the murderous convict in *Demons*, another victim of a 'father': because, as Stefan Verkhovensky's serf, he was sold into the army to pay off gambling debts (*Demons* 228, 487). Smerdyakov was found the day that Grigor's child is buried, as a newborn, replacement child, son of the dumb peasant Stinking Lizaveta, described as a 'holy fool' (97), and wholly excluded, though Fyodor Pavlovich said that she could be treated as a woman (i.e. raped) however animal-like she was (98: a Rabelaisian detail). 'Some' people say she was lifted over the garden fence into the Karamazov garden to give birth and die, or else was spirited over (99). So Lizaveta is, morally certainly, the mother of Smerdyakov by Fyodor Pavlovich, although Grigor insists the father is a well-known convict who had just escaped from prison and was living in 'our town' – called Skotoprigonyevsk (573), i.e. 'cattle-pen', a carnivalesque enough name, perhaps suiting Staraya Russa, south of Petersburg, where Dostoevsky had a summer house.

Smerdyakov has the same name and patronymic as his putative father, He is Pavel Fyodorovich Smerdyakov ('son of the stinking one', i.e. Lizaveta Smerdyashchaya). His strangeness and epilepsy (see 3.6), including an apparent propensity for hanging cats, then treating them as religious icons (he has a comparable sadism towards dogs, 535), associates popularly with the sense that he is a castrate (605; Peace 1992: 263). That, and his avarice – he kills for money – makes for an uncanny comparison with Chaucer's Pardoner. The account of him culminates in a comparison with Kramskoi's picture *The Contemplator* (1876): a red-haired peasant out of all relation to his wintry surroundings, his eyes wide open, looking as if frozen, in a trance, which may perhaps be epileptic. If Smerdyakov does something, he will either wander to Jerusalem to save his soul or take part in a *jacquerie*, or both, making him a little like Alyosha. The behaviour contrasts are as rapid as with the father's reaction to his first wife's death, and the word 'both' is a measure of the dualism, or lack of unified subjectivity, that so fascinates Dostoevsky. But if Kramskoi's painting is evoked for the reader to consider, it also suggests the alienated state of the peasant in Russian society, as a reminder that Smerdyakov is *not* a peasant. He is more upwardly mobile than that, though no less alienated. Alienation intimates the guilt that he inspires in others, and may account for his aggression, as when he refuses biblical teachings, for which Grigory slaps him. He shows Jesuitical skill (130): Jesuits (as Catholics, not of the Russian Orthodox Church) were associated with the Nihilists (Verhoeven 2009: 51). His gift is equivocating – as in his epileptic fits, whose certainty may be questioned – equivocation including the ability to enter into and inhabit another person's discourse. He asks where light shone from before the fourth day of creation, the Manichean challenge to Augustine (Augustine 2002: 51–53). Yet that teasing buffoonery must not be simplified, as Ivan, who spent some time talking to him, knows, being 'unable to understand what it was that could so... trouble "this contemplator"... Ivan was soon convinced that the sun, moon and stars [of the fourth day of creation] were not the point at all... he was after something quite different'. And Ivan also intuits a 'boundless' 'injured vanity' in Smerdyakov (266). The Manichee challenge points to a complacency within the 'official' Christian position, which has to be defended because it serves certain class interests (as Christianity may). Ivan's recoil from Smerdyakov may be because he cannot, ultimately, admit his right to equality in asking these questions. Just as, in *Othello*, Cassio says that the lieutenant must be saved before the ancient. Smerdyakov is after all, to be called the 'lackey', never recognised otherwise.[5]

Alyosha is to enter a monastery under the authority of the elder Zosima, who is first seen tending to women who are 'shriekers'. The narrator speaks of these as cases of demon-possession (47). The three brothers and the father are seen together first in the monastery, there to resolve a financial dispute between the father and Dmitri, where the father makes an ass of himself, and asks Zosima if he offends him, and Zosima replies by telling him to be at ease, and above all, not to be ashamed of himself, for that is the cause of everything (43): cause indeed of his buffoonery. Shame is placed at the heart of the book as a reactive state, as Nietzsche would call it, which protects itself by further reactive behaviour, which creates something worse. Shame, unlike guilt, implies the double: if I am ashamed of myself, that self-reflexivity implies looking at myself, doubling myself, becoming an object, and leading either to self-punishment, or to a desire to humiliate the self before others: this is what happens with the father. While everyone is waiting for Dmitri to arrive – it turns out that Smerdyakov gave him the wrong time – a debate develops over an article written by Ivan, the rationalist, but also the secret theologian. And if these things are the same, it is because both appeal to an absolute authority, reason or science in one case. God in the other.

Ivan's article has rejected the distinction between church and state, so that would mean that crime was judged to be an ecclesiastical offence, which he thinks should increase the severity of punishments. It would mean that crime was not treated in a utilitarian manner. Indeed, it would confirm the intimate relationship of the church with the criminal, which is not quite what Ivan was expecting, because his idea is to intensify punishment. It would be bad if the church might weaken such a power to punish, from a Manichean sense of that intimacy. In an anecdote (a Dostoevsky novel always becomes a retelling of anecdotes, whose origin and authority cannot be guaranteed: that equalising of all stories is part of the novels' dialogism), Ivan is credited as saying that there is no basis for law – certainly the utilitarian one is insufficient – except for belief in immortality. If this is taken away, evil-doing is 'the most necessary and most intelligent solution' (69). This statement of nihilism, where all values have turned illusory, is followed by the elder telling Alyosha to leave the monastery. The agenda here is to help Dmitri, whom Zosima intuits could murder the father.

5 The Grand Inquisitor

In Book 5, Alyosha meets Ivan, who speaks about his thirst for life as being a Karamazov trait (230), though he thinks he will be through with that by the age of thirty. He also mentions his love for the sticky buds of spring; i.e. for those fresh and clingy elements of life, especially sexual life, which defeat logic (as Mephistopheles told the student: 'Grau, teurer Freund, ist alle Theorie,/Und gründes Lebens goldner Baum' (2038–2039: theory, my friend, is all grey: only the tree of life is green). Ivan turns the subject towards theory: i.e. that there is no God, which he had told his father. His father had responded by asking who was laughing at mankind, to which Ivan replied that it 'must be the devil', before negating the devil's existence (134). Ivan quotes Voltaire by saying that if God did not exist he would have to be invented, and finds God to be a projection of man's. But, he says, if the world is God's creation, he will not accept it, pointing to the sufferings of children, so qualitatively different from adults – at least until they reach the age of seven. In this he shows his own vulnerability, since he was seven when his mother died: the mother/child relation, as with Alyosha, being separate from this debate, though protected in the memory. After giving instances of cruelty to children in front of the mother he says that if the devil does not exist, he has been created by humans in their likeness, repeating the point made about God, and equating the two. He accumulates stories of cruelty to children, getting Alyosha to say about one persecutor, with a 'twisted' smile, 'shoot him', a pure nihilism to which Ivan responds as having proved his point about the devil as a human creation: 'see what a little devil is sitting in your heart' (243). Ivan argues that children, as outside systems, and outside guilt, are the extra force which make thoughts of universal justice impossible. It makes him feel that he must return his ticket, in a refusal of this universe. All of this is directed at making Alyosha feel the more compromised in his faith. And he gives the question, which had been posed in *Père Goriot*: if happiness could be built on the basis of the suffering of one child, would that be acceptable?[6]

At this, Alyosha thinks of the Christian doctrine of Christ dying for all, and Ivan says that the previous year he had thought up a poem called 'The Grand Inquisitor' on this subject; that the rationalist thinks in terms of poetry is typically contradictory. He proceeds to give, not the poem, but a paraphrase of it (so what follows becomes a discourse about discourse), saying that the form belongs to a medieval drama tradition, where God and humans interact.

The chapter, 'The Grand Inquisitor' (5.5) is, then, framed so as to make it impossible to take it as an authoritative statement of Ivan's – let alone of any aspect of Dostoevsky – but Ivan's imagination is obviously fired by the telling, by the debate he has with his own rationalism. The account of the poem is in dialogue with Schiller's *Don Carlos*, and the Grand Inquisitor there, but also with Faust, who desired two incompatible things: to combine control with the gift of freedom to people. Christ has returned to sixteenth-century Seville. The Inquisitional authorities have imprisoned him, and the ninety-year-old Inquisitor visits him there. The Inquisitor's subject is the temptation of Christ (Matthew 4:1–11), at which time the devil, 'the dread and intelligent spirit, the spirit of self-destruction and of non-being', (more than Mephisto therefore, though from the description, it must include him) met Christ (251). Intelligence must, it seems, be defined as nihilism, as readiness to see through all values, which makes it a double quality (Connolly 2013: 26–28). The three temptations, or questions, are momentous, and must be interpreted.

The first is that Christ should provide bread for people who can only be controlled by that, since modernity will produce a sense that there is no crime, nor sin, but only hunger, which must be catered for before there can be virtue. In their disappointment that the 'Tower of Babel' remains unbuilt, the Grand Inquisitor envisages the people asking him and his like for help, disappointed that they were not given 'fire from heaven'. The people, in other words, are interpreted as wanting another Prometheus, the archetypal Satan of Romanticism. Prometheus, in stealing from heaven for the people, was both a populist, and demonic, in negating the divine hierarchy. Here, the Grand Inquisitor, who speaks as one experienced in control, envisages the emergence of a new power and authority, centred on the person who presents himself as a Prometheus: the nihilist of the nineteenth century, who undoes existing power with its attendant ideology, for 'nihilism does not transform something into nothing but shows that nothing which has been taken for something is an optical illusion, and that every truth, however it contradicts our favourite ideas, is more wholesome than that' (Gillespie 1995: 139). We can see the Grand Inquisitor as both a nihilist and the person who shows that nihilism is a form of control, and therefore no more than another ideological formation. The person who gives fire from heaven in the form of 'bread and circuses', banal satisfaction, will have the people's consent to enslave them. Christ, in not doing this, laid the basis for the destruction of his own kingdom: in that sense, Christ is an alternative form of nihilism, in willing to bring about the end of his own rule.

The second temptation was for Christ to throw himself from the pinnacle of the temple, which he refused to do since that would imply performing a miracle, and ignoring people's need to have miracles created for them. The weak soul cannot tolerate such a demand, which implies his freedom to choose. The Inquisitor speaks of the power that he and the church have assumed, of control, indeed of enslaving, permitting 'rebellion' (the title of the previous chapter, when Ivan was resisting God's universe) as 'a child and a schoolboy' (256). Rebellion only demonstrates the superiority of a controlling power which contains it, and so shows up the puerility of the rebellious. Allowance of rebellion is a strategy of containment. So the church, as paradigmatic of modern rule, corrects the weakness of Christ in not offering a miracle by imposing 'miracle, mystery and authority'. The result is that people become dependent, like sheep. As the Inquisitor tells this to Christ, his anger with himself becomes evident as he says that 'we are not with you, but with *him*' (257). The church is diabolical, and the Grand Inquisitor speaks as the devil's avatar.

He then reaches the third temptation, which comprises Christ's refusal to adopt Caesar's universal empire for himself. The church has done that where Christ would not. The Grand Inquisitor anticipates the day when that will be recognised – there will be no more 'lawlessness of free reason' (258). People will be convinced that they have freedom when they give their freedom over. The discourse of freedom, of course, conflicts sharply with what Faust wants (*Faust*, 11,575), though it could be argued that the Grand Inquisitor is a critique of that agenda, since 'freedom' now seems forced on people as freedom to consume (the hidden hand in the free market). The Grand Inquisitor also recalls Mephisto's soliloquy in *Faust* Part One (lines 1851–1867) in offering banality, and freedom to people to amuse themselves, under the permission of the central authority, while, he says, the people will have no secrets from us. There is a free acknowledgement, too, that this will all be purchased through systematic lying to the people.

He concludes by telling Christ that he was once like him, in the wilderness, and ate locusts and roots, like John the Baptist (Matthew 3:1–4), but adds that 'I awoke, and did not want to serve madness' (260). There is a tragedy in that last sentence. Madness, which contrasts with the devil as 'intelligent', rational enough to control people, associates with holy fools, who are carnivalesque in their folly.[7] Behind the Inquisitor's words is a deep refusal of carnival in favour of monological utterance with firm originating authority behind it, and a commitment to 'correcting' Christ's holy foolishness.

The statement which gives the rationale of the Grand Inquisitor is, however, as Alyosha says, really praise of Jesus, an instance of the impossibility of monologism, how everything that it represses returns. And perhaps Ivan knew that: hence he wrote a poem, not discursive prose. The piece is really in praise of the heterogeneous and despised Christ, about to suffer an auto-da-fé, as demonstrated by the Grand Inquisitor's sheer obsessiveness. Ivan is left trying to defend his psychology and his intelligence, and to show that his Faustian alliance with what is now called 'the dread spirit of death and destruction' (261 – Blake's 'God of this world'), includes willing acceptance of lies and deceit; that he is a nihilist, in the sense that the death of God has occurred, but, he is an incomplete nihilist, since in the name of control he wants to preserve the old values while recognising that they have no foundation. He calls those in the desert 'proud', because they are few, and therefore might think of themselves as exceptional, and calls the others, whom he controls, the humble. And that also feeds into Nietzsche's analysis, in *The Genealogy of Morals*, which calls institutionalised Christianity the triumph of the weak, and recalls the statement in Nietzsche's later notebooks, which Deleuze cites, 'the strong always have to be defended against the weak' (Deleuze 1983: 58).

The reported ending of the poem shows Christ silently kissing the Grand Inquisitor, an action Alyosha repeats with Ivan, making him, the Grand Inquisitor, and the 'poem' autobiographical. The old man silently releases him into the 'dark squares of the city'. The Grand Inquisitor's anger is that something has escaped his enframing of the world into his single system, something that remains silent, like the woman in *The Meek One* (a significant name). But what else may be said of the silence and the gesture? Is Ivan, in scripting the kiss, showing signs of a desire for Christ? Or suggesting that Christ will win, so that the Grand Inquisitor's nihilism is pointless? More teasingly, does the silence suggest that Christ recognises that the Grand Inquisitor is also right? – and that he has no answer for him?

What is also evident is the nihilism that 'poem' reveals: that all European power structures use Christianity to represent and support themselves, which makes the 'poem' a potentially radical statement from a member of the 'young generation' that Ivan represents. It also means that the poem could never be a challenge to Christ, only to how

Christ can be manipulated in Christianity. Ivan would have liked to have negated the existence of God insofar as this impinges on reality, and the 'poem' is his attempt at the 'new word' that Raskolnikov thought of. But he can only negate the ways in which God is represented in the world. God, like the devil, cannot be thought of outside ways in which he is represented, an argument used within 'negative theology'. In that way the father may resist the act of parricide elsewhere so desired in this novel, and which Freud's essay 'Dostoevsky and Parricide' rightly sees as Dostoevsky's subject (*SE* 21. 175–196). Nihilism, which would destroy the father's authority, is confuted, the old diabolism of the father must continue, but Freud indicates that the would-be parricide can only want that: he wishes his own defeat.

6 Parricide

The brothers' conversation concludes with Ivan holding to his view, as paraphrased by Dmitri, that 'everything is permitted'. As he walks off, Alyosha projects onto Ivan a sense of his crookedness in walking, left shoulder (the side of damnation (Matthew 25:33)) diabolically higher. Ivan has infected his thinking. Bosch's *Wayfarer*, too, has his left leg bandaged. (At the end of the following chapter, Ivan's walk is as if in spasms: as if he is epileptic.) Alyosha, noting Ivan, remembers 'several times later, in great perplexity' (264) that the meeting let him forget what he had come to do: i.e. find Dmitri, under the sense that something catastrophic was about to happen to him (222). The forgetting is like the father's quasi-epileptic lapse (138). It relates to Alyosha's double aims (he wants to be with his Zosima, called 'Pater Seraphicus' by Ivan out of Goethe (*Faust,* line 11,918), as if Alyosha was a young Faust). He also wants to be with Dmitri. The Ivan meeting shows that thinking can never work with such binaries; a devil gets into it, and abolishes such neatnesses. The parapraxis, one of many that constructs this novel, indicates too that Alyosha's motives towards Dmitri are not single. The unconscious within them makes all events and conclusions in the text much less resolved, more like compromise formations.

Ivan's dialogue prompts the idea of something Jesuitical within him. In accordance with that, the novel then tracks his meeting with Smerdyakov, where Ivan's repulsion does not stop him thinking that Smerdyakov's 'slightly squinting left eye' is winking as if saying that 'we two intelligent men' ought to talk. 'Intelligent' as a word gathers meaning from the 'Grand

Inquisitor' chapter, where it was applied to the devil. Smerdyakov – whose talking with Ivan, with its hints and echoing language, recalls Iago – seems Ivan's double. But though the text's dialogism, i.e. the impossibility of finding an originating, authorising statement in it, does not allow for such an idea of an 'original' self who can be doubled, and Smerdyakov's conversation with Ivan about his father's and Dmitri's mutual obsession over Grushenka, shows him, in its servility, as virtually their double, too; the double is not a symmetrical concept. The dialogue contains hints that Dmitri might kill his father, from jealousy over Grushenka and in order to steal. He hints that the father's death would be good for all the brothers. Otherwise the father might marry Grushenka, who would possess all his money, because, in Smerdyakov's characteristic use of unauthorised statements, 'I know myself that her merchant Sansonov told her . . . that it would even be quite a clever deal . . . ' (273). Ivan is being tempted by Smerdyakov to go to Chermashnya, which would put him out of reach during a putative murder by Dmitri of the father. Ivan would be implicated as a virtual accessory: suspecting that his father was to be killed but not doing anything.

The following chapter, 'It's Always Interesting to Talk with an Intelligent Man' continues Ivan's temptation since his father wants him to visit Chermashnya to deal with Gorstkin, whose honesty the father suspects. He is a characteristic liar, says the father (it takes a diabolical and carnivalesque one to know one). He apparently boasted that his wife was dead and that he had remarried, but his wife is still alive and beats him periodically, and his beard indicates whether he is lying or not . . . Only Ivan can detect all this, being 'intelligent', so the father says. Under this pressure, Ivan irrationally announces publicly that he is going to Chermashnya, and Smerdyakov says that it is true what they say, that 'it's always interesting to talk with an intelligent [i.e. diabolical] man'. He thus indicates that he has secured Ivan's connivance in being unable to prevent a murder, which Smerdyakov, of course, will commit. Though Ivan actually goes to Moscow, as though trying to evade the responsibility, he still feels he is a scoundrel, a word he had previously used about Smerdyakov, who finishes the chapter with an apparent serious epileptic fit. Does he have Ivan's fit vicariously?

Part Two finishes with the death of Father Zosima, whose life, death, relations to his brother, and writings receive three chapters. This narrative, which usually attracts attention as indicative of Dostoevsky's religious convictions, frames Zosima within the typology of Job, whose life and temptations he takes as exemplary for all. If this, writing in hagiographical mode, reads as isolated from the dialogical interest of the novel, it needs emphasising that Zosima is a creation of Alyosha's text, reconstructing fragmentary conversations, putting them into order from memory after Zosima's death, and after the events of the novel. Neither is the record said to be uncontroversial (286). This 'Zosima' comes from Alyosha's desire to create a father figure who is outside the flow of events and of dialogue, and who contrasts with the trauma which Alyosha experiences at the opening of Book 7, since Zosima's now corrupt and smelling dead body, reminiscent of Stinking Lizaveta, and this linking the holy fool with the saint (Ziolkowski 1988: 153–169), causes a crisis which drives Alyosha out of the monastery. The logic also connects Zosima with Smedyakov, but Alyosha literally cannot see that kinship ('Will my brother Dmitri be back soon?' he says to Smerdyakov (226)).[8] This is one of the gaps in Alyosha's being, already noticed – his forgetfulness – but at some level, it induces, apparently, epilepsy, as a crisis of faith, which the cynical and hence nihilistic career monk Rakitin notices (7.2). Rakitin's effect on Alyosha is to make him adopt Ivan's words about not accepting God's word, and eating a sausage, during Lent.

When we turn from that to Grushenka, and the account of Samonov, her 'patron' – this older lover is another 'father' – it becomes apparent that the novel is structured on relationships which resemble Mephisto acting towards to a person who can be tempted. Nearly everyone has the potential to be a Mephisto, lowering the estimate of something, nihilistically devaluing it. Grushenka, for instance, has tried tempting Alyosha, promising Rakitin, with echoes of Judas, twenty-five roubles to bring her Alyosha, before she disappears to an assignation with a Pole. She thus betrays Dmitri, and Orthodoxy, focusing the former's jealousy, making him an Othello (8.3), that other famous epileptic. So Dmitri, in Book 8 – which contains the father's murder, and Dmitri's rash assault on Grigory, about which he feels complete remorse (9.2) – rushes headlong to and fro, unable to complete an action, and feeling near to 'brain fever' (364). His arrest, charged with his father's murder, completes Book 9.

7 Ivan's Devil

While Book 10 is Alyosha's, Book 11 is about Ivan, who only returned from Moscow five days after the murder, so missing the burial. The unconscious meanings of that delay must be pondered on. Ivan is alluded to repeatedly in chapter 4, when Alyosha talks to Dmitri in prison. In chapter 5, it is apparent that Ivan is undergoing a breakdown, which first takes the form of tearing a letter to pieces from 'that little demon' Liza. As Alyosha and Ivan walk together, Ivan asks who the murderer was, naming Smerdyakov (whom Alyosha has repeatedly accused, it seems, while Ivan thinks Dmitri was guilty). Alyosha repeats 'You know who', then adding that it was not Ivan, and saying that Ivan has told himself several times that he was the murderer, self-accusing, as if he was his own double, who shames, and accuses.

Ivan replies to this vindication, which Alyosha says came to him from God, by saying 'you were in my room at night when he came . . . confess . . . you saw him'. Who 'he' is remains unclear. He is certainly the accuser, which also implies the Freudian superego, that part of the ego which replaces the dead, and vengeful father.[9] (It will later become apparent that 'he' is the devil.) But then Ivan becomes rational, and ultra-formal, saying he cannot bear prophets and epileptics, messengers from God especially. Is he calling Alyosha an epileptic? On the previous page he called Smerdyakov 'that mad epileptic idiot' (601).

The brothers separate, and Ivan, instead of going home, goes to Smerdyakov's lodging; it being specified that this is the third visit he pays him – the third time is as climactic as the card-playing which ends *The Queen of Spades* – and the earlier visits are then recorded. The first was in the hospital where Smerdyakov has been since his epileptic fit on the night of the murder. That dialogue is now reported, and Smerdyakov in rerunning the conversation he had with Ivan (3.6,7) indicates that he was reproaching Ivan for abandoning his parent (saying that he wanted him to go to Chermashnya, not Moscow, if he had to go anywhere, because Chermashnya was nearer to home). The second visit (11.7) is to Smerdyakov's lodgings, and by now, Ivan has thoroughly internalised the idea that he had wished for his father's death, at Dmitri's hands, and he wants to question Smerdyakov about the conversation he had had with him (Book 5). Had he entered into some league (unconsciously) with him? The Faustian suggestion is strong. Smerdyakov's reply is to say that Ivan had wished for his father's death, for which Ivan slaps him (614), knowing the statement has a partial truth in it (617). There are echoes of David Copperfield slapping Uriah Heep (Dickens 2004: 626: Dostoevsky read Dickens keenly). That act of aggression exposes Copperfield because, or as, weak. In both cases, such direct action, which implies the loss of temper, and so of self-possession, has the damaging effect of affirming a class division. It is the reactive behaviour of the strong, who is thus identified with the weak, while the weaker person can claim a moral victory over him. It recalls how Smerdyakov is repeatedly called a lackey – a term Ivan also applies to the devil (648). Ivan accuses Smerdyakov of killing the father. The latter replies by saying that an 'intelligent' man (he repeats this) should have no such thought. Smerdyakov's victory over Ivan is to accuse him successfully of *wanting* to kill his father, creating guilt, so that he considers himself a murderer as much as the Dmitri he has blamed hitherto.

On the way to the third meeting (11.8) – remembering that Ivan still considers Dmitri to be, formally, the murderer (see 624) – Ivan knocks down a peasant – perhaps substituting for Smerdyakov – who was singing drunkenly; 'Ah, Vanka [the same name as Ivan]'s gone to Petersburg/And I'll not wait for him', which could even be Smerdyakov's language for what he could do with Ivan out of the way. Ivan's gesture violently repudiates this interpretation, which would align the two with each other. He repeats the slap, in more violent mode. Smerdyakov this time looks sick – yellow, as a devilish, jaundiced, colour is played on several times – and has a book, the works of Isaac the Syrian: the sacred text has its way of being read demonically, or becoming demonic, or perhaps was always demonic: a point for Bosch. Ivan wants to know if Katerina – who wants to blame Dmitri for the death, so that she can love him in a more controlling way – has been to see him. Smerdyakov refuses to answer but tells him to go, repeating Alyosha's words, 'it was not you who killed him' (623). Alyosha had meant to free Dmitri and Ivan from any guilt: but when Smerdyakov repeats it, he wants to implicate Dmitri, and Ivan, because the meaning is also: 'I killed him', a sense Ivan grasps: and also: 'if I killed him, you killed him, because I was your lackey'.

When Ivan thinks he is unreal, a dream or a ghost (an intimation of the devil), Smerdyakov's reply emphasises his own reality – which Ivan cannot quite take – and then de-realises everything by saying a third is with them now, which he qualifies by saying he means God, though his original meaning could make the devil the third. He produces out of his left-leg stocking the 3000 roubles which he stole – his motive for murder (compare John 12:6) and which Dmitri was accused of stealing – returning these to Ivan is Judas-like; so is the number (3000 roubles versus thirty pieces of silver), and so are the consequences, for Judas and Smerdyakov both hang themselves (Matthew 27:3–5). The gesture causes convulsive fear in Ivan, abjection, from the contiguity with the body (there is a sexual frisson there; further, the stocking's whiteness connotes castration (Peace 1992: 262)). Smerdyakov insists on bringing Ivan into a sodality with himself, deflecting his own hatred for the father onto him, and indicating how much he wanted to have Ivan as his guilty patron. Further, he keeps quoting Ivan's words, intended partly for intellectual debate, about everything being permitted, as if invading his consciousness, or suggesting that he was inhabited by Ivan's consciousness (his 'intelligence' – a word whose constant repetition, in an increasingly ironic context, suggests the equivalent 'Brutus is an honourable man' in *Julius Caesar* 3.2 (Terras 1981: 379)). Finally, he tells Ivan that he is the most like his father, and would not want to take 'shame' upon himself in the court by accusing Smerdyakov, because that would also shame him. And indeed, Ivan lacks that carnival possibility of being, like his father, a buffoon. He returns to his lodgings, but on the way, makes reparation, which lasts an hour, to the peasant whom he had knocked over.

There is more I will say about Smerdyakov, but I will proceed to the next chapter: 'The Devil. Ivan Fyodorovich's Nightmare' is of delirium and of seeing the devil, as a faded figure of bare respectability around the age of fifty, either a bachelor or a widower, one likely to forget his children (so like the novel's father), and a sponger: a figure of banality (647). He may be an 1840s figure, like Stepan Verkovensky, another sponger (a parasite), so one of the 'Fathers' who is partly responsible for Ivan, as the nihilist (Terras 1981: 386). Certainly, he is twice Ivan's age, his ideas borrowed, like the French he is associated with ('qui frisait la cinquantaine' and 'du bon ton' both appear in his initial description; interestingly, Smerdyakov was also learning French (616–617)), and he does not want to be excluded. It seems rather that the devil's desire is to be bourgeois and to be accepted. The question whether he is real or not shows the split within Ivan's cultural formation, between a Russian traditional belief, which might agree that he is, and a city-based Western viewpoint which would regard any such belief as evidence of breakdown. This is not his first visit; though Ivan insists that his voice is talking, he cannot quite refute belief in the devil's objectivity, which the devil wants to maximise. And indeed, if he did believe it, that would create a simpler world; it would make things easier for Ivan, whose struggle against belief in the devil, then, is an attempt to hold onto sanity, even if it means that he is schizophrenic.

The 'devil', subtle as Smerdyakov, parasitic in another way, insists on his reality. He reminds Ivan that he spoke to Alyosha that night of seeing 'him'. Talking incessantly, comparing himself with Mephisto, he denies that his function is to negate (642). He deals in affirmation, and wants bourgeois security. He says that Ivan wants, secretly, to identify with those who eat locusts in the desert; this being the secret meaning of his poem 'The Grand Inquisitor'. Victories over desert fathers are the devil's most precious:

> some of them . . . are not inferior to you in [intellectual] development . . . They can contemplate abysses of belief and disbelief at one and the same moment that really, it sometimes seems that another hair's breadth and a man would fall in 'heel-over headed' as the actor Gorbunov says. (645)

Such 'desert fathers' can think in schizoid fashion, which, as the opposite of bourgeois thinking, is their strength and their danger. Though the 'Grand Inquisitor' poem is only mentioned later (648), it ghosts this dialogue. The devil's greatest success was to have co-opted the Grand Inquisitor into his own scheme, as a figure who was in the wilderness, like Christ, a holy fool; and to have turned him towards himself, with all the non-bourgeois concern for central control the Grand Inquisitor has. In contrast, falling into the abyss head first recalls Dmitri's sense that a Karamazov falls in carnival fashion, with the showmanship of the actor Ivan Gorbunov, a Dostoevskian contemporary. The very equivocating, Jesuitical, style of these figures of the desert is carnivalesque. The devil has captured the carnival. So he says he works in the sphere of comedy and wordplay, which give him his chance; confessional booths give the perfect opportunity for Jesuitical casuistry.

His nihilism is to 'destroy the idea of God in mankind' which may quote Ivan's words. The result of that will not open life up to the new, and to Nietzschean 'becoming'. It will, rather, produce the perfected, controlled, consumer society. Indeed, at that point he sounds like the Grand Inquisitor himself. People who can talk about everything being permitted will proceed to produce worse actions, conquering nature, as the 'man-god' (649; not even Kirillov's self-assertive God-man). When Ivan throws the glass of tea at him, like Luther with the inkpot thrown at the devil, a knocking comes from outside. Does this uncanny moment replace the devil with something worse? Alyosha is there to tell Ivan that Smerdyakov hanged himself an hour previously, immediately after Ivan left him, as if increasing Ivan's guilt. Has something of Smerdyakov passed into the devil? Ivan says that he knew Smerdyakov had hanged himself, though the devil said no such thing: 'He said that' is the chapter title. 'He told me' (651) leaves ambiguous whether Smerdyakov is the devil. Eventually Ivan says that the devil has visited three times, matching, doubling the visits to Smerdyakov. Alyosha objects that the devil could not have told him about Smerdyakov's death, but Ivan's replies, a mixture of Smerdyakov's and the devil's language, and his delirium, which is also his impression of these conversations, only prove how there is no unambiguous meaning within language, which instead, picks up and drops its individual speakers and passes on to another. The events of chapters 11.8 and 11.9 have given Ivan a memory which does not coincide with what literally happened – but what has 'literally' happened? Ivan says that he will not commit suicide, which is where Smerdyakov's, or more, the devil's logic would lead him.

Like all suicides discussed in this chapter, there remains something for speculation in Smerdyakov's suicide. It is not wholly explicable, though it may respond to a disappointment with Ivan, and a hatred of being the lackey: the 'whoreson', to recall the language of Gloucester talking about his bastard son Edmund in *King Lear* (1.1.22). Smerdyakov is not acknowledged, not even by Alyosha, who tells Kolya 'the lackey killed him [the father], my brother is innocent' (768); another Alyosha forgetting because failing to make connections (the lackey was also my brother). Perhaps that grievance Smerdyakov has against Ivan is one reason why he says that Ivan is most like his father. Neither of those two have acknowledged him. His suicide may not be simply nihilistic, a response to being found out in his theft and murder. It is entrapping. As a fall-back to the idea that Ivan would not, in the event, accuse him, because that would implicate himself, it continues to cast Dmitri as the murderer. Ivan cannot testify meaningfully against Smerdyakov because of the latter's ambivalent suicide note: 'I exterminate my life by my own will and liking, so as not to blame anybody' (651), which is his revenge, for it expects that people will start blaming each other, accusing some survivor. It means that he denies murder. He leaves the blame on Dmitri's shoulders. Is it a weak way of reminding the world that everything is permitted (632)? Yet the absence of grammar in the suicide note, which Terras notes (1981: 397) points to a failure which also characterises the suicide; a breakdown which makes two halves of a sentence disconnected, and pronounces Smerdyakov another 'poor devil'. The man reading Isaac the Syrian on the day of his death – as he was read by Grigory, before his birth – may be halfway towards a despairing repentance which will kill him. The ambiguities in the third interview bring out a desire for Ivan, that he would endorse him, or recognise him. It is clear he has invested something in him which Ivan has not returned, and this constructs his ambiguity towards him, entrapping him, but trying to release him by appealing to his self-interest, and saying goodbye. And he has already said he no longer needs the money, which is another way of declaring himself on the way to suicide. In which case the grammatical break in the suicide note may mean that he both says everything is permitted, and in contradiction, that he wants no one blamed – or everyone blamed. Such a splitting makes the appearance of the devil, as a reminder to Ivan of his own egotism as exhibited in the devil, a warning of how all motivations fail to be single; all are characterised by a break, a discontinuity within them.

Ivan notes how the devil points up such contradictions of behaviour in him: in that way we can say that one aspect of diabolism is to try to insist on the continuity and consistency of the single subject, and to torment splits in identity. It is of a piece with that that Ivan does not know if the devil was real, or his dream, or delusion. The force that impels single subjectivity is both real and absent, nowhere singly attributable. In the following day's trial, Ivan affirms his own guilt, and knows the devil is everywhere and nowhere, perhaps under the table which has the evidence stacked on it (686–687). The trial has its own, other diabolism. It produces an appallingly carnivalesque series of mistakes whose comedic injustice, like the trial of Pickwick in Dickens, convicts the wrong man, in this case Dmitri, though there is a sense that all three brothers may gain something else from the events, and from the sentence. Certainly, the text closes with the sense of its own unfinishedness; it does not have the single cohesive identity in it whose lack the devil accuses; it is too full of heterogeneous detail to let a unified reading of it stand. And the issues in it must be rolled over into the next chapter, in looking especially at Thomas Mann.

Notes

1. Nozdryov was a crazily comic landowner in *Dead Souls* (chapter 4), his every word a braggadocio's lie, e.g.: '.... he had given [Chichikov, at school] a bit of a going over, which later made it necessary to apply two hundred and forty leeches to his temples alone, that is, he meant to say forty but two hundred somehow popped out all by itself...' (Gogol 2004: 236).
2. *A Writer's Diary*, of incalculable significance for studying Dostoesvky, began as occasional pieces in 1873–1874 as a literary column in a journal, *The Citizen*, which he edited, but which became an independent magazine (1876–1877). It was suspended in 1878 and 1879 for *The Brothers Karamazov*, which it had prepared for, resuming in single issues in August 1880 and January 1881 (Dostoevsky died February 1881).

3. Dostoevsky, of course, was epileptic. In *The Idiot*, Myskhin, about to suffer an epileptic fit himself thinks of the moment it occurs as supreme, when 'there should be time no longer'. It was 'the same second in which the epileptic Mahomet's overturned water-jug failed to spill a drop, while he contrived to behold all the mansions of Allah' (Dostoevsky 1992: 238). The passage is virtually quoted in *The Satanic Verses*: see next chapter. See also Fung 2014.
4. John Donne wrote *Biathanatos*, subtitled 'A Declaration of that Paradoxe, or thesis, that Selfe-Homicide is not so Naturally Sinne, that it may never be Otherwise' in 1608, justifying suicide; it was published posthumously.
5. The meaning of 'lackey' for Dostoevsky would also include beyond its class sense the sense of 'nihilist' and 'Westerniser'; it indicates how much anxiety is being dumped upon Smerdyakov: see Kanevskaya 2002: 367–368.
6. In Balzac, it is a Chinese Mandarin: see Balzac 1991: 124.
7. As a related point, it should be noted how the holy fool – divinely mad – is central to Dostoevsky (Murav 1992: 124–169).
8. The play on Genesis 4:9 which Smerdyakov quotes back to Alyosha, without saying 'brother' because he is excluded, and the repetition of the phrase by Ivan with reference to Dmitri (231), is significant: Cain, of course, as the vagabond on the earth, is the poor devil.
9. There are differences, too. Freud's 'superego' has as part of its power, the function of enforcing the ego's single identity. Freud calls what holds sway in the superego a 'pure culture of the death instinct', adding that it can drive the ego into death ('The Ego and the Id', *SE* 19.53).

Chapter 8: Bulgakov, Mann, Adorno, and Rushdie

Thomas Mann's *Doctor Faustus* and Mikhail Bulgakov's *The Master and Margarita* respond to both Dostoesvky, and Goethe. In Mann's *Lotte in Weimar* (1939), his historical novel which recalls Goethe's early frustrated love for Charlotte Buff, Goethe's demonism is described in terms of being a nihilistic 'all-embracing irony'. Mann is fascinated by the artist as cold; an example of this comes when Goethe is quoted as saying that nothing has savour without irony (Mann 1968: 72). *Doctor Faustus: The Life of the German Composer Adrian Leverkühn as told by a Friend* (1947) uses *Faust*, and Spies' *Faustbuch* (Ball 1986; Bergsten 1969), to place a 'cold' musician at its centre, and it reads post-Lutheran German history antagonistically, taking Luther, in the discussions of theology at the University of Halle (chapters 11 to 13), as thoroughly retrograde; nationalistic, irrational, and hostile to women.

Before Mann was to write his novel, Bulgakov (1891–1940), born in Kiev – not the least of his associations with Gogol – began *The Master and Margarita,* in 1929. His third wife, Yelena Shilovskaya, saw it through to publication in 1966, when censorship permitted it (Barratt 1987: 11–130). Like Hoffmann, Pushkin, Gogol, and Dostoevsky, Bulgakov explores the double, as in 'Diaboliad' (1924), 'The Story of How Twins Destroyed a Clerk'. The setting is Moscow, where he lived after 1921; the subject, the identity loss implied in Soviet bureaucratisation, summed up in *The Master and Margarita* with the devil Koroviev's mockery of its language: 'no papers, no person' (Bulgakov 1997: 289). Both Bulgakov's and Mann's

J. Tambling, *Histories of the Devil*,
DOI 10.1057/978-1-137-51832-3_9

novels are self-reflexive, telling plural tales. Bulgakov's is both a novel about Moscow in the 1920s and 1930s, and at the same time about Pilate in Jerusalem. *Doctor Faustus*' narrator is Serenus Zeitblom, antithesis of Adrian Leverkühn. Perhaps these are split selves, part of a disunited narration, which acts, and comments, and shows that the events narrated cannot be closed off. If Bulgakov's modernist narrators tell a traditional story, about Pilate, Mann's traditional narrator, Zeitblom, classical scholar and Humanist, tells a modernist tale about Adrian. The Pilate narrative, of a judge faced with what he cannot comprehend, offers an alternative history, both to traditional (i.e. Tsarist), and to Soviet thinking, with its official 'atheism'.

Writing about Pilate cannot for Bulgakov be part of a religious history remembered nostalgically, nor from a superior position, taking the present as progress, and disavowing or rewriting the past. Bulgakov and Mann are historical in writing their present, knowing how many pasts are sedimented within it. Both ask what future there can be; either after Stalinism, which tolerates no heterogeneity; or, after a history culminating in Auschwitz. In Bulgakov, the diabolical affirms a possible way forward. Mann makes it ambiguously constitutive of Germany, but also an art outside German nationalism and Fascism. In this last chapter, I consider the diabolism in both, closing with a third text: Salman Rushdie's *The Satanic Verses* (1988). Impossible *not* to include the latter, which, considering the devil from texts discussed earlier, *Othello*, Milton, Defoe, Blake, studies the effects of migrancy on the migrant, critiques British racism and imperialist history, and includes awareness of Islamic monotheism, which led to its comprehensive bannings and the *fatwa*. In questioning it, I will try, as a conclusion, to summarise this book's thoughts about both theology and 'evil'.

1 Woland and Margarita: The Uses of Madness

One idea for Bulgakov's novel was the Blakean 'gospel according to the devil' (Proffer 1984: 525). Berlioz, the authoritative editor in the Stalinist literary world, begins by telling the younger poet Ivan, whose patron he is, that Christ never existed, in which he follows the J.G. Frazer-inspired mythologizing of the New Testament. Berlioz should know better, on the basis of his name, which recalls the composer of the *Symphonie Fantastique* whose subject, a masochistic version of Faust tortured by Gretchen, goes to the guillotine, while the Fifth Movement is a witches' Sabbath. An ennui-ridden Faust gives character to Berlioz' oratorio/opera *Damnation de Faust*. Bulgakov's Berlioz does not respond to the allegory implicit in his name. Immediately the devil appears to Berlioz and Ivan, as an apparently German professor whose speciality is black magic; a historian, he has come to examine the papers of the tenth-century Pope Gerbert of Aurillac, a Faustian figure of learning, deriving much from Muslim learning, and accused of dealings with the devil. Perhaps quoting Junker Voland in Goethe's *Faust* (line 4023), he calls himself Woland in chapter 7 (Lowe 1996: 279–286). By then, he has entered the apartment of the late Berlioz and Likhodeev, no. 50 on Sadovaya Street – which he means to possess – and greets the hungover director of the Variety Theatre, at which venue a diabolical performance will take place, using the words used by Gounod's Mephistopheles when greeting Faust, whilst holding a Faustian contract which Likhodeev cannot remember signing.

Woland affirms Jesus' historical existence, and tells Berlioz and Ivan a story, which, as he begins, fades into chapter 2, which gives an unattributed account of Pilate and of Ieshua (Jesus), who is on trial before him, on the morning of 14 Nisan in Yershalaim (Jerusalem), the equivalent time in Jerusalem to these events in Moscow. Ieshua, no literal son of God, more a *picaro* or holy fool, complains that his utterances have been wrongly quoted, and that this ensuing 'confusion [i.e. Christianity] may go on for a very long time' because his disciple, Matthew Levi, 'writes down the things I say incorrectly' (Bulgakov 1997: 23). The chapter finishes; and in the next, in Moscow, reacting to Woland telling this tale, Ivan feels that he has been hearing a dream. Perhaps Berlioz does, too, because he says that the 'story' is very interesting even though it does not coincide with the Gospel stories. At this the Professor says that nothing of what is written in the Gospels actually happened, and 'if we start referring to the Gospels as an historical source . . . ' (42) – which sentence repeats what Berlioz was saying to Ivan, but it remains unfinished, so leaving interpretation open. The novel's epigraph quotes Goethe's Mephisto as saying he is the spirit which desires evil but does good (*Faust* 1334–1336), in the context of being the spirit that denies – but as Woland negates the Gospels, that introduces a new form of thinking, which countermands the flat literality of Berlioz the atheist, and Ivan who denies that the devil exists (Bulgakov 1997: 44).

An allegorical reading of this seems possible; historical documents remain open, and, as Woland tells the Master later, 'manuscripts don't burn' (287): they survive.

The Master, in despair, had burned his novel – part of which Woland has retold – in manuscript form because it was rejected by the censors, who in themselves suggest one form of diabolism, which is intimated in the censor's name Ariman.[1] This censor accuses the Master of writing an apology for Christ. Another critic, Mstislav Lavrovich, accuses him of 'Pilatism' and of being an 'icon-dauber', i.e. of being a nostalgic historian. A third, Latunsky, calls him an Old Believer (144–145), so associating him with Dostoevsky's Castrates and Flagellants and holy fools, as dualistic, seeing the world as under the control of the devil, and, constituting, since all they date from their various formations in the seventeenth century, anti-modernising tendencies (Heretz 2008: 42–75, 81–97). These secular critics are nonetheless 'devils' in their irrational and primitive rationalism. The Master sees them as inherently insincere, not writing what they want to say, which is their cowardice. Their rage springs from that (145). Yet they are not Pilates, but lesser than him, because they are less challenged by what Ieshua and Pilate represent. Their effect is to make the Master give up, showing the impossibility now of Faustian striving.

Yet if 'manuscripts don't burn', neither documents, nor people, can be lost to history, though the Nazi gas ovens challenge that; but if manuscripts are to survive, their value depends on not being confined to literal readings. As the devil Behemoth, a cat, says: 'we don't put dates, with a date the document becomes invalid' (291). An earlier chapter discussed Benjamin on *apokatastasis*: he tells Gershom Scholem 'the series of years are doubtless countable, but not numerable' (Fenves 2011: 107). We can explicate this by saying that counting is essential for memory, taking account of what has happened, but in contrast, what is numerable implies reducing the years to numbers and dates. Chronology produces the concept of progress, which makes past things dispensable, exchangeable, but each year is unique; 'historical years are names' (Benjamin, quoted in Fenves 2011: 107), and 'to write history means giving dates their physiognomies' (Benjamin 1999: 476). It means to ascribe a face to each year, to singularise it, making it not exchangeable, hence not datable; since that reduces everything into a single chronology.

Pilate, and his encounter with Ieshua, once introduced in chapter 2, is continually recalled. Woland first tells it but the Master wrote it in novel form (Bulgakov 1997: 286). Ivan dreams a further episode in it (chapter 16), while Margarita has retrieved a section of the Master's burned manuscript which she reads (chapter 19, 220). Phrases from that manuscript, like a Wagnerian leitmotif, are repeated by Azazello, another devil (226) before Margarita rereads them in the now unburned manuscript, at the end of chapter 24. That leads into two further chapters dealing with Pilate. His words in chapter 2, when he desires poison for himself, are not forgotten, for they are heard at the ball held by the members of the Soviet literary club, MASSOLIT, at a house supposed to be associated with Griboedov (1795–1829). His play *Woe From Wit* (1825) satirised nineteenth-century Moscow. It therefore has a message for these metropolitan critics, whose ball is like hell (61). Perhaps so many people can narrate from the novel because single authorship is an impossibility, since nothing has single ownership. The way history continues to resonate in different voices indicates that; as does, incidentally, the character of Pilate in subsequent Soviet fiction (Ziolkowski 1992: 164–181). The novel's unfinished nature shows in that Pilate and Ieshua must meet again (381–382); that Ivan may write a sequel (373). Indeed, Ivan, now become a Professor of History himself (he will write no more bad verse) will in dream continue the themes of reconciliation, and *apokatastasis*, which were implicit in the narrative (319, 395–396).

In chapter 13, the Master tells Ivan why he as a historian burned his own novel, internalising its negative criticism, becoming paranoid, having dreams and sensations of being caught by an octopus-like force, which more terrifyingly suggesting the abject because of its formlessness, its absence of shape and outline. It is matter which clings and cannot be escaped from. He turns himself into the psychiatric clinic. In writing a novel about Pontius Pilate, the Master deals with a figure who, as indicated by his afterlife in medieval drama, was supposed to have been fingered by the devil. Pilate was pictured as subject to demons whispering in his ear, as in a thirteenth-century miniature in the Psalter of Robert de Lindsey (Hourihane 2009: 267–268). He was made either anti-Jewish, or Jewish himself, according to prejudice. Certainly, he was seen as a suicide at the end, as *The Golden Legend* confirmed (Voragine 1993: 2.215–214; Bond 1998). His wife, named Procula in legend, who warned Pilate not to have anything to do with Christ, because of a dream she had had (Matthew 27:19), was also supposed to have been visited by demons who did not want Christ crucified. For that, in salvation terms, would mean their defeat (Hourihane 2009: 126–142). Bulgakov, who wrote a life of Molière, and knew all about the theatre, had had occasion to think about unjust judges. He had played a comic myopic Judge, in a dramatisation of *Pickwick Papers* in the Moscow Art Theatre in 1934, Justice Stareleigh, an apt figure for the Soviet state, who gives judgment on Pickwick, another Christ-like holy fool (Proffer 1984: 389). And Bulgakov had access to the apocryphal Acts of Pilate, which gave him the names of the thieves crucified with Christ, Dysmas and Gestas (Elliott 1993: 176). Legends of Pilate which appeared after the Gospel accounts, and historians and writers such as Philo and Josephus, attempted to diabolise the whole proceedings, to give to the history and theology of the Pilate/Christ encounter a whole new irrational force, to supplement the Gospels. That increases with the addition of Judas to the narrative. Bulgakov's Pilate orders him to be killed, to revenge his betrayal of Christ.

The legends gave Pilate and Judas parallel lives. Hourihane (2009: 324–328) quotes the view that Punch and Judy stem from Pontius and Judas in late medieval drama. But Judas' medieval afterlife was richer than Pilate's: *The Golden Legend* makes him an Oedipus, cast out at birth, but returning to Judaea, coming into favour with Pilate and stealing fruit from his father's orchard for him. He kills his father and marries his mother before he becomes Christ's disciple. Later he betrays Christ and then despairs and hangs himself (Voragine 1993: 1.167–169). Judas is the classic sinner who belongs to the devil, but the German medieval writer, Hartman von Aue (1165–1210), took an absolutely parallel case to this pre-life of Judas, and made his character Gregorius become Pope – though he had been, in his actions, both an Oedipus and Judas. Thomas Mann retold the story of Gregorius in his last novel, *The Holy Sinner* (*Die Erwählte*, 1951), which is a coda to *Doctor Faustus.* But the latter novel itself refers to the medieval narrative (Mann 1980: 426–430; 1996: 317–320) contained within the *Gesta Romanorum*, of what is called its *Gottgeistig* 'Godwitted' – i.e. mad material (*Doctor Faustus* 429, 319).[2] Judas, devil-possessed, recalling John 13:27, shades into Faustus in the Middle Ages. Their careers fuse, as having sold their souls to the devil makes them melt into each other. And Judas' sin is not Christ's betrayal but the Satan-induced despair which produces his suicide (Ohly 1992: 74, 93); despair, loss of hope of God's grace, the Calvinist state felt by Cowper and recorded by Hogg.

Bulgakov works with material which is saturated in diabolism, but his version of Pilate secularises that, and makes Pilate/Judas a psychological novel, which allegorises the conditions of justice in Stalinism. Bulgakov's Pilate is unwell, and even a potential suicide, his mind dwelling on poison. His failure is his cowardly decision to yield to the malice of Caiaphas, the High Priest, in fear of losing his post. The charge of cowardice is a key to the text (Bulgakov 1997: 305, 319, 329). During his encounter with

Ieshua, he suffers a slow inward collapse (29), undergoing an anguish which 'visits' him (35) just as Woland visits Berlioz in his unaccountable sudden anguish (8). Pilate is challenged by Ieshua's words, spoken as a Nietzschean nihilist, that all power is violence, though there is a 'kingdom of truth' (30), where 'truth' seems to be madness, the rule of carnival. That makes Pilate like the Grand Inquisitor before Christ in prison, where utilitarian reason and a commitment to government as requiring above all security (everything is cordoned off around the palace) encounters the opposite: truth as heterogeneity, what cannot be fitted in. The Master's version of Pilate is Ivan Karamazov's Grand Inquisitor in revised form, as Dostoevsky's Ivan reappears as Bulgakov's Ivan.

Pilate and Ieshua confront each other as different forms of madness. A clue appears in chapter 6's title, 'Schizophrenia, As Was Said', or in chapter 11: 'Ivan Splits in Two'. Splitting happens when Berlioz, who has been pre-warned by Woland, loses his head when he is killed by a tram at the end of chapter 3. At the black magic performance the Master of Ceremonies, Bengalsky, has his head removed by Behemoth, and then replaced (126–127), after which he feels he has lost his head. Ivan, traumatised by witnessing the decapitation of Berlioz, and by seeing Behemoth, is haunted by Pilate as a buried name in history, as an indicator of something wrong in the organisation and control within Moscow. He is taken into a psychiatric clinic to be treated by a Dr Stravinsky. At this point he rejects the poetry he has written as only in the service of the state (90). He meets the Master, also in the clinic, who begins by telling Ivan that a new arrival has just come to room 119. This is Nikanor Ivanovich, chairman of the tenants' association of the building which contains the apartment where Woland now lives. He has been driven mad by the devils (102, 134–135, 159), a just punishment on anyone who holds such command over tenants in an era of lack of housing supply. A little later, Bengalsky arrives at room 120, wanting his head back (148). He is another product of the devils' work. The neatness of the ascending room numbers tells a story of accumulating madness. Unlike Ivan, the Master knows at once that the person he met the previous evening (Woland) was Satan, referencing, however, not Goethe but Gounod (136). He tells Ivan that what unites them both is Pilate: Ivan for talking about him, the Master for writing about him. Pilate, then, agent of Caesar, is the repressed figure, with something faintly diabolical within him, who provides a way of reading Moscow's official negations; he symbolises such bureaucratic power.

Woland, as Satan, referred to by this name again in the title for chapter 23, and also named 'the non-existent one' (253) on account of what Ivan had said about him in the beginning, embodies an energy and spreads a carnivalesque anarchy which official Moscow cannot acknowledge. The force he appeals to is Margarita, who corresponds to Margarete in *Faust*, since she has willingly and completely given herself to the Master. The second part of the book shows her becoming Faustian in her agreement to go to the devil and beyond (229). She becomes a witch: in the kitsch form of the Satanic Mass, where a jazz band is conducted by the waltz king, Johann Strauss, playing 'Allelulia' (262–263), she is in hell, in the same way as Mary is, in Ivan's narrative of the Grand Inquisitor. That narrative includes in it a little monastery poem, in the Greek tradition, called 'The Mother of God Visits the Torments'. It tells how the Virgin visits Hell, and secures release from its torments for all sinners between Holy Friday and Pentecost (Dostoevsky 2004: 247; Ericson 1974: 20–36). At the Great Ball, which is not much more than a parody of the ball at Griboedov's and which quotes from it, the kitsch sounds of the present-day music cannot drown out the past. Equally, the site of Satan's ball, the apartment where Woland has taken up residence, is a house where people have disappeared through Stalinist purges. The chapter combines Gothic surprise with political comment (75–76; Maguire 2012: 74–76). The writing of this Mass parodies popular ideas of what satanic rituals comprise. Woland addresses the head of Berlioz, who had pronounced death as 'non-being'. From that head, which becomes a skull, Woland drinks 'to being' (273). Clearly, the writing associates the state of being with the Dionysian, because of the grapevines which are the source of the wine that is the skull out of which Marguerite is to bid to drink: the devils are on the side of the bacchic (275).

These devils who have visited Moscow to see it for themselves, and to judge it, do not do so negatively (122–123, 126), but do see contemporary Moscow citizens as suffering from a severe housing shortage. However Christianity, which is represented by Matthew Levi, cannot accept Woland, because he is beyond good and evil, which are Christianity's values. Levi calls Woland a 'spirit of evil and sovereign of shadows' (360). Woland replies that Levi's statement means that he is acknowledging neither shadows nor evil as being, which means that the Christian is the nihilist. But, he says, 'consider what would your good do if evil did not exist, and what would your earth look like if shadows disappeared from it?' The Christian has the fantasy of mere 'bare light'. Shadows, of course, are non-existent, and perhaps evil is, too; Woland does not commit himself to being, but he does criticise the belief in pure presence, which is the Christian's dream.

Yet Woland's intervention with his retinue works on the level of changing the few lives with which it catches up. For the rest, the people not reached and not affected, the madness of this world will continue. And though the novel is drily aware of Stalinist persecutions, which would, in scale, and numbers of deaths, ultimately top even those of Nazism, even though much of that slaughter postdated Bulgakov's death, its sphere is that of a carnival intervention within Moscow. It is less a critique of twentieth-century modernity than *Doctor Faustus* presents itself as being, and is more locally transgressive than that text, to which I now turn.

2 Doctor Faustus

Adrian Leverkühn, who finds music always a strange power, is shown as having a musical education which includes Romantic opera: Mozart's *The Magic Flute* (1791) and *The Marriage of Figaro* (1786), *Der Freischütz* (Weber, 1821), and Marshner's *Hans Heiling* (1833), whose plot derives from Hoffmann's *Undine* in that it shows a self-divided demonic figure who lives in two spheres, and wants to marry a human, despite the advice of his mother, the Queen of the Erdgeister. Also mentioned in Mann's novel are Wagner's *The Flying Dutchman* (1843) and Beethoven's *Fidelio* (1805) (108, 77–78). *Fidelio*'s frenzied Pizarro, like Kaspar in *Der Freischütz*, an opera discussed by Adrian and the devil (307, 227–28; 328, 243), derives from the *The Magic Flute*'s Queen of the Night. All these have the violence of demonic revenge (*die Rache*) in common. The devil in *Der Freischütz* is Samiel, a huntsman in green, whose diminished seventh, and C minor tonality, placed against the C major, heard, for instance, in the Overture, intimate despair (Warrack 1968: 201–230). To him may be added his ally Kaspar, an Iago-figure who tells Max, whom he is trying to ruin, how he was associated with Tilly, the Catholic, Pro-Imperial commander in the Thirty Years War (1618–1648), at the 'Magdeburger Tanz' – the dance of death at Magdeburg. Destroying that city in 1631 became, historically, a marker of wanton cruelty (Warrack 2001: 306; Wilson 2009: 467–470). It is, of course, a context for Germany in the twentieth century.

The devil comments on Adrian reading Kierkegaard's *Either/Or*, on *Don Giovanni* (Mann 1996: 301, 223; 326, 242). That is illuminated by a note recorded by Mann:

> [Kierkegaard's] mad love for Mozart's *Don Juan*. Sensuality, discovered by Christianity along with spirit. Music as a demonic realm.... (Mann 1961: 86)

Either/Or, makes 'music the daemonic': in 'the erotic-sensuous genius' music has its 'absolute object' (Kierkegaard 1959: 1.63). It wants no less than that, and is inherently demonic in reaching it. As the devil says, following Theodor Adorno (1903–1969), whose music criticism comprises a third of all his writings on critical theory, and derives, like the rest of his writing, from a sustained encounter with Benjamin, 'the devil ought to understand music' (Mann 1996: 326, 242).

Another demonism is implicit from Wagner's *Die Meistersinger* (1868), the Prelude to whose Act Three is described, though not named as such, when Adrian Leverkühn listens to nineteenth-century music (Mann 1996: 65, 85, Tambling 2012b: 208–221). The Prelude succeeds the riotous – and apparently unmotivated – violence which ended Act Two: as Sachs sings, thinking about that affray and its sources, 'ein Kobold half wohl da': a goblin must have been involved. Adrian's letter on this music is followed by: 'Lieber Freund, warum muss ich lachen?' and

> Warum müssen fast alle Dinge mir als ihre eigene Parodie erscheinen? Warum muß es mir vorkommen, als ob fast alle, nein, alle Mittel und Konvenienzen der Kunst *heute nur noch zur Parodie taugten?* (Mann 1980: 182)

> why must I laugh.... why must almost everything appear to me as its own parody? Why must it seem to me that nearly everything, no everything, of the methods and conventions of art are today only good for parody only? (134)

Laughing, implying irony, and so recalling what Baudelaire said about it, is Adrian's element of diabolism. Zeitblom fears it as an element of barbarism (506, 378). Everything of music for the age of realism, and indeed of realist art, which purports to give a sense of how the world is, parodies that world, but may do so unwittingly, because realism's danger is to be on the side of those who do not want to change existing reality, and whose interest is in conserving their own values (Wagner's 'traditional' Nürnberg), so that the mere recital of its interests and values is likely to become parodic. This is nihilism and diabolism together; and applicable also to Bulgakov, who, however, is a conscious parodist of Stalinist oppression, whose 'socialist realism' replaced the older oppression of bourgeois realism. Mann thought his *Doctor Faustus* traditional when put alongside *Finnegans Wake*, but he noted Harry Levin's comments about James Joyce taking his subject as 'the decomposition of the middle class', and further drew on T.S. Eliot to ask 'whether in the field of the novel nowadays the only thing that counted was what was no longer a novel' (Mann 1961: 76). To write what is not a novel is to accept that a 'novel' must now parody itself, as Antichrist to the church's Christ. It cannot underwrite the values of the bourgeoisie, who are no longer revolutionary, as perhaps they were in the days of the *Communist Manifesto*, and of Goethe's *Faust* as modern man. The bourgeoisie are now figures of reaction and of Nietzschean *ressentiment*, yet, ironically, they are nonetheless the expected readers of this text. Writing must embody and indicate the parody which is already inherent in the recital of bourgeois values, but it must also parody actively, which presents problems of superiority in its 'aristokratischen Nihilismus' (327): 'aristocratic nihilism' (241).

These critical points inform the writing and the content of *Doctor Faustus*, both with Zeitblom, the bourgeois narrator, and Adrian, the musician who parodies, who is avant-garde in his music, and is also, it seems, diabolically transgressive. Mann started writing the novel in exile in Los Angeles, in summer 1943, receiving, on 1 July 1943, the assistance provided by the manuscript of Theodor Adorno's *Philosophy of New Music.*[3] Adorno and Horkheimer went on to publish *The Dialectic of Enlightenment* in 1947; *The Philosophy of New Music* (1948) was an 'extended appendix' to it. Mann was also reading fragments from Adorno's *In Search of Wagner*, completed in 1939, and published in 1952. Adorno's essay 'Spätstil Beethovens' ('Late Style in Beethoven'), another essential text for *Doctor Faustus*, had appeared in 1937. Adorno's letter to Mann of 5 July 1948 includes Adorno's curriculum vitae, distinguishing amongst his writings *The Philosophy of New Music*, where Schoenberg (1874–1951), is called the greatest living composer on account of his dodecaphonic technique (Gödde and Sprecher 2006: 24–27).

Schoenberg works through three stages of musical writing; the first, a 'late Romantic'; the second, where he writes atonally; the third, where the music is utterly ordered and rational, according to the pattern set by a specific 'tone-row' of notes which may be played forward, or in retrograde, or inverted, or inverted and in retrograde. Here, it seems that the equivocal – that which can go forward or back – has been raised into a system; or else that Schoenberg's system recognises the equivocal, as Freud notes, at the end of 'The Antithetical Meaning of Primal Words', discussing how the reversal of sounds comprises an ambiguity inherent in all language (*SE* 11.160–161). Whereas Schoenberg's second stage of writing expressed a desire for subjectivity in the conditions of alienation, the third witnesses to alienation by its own constrained state, as ordered, organised. Stravinsky's modernism, Adorno contends, is regressive by comparison, its modernism and objectivity – as if it has yielded to the idea of a wholly rationalised society – pretends by its free quotation of the music of different historical periods that there is no alienation; that the composer has no constraints. Yet, adding to the equivocal: the tone-row that Adrian writes also encyphers the erotic: the name of a woman (209–210, 155–156; 258, 191), so that the coldly unemotional is also its opposite.

Mann and Adorno's informal collaboration produced what remains the best introduction to Adorno on music, while Adorno appears in *Doctor Faustus* as Herr Kretzschmar, a lecturer in music. The *z* in his name, omitted in Lowe-Porter's translation, but not in Woods' (1997), hints at the co-presence of Nietzsche – a montage effect – and the devil. As the latter, seen in chapter 25, his advice comments on the impossibility in the contemporary world of any conventional art, underpinning what he said as Kretzschmar (321–329; 237–243). Adorno and critical theory are, then, part of the diabolical in the text, as much as music is. The novel itself is not free from problems; for instance, it is open to the accusation of caricature, as with the Jewish impresario Fitelberg. He attempts to persuade Adrian, in Mephistophelean fashion, to leave Germany for France. After declaring Germany to be essentially anti-Semitic, he distinguishes Gounod's *Faust* from Goethe's. The French is 'a pearl – a marguerite, full of the most ravishing musical inventions' (545; 407); but he implies that that beauty, associated with the opera's constant evocation of Marguerite, has nothing to do with Goethe's sense of Faust. Goethe is more intense, less about the power of the meretricious in securing Marguerite, more probing about the diabolical, which, in comparison, is hardly a serious issue for Gounod. By implication, because of its diabolism, Goethe's *Faust* belongs to a national culture. For Fitelberg there are only two nationalisms, German and Jewish; French and France being in comparison cosmopolitan:

> ein deutscher Schriftsteller könnte sich nich gut 'Deutschland' nennen, so nennt man höchstens ein Kriegsschiff. Er müsste sich mit 'Deutsch' begnügen, – und da gäbe einen jüdischen Namen, – oh la, la! (546)

> a German writer could not well call himself Germany; one gives, at the most, such a name to a battleship. He has to call himself German – and that is a Jewish name, oh la la! (408)

When one language (Yiddish) is, inherently, inside another (German), there can be no national or separate identity. That indicates the strength – and decided weakness – of the novel: while unremitting in its focus on Germany as distinctive, its political analysis is weak. It takes not enough heed of anti-Semitism, being too intent on seeing diabolism as a post-Lutheran German anti-rationalism. It repeats the nationalism it mocks, and its sense of German 'exceptionalism' prevents it from closing with the question of who was to blame for what happened in the 1930s: Germany, or international financial capitalism? – for which it had been convenient to blame the Jews.

The novel opens with Zeitblom, aged sixty, sitting down to write on 27 May 1943, three years after the death of Adrian, whose life he is writing in the form of a hagiography, like Alyosha Karamazov's in *The Brothers Karamazov*. Adrian was born in Saxony in 1885, like Alban Berg. He transfers from studying Lutheran theology at Halle to music composition at Leipzig. In 1906 he comes into contact with a prostitute, actively seeks her out and is infected with syphilis, which may mark the devil's influence. He becomes a Schoenberg-like composer, working with dodecaphony, which also influenced Berg, and Webern, both of whom, like Nietzsche, form part of Adrian, who is a composite (in 1948, Mann had to include a postscript to the novel, disavowing its relation to Schoenberg since the latter regarded Mann as plagiarising him). In 1911, he has an encounter with the Devil, like Ivan Karamazov; the devil promises him continuance in composition, so that Adrian goes through the First World War, surviving until 1930, when tertiary syphilis causes complete breakdown.

This, and his death in 1940, evokes Nietzsche, who according to Paul Deussen's memoir (1901), suffered similarly from contracting syphilis in Cologne. Mann also related Dostoevsky's epilepsy to a sexual crisis (Bergsten 1969: 59–61, 69–70). Yet Adrian suffers from migraines prior to syphilis, so that nothing is single here nor fits a chronology of 'before' and 'after'. Further, there is every reason to question the syphilis diagnosis for Nietzsche, as opposed to schizophrenia (Schain 2001: 97–105). If madness is always Nietzsche's subject, whether as the expression of Dionysus, or because it is inherent in a thinking based on difference, not on single identity, then the madness which confronted him develops out of that non-stable identity.

Adrian's decisive moment is the encounter with Wendell Kretzschmar, who in evening classes, plays Beethoven's late piano sonata Opus 111 (no. 32), in C minor, in two movements only. The second contains a single arietta which then receives a series of variations which sound intensely personal, subjective. Kretzschmar distinguishes between *harmonic subjectivity* and *polyphonic objectivity*, saying that the latter associates with the ability to write a fugue, which Kretzschmar contends Beethoven could hardly do. But Beethoven had been more subjective in his middle period. Now in the late piano sonatas, his music gains a new objectivity; the subjective and the conventional (i.e. the objective) reach a new relationship, 'ein Verhältnis, bestimmt vom Tode' (74), 'a relationship conditioned by death' (53), death being the ultimate objective state, and the weapon of the Fascist state; and, as diabolical, bringing terror in mourning (Benjamin 1977: 229). Death, as stuttered out by Kretzschmar (stuttering shows the divided subject) sounds like machine-gun fire: that violence, i.e. music and warfare together, is its ambiguity. Kretzschmar plays the tender and innocent arietta theme which opens the second movement, interpreting it as an 'Abschied', a farewell, which acquires an added C sharp before the DGG, which intensifies the implicit utterance in the simple tune, making it 'O – du Himmelsblau . . . Grüner Wiesengrund [punning on Adorno's name], Leb' – mir ewig wohl' (77), 'O thou heaven's blue, greenest meadowland, fare thee well for ever' (55). He adds that the C sharp-effect is erotic, like having the cheek stroked: a Kierkegaardian emphasis about music. Then everything 'breaks off' (Spitzer 2006: 156–157). The music comprises fragmentation, the caesural, the traumatic, the irresolvable; all these being characteristic of Beethoven's 'late style', since 'in the history of art, late works are the catastrophes' (Adorno 1998: 126). Catastrophe and farewell combine as the music echoingly bids farewell, to life, to art's innocence, and to Germany, making a third movement, a return, impossible.

Echoing associates with the child, Nepomuk, nicknamed 'Echo'; he dies of meningitis while staying with Adrian (chapters 44, and 45). Adrian's name suggests 'Ariadne', whom Nietzsche associated with music (Krell 1986: 15–31). He is the Nietzschean nihilist 'taking back' the affirmativeness of Beethoven's Ninth Symphony (639, 478). His final composition before his madness, written while Echo is dying, is the oratorio *The Lamentation of Dr Faustus* ('Dr Fausti Weheklag', 645, 483). This sets as a tone-row the words from Spies' *Faustbuch*, 'Denn ich sterbe als ein böser und gutter Christ' (654), 'then I die as a bad and good Christian' 654, 487), words discussed in the first chapter. The lamentation may make Adrian the embodiment of Germany as itself the exemplary Christian, or Christ, though nonetheless diabolical. It assumes the language of the 'holy sinner'. While how much this exculpates Germany (but of what, in Germany?) is a question for the text, it comes within a discussion of lamentation as expression (*Ausdruck*), and expression as lament, because, it is said, music becomes lament, when it becomes modern, conscious of itself, as it slowly moves out of the sphere of the church as written for it, becoming 'art', subjective, and no longer a function of and for the community.

Music's keynote is 'lasciatemi morire' (let me die), which is Ariadne's death wish in Monteverdi's opera, *L'Arianna* (1608). Zeitblom notes Monteverdi's interest in echoing, as a baroque effect. The text virtually identifies echoing and lamentation; earlier on, Adrian had noted an 'outburst of modernity in Monteverdi's musical devices' (240, 177). When echoing is heard in the Wolf's Glen scene in *Der Freischütz*, it is diabolical, and partakes of Samiel's pervasive laughter, which is always echoing. Lamentation as a topic here implies the influence of Benjamin, writing on German *Trauerspiel*, the German baroque mourning plays, appropriate for modernity, in the era of total warfare, as anticipated in the Thirty Years' War. These plays work by allegory, and evoke the fragment as appropriate for history as it records the 'untimely, sorrowful, unsuccessful' (Benjamin 1977: 166). As discussed before, the fragment is typically expressed in the mask which is the death's head, like Yorick's skull, the trace of the diabolical.

Music is sensuous, but in *Don Giovanni* it contains something else: anxiety (dread), but 'this dread is precisely the demonic joy of life' (Kierkegaard 1959: 128–129). As Echo, the child dies, Adrian, the Prospero/magus, says, as if speaking to Ariel, 'Then to the elements. Be free and fare thee well' (641, 479), which, as Ohly (1992: 193) says, evokes Prospero's own plight: 'And my ending is despair' (*The Tempest* 5.1.317–318, 333). Prospero is in the Faustian situation: he fears death, like Marlowe's Faustus, so coming close to Judas, and to Richard III, whilst also sensing that there is no alternative to despair in death (Sachs 1964: 625–647), which may also be the state of Smerdyakov.

As Augustine said of Judas: 'when he hanged himself he did not atone for the guilt of his detestable betrayal but rather increased it, since he despaired of God's mercy and in a fit of self-destructive remorse left himself no chance of a saving repentance' (Augustine 1972: 27). Lamentation, like *Trauerspiel*, seems to be, in modernity, essential to art: the recognition of death, and the fear that there may be nothing except despair. As Adorno writes near the close of his posthumuously published *Aesthetic Theory*: 'what would art be, as the writing of history, if it shook off the memory of accumulated suffering?' (Adorno 1997: 261). As directed, and commissioned, whether in relationship to the church, or the concert hall and opera house as places of entertainment, as part of a 'culture industry', music must, enforcedly, be celebratory, reconciling personal suffering within a whole, and Adorno sees this as a falsity, a concession to Hegel's sense of reconciling everything within a 'totality'. It is untrue to a writing of history which sees the latter as Benjamin described it in 1940: 'one single catastrophe, which keeps piling wreckage upon wreckage' (Benjamin 2003: 392). Adorno's work, much of it written after Auschwitz, negates, in its character of 'negative dialectics', not willing to reach a further synthesis, or unity of thought, as in Hegel, but refusing that idea, that there can be a unified totality. He sees it as authoritarian, because eliminating non-reconcilable difference(s), in the name of communal identity. As Ivan Karamazov also feels, talking to Alyosha, that art cannot speak of reconciliation achieved, because this would mean that injustice would remain; it would just not be registered as such. In contrast, Adorno proposes the significance of 'non-identity' within the modern artwork, saving new art from being what art has been before (Adorno 1997: 23). And non-identity may be the presence of the diabolical; that which disturbs art's affirmatory power, and insinuates the different.

3 Adrian's Music: Risking Barbarism

Music becomes 'Zweideutigkeit': 'ambiguity' (67; 47), and so contains the possibility of non-identity. Adrian's music is discussed in theoretical terms in *Doctor Faustus* chapters 21, 22, and 25, but the starting point is chapter 8, with Kretzschmar's sense that music, separated from church services, as happened in Beethoven's time, gained a new theological intensity in itself, as absolute art; and that this has been used, discursively and nationalistically, historically, and in the present to separate art and 'culture' from 'barbarism'. ('We [meaning the British] have culture, the BBC, the RSC, which is the envy of the rest of the world . . . '.) An epoch which does possess culture would be unselfconscious in that; one which talks about culture and elevates itself as possessing it uniquely, needs to define itself in relation to a 'barbarism' which, it believes, is incapable of culture. The society which *talks* about culture knows neither it nor the so-called primitive barbarism which it has to attack, perhaps in the name of anti-semitism; the 'cultured' bit of that society forgetting that the barbarians are already inside their own gates. There is no need to wait for them. A society which thinks it is cultured has forgotten its own barbarism.

Yet 'barbarism', thought to be applicable to the new music because it is does not sound harmonious or tonal, and so is rejected by a comfortable bourgeois audience, challenges talk of culture but in the novel is also thought of as diabolical. Yet it even risks a worse, Fascist, barbarism (part of the ambiguity the novel discusses). The debate about culture in chapter 8 is resumed in chapter 24, where Leverkühn has made an opera out of *Love's Labour's Lost*, which, as in Shakespeare, mocks the over-refinement of the cultured, who want to set aside life and women in the pursuit of abstract knowledge. Berowne, who has most to lose in joining these *precieux*, tells them that he has already, in the past:

> for barbarism spoke more
> Than for that angel knowledge you can say.
> (*Love's Labour's Lost*,
> 1.1.112–113)

Zeitblom, the complacent Humanist, dislikes relegating culture ('knowledge') in favour of nature ('barbarism'), but notes that Adrian's music does not actually endorse 'Natur und Menschlichkeit' (nature and humanity): 'Das, was der Ritter Biron "barbarism" nennt, das Spontane und Natürliche also eben, feierte in ihr keine Triumphe' (293) 'what Sir Berowne calls "barbarism", even the spontaneous and natural, finds here [in the opera] no triumph' (217). But Zeitblom is equally uncomfortable with Adrian's dismissal in music of what Zeitblom thinks of as nature and natural instincts. Leverkühn has not written Romantic music, nor, like Stravinsky's modernist *Rite of Spring* (1913) does it celebrate primitive nature. His aim has been that the antithesis culture/barbarism be deconstructed. These two cannot exist separately; and nature is not to be thought of as preceding culture, or history. And *every culture is constituted by what it excludes by calling it barbarism*; 'barbarism' being, as how it is commonly spoken about by those who profess culture, what Adorno calls the 'non-identical'.

The point is reiterated by the devil, who challenges Leverkühn in his music to become barbaric twice over (328, 243). 'Twice': because (a) such barbarism comes after bourgeois refinement, (b) because such new barbarism must be self-conscious, deliberately created; but then also it will be more dangerous, because that barbarism has the ambiguity of being destructively mad, creating the 'march of the future' (der Zukunft den Marsch) This has militaristic, if not Nazi implications. And another take on the topic returns in the third of *three* chapters in the novel all called chapter 34, which as a number invokes the magic number 34 in Dürer's *Melencolia I* (127, 92; 260, 192). This third chapter of three, which has several recalls of chapter 8, meditates on the word 'barbarian', in discussing Leverkühn's composition called *Apocalypsis cum figuris* which follows on from Dürer's woodcuts of the Apocalypse (1498), with added passages from Psalms, and Jeremiah's Lamentations (*Klageliedern*).

Mann asked Adorno about this imaginary music: 'how you would compose the music if you yourself were in league with the devil?' (Gödde and Sprecher 2006: 13). The piece is to be imagined as performed in 1926, conducted by Otto Klemperer, one of those who pioneered Mahler's music. Here, Adrian's barbarism is not outlandish, but the opposite: close to aestheticism: art for art's sake. Benjamin (SW3: 122) famously attacked such art as being Fascist in tendency. Similarly, Judge William in *Either/Or* describes fascination with the musical erotic of *Don Giovanni* as abiding at the aesthetic stage of life. The aesthetic as Fascist shows how art can be distanced from life, and from suffering; how even ruin, which speaks of disaster, can be made to seem beautiful. In contrast, the aesthetic as Adorno writes about it gives space to the disintegrated, the non-identical, the fragment which cannot be absorbed into reality as the bourgeois accepts this. If art is to be mimetic, it is *not* as a copy of what is, but of what is not recognised:

> what is essential to art is that in it which is not the case, that which is incommensurable with the empirical measure of all things. (Adorno 1997: 335)

Adorno says that 'art has truth as the semblance of the illusionless' ['Schein des Scheinlosen'], and that in artworks, the 'truth content ['Wahrheitsgehalt'] is not null; every artwork, and most of all works of absolute negativity mutely say: *non confundar*' (Adorno 1997: 132). 'Non confundar' translates the end of Psalm 31:1: 'In thee, O Lord, do I put my trust, let me never be ashamed'. Adorno continues: The 'object of art's longing' is 'the reality of what is not'. This states something which appears in the analysis of *The Lamentation of Dr Faustus* (645–657, 482–491): 'questioning negativity stands as an allegory of hope' (Gödde and Sprecher 2006: 126). Art deals with the illusion of what is not an illusion, what cannot be reduced to being mimesis (representation) of the familiarly known. (The duality in *The Birth of Tragedy* between Nietzsche's Apollo, the sphere of illusion, and Dionysus, quite outside what can be individuated, may be recalled.) Given art's 'longing', implicit in Beethoven's Opus 111, discussed above, the truth content of the work of art cannot be defined, or pre-known, or predicted. It is essential that it should exist, so that there should not be despair, which is of the devil. And the truth content will be no total statement. Rather, following Adorno:

> artists discover the compulsion towards disintegration... it moves them to set aside the magic wand as does Shakespeare's Prospero. (Adorno 1997: 45)

The magic wand is the magus' pretence to unity, to wholeness, which a fake diabolical magic secures.

Adrian's *Apocalypsis cum figuris* combines 'blutigen Barbarismus' with 'blutlosen Intellectualität' (501, 374). It is subjective in its extremity – sounding like bloody barbarism – as well as being intellectually ordered as bloodless intellectuality, in an objective systematicity which Adrian endorses (95, 68; 257, 190). Both sides, the barbarism, and the bloodlessness, are, as we have seen, ambiguous in themselves. This music makes dissonance express the wounded spirit, and suffering, while its diatonicism, its harmony, is on the side of the 'Welt der Hölle', and the 'Welt der Banalität und des Gemeinsplatzes' (503) 'the world of hell, and the world of banality and commonplaces' (375). Banality fits with what the Karamazov devil wants to take hold of: a world of commonplaces.

The 'barbarism' charge directed against *Apocalypsis cum figuris* includes the criticism that this music is not pro-progress. In comparison, Beethoven's intense rhythmic sense could be seen as barbaric, or primitive, while being, of course, absolutely technically advanced. Zeitblom tells of the German pastor Beissel, in America in the eighteenth-century, who lived as if he was in the wilderness (there are several echoes here of the Grand Inquisitor's narrative). Beissel created a wholly ordered, so objective music for his congregation. Back in Germany, 'Ludwig' (i.e. Beethoven), almost contemporaneously, was working outside this kingdom of the spirit, to which his music aspired in an alternative, subjective mode (91; 65). Different senses of rhythm are evoked and juxtaposed: one regular, ordered (Beissel), one breaking away from the measured order imposed by the bar line (Beethoven). Music is both old and young, and outside all chronology, defeating a single linear history; uniquely ambiguous, having a form which only questionably wants to address itself to the ear, because it is a mathematical code. Hence Kretzschmar says that perhaps music wishes not to be heard at all (that is its intellectualism, its rationality) but it also wants a seductive, sensuous realisation: like Kundry (see Wagner's *Parsifal* (1882) Act Two, where the witch – the outcast, the Wandering Jew as female – tries to seduce Parsifal, the holy fool), music, as a woman, wills not what she does and flings soft arms of lust round Parsifal's neck (86, 61). Music is a woman; she unmans the man.

The human voice (e.g. that of Kundry) 'das stallwärmste Klangmaterial ist, das sich erdenken läßt' (96) 'the most stable-warm imaginable thing in the world of sound' (68). This comment is explained from Adrian's memory of the stable girl singing 'abends auf der Bank unter der Linde' (42); 'on the bench under the linden tree' (27): a reference to the national tree (compare 'Lindenbaum' in Schubert's *Winterreise*). Nationalism, sexuality, music, and the demonic-Faustian come together. Adrian adds that while music is abstract, it also has the Baubo-like quality of confronting the male with the woman's nakedness:

> Abstrakt mag sie sein, die menschliche Stimme, – der abstrakte Mensch, wenn du willst. Aber das ist eine Art von Abstraktheit, ungefähr, wie der entkleidete Körper abstrakt ist, – es ist ja beinahe ein pudendum. (96)
>
> (Abstract it may be, the human voice – the abstract human being if you like. But that is a kind of abstraction more like that of the naked body – it is after all more a pudendum. (68))

Baubo, Demeter's nurse, seen in the Walpurgisnacht (*Faust* 3962), and so one of Goethe's many 'Mothers', is the obscene diabolical pagan figure who would confront and terrify a will to truth in Western philosophy (Nietzsche 1974: 38, Kofman 1988: 175–202). Music, which could potentially stand outside the fetishistic structures of capitalist modernity, is cool and hot simultaneously, as Adrian makes his music (240, 178). Zeitblom's passage describing this music, which is said to be demonic, ends in words which are not translated by Lowe-Porter: 'und mich stets an den feurigen Riss erinnerte, welchen der Sage nach ein Jemand dem zagenden Baumeister des Kölner Doms in den Sand zeichnete' ('and it makes me recall the fiery outline which the legend says that a Someone drew in the sand for the reluctant architect of Cologne cathedral' (Mann 1980: 240, Woods 1997: 189). The Gothic, and the sense of Cologne as a national shrine are both included in this diabolism; in *Faust* a diabolical Archbishop, publicly objecting to Faust as a necromancer, presses for Cologne's completion (11,005–11,020) with high towers 'wie sie zum Himmel streben' (11,013), which will strive against heaven.

To these ambiguities – music as sensuous *and* abstract – may be added two more: first, music's questioning of gender. Kierkegaard (1959: 1.102) makes music masculine, like the will of Don Giovanni. But it is feminine, too, as with Kundry. Second, music questions chronological history, as when Zeitblom says that he remembers a chaconne of Jacopo Melani (1623–1676) which literally anticipates a passage in *Tristan* (1865) (648; 484). Zeitblom makes music's own history – playing with gender and chronology, disallowing the latter, and combining absolute order with subjectivity – almost the biography of the devil. And Mann makes music metaphorical for German history: if 'Germany' is read, as in *Faust*, as an exemplar of 'modernity', that is also Adorno's understanding, explaining why he sees Beethoven as paradigmatic, especially for his 'late style' (Subotnik 1976: 242–275). German modernism, like others, intensifies its conservatism; its technological development supports the retrograde violence of Fascism, in banal mode.

What does Adrian's music signify? As a modern discourse, it possesses order and organisation, parallel to Nazism. The text allows for the thought that this music, like Germany, as *Mephisto* argues, has made a pact with the devil. Zeitblom's chapter 46 records America's General Eisenhauer on 25 April 1945, making the people of Weimar file past the crematoria at the concentration camp at Buchenwald (643, 481). Music is used to open up the extent of Nazi maliciousness, which the devil hints at when he speaks of soundless cellars and thick walls and of hopelessness: of the machinery of Nazi Germany's persecution and criminality (330; 244). Writing about the devil ends up, then, in approaching the subject of Auschwitz, which silences any confidence in the art of bourgeois Humanism – that is what this art was impotent against, if not complicit with. Adrian mocks such a sense of bourgeois music in chapter 21. There too, he says that music would like to stop being pretence and play (entertainment for the bourgeois), and become knowledge ('Erkenntnis', 244, 181; compare Adorno 1973: 41). Such an *Erkenntnis*, which Woods (193) translates as 'comprehension', would mean that it contained the 'truth content' which negates the complacency of what exists for 'the possibility of the non-existing' (Adorno 1997: 132). Adrian's point is enlarged upon by the devil: 'only the non-fictional is still permissible, the unplayed, the undisguised and untransfigured expression of suffering in its actual moment' (324–325, 240).

4 In Conclusion: Mann, The Satanic Verses, and 'Evil'

Analysing Goethe's daemonic, Kirk Wetters 2014: 195) notes how belief in the rationality of modern forms and systems represses the point that these are tied to ambiguous forms of older systems, on which, without quite acknowledging it, they are constructed. We cannot presuppose the dominance of the modern rational, because it cannot shed the older, mythological, premises on which it relies. What precedes that rationality, which depends on it, is not rational.

Freud quotes the psychologist Wilhelm Wundt on the origins of the taboo being 'fear of "daemonic" powers' which are resident in the tabooed object (*SE* 13.24). So all 'custom, and tradition, and law' are based on this irrational premise. Freud's rationalism dislikes this argument, since he says the 'daemonic' was the human mind's creation. For Wundt, the tabooed object preceded the distinction between the sacred and the unclean, giving rise to it: the 'demonic' was what may not be touched, the tabooed (*SE* 13.66), sacred *and* profane. Freud, however, finds in the word 'taboo' an ambivalence which makes things to be wanted and therefore forbidden. A 'taboo' arouses a contrary idea in the person acknowledging its existence and force. This accords with 'The Antithetical Meaning of Primal Words', which indicates that language comprises words which mean the same, *and* their opposite. Like 'taboo': which means something forbidden, and something (therefore) desired. Impossible to build rational, modern systems of law on that basis.

But so theology builds. In *Doctor Faustus*, Adrian tells Zeitblom that Christian marriage domesticated sex, 'which is evil by nature' (252, 187). Zeitblom objects to this Puritanism: he says that denying the work of God (including sex) entails becoming the advocate of nothing: which associates with the devil. Adrian replies that he spoke jokingly, as if he was a theologian. But Zeitblom has noted a serious issue. Rejection of the natural is of what theologians dub as evil, since theology separates sexual life into two: the free, subjective, and therefore evil, and the ordered, typified by marriage. Calling something 'evil' is always theological because this is dualistic thinking. Theological thinking, looking for a centre – if only an absent centre in apophatic theology – must involve hostility to something which it counts as 'other', and which it resists, however it masks its opposition. Adrian knows this, and in strange alliance to his diabilically theological comments about sex, writes music which subordinates freedom to order. This in Schoenberg indicates alienation, lack of freedom, knowing that reality has been commodified, reified (meaning that capitalism treats people as things). Adrian is fascinated that this tendency in music goes forward and backward simultaneously, being progressive *and* regressive. But interesting phenomena, he says, have the double face of past and future: they 'zeigen die Zweideutigkeit des Lebens selbst' (261); 'show the double-meaning of life itself' (193).

One value of theology may be to indicate and open up such ambiguity, whereas bourgeois culture more banally ignores it, living off its own universal commodification, where everything tends towards the homogeneous if not towards kitsch. Why does Adrian subordinate his music to an order? Because *any* statement, whenever made, and by whoever, needs countering. Any single expression, such as that of the Romantic 'I', must enter a dialectic, and be answered by another; not in a Hegelian dialectic, which presumes that there is an inherent progression inherent within that opposition, a view which is therefore theological, because it has a telos, but because no statement can be absolute, or allowed to be so, because every statement has its unconscious, and so other meaning. Call the opposition 'negative dialectics' or deconstruction, all statements are equivocal, however much that is repressed within any statement which makes unambiguous distinctions, such as good/evil.

In chapter 25, not Zeitblom but Adrian writes the account – on music manuscript, as though his soliloquy was itself music – of meeting the devil, who is an 'other' shifting between four identities. Michael Maar, who finds evidence of a real, or fantasised crime of blood activating all Mann's writings, including a sexual desire to let blood, says that the devil's first manifestation is the same as the Neapolitan pimp-comedian who lures on Aschenbach in *Death in Venice* (Maar 2003: 84). That suggests both the sexual, and how 'the homosexual plays an impish part' (Mann 1961: 80) in *Doctor Faustus*, and in its music. Maar thinks that in 1897, Mann had some encounter with the devil, in Palestrina, apparently then, as part of southern Italy, 'the centre of European Satanism' (Maar 2003: 44, 96, 100, 134). Leverkühn's devil is equivocal, first, like Ivan Karamazov's, negative, voicing Adrian's syphilis, but then, drawing on life as equivocal. Even death and life, he says, are not opposites, nor sickness and health. The 'Pfahlbürger' – the petit-bourgeois, the Philistine, cannot be allowed the last word here on what is sick/not sick (318, 235). Illness and madness are essential for creativity; what is of hell, and what is 'merely' Dürer's melancholia – and in Aristotelian terms, essential for creativity (Benjamin 1998: 148–151) – may be indistinguishable. So, 'der Künstler ist der Bruder des Verbrechers und des Verrückten' (319), 'the artist is the brother of the criminal and the madman' (236). All creativity comes from the devil, who seems here spontaneous, not Goethe's negating figure. But spontaneity is ambiguous, being what Fascism wants: banal affirmatory creation of unthinking allegiance to the national cause.

Saying this, the devil mutates into a more Adorno-like figure (321, 123), his subject art today, and how 'das Komponieren selbst ist zu schwer geworden, verzweifelt schwer' (322), 'composing itself has become too hard, desperately too hard' (238). The tonal conventions of musical composition creating a self-defined autonomous piece no longer work. Art becomes 'critique', and 'reflection', exceeding spontaneity. The devil insists on Kierkegaard as a theologian, loving but still damning *Don Giovanni*. He could only love such music for being ambiguous, ironical, questionable. Pushing it in either direction of that ambiguity would destroy it. Putting life into categories of good and evil attempts, fearfully, to eradicate ambiguity. This Adorno-figure repeats what the devil had said: life does not begin as moral, nor does the moral spur it on; everything works by untruth, 'Unwahrheit' (327, 242) and by disease. This devil, this 'Sammael', the fuller, Talmudic, version of *Der Freischütz*'s 'devil Samiel', urges Adrian to allow his madness to break through the cultural epoch and to become 'barbaric', in contrast to bourgeois refinement which has never permitted 'excess, paradox, mystic passion' (328, 243), qualities of mysticism, even Lutheran.

Then the devil fades into the older form. Positively, he advises exceeding the bourgeois categories of good and evil, where the bourgeois consider their values as 'good', excluding as evil what they neither know, nor wish not to know. That, negatively, risks a subjectivism which knows no critique, and endorses a cult of the feelings which takes these as absolute: the context for Fascism. Morphing, transiting from one form to another, the devil repeats that he is a theologian; indeed, the only one.

That makes two points: (a) theological discourse directs attention to the equivocal – in which case, it should join with psychoanalysis, and literature, and critical theory – and (b) it sanctions massive exclusions, as the Grand Inquisitor knows, and as all fundamentalists practise, whether in North American Republicanism and its congeners, or in current 'radical' Islam. Hence in the third manifestation, before making a final mutation to speak of Adrian's twenty-four years of creativity before everything ends for him, the devil, describing the hell of the concentration camp, thinks not of the end of art, but of the end of speech: 'hier alles aufhört' (330), 'everything ceases' (245). The reality of the horror of the death camps exceeds representation; art cannot pretend to encompass it.

Adrian asks whether total abandonment, producing utter despair, cannot be a way to salvation, in theological terms, since mediocrity ('Mittelmässigkeit', 333, 247) can neither interest theology nor God; one must be a Faust, or Cain, or holy sinner. That may endorse the sense that something theological constructs Mann's own interests. It asks how a sense of guilt over a forbidden sexuality indulged in deliberately transgressively (Leverkühn's syphilis), articulates with the political critique, that Germany has allowed itself to become Nazi. Why is guilt the proper reaction to either, especially Nazism? There might be special cases where guilt was appropriate. 'Guilt' means that the novel cannot step outside its own theological allegory; despite its Nietzschean tendency to allow for dissonance, so decentring itself, it still centres itself, through Zeitblom's thinking that *Germany* has sinned uniquely, on Adrian's analogy of the holy sinner, and is, therefore, bound to return. Neither the nationalism, nor the talk of sin, is the point. They endorse the wrong analysis, which is already too influential and apolitical: the Nazis were 'evil', so separating them, and any other group from 'us' and our 'core values', which may perhaps be those of what US politicians, monologising and coercing, in an effort at identity-thinking, call 'the American people'.

But misnaming is at the heart of everything, causing the primary constructions of good/evil to be premised on the idea of the unitary subject. When any group or act or person is called evil (or 'barbaric'), it stops debate by essentialising, fixing those values nihilistically, because refusing to admit the other. It has preselected what it wants to keep, and projects what it disavows in itself, onto an imaginary other. In Freud's essay 'Negation', someone engages in 'rejection, by projection' of ideas that are considered unacceptable (*SE* 19.235): what I do not accept in myself I identify in you. Such projection is inseparable from personification-allegory: naming a quality in another ('Evil') separates that, and the person, from me, and enables an ambivalent and fascinated attitude towards it.

Accusation involves projection; the devil as accuser works theologically, embracing the wrong side: power. But thinking diabolically also means that the dominant group, possessing power to name (for example, to pronounce mad) possesses what it negates; that point appears throughout *The Master and Margarita*. The devil as the principle of equivocation points to the instability of naming. The diabolical is on either side of theology's binary oppositions, and in the middle too, as the deconstructive principle which creates theology as a reaction to doubleness, wishing to disambiguate, to self-simplify, to bring about closure, to make irony only a concept, not an active principle. 'The Antithetical Meaning of Primal Words' declares that there can be no primary 'no', certainly not in dream-thought (*SE* 11.155). This fundamental ambiguity makes all interpretation selective, political, strategic; or, negatively, simplifying, disavowing. Perhaps the question to ask is how to go on, knowing such doubleness constructs everything: how to live double?

That recurs with the dual Muslim actor-heroes in Salman Rushdie's *Satanic Verses* (1988). Saladin Chamcha, Anglophile Indian, becomes what English racist discourse makes him: demonic; and Gibreel Farishta, born Ismail Najmuddin ('star of faith'). Saladin, returning from England, reconciles with his father. Gibreel, the outcast, like *Moby-Dick*'s Ishmael (compare Genesis 21:9–21), becomes a case of paranoid schizophrenia (Rushdie 1988: 429, like Freud's Judge Schreber), which is induced because of the impossibility, the double bind, involved in relating to two separate cultures simultaneously. The problem is more acute than even for the postcolonial Joyce, whose innovatory language, ridden with portmanteau words, influences Rushdie. Gibreel fantasises himself as Mohammed, the medieval Mahound, the devil's synonym (Rushdie 1988: 93), and as the Gabriel who speaks to Mahound, and as the Persian scribe, Salman, who may also be Shaitan (367).

Thus the 'satanic verses', whose subject is women, get inserted into the Qur'an: 'Have you thought upon Lat and Uzza, and Manat, the third, the other? ... they are the exalted birds, and their intercession is desired indeed' (114). These words, problematising alike monotheism and its patriarchy, apparently emanate from Gibreel's schizophrenia. This is described through the language of Milton's Satan addressing another Gabriel: 'Lives there who loves his pain' (*PL* 4.388), as though that Satan was schizophrenic; and 'in the Beckettian formula, *Not I. He*' and through the idea of Jekyll and Hyde. It makes Gibreel speak in Arabic, 'a language he did not know', words translated as 'these are exalted females whose intercession is to be desired' (340). (The girl/bird elision is discussed by Freud in relation to Schreber's fantasies (*SE* 12.36).) The words must be rescinded, but they give Mahound the sense that both versions are 'unreliable', that, as Gibreel thinks, '*it was me both times, baba, me first and second also me*' (123, compare 111). He collapses, as unknowable, the difference between the godly and the satanic. Yet schizophrenia, while taking personal forms for Gibreel (21–22), is not the self's problem, and cannot be solved by it, for 'the splitting was not in him but in the universe' (351). The statement may be reconcilable with Deleuze and Guattari in their writings on capitalism and schizophrenia in *Anti-Oedipus* and *Thousand Plateaux*: individual sickness – or pain, which the subject *does* love, through repression – issues from irreconcilable social and public pressures, tending towards de-territorialisation (loosening of categories and distinctions) and re-territorialisation simultaneously; towards de-centredness and recentring the self in a centred national/family-based/religious framework: a maddening double bind, politically and socially imposed.[4]

Theology creates Gibreel's self, torn between the two forms of angels dictating. Sanity lies in adhering to the 'good', but theology on that basis serves a splitting which predates it and which produces racism, as when a link is forged between the words *black* and *blasphemy* (288). Blasphemy becomes the novel's subject – and so gives the language for Iran's condemnation of it – as when, in the book, a film about Mohammed is discussed. Someone asks 'would it not be seen as blasphemous, a crime against . . . ' (272). But *what* it would blaspheme is unsaid. Again, Salman the Persian, Mahmoud's amanuensis, who changed the words which were dictated to him (being as devilish as Mahmoud, or Gibreel) is accused by Mahmoud of blasphemy, of setting his words against those of God (374). But if that defines blasphemy, there is no getting outside it. Gibreel 'caught himself in the act of forming blasphemous thoughts' as a boy going off to sleep (22). The reflexive form shows that his superego is policing his thinking, which cannot be allowed to come from him as 'I'. Any 'I' is inherently split, and must, then, set the word against the word, consciously or unconsciously. If the self is counted responsible for its 'blasphemous thoughts', that act of self-centring will always be contested by other un-delimited words. The single subject produces theologically orientated thought, making any other thought transgressive, blasphemous.

Thinking non-theologically, beyond the thought of the death of God, requires a non-logocentrism which ends the single subject, and allows the thought of the other. That would exceed what the devil permits, since, though the language of the devil points to something else, and suggests that in the beginning was perversity, diabolism was created by, and depends on, a thought which centres itself. This, in modernity, reacts to its decentring, which tends towards feelings of abjection, with the intolerance of an apocalyptic fury: unveiling the other and fighting it. Calling it 'the devil' in attempting to cast it out comes from the horror of the abject, in Kristeva's terms. Being decentred within the other approaches the mysticism we have noted with, for instance, de Certeau: a more feminine state even if, as Dostoevsky noted, it commits suicide while holding the icon.

Notes

1. He is perhaps identifiable with the critic Leopold Averbakh, who disliked *Diaboliada*, and who became leader in 1928 of RAPP, i.e. the Russian Association of Proletarian Writers. Bulgakov saw him as one of those preventing him from writing, which he said, in a letter to the Soviet Government of 28 March 1930, was the same as burying him alive (Milne 1990: 273).
2. In quotations from *Doctor Faustus*, where two numbers are given, the first refers to the German (Mann 1980), the second to the Lowe-Porter (Mann 1996) translation. The *Gesta Romanorum* was a source-book of narratives heavily drawn on by Chaucer, Gower, and Shakespeare, compiled at the end of the thirteenth-century.
3. Mann had met Adorno in Los Angeles, where both had gone to escape the Third Reich; perhaps in 1942, certainly, by 29 March,1943 (Gödde and Sprecher 2006: 3–4). Gödde and Sprecher indicate Mann's knowledge of the then-current writing of *Minima Moralia*, and of Adorno's work on Alban Berg, his music teacher, on Kierkegaard (1959), and outstandingly, on Beethoven.
4. Gilles Deleuze (1925–1995) and Félix Guattari (1930–1992) produced these two volumes, with the umbrella title *Capitalism and Schizophrenia*, in 1972 and 1980 respectively.

Bibliography

Adorno, Theodor W. 1973. *Philosophy of Modern Music*. Trans. Anne G. Mitchell and Wesley V. Blomster. London: Sheen and Ward.

———. 1974. *Minima Moralia*. Trans. E.F.N. Jephcott. London: Verso.

———. 1997. *Aesthetic Theory*. Ed. Gretel Adorno and Rolf Tiedemann, trans. Robert Hullot-Kentor. Minneapolis: Minnesota U.P.

———. 1998. *Beethoven: The Philosophy of Music*. Ed. Rolf Tiedermann, trans. Edmund Jephcott. Cambridge: Polity.

Ainsworth, Maryan W. (ed.). 2010. *Jan Gossart's Renaissance: Man, Myth, and Sensual Pleasure*. New Haven: Yale U.P.

Alighieri, Dante. 1970–1975. *The Divine Comedy*. 3 vols. Ed. and Trans. Charles Singleton. Princeton: Princeton U.P.

Anderson, M.D. 1963. *Drama and Imagery in English Medieval Churches*. Cambridge: C.U.P.

Aquinas, Thomas. 2003. *On Evil*. Ed. Brian Davies, trans. Richard Regan. Oxford: O.U.P.

Arendt, Hannah. 1968. *The Origins of Totalitarianism*. New York: Harcourt Brace.

———. 1977. *Eichmann in Jerusalem: A Report on the Banality of Evil*. Harmondsworth: Penguin.

Astell, Ann W. 1994. *Job, Boethius, and Religious Truth*. Ithaca: Cornell U.P.

Astington, John. 1985. '"Fault" in Shakespeare'. *Shakespeare Quarterly* 36: 330–334.

Atkins, Stuart. 1958. *Goethe's Faust: A Literary Analysis*. Cambridge, MA: Harvard U.P.

J. Tambling, *Histories of the Devil*,
DOI 10.1057/978-1-137-51832-3

Augustine. 1972. *City of God*. Trans. Henry Bettenson. Harmondsworth: Penguin.

———. 1992. *Confessions*. Trans. Henry Chadwick. Oxford: O.U.P.

———. 1997. *On Christian Teaching*. Trans. R.P.H. Green. Oxford: O.U.P.

———. 2002. *On Genesis*. Ed. John E. Rotelle, trans. Edmund Hill. New York: New City Press.

Awn, Peter J. 1983. *Satan's Tragedy and Redemption: Iblis in Sufi Psychology*. Leiden: E.J. Brill.

Bakhtin, Mikhail. 1984a. *Rabelais and his World*. Trans. Hélène Iswolsky. Bloomington: Indiana U.P.

———. 1984b. *Problems of Dostoevsky's Poetics*. Ed. Caryl Emerson. Manchester: M.U.P.

Bakker, Boudewijn. 2012. *Landscape and Religion from Van Eyck to Rembrandt*. Trans. Diane Webb. Aldershot: Ashgate.

Baldass, Ludwig von. 1960. *Hieronymus Bosch*. London: Thames and Hudson.

Ball, J.T. 1986. *Thomas Mann's Recantation of Faust: Doktor Faustus in the Context of Mann's Relationship to Goethe*. Stuttgart: Hans-Dieter Heinz.

Balzac, Honoré de. 1991. *Père Goriot*. Trans. A.J. Krailsheimer. Oxford: O.U.P.

Barber, C.L. 1988. 'The Form of Faustus' Fortunes Good or Bad'. In Richard Wheeler (ed.), *Creating Elizabethan Tragedy: The Theatre of Marlowe and Kyd*. Chicago: Chicago U.P.

Barnes, Jonathan. 1987. *Early Greek Philosophy*. Harmondsworth: Penguin.

Baron, Frank. 1978. *Doctor Faustus: From History to Legend*. Munich: Wilhelm Fink.

Barratt, Andrew. 1987. *Between Two Worlds: A Critical Introduction to the Master and Margarita*. Oxford: O.U.P.

Barthes, Roland. 1977. *Image-Music-Text*. Trans. Stephen Heath. London: Fontana.

Bate, Jonathan. 1989. *Shakespeare and the English Romantic Tradition*. Oxford: Clarendon.

Baudelaire, Charles. 1972. *Selected Writings on Art and Artists*. Trans. P.E. Charvet. Harmondsworth: Penguin.

———. 1986. *Baudelaire: The Complete Verse*. Trans. Francis Scarfe. London: Anvil Press.

———. 1998. *The Flowers of Evil*. Trans. Jonathan Culler. Oxford: O.U.P.

Beer, John. 1979. 'Influence and Independence in Blake'. In Michael Phillips (ed.), *Interpreting Blake*. Cambridge: C.U.P.

Behrendt, Stephen C. 1983. *The Moment of Explosion: Blake and the Illustration of Milton*. Lincoln: University of Nebraska Press.

Beier, A.L. 1985. *Masterless Men: The Vagrancy Problem in England 1560–1640*. London: Methuen.

Belknap, Robert L. 1990. *The Genesis of The Brothers Karamazov: The Aesthetics, Ideology and Psychology of Making a Text.* Evanston: Northwestern U.P.

Bell, Millicent. 1953. 'The Fallacy of the Fall in *Paradise Lost*'. *PMLA* 68: 863–883.

———. With Wayne Shumaker. 1955. 'The Fallacy of the Fall in *Paradise Lost*'. *PMLA* 70: 1185–1203.

Belsey, Catherine. 1985. *The Subject of Tragedy: Identity and Difference in Renaissance Drama.* London: Methuen.

Benjamin, Walter. 1977. *The Origin of German Tragic Drama.* Trans. John Osborne. London: Verso.

———. 1996–2003. *Selected Writings.* 4 vols. Ed. Marcus Bullock, Michael W. Jennings, Howard Eiland, and Gary Smith. Cambridge, MA: Harvard U.P. (quoted as *SW* plus volume and page).

———. 1999. *The Arcades Project.* Trans. Howard Eiland and Kevin McLaughlin. Cambridge, MA: Harvard U.P.

Bentley, G.E., Jr. 2001. *The Stranger from Paradise; A Biography of William Blake.* New Haven: Yale U.P.

Bergsten, Gunilla. 1969. *Thomas Mann's Doctor Faustus: The Sources and Structure of the Novel.* Trans. Krishna Winston. Chicago: Chicago U.P.

Berman, Marshall. 1983. *All that is Solid Melts into Air: The Experience of Modernity.* London: Verso.

Berrong, Richard. 1986. *Rabelais and Bakhtin: Popular Culture in Gargantua and Patangruel.* Lincoln, NE: Nebraska U.P.

Bertz, Douglas. 1985. 'Prophecy and Apocalypse in Langland's *Piers Plowman*, B-Text, Passūs XVI to XIX'. *Journal of English and Germanic Philology* 84: 313–327.

Besserman, Lawrence L. 1979. *The Legend of Job in the Middle Ages.* Cambridge, MA: Harvard U.P.

Bevington, David M. 1962. *From Mankind to Marlowe: Growth of Structure in the Popular Drama of Tudor England.* Cambridge, MA: Harvard U.P.

Bevington, David M. and Eric Rasmussen. 1993. *Christopher Marlowe: Doctor Faustus, A and B Texts 1604, 1616.* Manchester: M.U.P.

Bindman, David. 1977. *Blake as an Artist.* Oxford: Phaidon.

Blanchot, Maurice. 1982. *The Space of Literature.* Trans. Ann Smock. Lincoln: Nebraska U.P.

Blumenberg, Hans. 1985. *Work on Myth.* Trans. Robert M. Wallace. Cambridge, MA: MIT Press.

Blunt, Anthony. 1959. *The Art of William Blake.* New York: Columbia U.P.

Bond, Helen K. 1998. *Pontius Pilate in History and Interpretation.* Cambridge: C.U.P.

Bontea, Adriana. 2006. 'A Project in its Context: Walter Benjamin on Comedy'. *MLN* 121: 1041–1071.

Boureau, Alain. 2006. *Satan the Heretic: The Birth of Demonology in the Medieval West.* Trans. Teresa Lavender Fagan. Chicago: University of Chicago Press.

Boss, Valentin. 1991. *Milton and the Rise of Russian Satanism.* Toronto: Toronto U.P.

Boyce, Mary. 1984. *Textual Sources for the Study of Zoroastrianism.* Manchester: M.U.P.

Boyle, Nicholas. 1987. *Goethe: Faust Part One.* Cambridge: C.U.P.

———. 1991. *Goethe: The Poet and the Age, vol 1: The Poetry of Desire.* Oxford: O.U.P.

Brant, Sebastian. 1944. *The Ship of Fools.* Trans. Edwin H. Zeydel. New York: Dover.

Briggs, K.M. 1959. *The Anatomy of Puck: An Examination of Fairy Beliefs among Shakespeare's Contemporaries and Successors.* London: Routledge and Kegan Paul.

Bristol, Michael D. 1985. *Carnival and Theater: Plebian Culture and the Structure of Authority in Renaissance England.* London: Methuen.

Brockbank, J. Philip. 1962. *Marlowe: Doctor Faustus.* London: Edward Arnold.

Brown, Beatrice Daw. 1939. 'Marlowe, Faustus, and Simon Magus'. *PMLA* 54: 82–121.

Brown, Jane K. 1992. *Faust: Theatre of the World.* New York: Twayne.

Brown, Peter. 2000. *Augustine of Hippo: A Biography.* London: Faber.

Browne, Alice. 1977. 'Descartes' Dreams'. *Journal of the Warburg and Courtauld Institutes* 40: 256–273.

Brownlow, F.W. 1993. *Shakespeare, Harsnett, and the Devils of Denham.* Delaware: Delaware U.P.

Bruster, Douglas and Eric Rasmussen. 2009. *Everyman and Mankind.* London: Methuen.

Bulgakov, Mikhail. 1997. *The Master and Margarita.* Trans. Richard Pevear and Larissa Volokhonsky. London: Penguin.

Bunyan, John. 1987. *The Pilgrim's Progress.* Ed. Roger Sharrock. Harmondsworth: Penguin.

Butler, E.M. 1952. *The Fortunes of Faust.* Cambridge: C.U.P.

Butlin, Martin. 1981. *The Paintings and Drawings of William Blake.* 2 vols. New Haven: Yale U.P.

Campbell, Caroline. (ed.). 2007. *Temptation in Eden: Lucas Cranach's Adam and Eve.* London: Courtauld Institute of Art Gallery and Paul Holberton.

Casey, Timothy J. (ed.). 1992. *Jean Paul: A Reader.* Trans. Erika Casey. Baltimore: Johns Hopkins U.P.

Cawley, A.C. 1959. *The Wakefield Pageants in the Towneley Cycle.* Manchester: M.U.P.

Cazotte, Jacques. 1991. *The Devil in Love.* Trans. Judith Landry. London: Daedalus.

Certeau, Michel de. 1986. *Heterologies: Discourse on the Other.* Manchester: M.U.P.

———. 1988. *The Writing of History*. Trans. Tom Conley. New York: Columbia U.P.

———. 1992. *The Mystic Fable, vol. 1: The Sixteenth and Seventeenth Centuries*. Trans. Michael B. Smith. Chicago: Chicago U.P.

———. 2000. *The Possession at Loudun*. Trans. Michael B. Smith. Chicago: Chicago U.P.

Cervantes, Miguel de. 1998. *Exemplary Stories*. Trans. Lesley Lipson. Oxford: O.U.P.

Chambers, E.K. 1903. *The Medieval Stage*. 2 vols in one. New York: Dover.

———. 1923. *The Elizabethan Stage 4 vols*. Oxford: O.U.P.

Chaucer, Geoffrey. 1988. *The Riverside Chaucer*. Ed. Larry D. Benson. Oxford: O.U.P.

Chesterfield, Lord. 1992. *Lord Chesterfield: Letters*. Ed. David Roberts. Oxford: O.U.P.

Clark, Stuart. 1997. *Thinking with Demons: The Idea of Witchcraft in Early Modern Europe*. Oxford: Clarendon.

Cohen, Margaret. 1989. 'Walter Benjamin's Phantasmagoria'. *New German Critique* 48: 87–107.

Cohn, Norman. 1993. *Cosmos, Chaos, and the World to Come: The Ancient Roots of Apocalyptic Faith*. New Haven: Yale U.P.

Conley, Tom. 1992. *The Graphic Unconscious in Early Modern French Writing*. Cambridge: Cambridge U.P.

Connolly, Julian W. 2013. *Dostoevesky's The Brothers Karamazov*. London: Bloomsbury.

Constantine. 2005, 2009. *Johann Wolfgang von Goethe: Faust, Part I, Faust Part 2*. London: Penguin.

Cornish, Alison. 2000. *Reading Dante's Stars*. New Haven: Yale U.P.

Cowper, William. 1934. *The Poetical Works of William Cowper*. Ed. H.S. Milford. Oxford: OUP.

Cox, John D. 2000. *The Devil and the Sacred in English Drama, 1350–1642*. Cambridge: C.U.P.

Craik, T.W. 1958. *The Tudor Interlude: Stage, Costume, and Acting*. Leicester: Leicester U.P.

Daemmirch, Horst S. 1973. *The Shattered Self: E.T.A. Hoffmann's Tragic Vision*. Detroit: Wayne State U.P.

Damon, S. Foster. 1966. *Blake's Job: William Blake's Illustrations of the Book of Job*. Providence: Brown U.P.

Daniel, Howard. 1974. *Callot's Etchings*. New York: Dover.

De Jonge, Alexis. 1973. 'Gogol'. In John Fennell (ed.), *Nineteenth-Century Russian Literature: Studies of Ten Russian Writers*. Faber: London.

De Man, Paul. 1996. 'Sign and Symbol in Hegel's *Aesthetics*'. In Andrez Warminski (ed.), *Aesthetic Ideology*. Minneapolis: Minnesota U.P.

Defoe, Daniel. 1972. *Robinson Crusoe*. Ed. J. Donald Crowley. Oxford: O.U.P.

———. 2005. *The Political History of the Devil.* Ed. John Mullan. London: Pickering and Chatto.

Deleuze, Gilles. 1983. *Nietzsche and Philosophy.* Trans. Hugh Tomlinson. London: Athlone.

Derrida, Jacques. 1976. *Of Grammatology.* Trans. Gayatri Chakravorty Spivak. Baltimore: John Hopkins U.P.

———. 1978. *Writing and Difference.* Trans. Alan Bass. London: Routledge and Kegan Paul.

———. 1981. *Dissemination.* Trans. Barbara Johnson. Chicago: Chicago U.P.

———. 1987. *The Postcard: From Socrates to Freud and Beyond.* Trans. Alan Bass. Chicago: Chicago U.P.

Descartes, René. 1988. *Selected Philosophical Writings.* Trans. John Cottingham, Robert Stoothoff, Dugald Murdoch. Cambridge: C.U.P.

Dews, Peter. 2008. *The Idea of Evil.* Oxford: Blackwell.

Dickens, Charles. 2004. *David Copperfield.* Ed. Jeremy Tambling. London: Penguin.

Dijkhuzen, Jan Frans Van. 2007. *Devil Theatre: Demonic Possession and Exorcism in English Renaissance Drama, 1558–1642.* Woodbridge: D.S. Brewer.

Diller, Hans-Jurgen. 1992. *The Middle English Mystery Play: A Study in Dramatic Speech and Form.* Cambridge: C.U.P.

Dostoevsky, Fydor. 1964. *Crime and Punishment.* Ed. George Gibian, trans. Jessie Coulson. New York: Norton.

———. 1972. *Notes from Underground and the Double.* Trans. Jessie Coulson. Harmondsworth: Penguin.

———. 1992. *The Idiot Trans. Alan Myers.* Oxford: O.U.P.

———. 1994a. *Demons*, Trans. Richard Pevear and Larissa Volokhonsky. London: Vintage.

———. 1994b. *A Writer's Diary.* 2 Vols. Trans. Kenneth Lantz. Evanston: Northwestern U.P.

———. 2004. *The Brothers Karamazov.* Trans. Richard Pevear and Larissa Volokonsky. London: Vintage.

Duchesse-Guillemin, Jacques. 1958. *The Western Response to Zoroaster.* Oxford: O.U.P.

Dunbar, Pamela. 1980. *William Blake's Illustrations to the Poetry of Milton.* Oxford: Clarendon.

Dye, Ellis. 2001. 'Figurations of the Feminine in Goethe's *Faust*'. In Paul Bishop (ed.), *A Companion to Goethe's Faust, Parts I and II.* Rochester, NY: Camden House.

Eaves, Morris, Robert N. Essick, and Joseph Viscomi. 1993. *William Blake: The Early Illuminated Books.* London: Tate Gallery.

Eckermann, Peter. 1970. *Conversations with Goethe.* Trans. John Oxenford. London: Dent.

Eliot, George. 1967. *Daniel Deronda*. Ed. Barbara Hardy. Harmondsworth: Penguin.

———. 1985. *Adam Bede*. Ed. Stephen Gill. Harmondsworth: Penguin.

Eliot, T.S. 1951. *Selected Essays*. London: Faber.

Elliott, J.K. (ed.). 1993. *The Apocryphal New Testament*. Oxford: O.U.P.

Emmerson, Richard Kenneth. 1981. *Antichrist in the Middle Ages*. Manchester: M.U.P.

Empson, William. 1951. *The Structure of Complex Words*. London: Chatto and Windus.

———. 1961. *Milton's God*. Cambridge: C.U.P.

———. 1965. *Some Versions of Pastoral* (1935). Harmondsworth: Penguin.

———. 1981. *Milton's God*. Cambridge: C.U.P.

———. 1987. *Faustus and the Censor: The English Faust-Book and Marlowe's Doctor Faustus*. Ed. John Henry Jones. Oxford. Basil Blackwell.

Erasmus, Desiderius. 1971. *Praise of Folly*. Harmondsworth: Penguin.

———. 1991. *Collected Works 33*. Trans. R.A.B. Mynors. Toronto: Toronto U.P.

Erdman, David V. 1975. *The Illuminated Blake*. Oxford: O.U.P.

———. 1977. *Blake: Prophet Against Empire*. Princeton: Princeton U.P.

———. 1982. *The Complete Poetry and Prose of William Blake*. Berkeley: California U.P.

Ericson, Edward E. 1974. 'The Satanic Incarnation: Parody in Bulgakov's *The Master and Margarita*'. *Russian Review* 33: 20–36.

Evans, J.M. 1968. *Paradise Lost and the Genesis Tradition*. Oxford: Clarendon.

Fairley, Barker. 1953. *Goethe's Faust: Six Essays*. Oxford: Clarendon Press.

Febvre, Lucien. 1982. *The Problem of Unbelief in the Sixteenth Century: The Religion of Rabelais*. Trans. Beatrice Gottlieb. Cambridge, MA: Harvard U.P.

Fenves, Peter. 2011. *The Messianic Reduction: Walter Benjamin and the Shapes of Time*. Stanford: Stanford U.P.

Ferber, Sarah. 2004. *Demonic Possession and Exorcism in Early Modern France*. London: Routledge.

Fernie, Ewan. 2013. *The Demonic: Literature and Experience*. London: Routledge.

Ferreiro, Alberto. 2005. *Simon Magus in Patristic, Medieval and Early Modern Traditions*. Leiden: Brill.

Foakes, R.A. (ed.). 1997. *King Lear*. London: Thomas Nelson.

Forsyth, Neil. 1987. *The Old Enemy: Satan and the Combat Myth*. Princeton: Princeton U.P.

———. 2003. *The Satanic Epic*. Princeton: Princeton U.P.

Foucault, Michel. 2006. *History of Madness*. Ed. Jean Khalfa, trans. Jonathan Murphy and Jean Khalfa. London: Routledge.

Frame, Donald. 1977. *François Rabelais: A Study*. New York: Harcourt Brace Jovanovich.

———. 1991. (trans.). *The Complete Works of Francois Rabelais.* Berkeley: California U.P.

Fränger, Wilhelm. 1952. *The Millennium of Hieronymus Bosch: Outlines of a New Interpretation.* Trans. Eithne Wilkins and Ernst Kaiser. London: Faber.

Frank, Joseph. 1977. *Dostoevsky: The Seeds of Revolt, 1821–1849.* Princeton: Princeton U.P.

———. 1986. *Dostoevsky: The Stir of Liberation, 1860–1865.* Princeton: Princeton U.P.

———. 1990. *Dostoevsky: The Years of Ordeal, 1850–1859.* Princeton: Princeton U.P.

———. 1995. *Dostoevsky: The Miraculous Years, 1965–1871*, Princeton: Princeton U.P.

———. 2002. *Dostoevsky: The Mantle of the Prophet (1871–1881).* Princeton: Princeton U.P.

Frank, Maria Esposito. 2007. 'Dante's Muhammad: Parallels between Islam and Arianism'. *Dante Studies* 125: 185–206.

Freccero, Carla. 1991. *Father Figures: Genealogy and Narrative Structure in Rabelais.* Ithaca: Cornell U.P.

Freccero, John. 1986. *Dante: The Poetics of Conversion.* Ed. Rachel Jacoff. Cambridge, MA: Harvard U.P.

Freeborn, Richard. 1960. *Turgenev: The Novelist's Novelist.* Oxford: O.U.P.

Freud, Sigmund. *Standard Edition of the Complete Psychological Works.* 24 vols. Ed. James Strachey. London: Hogarth Press. (quoted as *SE* plus volume and page).

Frieden, Ken. 1985. *Genius and Monologue.* Ithaca: Cornell U.P.

Fung, Paul. 2014. *Dostoevsky and the Epileptic Mode of Being.* Oxford: Legenda.

Gardner, Iain and Samuel N.C. Lieu. 2004. *Manichean Texts from the Roman Empire.* Cambridge: C.U.P.

Gardner, John. 1967. '*The Canon Yeoman's Prologue and Tale*: An Interpretation'. *Philological Quarterly* 46: 1–17.

Garside, P.D. (ed.). 2006. *James Hogg: The Private Memoirs and Confessions of a Justified Sinner.* Edinburgh: E.U.P.

Gearey, John. 1992. *Goethe's Other Faust: The Drama, Part II.* Toronto: Toronto U.P.

Gibson, Marion. 2006. *Possession, Puritanism, and Print: Possession, Darrell, Harsnett, Shakespeare and the Elizabethan Exorcism Controversy.* London: Pickering and Chatto.

Gibson, Walter S. 1973. *Hieronymus Bosch.* London: Thames and Hudson.

———. 1977. *Bruegel.* London: Thames and Hudson.

———. 2006. *Pieter Bruegel and the Art of Laughter.* Berkeley: University of California Press.

Gillespie, Michael Allen. 1995. *Nihilism Before Nietzsche.* Chicago: Chicago U.P.

———. 2008. *The Theological Origins of Modernity.* Chicago: Chicago U.P.

Gilson, Simon A. 2001. 'Medieval Magical Lore and Dante's *Commedia*: Divination and Demonic Agency'. *Dante Studies* 119: 27–66.

Gödde, Christoph and Thomas Sprecher. (eds.). 2006. *Theodor Weisengrund Adorno and Thomas Mann: Correspondence 1943–1955*. Trans. Nicholas Walker. Cambridge: Polity.

Goethe. 2005. *Faust: Eine Tragödie*. Kommentiert von Erich Trunz. München: C.H. Beck.

———. 2013. *The Sufferings of Young Werther*. Trans. Stanley Corngold. New York: Norton.

Gogol, Nikolai. 1985. *The Complete Tales of Nikolai Gogol*. 2 vols. Trans. Constance Garnett, revised Leonard J. Kent. Chicago: Chicago U.P.

Gogol, Nikolay. 2004. *Dead Souls*. Trans. Robert A. Maguire. London: Penguin.

Gombrich, E.H. 1976. *The Heritage of Apelles: Studies in the Art of the Renaissance*. London: Phaidon.

Grady, Hugh. 1996. *Shakespeare's Universal Wolf: Studies in Early Modern Reification*. Oxford: Clarendon Press.

Gray, Ronald. 1952. *Goethe the Alchemist: A Study of Alchemical Symbolism in Goethe's Literary and Scientific Works*. Cambridge: C.U.P.

Graziani, René. 1973. 'Pieter Bruegel's "Dulle Griet" and Dante'. *Burlington Magazine* 115: 109–119.

Greenblatt, Stephen. 1989. *Shakespearian Negotiations*. Berkeley: California U.P.

Greene, Robert. 1969. *Friar Bacon and Friar Bungay*. Ed. J.A. Lavin: New Mermaids. London: Ernest Benn.

Grimm, Jacob and Wilhelm Grimm. 1948. *Grimm's Fairy Tales*. Trans. Margaret Hunt and James Stern. London: Routledge and Kegan Paul.

Grossmann, F. 1966. *Bruegel: The Paintings*. London: Phaidon.

Hagstrum, Jean H. 1964. *William Blake: Poet and Painter*. Chicago: Chicago U.P.

Hall, Jonathan. 1995. *Anxious Pleasures: Shakespearean Comedy and the Nation-State*. Madison: Fairleigh Dickinson U.P.

Hamilton, Donna. 1992. *Shakespeare and the Politics of Protestant England*. Lexington: Kentucky U.P.

Hamlin, Cyrus. 1994. 'Tracing the Eternal-Feminine in Goethe's *Faust II*'. In Jane K. Brown, Meredith Lee, Thomas P. Saine, Paul Hernadi and Cyrus Hamlin (eds.), *Interpreting Goethe's Faust Today*. Columbia, SC: Camden House.

Hampton, Timothy. 1993. '"Turkish Dogs": Rabelais, Erasmus, and the Rhetoric of Alterity'. *Representations* 41: 58–82.

Happé, Peter. 1972. *Tudor Interludes*. Harmondsworth: Penguin.

———. 1975. *English Mystery Plays*. Harmondsworth: Penguin.

———. 1979. *Four Morality Plays*. Harmondsworth: Penguin.

———. 1994. *Ben Jonson: The Devil is an Ass*. Manchester: M.U.P.

Hartman, Geoffrey H. 1970. *Beyond Formalism: Literary Essays 1958–1970.* New Haven: Yale U.P.

Havely, Nick. 2004. *Dante and the Franciscans: Poverty and the Papacy in the Commedia.* Cambridge: C.U.P.

Hawkes, David. 2007. *The Faust Myth: Religion and the Rise of Representation.* London: Palgrave Macmillan.

Hayes, E. Bruce. 2007. 'Putting the "Haute" Back into the "Haute Dame de Paris": The Politics and Performance of Rabelais's Radical Farce'. *French Forum* 32: 39–52.

Heidegger, Martin. 1971. *Poetry, Language, Thought.* New York: Harper and Row.

———. 1977. *The Question Concerning Technology and Other Essays.* Trans. William Lovitt. New York: Harper and Row.

Heretz, Leionid. 2008. *Russia on the Eve of Modernity: Popular Religion and Traditional Culture Under the Last Tsars.* Cambridge: C.U.P.

Hieatt, Kent A. 1980. 'Eve as Reason in a Tradition of Allegorical Interpretation of the Fall'. *Journal of the Warburg and Courtauld Institutes* 43: 221–226.

———. 1983. 'Hans Baldung Grien's Ottawa Eve and its Context'. *Art Bulletin* 65: 290–304.

Hill, Christopher. 1979. *Milton and the English Revolution.* London: Faber.

Hingley, Ronald. 1967. *Nihilists: Russian Radicals and Revolutionaries in the Reign of Alexander II (1855–1881).* London: Weidenfeld and Nicolson.

Hirschkop, Ken. 1999. *Mikhail Bakhtin: An Aesthetic for Democracy.* Oxford: O.U.P.

Hobbes, Thomas. 1968. *Leviathan.* Ed. C.B. McPherson. Harmondsworth. Penguin.

Hoffmann, E.T.A. 1969. *Die Elixiere des Teufels.* Munchen: Winkler-Verlag.

———. 1992. *The Golden Pot and Other Tales.* Trans. Ritchie Robertson. Oxford: O.U.P.

———. 2008. *The Devil's Elixirs.* Trans. Ronald Taylor. London: Oneworld Classics.

Hogg, James. 1969. *The Private Memoirs and Confessions of a Justified Sinner.* Ed. John Carey. Oxford: O.U.P.

Holquist, Michael. 1977. *Dostoesvky and the Novel.* Princeton: Princeton U.P.

Honigmann, E.A.J. (ed.). 1997. *Shakespeare: Othello.* London: Thomas Nelson.

Hornback, Robert. 2009. *The English Clown Tradition from the Middle Ages to Shakespeare.* Cambridge: D.S. Brewer.

Hourihane, Colum. 2009. *Pontius Pilate, Anti-Semitism, and the Passion in Medieval Art.* Princeton: Princeton U.P.

Hudson, Nicholas. 1988. '"Why God no Kill the Devil?" The Diabolical Disruption of Order in *Robinson Crusoe*'. *Review of English Studies* 39: 494–501.

Jenkins, Harold. (ed.). 1982. *Shakespeare: Hamlet.* London: Methuen.

Jennings, Margaret. 1975. 'Tutivillus: The Literary Career of the Recording Demon'. *Studies in Philology* 74: 1–95.

Johnson, Christopher. 1993. *System and Writing in the Philosophy of Jacques Derrida*. Cambridge: C.U.P.

Johnson, James H. 2001. *Venice Incognito: Masks in the Serene Republic*. Berkeley: California U.P.

Jonassen, Frederick B. 1991. 'The Meaning of Falstaff's Allusion to the Jack-a-Lent in *The Merry Wives of Windsor*'. *Studies in Philology* 88: 48–68.

Jones, John Henry. 1994. *The English Faust Book: A Critical Edition Based on the Text of 1592*. Cambridge: C.U.P.

Jonson, Ben. 1988. *The Staple of News*. Ed. Anthony Parr. Manchester: M.U.P.

Kaiser, Walter. 1964. *Praisers of Folly: Erasmus, Rabelais, Shakespeare*. London: Victor Gollancz.

Kanevskaya, Maria. 2002. 'Smerdiakov and Ivan: Dostoevsky's *The Brothers Karamazov*'. *The Russian Review* 61: 358–376.

Kaula, David. 1975. *Shakespeare and the Archpriest Controversy*. The Hague: Mouton.

Kavaler, Ethan Matt. 1999. *Pieter Bruegel: Parables of Order and Enterprise*. Cambridge: C.U.P.

Kelly, Henry Ansgar. 2006. *Satan: A Biography*. Cambridge: Cambridge U.P.

Keynes, Geoffrey. 1971. *Blake Studies: Essays on His Life and Work*. Oxford: Clarendon.

Kierkegaard, Søren. 1959. *Either/Or*. 2 vols. Trans. David F. Swenson and Lillian Marvin Swenson, revised Howard A. Johnson. Princeton: Princeton U.P.

———. 1980. *The Concept of Anxiety*. Trans. Reidar Thomte and Albert B. Anderson. Princeton: Princeton U.P.

Kinser, Samuel. 1990. *Rabelais' Carnival: Text, Context, Metatext*. Berkeley: California U.P.

Knights, L.C. 1964. *Explorations*. Harmondsworth: Penguin.

Koch, Robert A. 1974. *Hans Baldung Grien: Eve, the Serpent, and Death*. Ottawa: National Gallery of Canada.

Kofman, Sarah. 1988. 'Baubô: Theological Perversion and Fetishism'. In Michael Gillespie and Tracy B. Strong (ed.), *Nietzsche's New Seas*. Chicago: Chicago U.P.

———. 1991. *Freud and Fiction*. Trans. Sarah Wykes. Cambridge: Polity.

Koldeweij, A. M, Vandenbroeck, P., and Vermet, B. 2001. *Hieronymous Bosch: The Complete Paintings and Drawings*. Amsterdam: Ludion Ghent.

Kolve, V.A. 1966. *The Play Called Corpus Christi*. Stanford: Stanford U.P.

Krailsheimer, A.J. 1963. *Rabelais and the Franciscans*. Oxford: Clarendon.

Krell, David Farrell. 1986. *Postponements: Women, Sexuality, Death in Nietzsche*. Bloomington: Indiana U.P.

Kreyenbroek Philip, G. 1995. *Yezidism – Its Background, Observances and Textual Tradition*. Lewisten, NY: Edwin Mellen Press.

Kristeva, Julia. 1981. *Powers of Horror: An Essay on Abjection*. Trans. Leon Roudiez. New York: Columbia U.P.

La Charité, Raymond. 1975. 'Devildom and Rabelais's Pantagruel'. *The French Review* 49: 42–50.

Laan, J.M. van der, and Andrew Weeks. 2013. *The Faustian Century: German Literature and Culture in the Age of Luther and Faustus*. Rochester, NY: Camden House.

Lacan, Jacques. 1992. *The Ethics of Psychoanalysis 1959–1960: The Seminar of Jacques Lacan*. Ed. Jacques Alain-Miller, trans. Dennis Porter. London: Routledge.

———. 2002. *Ecrits*. Trans. Bruce Fink with Héloïse Fink and Russell Grigg. New York: W.W. Norton.

Lamb, Jonathan. 1995. *The Rhetoric of Suffering: Reading the Book of Job in the Eighteenth Century*. Oxford: Clarendon.

Lawrence, D.H. 1956. *Selected Literary Criticism*. Ed. Anthony Beal. London: Heinemann.

Leatherbarrow, W.J. 2005. *A Devil's Vaudeville: The Demonic in Dostoesvky's Major Fiction*. Evanston: Northwestern U.P.

Leavis, F.R. 1952. *The Common Pursuit*. Harmondsworth: Penguin.

———. 1964. *Revaluation: Tradition and Development in English Poetry*. Harmondsworth: Penguin.

Lehning, Arthur. (ed.). 1973. *Mikhail Bakunin: Selected Writings*. Trans. Steven Cox and Olive Stevens. New York: Grove Press.

Leonard, John. 1990. *Naming in Paradise: Milton and the Language of Adam and Eve*. Oxford: Clarendon.

Levin, Harry. 1954. *The Overreacher: A Study of Christopher Marlowe*. London: Faber.

———. 1967. 'From Terence to Tabarin: A Note on Les Fourberies de Scapin'. *Yale French Review* 38: 128–137.

Lewis, C.S. 1936. *The Allegory of Love: A Study in Medieval Tradition*. Oxford: O.U.P.

Lieu, Samuel. 1985. *Manichaeism in the Later Roman Empire and Medieval China: An Historical Survey*. Manchester: M.U.P.

Linden, Stanton J. 1991. *Darke Hierogliphicks: Alchemy in English Literature from Chaucer to the Restoration*. Lexington: Kentucky U.P.

———. 2003. *The Alchemy Reader: From Hermes Trismegistus to Isaac Newton*. Cambridge: C.U.P.

Linfert, Carl. 1972. *Hieronymus Bosch*. London: Thames and Hudson.

———. 1989. *Bosch*. London: Thames and Hudson.

Lowe, David. 1983. *Turgenev's Fathers and Sons*. Ann Arbor: Ardis.

———. 1996. 'Gounod's Faust and Bulgakov's *The Master and Margarita*'. *Russian Review* 55: 279–286.

Löwy, Michael. 2005. *Fire Alarm: Reading Walter Benjamin's 'On the Concept of History'*. Trans. Chris Turner. London: Verso.

Lukacher, Ned. 1994. *Daemonic Figures: Shakespeare and the Question of Conscience*. Ithaca: Cornell U.P.

Lukács, Georg. 1968. *Goethe and his Age*. Trans. Robert Anchor. London: Merlin Press.

Luke, David. 1987, 1994. *Goethe: Faust Part One, and Faust Part Two* (trans.) Oxford: O.U.P.

Luther, Martin. 1969. *Luther and Erasmus: Free Will and Salvation*. Trans. and Ed. E. Gordon Rupp and others. London: SCM.

Maar, Michael. 2003. *Bluebeard's Chamber: Guilt and Confession in Thomas Mann*. Trans. David Fernbach. London: Verso.

Macalpine, Ida, and Richard A. Hunter. 1956. *Schizophrenia 1677: A Psychiatric Study of an Illustrated Autobiographical Record of Demoniacal Possession*. London: William Dawson.

MacDonald, Michael. 1983. *Mystical Bedlam: Madness, Anxiety and Healing in Seventeenth-Century England*. Cambridge: C.U.P.

Maguire, Muireann. 2012. *Stalin's Ghosts: Gothic Themes in Early Soviet Literature*. Oxford: Peter Lang.

Makhov, Alexander E. 2011. '... *In diversas figuras nequitiae*: The Devil's Image from the Viewpoint of Rhetoric'. In Gerhard Jaritz (ed.), *Angels, Devils: The Supernatural and its Visual Representation*. Budapest: Central European U.P.

Mann, Klaus. 1983. *Mephisto*. Trans. Robin Smyth. Harmondsworth: Penguin.

———. 1987. *The Turning Point: An Autobiography*. London: Serpent's Tail.

Mann, Thomas. 1961. *The Genesis of a Novel*. Trans. Richard and Clara Winston. London: Secker and Warburg.

———. 1968. *Lotte in Weimar*. Trans. Helen Lowe-Porter. Harmondsworth: Penguin.

———. 1980. *Doktor Faustus: Das Leben des Deutschen Tonsetzers Adrian Leverkühn, Erzählt von einem Freunde*. Ed. P. De Mendelssohn. Frankfurt: S. Fischer.

———. 1996. *Doctor Faustus*. Trans. Helen Lowe-Porter. London: Vintage.

Marlowe Christopher. 2003. *The Complete Plays*. Ed. Frank Romany and Robert Lindsey. London: Penguin.

Marston, John. 1997. *The Dutch Courtesan*. Ed. David Crane. London: A.C. Black.

Marrow, James H., and Shestack, Alan. eds. 1981. *Hans Baldung Grien: Prints and Drawings*. New Haven, CT: Yale University Art Gallery.

Martin, Nicholas. 2008. 'Nietzsche's Goethe: In Sickness and in Health'. *Publications of the English Goethe Society* 57: 115–124.

Marx, Karl. 1973a. *Surveys from Exile*. Ed. David Fernbach. Harmondsworth: Penguin.

———. 1973b. *The Revolutions of 1848*. Ed. David Fernbach. Harmondsworth: Penguin.

———. 1975. *Early Writings*. Trans. Rodney Livingstone and Gregor Benton. Harmondsworth: Penguin.

Mason, Eudo C. 1967. *Goethe's Faust: Its Genesis and Purport*. Berkeley: California U.P.

Maturin, Charles Robert. 2000. *Melmoth the Wanderer*. Ed. Victor Sage. London: Penguin.

McAlindon, T. 1981. 'The Ironic Vision: Diction and Theme in Marlowe's *Doctor Faustus*'. *RES* 32: 129–141.

McGinn, Bernard. 1985. *The Calabrian Abbot: Joachim of Fiore in the History of Western Thought*. New York: Macmillan.

———. 2000. *Antichrist: Two Thousand Years of the Human Dascination with Evil*. New York: Columbia U.P.

Mebane, John. 1989. *Renaissance Magic and the Return of the Golden Age: The Occult Tradition and Marlowe, Jonson, and Shakespeare*. Lincoln: Nebraska U.P.

Meganck, Tine Luk. 2014. *Pieter Bruegel the Elder: Fall of the Revel Angels*. Milan: Silvana Editoriale.

Merezhkovsky, Dmitry. 1974. 'Gogol and the Devil'. In Robert A. Macguire (ed.), *Gogol from the Twentieth Century*. Princeton: Princeton U.P.

Middleton, Christopher. (ed.). 1983. *Johann Wolfgang von Goethe: Selected Poems*. London: John Calder.

Middleton, Thomas. 2007. *The Collected Works*. 2 vols. Ed. Gary Taylor and John Lavagnino. Oxford: O.U.P.

Midelfort, H.C. Erik. 1972. *Witch Hunting in Southwestern Germany 1562–1684: The Social and Intellectual Foundations*. Stanford: Stanford U.P.

Milne, Lesley. 1990. *Mikhail Bulgakov: A Critical Biography*. Cambridge: Cambridge U.P.

Milton, John. 1998. *The Complete Poems*. Ed. John Leonard. Harmondsworth: Penguin.

———. 2007. *Paradise Lost*. Ed. Alastair Fowler. London: Longman.

Molière. 1968. *The Misanthrope and Other Plays*. Trans. Donald M. Frame. New York: Signet.

Morley, Edith J. 1938. *Henry Crabb Robinson on Books and their Writers*. 3 vols. London: Dent.

Muchembled, Robert. 2003. *A History of the Devil: From the Middle Ages to the Present*. Trans. Jean Birrell. Cambridge: Polity.

Muir, Kenneth. 1951. 'Samuel Harsnett and *King Lear*'. *RES* 2: 11–21.

Murav, Harriet. 1992. *Holy Foolishness: Dostoevsky's Novels and the Poetics of Cultural Critique*. Stanford: Stanford U.P.

Murray, Penelope. (ed.). 1989. *Genius: The History of an Idea*. Oxford: Basil Blackwell.

Nauert, Charles G., Jr. 1965. *Agrippa and the Crisis of Renaissance Thought*. Urbana: Illinois U.P.

Negus, Kenneth G. 1958. 'The Family Tree in E.T.A. Hoffmann's *Die Elixiere des Teufels*'. *PMLA* 73: 516–520.

Nicholls, Angus. 2006. *Goethe's Concept of the Daemonic: After the Ancients*. Rochester, NY: Camden House.

Nicoll, Allardyce. 1963. *The World of Harlequin: A Critical Study of the Commedia dell' Arte*. Cambridge: C.U.P.

Nietzsche, Friedrich. 1956. *The Birth of Tragedy and the Genealogy of Morals*. Trans. Francis Golffing. New York: Doubleday Anchor.

———. 1974. *The Gay Science*. Trans. Walter Kaufmann. New York: Vintage.

———. 1982. *Daybreak: Thoughts on the Prejudices of Morality*. Trans. R.J. Hollingdale. Cambridge: Cambridge U.P.

———. 1995. *Unfashionable Observations*. Trans. Richard Gray. Stanford: Stanford U.P.

———. 1999. *Kristische Studienausgabe*. 15 vols. Ed. Giorgio Colli and Mazzino Montarini. Munich: de Gruyter.

———. 2005. *Thus Spoke Zarathustra*. Trans. Graham Parkes. Oxford: O.U.P.

Nordvig, Gerda S. 1993. *Dark Figures in the Desired Country: Blake's Illustrations to The Pilgrim's Progress*. Berkeley: California U.P.

Oberman, Heiko A. 1989. *Luther: Man Between God and the Devil*. Trans. Eileen Walliser-Schwarzbart. New Haven: Yale U.P.

Ohly, Friedrich. 1992. *The Damned and the Elect: Guilt in Western Culture*. Trans. Linda Archibald. Cambridge: C.U.P.

Orenstein, Nadime M. 2001. *Pieter Bruegel the Elder; Drawings and Prints*. New Haven: Yale U.P.

Paley, Morton D. 1970. *Energy and the Imagination: A Study of the Development of Blake's Thought*. Oxford: Clarendon.

———. 2003. *The Traveller in the Evening: The Last Works of William Blake*. Oxford: O.U.P.

Pan, Daniel. 2011. 'The Structure of Aesthetic Pleasure in the Nazi Reception of Goethe's *Faust*'. In Pamela Swete and others (eds.), *Pleasure and Power in Nazi Germany*. Basingstoke: Palgrave.

Paperno, Irina. 1997. *Suicide as a Cultural Institution in Dostoevsky's Russia*. Ithaca: Cornell U.P.

Parker, Patricia and Geoffrey Hartman. (eds.). 1985. *Shakespeare and the Question of Theory*. Methuen: London.

———. 1993. '*Othello* and *Hamlet*: Delation, Spying, and the "Secret Place" of Woman'. *Representations* 44: 60–95.

Passage, Charles. 1954. *Dostoevski the Adapter: A Study in Dostoevski's Use of the Tales of Hoffmann.* Chapel Hill: North Carolina U.P.

———. 1963. *The Russian Hoffmannists.* The Hague: Mouton.

———. 1976. 'E. T. A. Hoffmann's "The Devil's Elixirs": A Flawed Masterpiece'. *JEGP* 75: 531–546.

Pastoureau, Michel. 2011. *The Bear: History of a Fallen King.* Trans. George Holoch. Cambridge, MA: Harvard U.P.

Patrides, C.A. 1966. *Milton and the Christian Tradition.* Oxford: Clarendon.

Peace, Richard. 1992. *Dostoevsky: A Study of the Major Novels.* Bristol: Bristol Classical Press.

Pearsall, Derek. 1994. *William Langland: Piers Plowman, the C Text.* Exeter: Exeter U.P.

Pelikan, Jaroslav. 1996. *Faust the Theologian.* New Haven: Yale U.P.

Philip, Lotte Brand. 1953. 'The Prado Epiphany by Jerome Bosch'. *Art Bulletin* 35: 267–293.

Pointon, Marcia R. 1970. *Milton and English Art.* Manchester: M.U.P.

Pollard, Alfred W. 1897. *The Towneley Plays, Redited from the Unique MS by George England.* EETS. Oxford: O.U.P.

Popkin, Richard H. 2003. *The History of Scepticism: From Savonarola to Bayle.* Oxford: O.U.P.

Powys T.F. 1967. *Mr. Weston's Good Wine.* Introduction by David Holbrook. London: Heinemann.

Pressly, William J. 1983. *James Barry: The Artist as Hero.* London: Tate Gallery.

Proffer, Ellendea. 1984. *Bulgakov: Life and Work.* Ann Arbor: Ardis.

Purdon, L.O. 1992. 'The Pardoner's Old Man and the Second Death'. *Studies in Philology* 89: 334–349.

Pushkin, Walter. 1984. *Collected Narrative and Lyrical Poetry.* Ed. and Trans. Walter Arndt. Ann Arbor: Ardis.

Puyvelde, Leo Van. 1946. *Pieter Bruegel's Dulle Griet.* London: Percy Lund: Gallery series no. 10.

Rabelais, François. 1955. *Oeuvres Complètes.* Ed. Jacques Boulenger and Lucien Scheler. Paris: Gallimard.

———. 2006. *Gargantua and Pantagruel.* Trans. M.A. Screech. London: Penguin.

Rapaport, Herman. 1983. *Milton and the Postmodern.* Lincoln: Nebraska U.P.

Rapley, Robert. 1998. *A Case of Witchcraft; The Trial of Urbain Grandier.* Manchester: M.U.P.

Raraty, M. M. 1964. 'Hoffmann and his Theatre'. *Hermathena* 98: 53–67.

———. 1972. *Hoffmann, Prinzessin Bramilla.* Oxford: O.U.P.

Rice, James L. 1985. *Dostoevsky and the Art of Healing: An Essay in Literary and Medical History*. Ardis: Ann Arbor.

———. 2009. 'The Covert Design of *The Brothers Karamazov*: Alesha's Pathology and Dialectic'. *Slavic Review* 68: 355–375.

Richardson, Miles. 1974. *The Human Mirror: Material and Spatial Images of Man*. Baton Rouge: Louisiana University Press.

Rist, John M. 1994. *Augustine: Ancient Thought Baptized*. Cambridge: C.U.P.

Robertson, D.W., Jr. 1954. 'Why the Devil Wears Green'. *Modern Language Notes* 69: 470–472.

———. 1962. *A Preface to Chaucer*. Princeton: Princeton U.P.

Robson-Scott, W.D. 1965. *The Literary Background of the Gothic Revival in Germany*. Oxford: Clarendon.

Röder-Bolton, Gerlinde. 1998. *George Eliot and Goethe: An Elective Affinity*. Amsterdam: Rodopi.

Rossiter, A.P. 1950. *English Drama From Early Times to the Elizabethans*. London: Hutchinson.

———. 1961. *Angel with Horns*. Ed. Graham Storey. London. Longman.

Rowland, Christopher. 2010. *Blake and the Bible*. New Haven: Yale U.P.

Rubenstein, Emanuela Barasch. 2015. *Mephisto in the Third Reich: Literary Representations of Evil in Nazi Germany*. Oldenbourg: de Gruyter.

Ruprecht Laura. 2006. *Dances of the Self in Heinrich von Kleist, E.T.A. Hoffmann and Heinrich Heine*. Farnham: Ashgate.

Rushdie, Salman. 1988. *The Satanic Verses*. London: Random House.

Russell, Jeffrey Burton. 1977. *The Devil: Perceptions of Evil from Antiquity to Primitive Christianity*. Ithaca: Cornell U.P.

———. 1981. *Satan: The Early Christian Tradition*. Ithaca: Cornell U.P.

———. 1985. *Lucifer: The Devil in the Middle Ages*. Ithaca: Cornell U.P.

———. 1986. *Mephistopheles: The Devil in the Modern World*. Ithaca: Cornell U.P.

Sachs, Arieh. 1964. 'The Religious Despair of Doctor Faustus'. *JEGP* 63: 625–647.

Salingar, Leo. 1974. *Shakespeare and the Traditions of Comedy*. Cambridge: C.U.P.

———. 1986. *Dramatic Form in Shakespeare and the Jacobeans*. Cambridge: C.U.P.

Samuel, R.H. 1968. *Johann Wilhelm Goethe's Faust in the Original Version*. London: Macmillan.

Schain, Richard. 2001. *The Legend of Nietzsche's Syphilis*. Westport, CN: Greenwood Press.

Schmidt, A.V.C. 1974. *Geoffrey Chaucer: The General Prologue to The Canterbury Tales and The Canon Yeoman's Prologue and Tale*. London: London U.P.

———. 2011. *William Langland: Piers Plowman: A Parallel-Text Edition of the A,B,C and Z Versions*. 2 vols., 2nd edition. Kalamazoo: Medieval Institute Publications, Western Michigan University.

Schwartz, Jerome. 1990. *Irony and Ideology in Rabelais: Structures of Subversion.* Cambridge: C.U.P.

Segal Erich. 1968. *Roman Laughter: The Comedy of Plautus.* Cambridge, MA: Harvard U.P.

Sewell, Arthur. 1939. *A Study in Milton's Christian Doctrine.* Oxford: O.U.P.

Shakespeare, William. 1997. *The Norton Shakespeare.* Ed. Stephen Greenblatt. New York: Norton.

Shneidman, N.N. 1984. *Dostoesvky and Suicide.* New York: Mosaic Press.

Shock, Peter A. 1993. 'The Marriage of Heaven and Hell: Blake's Myth of Satan and its Cultural Matrix'. *ELH* 60: 441–470.

Sillars, Stuart. 2006. *Painting Shakespeare: The Artist as Critic 1720–1820.* Cambridge: C.U.P.

Simpson, James. 1998. *Goethe and Patriarchy: Faust and the Fates of Desire.* Oxford: Legenda.

Sinclair, John D. 1939. *Dante: The Divine Comedy I: Inferno.* Trans. John D. Sinclair. Oxford: O.U.P.

Skiffingham, Lloyd A. 1985. *The History of English Soliloquy: Aeschylus to Shakespeare.* Lanham, MD: America U.P.

Sloterdijk, P. 1988. *Critique of Cynical Reason.* Minneapolis: University of Minnesota Press.

Smiles, Sam. 1994. *The Image of Antiquity: Ancient Britain and the Romantic Imagination.* New Haven: Yale U.P.

Southern, Richard. 1975. *The Medieval Theatre in the Round: A Study of the Staging of The Castle of Perseverance and Related Matters.* London: Faber.

Speirs, John. 1957. *Medieval English Poetry: The Non-Chaucerian Tradition.* London: Faber.

Spitzer, Leo. 1939. 'Le pretendu realism de Rabelais'. *Modern Philology* 37: 139–150.

———. 1944. 'The Farcical Elements in *Inferno* cantos XXI–XXIII'. *Modern Language Notes* 59: 83–88.

Spitzer, Michael. 2006. *Music as Philosophy: Adorno and Beethoven's Late Style.* Bloomington: Indiana U.P.

Spivack, Bernard. 1968. *Shakespeare and the Allegory of Evil: The History of a Metaphor in Relation to his Major Villains.* New York: Columbia U.P.

Stachniewski, John. 1991. *The Persecutory Imagination: English Calvinism and the Literature of Religious Despair.* Oxford: Clarendon.

Stallybrass, Peter and Allon White. 1986. *The Politics and Poetics of Transgression.* London: Methuen.

Stephens, Walter. 1989. *Giants in those Days: Folklore, Ancient History, Nationalism.* Lincoln: Nebraska: Nebraska U.P.

Stevens, Martin. 1987. *Four Middle English Mystery Cycles: Textual, Contextual, and Critical Interpretations.* Princeton: Princeton U.P.

Stewart, Alison G. 2008. *Before Bruegel: Sebald Beham and the Origins of Peasant Festival Imagery.* Aldershot: Ashgate.

Stieg, Elizabeth. 1990. 'Reinterpreting the Old Testament: Blake's Tiriel as Prophet'. *Studies in Romanticism* 29: 273–296.

Stiegler, Bernard. 1998–2011. *Technics and Time.* 3 vols. Trans. Richard Beardsworth and George Collins. Stanford: Stanford U.P.

Stridbeck, C.G. 1956. '"Combat between Carnival and Lent" by Pieter Bruegel the Elder: An Allegorical Picture of the Sixteenth Century'. *Journal of the Warburg and Courauld Institutes* 19: 96–109.

Subotnik, Rose Rosengard. 1976. 'Adorno's Diagnosis of Beethoven's Late Style: Early Symptom of a Fatal Condition'. *Journal of the American Musicological Society* 29: 242–275.

Sullivan, Margaret A. 1977. Madness and Folly: 'Peter Bruegel the Elder's "Dulle Griet"'. *Art Bulletin* 59: 55–66.

Szbari, Antónia. 2005. 'Rabelais Parrhesiastes: The Rhetoric of Insult and Rabelais's Cynical Mask'. *MLN* 120: S84-S123.

Szittya, Penn. 1975. 'The Green Yeoman as Loathly Lady: The Friar's Parody of the Wife of Bath's Tale'. *PMLA*, 386–394.

Szittya, P. R. 1986. *The Antifraternal Tradition in Medieval Literature.* Princeton, NJ: Princeton U.P.

Tambling, Jeremy. 1990. *Confession: Sexuality, Sin, the Subject.* Manchester: M.U.P.

———. 2003. 'Monomania of a Whale-Hunter: *Moby-Dick*'. *English* 52: 101–124.

———. 2004. 'Levinas and *Macbeth*'s Strange Images of Death'. *Essays in Criticism* 54: 351–372.

———. 2005a. *Blake's Night Thoughts.* London: Palgrave.

———. 2005b. 'On Not Being Able to Sing: Filming *Les contes d'Hoffmann*'. *FMLS* 42: 22–37.

———. 2009. 'Law and Will in *Measure for Measure*'. *Essays in Criticism* 59: 189–210.

———. 2012a. *On Reading the Will: Law and Desire in Literature and Music.* Brighton: Sussex Academic Press.

———. 2012b. 'Opera and Novel Ending Together: *Die Meistersinger* and *Doktor Faustus*'. *FMLS* 48: 208–221.

———. 2012c. *Literature and Psychoanalysis.* Manchester: Manchester U.P.

———. 2015. 'Hoffmann's *Die Elixiere des Teufels*: The Double, the Death-drive, and the Apotropaic'. *FMLS* 51: 379–393.

Tamburr, Karl. 2007. *The Harrowing of Hell in Medieval England.* Cambridge: D.S. Brewer.

Tanner, John S. 1992. *Anxiety in Eden: A Kierkegaardian Reading of Paradise Lost.* Oxford: O.U.P.

Terras, Victor. 1981. *A Karamazov Companion.* Madison: Wisconsin U.P.

Thompson, Diane Oenning. 1991. *The Brothers Karamazov and the Poetics of Memory.* Cambridge: C.U.P.

Thurn, David H. 1993. 'Fideikommißsbibliothek: Freud's "Demonological Neurosis"'. *MLN* 108: 849–874.

Traister, B. H. 1984. *Heavenly Necromancers: The Magician in English Renaissance drama.* Columbia: University of Missouri Press.

Turgenev, Ivan Sergeyevich. 1907. *A Lear of the Steppes etc.* Trans. Constance Garnett. London: William Heinemann.

———. 1975. *Fathers and Sons.* Trans. Rosemary Edmonds. Harmondsworth: Penguin.

Turner, James Grantham. 1987. *One Flesh: Paradisal Mariage and Sexual Relations in the Age of Milton.* Oxford: Clarendon.

Vaget, Hans Rudolf. 1994. 'Act IV Revisited: A "Post-Wall" Reading of Goethe's *Faust*'. In Jane K. Brown (ed.), *Interpreting Goethe's Faust Today.* Columbia, SC: Camden House.

Vandenbroeck, Paul. 1984. 'Verbeeck's Peasant Weddings: A Study of Iconography and Social Function'. *Simiolus: Netherlands Quarterly for the History of Art* 14: 79–124.

Verhoeven, Claudia. 2009. *The Odd Man Karakazov: Imperial Russia, Modernity and the Birth of Terrorism.* Ithaca: Cornell U.P.

Vernant, Jean-Pierre and Pierre Vidal-Naquet. 1988. *Myth and Tragedy in Ancient Greece.* New York: Zone.

Vincent, Deidre. 1987. *The Eternity of Being: On the Experience of Time in Goethe's Faust.* Bonn: Bouvier.

Voltaire. 1990. *Candide and Other Stories.* Trans. Roger Pearson. Oxford: O.U.P.

von Goethe, J. W. 1900. *Autobiography and Annals*, Vol. London: George Bell and Sons.

Voragine, Jacobus de. 1993. *The Golden Legend: Readings on the Saints.* 2 vols. Trans. Willam Granger Ryan. Princeton: Princeton U.P.

Walker, D.P. 1964. *The Decline of Hell: Seventeenth-Century Discussions of Eternal Torment.* London: Routledge and Kegan Paul.

———. 1981. *Unclean Spirits: Possession and Exorcism in France and England in the Late Sixteenth and Early Seventeenth Centuries.* London: Scolar Press.

Warner Janet A. 1984. *Blake and the Language of Art.* Montreal: McGill U.P.

Warrack, John. 1968. *Carl Maria von Weber.* London: Hamish Hamilton.

———. 2001. *German Opera from the Beginnings to Wagner.* Cambridge: C.U.P.

Wasiolek, Edward. 1964. *Dostoevsky: The Major Fiction.* Cambridge, MA: MIT Press.

Webber, Andrew J. 1996. *The Doppelgänger: Double Visions in German Literature.* Oxford: Clarendon.

Webster, Charles. 2008. *Paracelsus: Medicine, Magic and Mission and the End of Time.* New Haven: Yale U.P.

Webster, John. 1972. *Three Plays.* Ed. David Gunby. Harmondsworth: Penguin.

Weimann, Robert. 1978. *Shakespeare and the Popular Tradition in the Theater*. Ed. Robert Schwartz. Baltimore. Johns Hopkins U.P.

Wellbery, David E. 1996. *The Specular Moment: Goethe's Early Lyric and the Beginnings of Romanticism*. Stanford: Stanford U.P.

Wells, Stanley. 1961. 'Tom o' Bedlam's Song and *King Lear*'. *Shakespeare Quarterly* 12: 311–315.

Wells, Stanley and Gary Taylor. 1997. *William Shakespeare: A Textual Companion*. New York: W.W. Norton.

Welsford, Enid. 1935. *The Fool: His Social and Literary History*. London: Faber.

West, M.L. 2010. *The Hymns of Zoroaster: A New Translation of the Most Ancient Sacred Texts of Iran*. London: I.B. Tauris.

Westerink, Herman. 2012. *The Heart of Man's Destiny: Lacanian Psychoanalysis and Early Modern Reformation Thought*. London: Routledge.

Wetters, Kirk. 2014. *Daemonic History: From Goethe to the Present*. Evanston: Northwestern U.P.

White, Ann. 1980. *Name and Nomenclature in Goethe's Faust*. London: University of London Institute of Germanic Studies.

Wickham, Glynne. 1966. 'Hell-Castle and its Door-Keeper'. *Shakespeare Survey* 19: 68–74.

Wicksteed, Joseph H. 1910. *Blake's Vision of the Book of Job*. London: J.M. Dent.

Williams, Arnold. 1950. *Characterisation of Pilate in the Towneley Plays*. Michigan: Michigan State College Press.

Williams, John R. 1987. *Goethe's Faust*. London: Allen and Unwin.

Williams, Raymond. 1983. *Writing in Society*. London: Verso.

Willoughby, L.A. (ed.). 1943. *Goethe's Urfaust and Faust: Ein Fragment*. Oxford: Blackwell.

Wilson, F.P. 1969. *The English Drama 1485–1585*. Oxford: Clarendon.

Wilson, Peter H. 2009. *Europe's Tragedy: A New History of the Thirty Years War*. London: Penguin.

Wilson, W. Daniel. 2008. 'Goethe, His Duke and Infanticide: New Documents and Reflections on a Controversial Execution'. *German Life and Letters* 61: 7–32.

Wittreich, Joseph Anthony, Jr. 1975. *Angel of Apocalypse: Blake's Idea of Milton*. Madison: Wisconsin U.P.

Woods, John E. 1997. *Doctor Faustus: A New Translation*. New York: Vintage.

Woolf, Rosemary. 1972. *The English Mystery Plays*. London: Routledge and Kegan Paul.

Wright, Elizabeth. 1978. *E.T.A. Hoffmann and the Rhetoric of Terror: Aspects of Language Used for the Evocation of Fear*. London: Institute of Germanic Studies, University of London.

Yates, Frances. 1964. *Giordano Bruno and the Hermetic Tradition*. Chicago: Chicago U.P.

Zambelli, Paola. 2007. *White Magic, Black Magic in the European Renaissance.* Leiden: Brill.

Zika, Charles. 2007. *The Appearance of Witchcraft: Art and Visual Culture in Seventeenth-Century Europe.* London: Routledge.

Ziolkowski, Margaret. 1988. *Hagiography and Modern Russian Literature.* Princeton: Princeton U.P.

———. 1992. 'Pilate and Pilatism in Recent Russian Literature'. In Sheelagh Duffin Grahm (ed.), *New Directions in Soviet Literature.* Basingstoke: Macmillan.

Zupančič, Alenka. 2008. *The Odd One In: On Comedy.* Cambridge, MA: MIT Press.

Index

J. Tambling, *Histories of the Devil*,
DOI 10.1057/978-1-137-51832-3

Printed by Printforce, the Netherlands